Microsoft

Step by Step

Microsoft® Office
Project 2003

Carl Chatfield, PMP, and Timothy Johnson, MCP

PUBLISHED BY
Microsoft Press
A Division of Microsoft Corporation
One Microsoft Way
Redmond, Washington 98052-6399

Library of Congress Cataloging-in-Publication Data
Chatfield, Carl S., 1964-
    Microsoft Office Project 2003 Step by Step / Carl Chatfield and Timothy Johnson.
        p. cm. -- (Step by step)
    Includes bibliographical references and index.
    ISBN 0-7356-1955-7
    1. Microsoft Project.   2. Project management--Computer programs.   I. Johnson, Timothy D., 1962- II. Title.   III. Step by step (Redmond, Wash.)

    HD69.P75.C463   2003
    658.4'04'02855369--dc22   2003058832

Printed and bound in the United States of America.

13 14 15   QWE   8 7 6

Distributed in Canada by H.B. Fenn and Company Ltd.

A CIP catalogue record for this book is available from the British Library.

Microsoft Press books are available through booksellers and distributors worldwide. For further information about international editions, contact your local Microsoft Corporation office or contact Microsoft Press International directly at fax (425) 936-7329. Visit our Web site at www.microsoft.com/mspress. Send comments to *mspinput@microsoft.com*.

Acquisitions Editor: Alex Blanton
Project Editor: Laura Sackerman

Body Part No. X10-00033

Contents

I Managing a Simple Project

Contents

16   Getting Your Project Back on Track   322

III   Special Subjects

17   Applying Advanced Formatting   342

18   Customizing Project   358

19   Measuring Performance with Earned Value Analysis   380

20   Consolidating Projects and Resources   390

What's New in Microsoft Office Project 2003

You'll notice some changes as soon as you start Project 2003. The toolbars and menu bar have a new look, and there are some new task panes available on the left side of your screen. But the features that are new or greatly improved in this version of Project go beyond just changes in appearance. Some changes won't be apparent to you until you start using the program.

New in Office 2003

To help you quickly identify features that are new or greatly enhanced with this version, this book uses the icon in the margin whenever new features are discussed or shown.

The following new or improved features are available in Project Standard and Project Professional:

To learn how to	Using this new feature	See
Connect to the Microsoft Web site for assistance	Office Online service	Chapter 1, page 8
More easily print a view	Project Guide	Chapter 11, page 233
Create a project summary report for an Office application	Copy Picture to Office Wizard	Chapter 13, page 259

The following new or improved features are available in a Project Server–based enterprise project management system:

To learn how to	Using this new feature	See
Develop a new plan	Enterprise template	Chapter 21, page 423
Replace generic resources with work resources	Resource Substitution Wizard	Chapter 21, page 429
Report progress on assignments directly in Outlook	Outlook integration add-in for Project Server	Chapter 22, page 448
Identify risks to projects or tasks	WSS Risks integration with Project Server	Chapter 23, page 466

(continued)

To learn how to	Using this new feature	See
Create and delegate issues relating to projects or tasks	WSS Risks integration with Project Server	Chapter 23, page 469
Upload documents relevent to projects or tasks	WSS Risks integration with Project Server	Chapter 23, page 472

For more information about the Project family of products, see *http://www.microsoft.com/office/project/*.

Getting Help

Every effort has been made to ensure the accuracy of this book and the contents of its CD-ROM. If you do run into problems, please contact the appropriate source for help and assistance.

Getting Help with This Book and Its CD-ROM

If your question or issue concerns the content of this book or its companion CD-ROM, please first search the online Microsoft Press Knowledge Base, which provides support information for known errors in or corrections to this book, at the following Web site:

http://www.microsoft.com/mspress/support/search.asp

If you do not find your answer at the online Knowledge Base, send your comments or questions to Microsoft Press Technical Support at

mspinput@microsoft.com

Getting Help with Microsoft Office Project 2003

If your question is about a Microsoft software product, including Project, and not about the content of this Microsoft Press book, please search the Microsoft Knowledge Base at

http://support.microsoft.com

In the United States, Microsoft software product support issues not covered by the Microsoft Knowledge Base are addressed by Microsoft Product Support Services. The Microsoft software support options available from Microsoft Product Support Services are listed at

http://support.microsoft.com

Outside the United States, for support information specific to your location, please refer to the Worldwide Support menu on the Microsoft Product Support Services Web site for the site specific to your country:

http://support.microsoft.com

Using the Book's CD-ROM

The CD-ROM inside the back cover of this book contains all the practice files you'll use as you work through the exercises in the book. By using practice files, you won't waste time creating samples and typing schedule data—instead, you can jump right in and concentrate on learning how to use Microsoft Office Project 2003.

What's on the CD-ROM

In addition to the practice files, the CD-ROM contains the following:

- 60-day trial of Microsoft Office Project 2003 Standard Edition
- Microsoft Office Project Standard 2003 demonstration video
- Enterprise Project Management Solution demonstration video
- *Microsoft Office Project 2003 Step by Step* in eBook format
- *Insider's Guide to Microsoft Office OneNote 2003* in eBook format
- *Microsoft Office System Quick Reference* in eBook format
- *Introducing the Tablet PC* in eBook format
- *Microsoft Computer Dictionary, Fifth edition,* in eBook format
- 25 business-oriented templates for use with the programs in the Microsoft Office System
- 100 pieces of clip art

System Requirements

To use this book, along with Project Standard 2003, you will need

Computer/Processor

Computer with a Pentium 133-megahertz (MHz) or higher processor

Operating System

Microsoft Windows 2000 with Service Pack 3 (SP3) or Microsoft Windows XP or later operating system

Memory

64 MB of RAM (128 MB recommended) plus an additional 8 MB of RAM for each program in the Microsoft Office System (such as Project) running simultaneously

Hard Disk

Hard disk space requirements will vary depending on configuration; custom installation choices may require more or less hard disk space.

■ 105 MB of available hard disk space with 70 MB on the hard disk where the operating system is installed.

■ An additional 9 MB of hard disk space is required for installing the practice files.

■ An additional 237 MB of hard disk space is required for installing the 60-day trial version of Microsoft Office Project 2003 Standard Edition.

Drive

CD-ROM drive

Display

Super VGA (800×600) or higher-resolution monitor with 256 colors or higher

Peripherals

Microsoft Mouse, Microsoft IntelliMouse, or compatible pointing device

Note Project Professional, Project Server, and Project Web Access are not required to complete the chapters in this book but are illustrated in Chapters 21 through 23. You can see the system requirements of these products here: http://www.microsoft.com/office/project/evaluation/sysreqs.asp

Installing the Practice Files

You need to install the practice files on your hard disk before you use them in the chapters' exercises. Follow these steps to prepare the CD's files for your use:

1 Insert the CD-ROM into the CD-ROM drive of your computer.

The Step by Step Companion CD End User License Agreement appears. Follow the onscreen directions. It is necessary to accept the terms of the license agreement in order to use the practice files. After you accept the license agreement, a menu screen appears.

Important If the menu screen does not appear, start Windows Explorer. In the left pane, locate the icon for your CD-ROM drive and click the icon. In the right pane, double-click the **StartCD** executable file.

2 Click **Install Practice Files**.

3 Click **Next** on the first screen, and then click **Yes** to accept the license agreement on the next screen.

4   If you want to install the practice files to a location other than the default folder (*My Documents\\Microsoft Press\\Project 2003 Step by Step*), click the **Change Folder** button, select the new drive and path, and then click **OK**.

5   Click **Next** on the Choose Destination Location screen, click **Next** on the Select Features screen, and then click **Next** on the Start Copying Files screen to install the practice files.

6   After the practice files have been installed, click **Finish**.

Within the installation folder are subfolders for each chapter in the book.

7   Close the Step by Step Companion CD window, remove the CD-ROM from the CD-ROM drive, and return it to the envelope at the back of the book.

Using the Practice Files

Each topic in the chapter explains how and when to use any practice files. The file or files that you'll need are indicated at the beginning of the procedure in blue type, as shown here:

BE SURE TO: Start Microsoft Office Project 2003 if it's not already open.

OPEN: Parnell Aerospace Promo 18a and Wingtip Toys Commercial 18b from the *My Documents\\ Microsoft Press\\Project 2003 Step by Step\\Chapter 18 Customizing* folder. You can also access the practice files for this book by clicking **Start**, **All Programs**, **Microsoft Press**, **Project 2003 Step by Step**, and then selecting the chapter folder of the file you want to open.

The following table lists each chapter's practice files.

Chapter	Folder	Files
1	Chapter 1 Getting Started	(no practice file)
2	Chapter 2 Simple Tasks	Wingtip Toys Commercial 2a
3	Chapter 3 Simple Resources	Wingtip Toys Commercial 3a
4	Chapter 4 Simple Assignments	Wingtip Toys Commercial 4a
5	Chapter 5 Simple Formatting	Wingtip Toys Commercial 5a, Logo
6	Chapter 6 Simple Tracking	Wingtip Toys Commercial 6a
7	Chapter 7 Advanced Tasks	Short Film Project 7a
8	Chapter 8 Advanced Resources and Assignments	Short Film Project 8a

(continued)

Chapter	Folder	Files
9	Chapter 9 Advanced Plan	Short Film Project 9a
10	Chapter 10 Advanced Formatting	Short Film Project 10a
11	Chapter 11 Printing	Short Film Project 11a
12	Chapter 12 Publishing Online	Short Film Project 12a
13	Chapter 13 Sharing	Short Film Project 13a, Letter To Client, Sample Task List
14	Chapter 14 Advanced Tracking	Short Film Project 14a, Short Film Project 14b, Short Film Project 14c, Short Film Project 14d
15	Chapter 15 Reporting Status	Short Film Project 15a
16	Chapter 16 Getting Back on Track	Short Film Project 16a
17	Chapter 17 Advanced Formatting	Parnell Film 17a
18	Chapter 18 Customizing	Parnell Aerospace Promo 18a, Wingtip Toys Commercial 18b
19	Chapter 19 Earned Value	Short Film Project 19a
20	Chapter 20 Consolidating	Wingtip Toys Commercial 20a, Parnell Aerospace Promo 20b
21	(no practice folder)	(no practice file)
22	(no practice folder)	(no practice file)
23	(no practice folder)	(no practice file)

Uninstalling the Practice Files

After you finish working through this book, you should uninstall the practice files to free up hard disk space.

1   On the Windows taskbar, click the **Start** button, and then click **Control Panel**.

2   In Control Panel, click **Add or Remove Programs**.

3   In the list of installed programs, click **Microsoft Office Project 2003 Step by Step**, and then click the **Remove** or **Change/Remove** button.)

4   In the **Uninstall** dialog box, click **OK**.

Important   If you need additional help installing or uninstalling the practice files, please see "Getting Help" on page xi. Microsoft's product support does not provide support for this book or its CD-ROM.

Conventions and Features

You can save time when you use this book by understanding how the Step by Step series shows special instructions, keys to press, buttons to click, and so on.

Convention	Meaning
New in Office 2003	This icon indicates a new or greatly improved feature in Microsoft Office Project 2003.
	This icon indicates a reference to the book's companion CD.
BE SURE TO	Following these words are instructions for actions you should take before beginning an exercise.
OPEN	Following this word are instructions for opening the practice files you'll need to use for an exercise.
CLOSE	Following this word are the names of practice files you should close before moving on to another topic in the book.
1 **2**	Numbered steps guide you through hands-on exercises in each topic.
●	A round bullet indicates an exercise that has only one step.
Tip	This section provides a helpful hint or shortcut that makes working through a task easier.
Important	This section points out information that you need to know to complete the procedure.
Troubleshooting	This section shows you how to fix a common problem.
💾 Save	The first time a button is referenced in a topic, a picture of the button appears in the margin area with a label.
Alt + Tab	A plus sign (+) between two key names means that you must press those keys at the same time. For example, "Press Alt + Tab" means that you hold down the Alt key while you press Tab.

(continued)

Convention	Meaning
Boldface type	Program features that you click or press are shown in black boldface type.
Blue boldface type	Text that you are supposed to type appears in blue boldface type.
Blue italic type	Terms that are explained in the glossary at the end of the book are shown in blue italic type within the chapter.

Quick Reference

Chapter 1 Getting Started with Project

Page 6 **To start Project Standard**

1   On the Windows taskbar, click the **Start** button.

2   On the **Start** menu, point to **All Programs** (in Microsoft Windows XP) or **Programs** (in previous versions of Windows), point to **Microsoft Office**, and then click **Microsoft Office Project 2003**.

10   **To start Project Professional and work offline**

1   On the Windows taskbar, click the **Start** button.

2   On the **Start** menu, point to **All Programs** (in Microsoft Windows XP) or **Programs** (in previous versions of Windows), point to **Microsoft Office**, and then click **Microsoft Office Project 2003**.

3   If the **Project Server Security Login** dialog box appears, click **Cancel**.

4   In the **Project Server Accounts** dialog box, under **Choose account** select **My Computer,** and then click **Work Offline**.

13   **To create a project plan from a template**

1   In the Getting Started task pane, click **Create a new project**.

2   In the New Project task pane, under **Template**, click **On my computer**.

3   In the **Templates** dialog box, click the **Project Templates** tab.

4   Click the template you want, and then click **OK**.

16   **To switch to a different view**

1   On the **View** menu, click the name of the view you want.

2   If the view is not listed, click **More Views**, and in the **More Views** dialog box, click the name of the view you want, and click the **Apply** button.

21   **To view a report in the Print Preview window**

1   On the **View** menu, click **Reports**.

2   Click a report category, or to see all reports, click **Custom**, and then click the **Select** button.

3   Select the report you want, and then click the **Select** or **Preview** button.

23 **To create a new project plan using the Project Guide**

    1   On the **File** menu, click **New**.

    2   In the New Project task pane, under **New**, click the **Blank Project** link.

    3   In the Tasks pane, click the **Set a date to schedule from** link (in Project Standard) or the **Define the project** link (in Project Professional).

    4   In the **Date** box, enter the project's start date.

    5   At the bottom of the pane, click **Done** (in Project Standard) or the **Save and go to Step 2** link (in Project Professional).

26 **To set nonworking days using the Project Guide**

    1   On the **Project Guide** toolbar, click the **Tasks** button.

    2   In the Tasks pane, click the **Define general working times** link, and then follow the instructions that appear on your screen.

29 **To enter properties about a Project plan**

    1   On the **File** menu, click **Properties**.

    2   In the **Properties** dialog box, click the **Summary** tab, and then enter the information you want.

Chapter 2 **Creating a Task List**

Page 34 **To enter tasks using the Project Guide**

    1   On the **Project Guide** toolbar, click the **Tasks** button.

    2   In the Tasks pane, click the **List the tasks in the project** link, and then follow the instructions that appear on your screen.

38 **To enter task durations**

    1   In the Gantt Chart view, click a cell in the **Duration** column.

    2   Type the task duration, and then press Enter.

40 **To enter a milestone**

    1   On the Entry table, enter a name for the milestone, and then press Tab.

    2   In the **Duration** field, type 0d, and then press Enter.

41 **To organize tasks into phases using the Project Guide**

    1   On the **Project Guide** toolbar, click the **Tasks** button.

    2   In the Tasks pane, click the **Organize tasks into phases** link, and then follow the instructions that appear on your screen.

4 In the **Material Label** field, enter the unit of measure you want to use for this resource. For example, you might measure cement in pounds or tons.

5 In the **Std. Rate** field, enter the cost per unit of measure for this material resource.

6 Enter whatever other resource information would be useful for your project.

7 Repeat steps 2 through 6 for each resource.

64 **To enter resource pay rates**

1 On the **View** menu, click **Resource Sheet**.

2 In the **Std. Rate** field, enter the resource's pay rate, including the duration of a pay period.

3 If the resource should accrue overtime pay, enter his or her overtime pay rate in the **Ovt. Rate** field.

4 If the resource accrues a per-use cost, enter that amount in the **Cost/Use** field.

5 In the **Accrue At** field, click the method by which the resource accrues cost.

6 Repeat steps 2 through 5 for each resource.

66 **To adjust working time for individual resources**

1 On the **Tools** menu, click **Change Working Time**.

2 In the **For** box, click the name of the resource whose working time you want to change.

3 In the calendar below the **Select Date(s)** label, click the date range or day(s) of the week for which you want to adjust working time.

4 Under **Set selected date(s) to**, click the options you want.

69 **To document resources with resource notes**

1 Switch to a resource view such as the Resource Sheet view.

2 Click the name of the resource for which you want to create a note.

3 On the Standard toolbar, click the **Resource Notes** button.

4 In the **Resource Information** dialog box, type the note you want associated with this resource.

Chapter 4 Assigning Resources to Tasks

Page 72 **To assign resources using the Project Guide**

1 On the **Project Guide** toolbar, click **Resources**.

2 In the Resources pane, click the **Assign people and equipment to tasks** link, and then follow the instructions that appear on your screen.

73 **To assign resources using the Assign Resources dialog box**

1 On the Standard toolbar, click **Assign Resources**.

2 In the Gantt Chart view, click the name of the task to which you want to assign a resource.

3 In the **Resource Name** column of the **Assign Resources** dialog box, click a resource, and then click the **Assign** button.

78 **To control how Project schedules the work on a task after assigning an additional resource**

1 Assign an additional resource to a task.

2 Click the **Smart Tag Actions** button, and choose the action you want.

82 **To assign material resources to tasks**

1 On the Standard toolbar, click **Assign Resources**.

2 In the Gantt Chart view, click the name of the task to which you want to assign a resource.

3 In the **Resource Name** column of the **Assign Resources** dialog box, click a resource, and in the **Units** column, enter the number of units of the material resource you want to assign.

4 Click the **Assign** button.

Chapter 5 **Formatting and Printing Your Plan**

Page 86 **To create a custom view**

1 On the **View** menu, click **More Views**.

2 In the **More Views** dialog box, do one of the following:

■ To create a view, click the **New** button. Click **Single view** or **Combination view** in the **Define New View** dialog box, and then click **OK**.

■ To redefine a view, click the view's name, and then click the **Edit** button.

■ To create a new view based on another view, click the view's name, and then click the **Copy** button.

3 In the **View Definition** dialog box, choose the options you want.

89 **To format Gantt bars with the Gantt Chart Wizard**

1 On the **Format** menu, click **Gantt Chart Wizard**.

2 Follow the instructions that appear on your screen.

92 **To draw a text box on a Gantt chart**

1   On the **View** menu, point to **Toolbars**, and then click **Drawing**.

2   On the **Drawing** toolbar, click the **Text Box** button, and then drag a small square anywhere on the chart portion of a Gantt Chart view.

3   In the square you just drew, type the text you want.

94 **To format a category of text in a view**

1   On the **Format** menu, click **Text Styles**.

2   In the **Item to Change** list, click the type of text you want to format.

3   Select the font and other formatting options you want.

97 **To format selected text in a view**

1   Click the cell that contains the text you want to format.

2   On the **Format** menu, click **Font**.

3   Select the font and other formatting options you want.

102 **To edit a report's header**

1   On the **View** menu, click **Reports**.

2   Click a report category, or to see all reports, click **Custom**, and then click the **Select** button.

3   Select the report you want, and then click the **Select** or **Preview** button.

4   On the **Print Preview** toolbar, click the **Page Setup** button.

5   In the **Page Setup** dialog box, click the **Header** tab, and select the options you want.

Chapter 6 **Tracking Progress on Tasks**

Page 108 **To save a baseline using the Project Guide**

1   On the **Project Guide** toolbar, click the **Track** button.

2   In the Track pane, click the **Save a baseline plan to compare with later versions** link, and then follow the instructions that appear on your screen.

110 **To display the Variance table in the Task Sheet view**

1   On the **View** menu, click **More Views to** display the **More Views** dialog box.

2   In the **Views** box, click **Task Sheet**, and click the **Apply** button.

3   On the **View** menu, point to **Table: Entry**, and click **Variance**.

111 **To track a project as scheduled**

1   On the **Tools** menu, point to **Tracking**, and click **Update Project**.

2   In the **Update Project** dialog box, make sure the **Update work as complete through** option is selected. In the adjacent date list, type or click the date you want, and click **OK**.

112 **To enter a task's percent complete using the Project Guide**

1   On the **Project Guide** toolbar, click the **Track** button.

2   In the Track pane, click the **Prepare to track the progress of your project** link.

3   Click the **Save and go to Step 2** link.

4   Click **Always track by entering the Percent of Work Complete**, and then click the **Save and Finish** link at the bottom of the Setup Tracking pane.

5   In the Track pane, click the **Incorporate progress information into the project** link.

6   In the **% Work Complete** field for a task, type or click the percent complete value you want, and then press Enter.

114 **To enter actual values for tasks using the Project Guide**

1   On the **Project Guide** toolbar, click the **Track** button.

2   In the Track pane, click the **Prepare to track the progress of your project** link.

3   Click the **Save and go to Step 2** link.

4   Click **Always track by entering the Actual Work Done and Work Remaining**, and then click **Save and Finish**.

5   In the Track pane, click the **Incorporate progress information into the project** link.

6   In the **Actual Work** field for a task, type or click the actual work value you want, and then press Enter.

116 **To enter actual start dates and durations of tasks**

1   Click the task for which you want to enter actual values.

2   On the **Tools** menu point to **Tracking**, and then click **Update Tasks**.

3   In the **Start** field in the **Actual** box on the left side of the **Update Tasks** dialog box, type or click the start date you want.

4   In the **Actual dur** field, type or click the duration value you want, and then click **OK**.

139   To create a new base calendar

1   On the **Tools** menu, click **Change Working Time**.

2   In the **Change Working Time** dialog box, click the **New** button.

3   In the **Name** box, type a name for the base calendar.

4   Click **Create new base calendar**, or click **Make a copy of** and then choose the base calendar on which you want to base the new calendar.

5   Click **OK**.

6   In the **Selected Date(s)** box, click the days of the week for which you want to change working and nonworking time.

7   Under **Set selected date(s) to**, click **Nonworking time** for those days you want to mark as nonworking time.

8   For working days, in the **From** and **To** boxes, enter the working time you want.

140   To apply a task calendar to a task

1   In the Gantt Chart view, click a task.

2   On the Standard toolbar, click the **Task Information** button.

3   In the **Task Information** dialog box, click the **Advanced** tab.

4   In the **Calendar** box, choose the task calendar you want to apply.

5   If you want the task calendar to override resource calendar settings, click the **Scheduling ignores resource calendars** box.

140   To change a task type

1   In the Gantt Chart view, click a task.

2   On the Standard toolbar, click the **Task Information** button.

3   In the **Task Information** dialog box, click the **Advanced** tab.

4   In the **Task Type** box, click the task type you want.

145   To enter a deadline date using the Project Guide

1   On the **Project Guide** toolbar, click the **Tasks** button.

2   In the Tasks pane, click the **Set deadlines and constrain tasks** link, and then follow the instructions that appear on your screen.

148   To enter a fixed cost

1   On the **View** menu, point to **Table: Entry**, and then click **Cost**.

2   In the **Fixed Cost** field for the task you want, type or click an amount, and press `Tab`.

3   In the **Fixed Cost Accrual** field, choose a method, and then press `Enter`.

4 In the **Resource Information** dialog box, click the **General** tab.

5 In the **Resource Availability** grid, enter the date ranges and unit values you want.

161 **To delay the start of an assignment**

1 On the **View** menu, click **Task Usage** or **Resource Usage**.

2 Click the assignment you want to delay.

3 On the Standard toolbar, click the **Assignment Information** button.

4 In the **Assignment Information** dialog box, click the **General** tab.

5 In the **Start** box, type or click the date on which you want the selected resource to start work on the assignment, and then click **OK**.

163 **To apply a contour to an assignment**

1 On the **View** menu, click **Task Usage** or **Resource Usage**.

2 Click the assignment for which you want to contour to an assignment.

3 On the Standard toolbar, click the **Assignment Information** button.

4 In the **Assignment Information** dialog box, click the **General** tab.

5 In the **Work Contour** box, click the contour you want, and then click **OK**.

166 **To apply a different cost rate to an assignment**

1 On the **View** menu, click **Task Usage** or **Resource Usage**.

2 Click the assignment for which you want to apply a different cost rate table.

3 On the Standard toolbar, click the **Assignment Information** button.

4 In the **Assignment Information** dialog box, click the **General** tab.

5 In the **Cost Rate Table** box, type or click the rate table you want to apply to this assignment, and then click **OK**.

168 **To enter a material resource consumption rate on an assignment**

1 In the Gantt Chart view, click the name of the task to which you want to assign a material resource.

2 On the Standard toolbar, click the **Assign Resources** button.

3 In the **Assign Resources** dialog box, in the **Units** field for the material resource, type the consumption rate you want in the format quantity/time period. For example, to specify 20 feet per hour, type 20/hr.

4 Click the **Assign** button.

Chapter 10 **Organizing and Formatting Project Details**

Page 198 **To sort data in a view**

1 Switch to the view or table you want to sort.

2 On the **Project** menu, point to **Sort**, and then click the field by which you want to sort the view. To specify a custom sort, click **Sort By**, and in the **Sort** dialog box, choose the options you want.

202 **To group data in a view**

1 Switch to the view or table you want to group.

2 On the **Project** menu, point to **Group By: No Group**, and then choose the criteria by which you want to group the view. To specify different grouping options, click **Customize Group By**, and then choose the options you want in the **Customize Group By** dialog box.

207 **To turn AutoFilter on or off**

● On the Formatting toolbar, click the **AutoFilter** button.

207 **To filter data in a view**

1 Switch to the view you want to filter.

2 On the **Project** menu, point to **Filtered For**, and click **More Filters**.

3 In the **More Filters** dialog box, choose the filter you want, and then click the **Apply** button.

208 **To create a custom filter**

1 On the **Project** menu, point to **Filtered For: All Tasks** (for task views) or **All Resources** (for resource views), and then click **More Filters**.

2 In the **More Filters** dialog box, click the **New** button.

3 In the **Filter Definition** dialog box, select the options you want.

210 **To remove a filter**

● On the **Project** menu, point to **Filtered For:<filter name>**, and then click **All Tasks** (for task views) or **All Resources** (for resource views).

229 **To work in the Print Preview window**

1 On the **File** menu, click **Print Preview**.

2 Do one of the following:

- ■ To navigate between pages of a multi-page print job, click a page navigation button.

- ■ To zoom out to see all pages of a print job, click the **Multiple Pages** button.

- ■ To change page setup options such as header or legend text, click the **Page Setup** button, and choose the options you want.

- ■ To display the **Print** dialog box and set other options, or to print what you see in the Print Preview window, click the **Print** button.

- ■ To exit the Print Preview window, click the **Close** button.

234 **To print a predefined report**

1 On the **View** menu, click **Reports**.

2 In the **Reports** dialog box, click the category of report you want, and then click the **Select** button.

3 In the dialog box that appears next, click the specific report you want to print, and click the **Select** button.

4 In the Print Preview window, click **Print**.

234 **To edit a predefined report**

1 On the **View** menu, click **Reports**.

2 In the **Reports** dialog box, click the category of report you want, and then click the **Select** button (or for custom reports, click the **Preview** button).

3 In the dialog box that appears next, click the specific report you want to edit, and then click the **Edit** button.

4 In the dialog box that appears next, choose the options you want.

Chapter 12 **Publishing Project Information Online**

Page 242 **To save a snapshot of a view as a GIF image**

1 Set up the view with the specific details (such as the table, filter, or group) you want.

2 On the Standard toolbar, click the **Copy Picture** button.

3   Under the **Render Image** label, click **To GIF image file**, and then specify the file name and location you want.

4   Select whatever other options you want, and click **OK**.

246   **To customize how Project saves a Web page**

1   On the **File** menu, click **Save As Web Page**.

2   Specify the file name and location you want, and click the **Save** button.

3   In the Export Wizard, select the options you want.

Chapter 13   Sharing Project Information with Other Programs

Page 256   **To copy text from a Project table to the Windows Clipboard**

1   Set up the table to display only the data you want to copy—for example, apply a filter or insert or hide columns.

2   Select the range of data you want to copy.

3   On the **Edit** menu, click **Copy Cell**, **Copy Task**, or **Copy Resource**.

258   **To copy a snapshot of a view to the Windows Clipboard**

1   Set up the view with the specific details (such as tables, filters, or groups) you want.

2   On the Standard toolbar, click **Copy Picture**.

3   In the **Copy Picture** dialog box, click either **For screen**, to optimize the snapshot for online viewing, or **For printer**, to optimize it for printing.

4   Select whatever other options you want, and then click **OK**.

260   **To create a new Project summary report for Word, PowerPoint, or Visio**

1   On the **View** menu point to **Toolbars**, and click **Analysis**.

2   On the **Analysis** toolbar, click the **Copy Picture to Office Wizard** button, and then follow the instructions that appear on your screen.

265   **To open a file in a different format in Project**

1   On the **File** menu, click **Open**.

2   In the **Files of type** box, click the file format you want.

3   Locate and click the specific file you want to open, and then click the **Open** button.

4   If the file you selected is not in Project format, the Import Wizard appears. Follow the instructions that appear on your screen.

305 **To filter for tasks that have slipped**

    1   On the **Project** menu, point to **Filtered For: All Tasks,** and then click **More Filters.**

    2   In the **More Filters** dialog box, click **Slipping Tasks,** and then click the **Apply** button.

306 **To see schedule variance**

    ●   On the **View** menu, point to **Table: Entry,** and then click **Variance.**

309 **To see task costs in a view**

    1   On the **View** menu, click **More Views.**

    2   In the **More Views** dialog box, click **Task Sheet** and then click **Apply.**

    3   On the **View** menu, point to **Table: Variance,** and click **Cost.**

312 **To see task costs and overbudget tasks using the Project Guide**

    1   On the **Project Guide** toolbar, click the **Report** button.

    2   In the Report pane, click the **See project costs** link.

    3   In the Project Costs pane under **Apply a filter,** click **Cost Overbudget.**

314 **To sort resources by cost**

    1   On the **View** menu, click **Resource Sheet.**

    2   On the **View** menu, point to **Table: Entry** and click **Cost.**

    3   On the **Project** menu, point to **Sort,** and click **Sort By.**

    4   In the **Sort** dialog box, in the **Sort By** box, click **Cost,** and then select the **Descending** option.

    5   Make sure the **Permanently renumber resources** check box is cleared, and then click the **Sort** button.

315 **To sort resources by cost variance**

    1   On the **View** menu, click **Resource Sheet.**

    2   On the **View** menu, point to **Table: Entry** and click **Cost.**

    3   On the **Project** menu, point to **Sort** and click **Sort By.**

    4   In the **Sort** dialog box, in the **Sort By** box, click **Cost Variance.**

    5   Make sure the **Permanently renumber resources** check box is cleared, and then click the **Sort** button.

354   To format bars in the Calendar view

1   On the **View** menu, click **Calendar**.

2   On the **Format** menu, click **Bar Styles**.

3   In the **Bar Styles** dialog box, select the options you want.

Chapter 18   Customizing Project

Page 361   **To copy a custom element from one project plan to another through the Organizer**

1   First open the project plan that contains the custom element (such as a custom table), and then open the project plan to which you want to copy the custom element.

2   On the **Tools** menu, click **Organizer**.

3   Click the tab name that corresponds to the type of custom element you want to copy.

4   In the **<Custom Elements> available in** drop-down list on the left side of the **Organizer** dialog box, click the name of the project plan that contains the custom element.

5   Click the **Copy** button.

365   To record a macro

1   On the **Tools** menu, point to **Macro**, and then click **Record New Macro**.

2   In the **Macro name** box, enter a name for the macro (no spaces allowed).

3   In the **Store macro in** box, click **This Project** to store the macro in the active project plan, or **Global File** to store it in the global template.

4   Click **OK**.

5   Perform the actions you want recorded in the macro.

6   On the **Tools** menu, point to **Macro**, and then click **Stop Recorder**.

368   To run a macro

1   On the **Tools** menu, point to **Macro**, and then click **Macros**.

2   In the **Macro name** box, click the name of the macro you want to run, and then click the **Run** button.

369   To edit a macro in the Visual Basic Editor

1   On the **Tools** menu, point to **Macro**, and then click **Macros**.

2   In the **Macro name** box, click the name of the macro you want to edit, and then click the **Edit** button.

3   In the Visual Basic Editor, edit the macro.

4   On the **File** menu in the Visual Basic Editor, click **Close and Return to Microsoft Project**.

374 **To create a custom toolbar**

1   On the **Tools** menu, point to **Customize**, and then click **Toolbars**.

2   Click the **Toolbars** tab.

3   Click the **New** button.

4   In the **Toolbar Name** box, type the toolbar name you want, and then click **OK**.

375 **To add a command to a custom toolbar**

1   On the **Tools** menu, point to **Customize**, and then click **Toolbars**.

2   Click the **Commands** tab.

3   In the **Categories** list, click the category you want.

4   Drag the command you want from the **Commands** list to the custom toolbar.

377 **To edit the graphic image and text that appears on a custom toolbar button**

1   On the **Tools** menu, point to **Customize**, and then click **Toolbars**.

2   Click the **Commands** tab.

3   Click the custom button you want to modify on the custom toolbar.

4   Click the **Modify Selection** button, and then point to **Change Button Image**.

5   In the list of images that appears, click the image you want.

6   Click **Modify Selection**, and in the **Name** box, type the text you want for the custom button name.

Chapter 19 Measuring Performance with Earned Value Analysis

Page 383 **To set the project status date**

1   On the **Project** menu, click **Project Information**.

2   In the **Project Information** dialog box, in the **Status Date** box, type or click the status date you want, and click **OK**.

383 **To view earned value schedule indicators**

1   On the **View** menu, click **More Views**.

2   In the **More Views** dialog box, click **Task Sheet** and then click **Apply**.

3   On the **View** menu, point to **Table: Entry**, and click **More Tables**.

4   In the **More Tables** dialog box, click **Earned Value Schedule Indicators**, and click the **Apply** button.

385 **To view earned value cost indicators**

1 On the **View** menu, click **More Views**.

2 In the **More Views** dialog box, click **Task Sheet** and then click **Apply**.

3 On the **View** menu, point to **Table: Entry**, and click **More Tables**.

4 In the **More Tables** dialog box, click **Earned Value Cost Indicators**, and click the **Apply** button.

Chapter 20 **Consolidating Projects and Resources**

Page 393 **To create a resource pool**

1 Create a new project plan.

2 Save the new project plan that will become a resource pool.

3 Open one of the project plans you want to make a sharer plan.

4 On the **Tools** menu, point to **Resource Sharing**, and click **Share Resources**.

5 Under **Resources for <Sharer Plan Name>**, click **Use resources**.

6 In the **From** list, click the name of your resource pool, and click **OK** to close the **Share Resources** dialog box.

7 If you have more than one sharer plan, open another sharer plan.

8 Repeat steps 3 through 7 for the other sharer plans.

397 **To view assignment details in the resource pool**

1 On the **View** menu, click **Resource Usage**.

2 In the **Resource Name** column, click the name of a resource.

3 On the **Window** menu, click **Split** to display the Resource Form.

400 **To update a resource's working time in the resource pool**

1 Open the resource pool as read-write.

2 On the **View** menu, click **Resource Usage**.

3 In the **Resource Name** column of the Resource Usage view, click the name of the resource whose working time you want to change, and click the **Resource Information** button.

4 In the **Resource Information** dialog box, click the **Working Time** tab.

5 In the calendar below the **Select Date(s)** label, drag the vertical scroll bar or click the up or down arrow buttons until the month and year you want appears.

6   Click the dates you want to designate as nonworking time.

7   Under **Set selected date(s) to**, click **Nonworking time**, and click **OK** to close the **Resource Information** dialog box.

To update working time for all sharer plans from the resource pool

1   Open the resource pool as read/write.

2   On the **Tools** menu, click **Change Working Time**.

3   In the **Change Working Time** dialog box, in the **For** box, click the base calendar you want to change, for example **Standard (Project Calendar)**.

4   In the calendar below the **Select Date(s)** label, drag the vertical scroll bar or click the up or down arrow buttons until the month and year you want appears, and then click the specific days you want to make nonworking time.

5   Under **Set selected date(s) to**, click **Nonworking time**.

6   Click **OK** to close the **Change Working Time** dialog box.

To link new project files to the resource pool

1   Open the resource pool as read/write.

2   On the Standard toolbar, click the **New** button.

3   On the **Tools** menu, point to **Resource Sharing**, and click **Share Resources**.

4   In the **Share Resources** dialog box, under **Resources for <File Name>**, click **Use resources**.

5   In the **From** list, click the name of the resource pool, and click **OK** to close the **Share Resources** dialog box.

6   Save the sharer plan and resource pool.

To edit a sharer plan and update the resource pool

1   Open a sharer plan.

2   When prompted, open the resource pool.

3   In the sharer plan, make changes to assignments.

4   On the **Tools** menu, point to **Resource Sharing**, and click **Update Resource Pool**.

To create a consolidated project plan

1   On the Standard toolbar, click the **New** button.

2   Save the new project plan.

3   On the **Insert** menu, click **Project**.

4 In the **Insert Projects** dialog box, locate and click the project plan you want to insert into the consolidated project plan. To select multiple plans, hold down the ⌃Ctrl key while you click the name of each plan.

5 Click the **Insert** button.

413 **To create task dependencies between projects**

1 Open the two project plans between which you want to create a task dependency.

2 Switch to the project plan that contains the task you want to make the successor task.

3 On the **View** menu, click **Gantt Chart**.

4 Click the name of the task you want to make the successor task.

5 On the Standard toolbar, click the **Task Information** button.

6 Click the **Predecessors** tab.

7 In the **ID** column, click the next empty cell below any other predecessor tasks, and enter the name of the predecessor task from the other project file in this format: *Filename\Task ID*.

8 Press ⏎Enter, and click **OK** to close the **Task Information** dialog box.

Chapter 21 Planning Work with Project Server

Note These procedures require Project Professional with access to Project Server.

Page 422 **To create a new plan based on a template (project manager activity)**

1 In Project Professional, on the **File** menu click **New**.

2 In the New Project pane, under **Templates** click **On my computer**.

3 In the **Templates** dialog box, click the **Project Templates** tab, and double-click the template you want.

427 **To run the Resource Substitution Wizard (project manager activity)**

1 In Project Professional, open an enterprise project plan that contains generic or work resources that you want to replace.

2 On the **Tools** menu, click **Substitute Resources**

3 In the Resource Substitution Wizard, follow the instructions that appear on your screen.

437 **To publish a project plan to Project Server (project manager activity)**

1   In Project Professional, develop a project plan to the point that you are ready to publish it to Project Server.

2   On the **Collaborate** menu point to **Publish,** and then click **All Information.**

3   To republish updated information, on the **Collaborate** menu point to **Publish,** and then click **New and Changed Assignments.**

Chapter 22 **Tracking Work with Project Server**

Note   These procedures require Project Professional or Project Web Access with access to Project Server, or Outlook with the Outlook integration add-in installed from Project Server.

Page 442 **To report task changes through Project Web Access (resource activity)**

1   Log in to Project Web Access.

2   Click the **Tasks** tab to display the Tasks Center.

3   In the Tasks Center, record the actual work, percent complete, or other task status you want.

4   Click **Update All.**

442 **To report upcoming nonworking time through Project Web Access (resource activity)**

1   Log in to Project Web Access.

2   Click the **Tasks** tab to display the Tasks Center.

3   Click the **Notify your manager of time you will not be available for project work** in the pane on the left.

4   Record the type of nonworking time you want to report, and then click **Submit.**

446 **To manage tasks through the Outlook calendar (resource activity)**

1   Start Outlook and display the calendar.

2   Do one of the following:

■   To import new or updated task assignments, click the **Import New Assignments** button on the **Project Web Access** toolbar.

■   To record progress on an assignment, double-click the assignment's appointment in the calendar, click the **Project Web Access** tab, and record the values you want.

451 **To accept task changes from resources (project manager activity)**

1 Log in to Project Web Access.

2 Click the **Updates** tab to display the Updates Center.

3 For the task changes you want to accept, click in the **Accept?** column and in the drop-down list that appears click **Accept**.

4 Click **Update**.

5 After Project Server updates the affected plans in Project Professional, evaluate the impact of the task changes on the overall schedule.

456 **To see multi-project status and drill into a specific project (executive or other stakeholder activity)**

1 Log in to Project Web Access.

2 Click the **Projects** tab to display the Project Center.

3 Change the display options or active view to see the projects published to Project Server.

4 To display information for a specific project, in the **Project Name** column click the name of the project you'd like to see.

Chapter 23 **Managing Risks, Issues, and Documents with Project Server**

Note These procedures require Windows SharePoint Services integrated with Project Server.

Page 464 **To create a new risk (executive, project manager, or resource activity)**

1 Log in to Project Web Access.

2 Click the **Resources** tab, and then select a project with which you want to associate a risk.

3 Enter the risk information you want.

467 **To create a new issue (executive, project manager, or resource activity)**

1 Log in to Project Web Access.

2 Click the **Issues** tab, and then select a project with which you want to associate an issue.

3 Enter the issue information you want.

470 **To upload a document (executive, project manager, or resource activity)**

1 Log in to Project Web Access.

2 Click the **Documents** tab, and then select a project with which you want to associate a document.

3 In the document library, click **Upload Document,** and locate the document you want.

I
Managing a
Simple Project

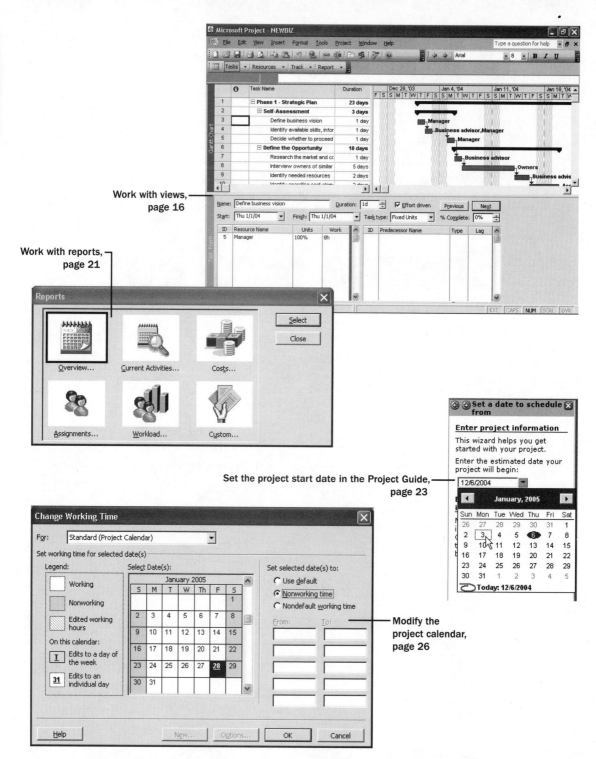

Work with views, page 16

Work with reports, page 21

Set the project start date in the Project Guide, page 23

Modify the project calendar, page 26

Chapter 1 at a Glance

1 Getting Started with Project

In this chapter you will learn to:

✔ Understand the family of Microsoft Office Project 2003 products.

✔ Understand what a good project management tool can help you do.

✔ Start Project Standard or Project Professional, and identify the major parts of the Project window.

✔ Use views to work with project plan details in different ways.

✔ Use reports to print project plan details.

✔ Create a project plan and enter a project start date.

✔ Set the working and nonworking time for a project.

✔ Enter a project plan's properties.

Project management is a broadly practiced art and science. If you're reading this book, there's a good chance that either you're seriously involved in project management, or you want to be.

At its heart, project management is a toolbox of skills and tools that help you predict and control the outcomes of endeavors your organization undertakes. Your organization might do other work apart from projects. *Projects* (such as a film project) are distinct from *ongoing operations* (such as payroll services) in that projects are temporary endeavors undertaken to create some sort of unique deliverable or end result. With a good project management system in place, you should be able to answer such questions as

■ What *tasks* must be done to produce the *deliverable* of the project?

■ Who will complete these tasks?

■ What's the best way to communicate project details to people who have an interest in the project?

■ When should each task be performed?

■ How much will it cost?

■ What if some tasks are not completed as scheduled?

Good project management does not guarantee the success of every project, but poor project management usually guarantees failure.

Microsoft Office Project 2003 should be one of the most frequently used tools in your project management toolbox. This book explains how to use Project to build project plans complete with tasks and resources, use the extensive formatting features in Project to organize and format the project plan details, track actual work against the plan, and take corrective action when things get off track.

See Also   If you are new to project management, stop right here and read Appendix A, "A Short Course in Project Management," before proceeding with this chapter. It won't take you long, and it will help you properly assess and organize your specific project scheduling needs and build solid plans in Project.

Most of the exercises in this book revolve around a fictitious film production company, Southridge Video and Film Productions. Chances are you don't work for a film production company, but you probably have seen a TV commercial or film recently. Each is its own project; some in fact are fairly complex projects involving hundreds of resources and aggressive *deadlines*. We think you'll be able to recognize many of the scheduling problems Southridge Video encounters and apply the solutions to your own scheduling needs.

This chapter walks you through the Project interface and presents the steps necessary to create a new project plan in Project.

 Important   To follow along with the exercises in this book, you need to install the practice files from the companion CD. (You cannot just copy the files.) You will find instructions for installing the files in "Using the Book's CD-ROM," on page xiii.

Managing Your Projects with Project

The best project management tool in the world can never replace your good judgment. However, the tool can and should help you accomplish the following:

- Track all the information you gather about the work, duration, costs, and resource requirements for your project.

- Visualize and present your project plan in standard, well-defined formats.

- Schedule tasks and resources consistently and effectively.

- Exchange project information with other Microsoft Office System applications.

■ Communicate with resources and other stakeholders while you, the project manager, retain ultimate control of the project.

■ Manage projects using a program that looks and feels like other desktop productivity applications.

The Microsoft Office Project 2003 family encompasses a broad range of products, including the following:

■ Microsoft Office Project 2003 Standard edition, a Windows-based desktop application for project management. The Standard edition is designed for the single project manager and does not interact with Project Server. The previous version, Project Standard 2002, could be used with Project Server for some collaborative functions, but Project Standard 2003 is a stand-alone product.

■ Microsoft Office Project 2003 Professional edition, a Windows-based desktop application that includes the full feature set of the Standard edition, plus—when used with Project Server—additional project team planning and communications features. Project Professional plus Project Server represents Microsoft's *enterprise project management* (EPM) product offering.

■ Microsoft Office Project 2003 Server, an intranet-based solution that enables enterprise-level project collaboration, timesheet reporting, and status reporting when used in conjunction with Project Professional.

■ Microsoft Office Project 2003 Web Access, the Internet Explorer–based interface for working with Project Server.

Tip   To learn more about the new features in Project 2003 and the differences between the Standard and Professional editions, type **What's new?** into the **Search** box in the upper right corner of the Project window. The **Search** box initially contains the text *Type a question for help*.

Most of the chapters in this book focus on the feature set of Project Standard, the entry-level desktop project management tool. The chapters in Part 4 introduce you to the enterprise project management features available with Project Professional and Project Server. All of the content in this book that applies to Project Standard also applies to Project Professional, so you can use either edition of Project to complete Parts 1 through 3 of this book. If you have Project Professional and access to Project Server, you can also explore the features introduced in Part 4. Otherwise, you can browse through Part 4 to help you decide whether you or your organization should be using Project Professional and Project Server.

What Can a Scheduling Engine Do for You?

Many projects are not managed with a real scheduling tool such as Project, but they should be. It's common to see task and resource lists from spreadsheet programs such as Excel, or even nicely formatted Gantt charts from drawing programs such as Visio. One big advantage Project has over such applications is that it includes a scheduling engine— a computational brain that can handle issues such as ripple effects when task 1 in a 100-task sequence changes its start date. This scheduling engine can also account for nonworking time such as weekends when calculating a task's start and finish dates. Applications such as Excel and Visio might have a place in your project management tool-box, but to be really successful you'll need a scheduling engine such as Project.

Starting Project Standard

Note   Follow the steps in this section if you have Microsoft Office Project Standard. If you have Microsoft Office Project Professional, skip this section and refer to the next section, "Starting Project Professional." If you don't know which edition of Project you have, Start Project, and on the **Help** menu click **About Microsoft Office Project**. The dialog box that appears indicates which edition you have.

Project Standard is a member of the Microsoft Office System, so much of what you see in Project is similar to what you see in Word, Excel, and Access. For example, Project's menu bar and toolbars are similar in organization, if not in content, to other Office applications.

In this exercise, you'll start Project Standard, create a file based on a *template* (a file containing some initial data that you can use as a starting point for a new project plan), and see the major areas of the default Project interface.

1   On the Windows taskbar, click the **Start** button.

     The **Start** menu appears.

2   On the **Start** menu, point to **All Programs** (in Microsoft Windows XP) or **Programs** (in previous versions of Windows), point to **Microsoft Office**, and then click **Microsoft Office Project 2003**.

     Project Standard appears. Your screen should look similar to the following illustration:

Menu bar Project plan window Search for Help box

Toolbars

Task pane

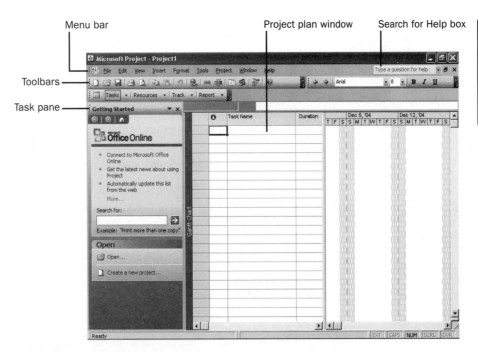

Toolbar Options

Important Depending on the screen resolution you have set on your computer and which toolbar buttons you use most often, it's possible that not every button on every toolbar will appear on your Project toolbars. If a button mentioned in this book doesn't appear on a toolbar, click the **Toolbar Options** down arrow on that toolbar to display the rest of the available buttons.

If you've used Office applications, or if you're upgrading from a previous version of Project, you'll be familiar with many of the major interface elements in the Project window. Let's walk through them:

■ The main menu bar enables you to give instructions to Project.

■ Toolbars provide quick access to the most common tasks; most toolbar buttons correspond to a menu bar command. Like other Office applications, Project customizes the menus and toolbars for you, based on how frequently you use specific commands or toolbar buttons. The most frequently used commands and buttons will remain visible on the menus and toolbars, whereas the commands and buttons you don't use will be temporarily hidden.

■ The project plan window contains a view of the active project plan. (We'll refer to the types of documents Project works with as *project plans*, not documents or schedules.) The name of the active view appears on the left edge of the view—in this case, the Gantt Chart view is displayed.

Search Help

New in Office 2003

■ The box labeled *Type a question for help* enables you to quickly search Project's Help for instructions on performing common activities in Project. Just type in a question and press ⊂Enter⊃. Throughout this book we'll suggest questions you can enter into this box to learn more about specific features. If your computer is connected to the Internet, your search query will go to assistance content on Office Online (part of the Microsoft Web site), and the results displayed will reflect the most up-to-date content available from Microsoft. If your computer is not connected to the Internet, the search results will be limited to the Help installed with Project.

■ The Getting Started task pane in Project is similar to the task panes you might see in other Office applications. It is a convenient list of recently opened files as well as another means of creating new files. In addition to this task pane, Project includes the Project Guide, which is discussed below.

Next you will view the templates included with Project and create a project plan based on one of them.

3   In the Getting Started task pane, click **Create a new project**.

The New Project task pane replaces the Getting Started task pane.

4   In the New Project task pane, under **Template**, click **On my computer**.

The **Templates** dialog box appears.

5   Click the **Project Templates** tab.

Your screen should look similar to the following illustration:

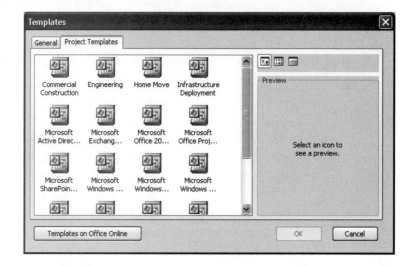

6   Click **New Business** (you may need to scroll down in the list of Project Templates to see it), and then click **OK**.

Important   Depending on how Project was installed on your computer, the templates included with Project might not be installed at this point. This "install on first use" setting is one of the setup choices for optional components included with Project. If you have never seen the templates included with Project before, spend some time browsing through them. You might find one that matches an upcoming project for which you'd like to develop a full plan. Starting with a predefined template can save you a lot of effort.

Project creates a project plan based on the New Business template, closes the New Project task pane, and displays the Tasks activity list in the Project Guide. Your screen should look similar to the following illustration:

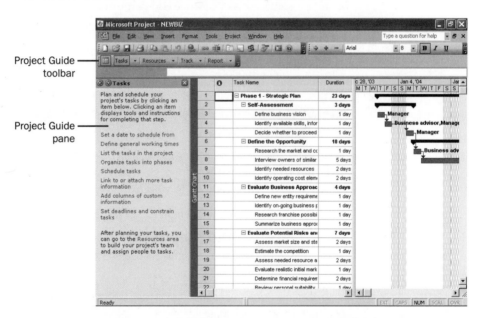

The Project Guide is a wizard-like interface you can use when creating or fine-tuning a project plan. In later chapters you will use the Project Guide to perform many common activities relating to tasks, resources, and assignments. You can view all activities in the Project Guide through the **Project Guide** toolbar. This toolbar is divided into the most common subject areas of Project (Tasks, Resources, Track, and Report).

For the next few exercises in this chapter, you will use the sample data provided by the template to identify the major parts of the Project interface.

Starting Project Professional

Note Follow the steps in this section if you have Microsoft Office Project Professional. If you have Microsoft Office Project Standard, skip this section and refer to the previous section, "Starting Project Standard." If you don't know which edition of Project you have, Start Project and on the **Help** menu click **About Microsoft Office Project**. The dialog box that appears indicates which edition you have.

Project Professional is a member of the Microsoft Office System, so much of what you see in Project is similar to what you see in Word, Excel, and Access. For example, Project's menu bar and toolbars are similar in organization, if not in content, to other Office applications.

In this exercise, you'll start Project Professional, create a file based on a *template* (a file containing some initial data that you can use as a starting point for a new project plan), and see the major areas of the default Project interface.

1 On the Windows taskbar, click the **Start** button.

The **Start** menu appears.

2 On the **Start** menu, point to **All Programs** (in Microsoft Windows XP) or **Programs** (in previous versions of Windows), point to **Microsoft Office**, and then click **Microsoft Office Project 2003**.

Depending on how your enterprise options have been set in Project Professional, you may be prompted to log into or choose a Project Server account. If so, complete steps 3 and 4. Otherwise, go to step 5.

3 If the **Project Server Security Login** dialog box appears, click **Cancel**.

You would see the **Project Server Security Login** dialog box only if Project Professional has been set up to log into a specific Project Server account using Project Server Security authentication.

4 In the **Project Server Accounts** dialog box, under **Choose account** select **My Computer**, and then click **Work Offline**.

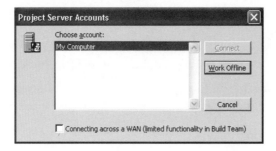

Choosing this option sets Project Professional to work independent of your Project Server and helps ensure that none of the practice file data you use for this chapter can accidentally be published to your Project Server.

Project appears. Next you'll review or adjust some enterprise options.

5 On the **Tools** menu point to **Enterprise Options,** and then click **Microsoft Office Project Server Accounts.**

The **Project Server Accounts** dialog box appears. Your screen should look similar to the following illustration:

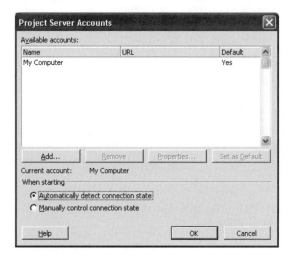

6 Note the **Current account** value.

If the **Current account** value is something other than **My Computer,** click **Manually control connection state,** click **OK,** and then complete step 7.

Or

If the **Current account** value is **My Computer,** click **Cancel,** and then skip step 7.

Choosing **Manually control connection state** will cause Project Professional to prompt you to choose an account to work with when you start Project Professional. This helps ensure that none of the practice file data you use for this chapter can accidentally be published to your Project Server.

7 Close and restart Project Professional. If prompted to choose an account, click **My Computer,** and then click **Work Offline.**

Project Professional appears. Your screen should look similar to the following illustration:

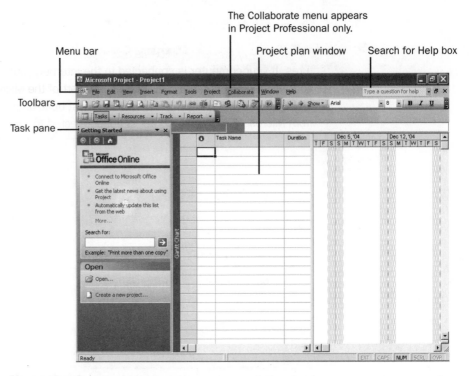

The Collaborate menu appears in Project Professional only.

Menu bar — Project plan window — Search for Help box

Toolbars —

Task pane —

Toolbar Options

Important Depending on the screen resolution you have set on your computer and which toolbar buttons you use most often, it's possible that not every button on every toolbar will appear on your Project toolbars. If a button mentioned in this book doesn't appear on a toolbar, click the **Toolbar Options** down arrow on that toolbar to display the rest of the available buttons.

If you've used Office applications, or if you're upgrading from a previous version of Project, you'll be familiar with many of the major interface elements in the Project window. Let's walk through them:

■ The main menu bar enables you to give instructions to Project.

■ Toolbars provide quick access to the most common tasks; most toolbar buttons correspond to a menu bar command. Like other Office applications, Project customizes the menus and toolbars for you, based on how frequently you use specific commands or toolbar buttons. The most frequently used commands and buttons will remain visible on the menus and toolbars, whereas the commands and buttons you don't use will be temporarily hidden.

■ The project plan window contains a view of the active project plan. (We'll refer to the types of documents Project works with as *project plans,* not documents or schedules.) The name of the active view appears on the left edge of the view—in this case, the Gantt Chart view is displayed.

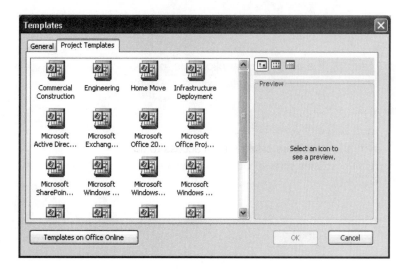

Type a question for help

Search Help

■ The box labeled *Type a question for help* enables you to quickly search Project's Help for instructions on performing common activities in Project. Just type in a question and press ⌊Enter⌋. Throughout this book we'll suggest questions you can enter into this box to learn more about specific features. If your computer is connected to the Internet, your search query will go to assistance content on Office Online (part of the Microsoft Web site), and the results displayed will reflect the most up-to-date content available from Microsoft. If your computer is not connected to the Internet, the search results will be limited to the Help installed with Project.

■ The Getting Started task pane in Project is similar to the task panes you might see in other Office applications. It is a convenient list of recently opened files as well as another means of creating new files. In addition to this task pane, Project includes the Project Guide, which is discussed below.

Next you will view the templates included with Project and create a project plan based on one of them.

8 In the Getting Started task pane, click **Create a new project**.

The New Project task pane replaces the Getting Started task pane.

9 In the New Project task pane, under **Template**, click **On my computer**.

The **Templates** dialog box appears.

10 Click the **Project Templates** tab.

Your screen should look similar to the following illustration:

11 Click **New Business** (you may need to scroll down in the list of Project Templates to see it), and then click **OK**.

Important Depending on how Project was installed on your computer, the templates included with Project might not be installed at this point. This "install on first use" setting is one of the setup choices for optional components included with Project. If you have never seen the templates included with Project before, spend some time browsing through them. You might find one that matches an upcoming project for which you'd like to develop a full plan. Starting with a predefined template can save you a lot of effort.

12 Project creates a project plan based on the New Business template, closes the New Project task pane, and displays the Tasks activity list in the Project Guide. Your screen should look similar to the following illustration:

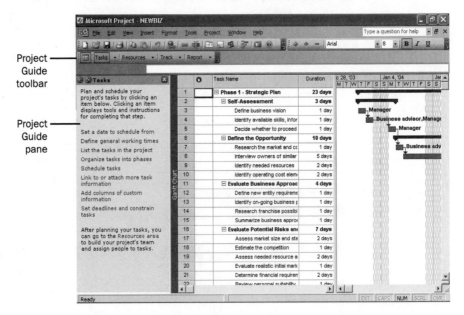

The Project Guide is a wizard-like interface you can use when creating or fine-tuning a project plan. In later chapters you will use the Project Guide to perform many common activities relating to tasks, resources, and assignments. You can view all activities in the Project Guide through the **Project Guide** toolbar. This toolbar is divided into the most common subject areas of Project (Tasks, Resources, Track, and Report).

For the next few exercises in this chapter, you will use the sample data provided by the template to identify the major parts of the Project interface.

Exploring Views

The working space in Project is called a *view*. Project contains dozens of views, but you normally work with just one view (sometimes two) at a time. You use views to enter, edit, analyze, and display your project information. The default view, the one you see when Project starts, is the *Gantt Chart view* shown here.

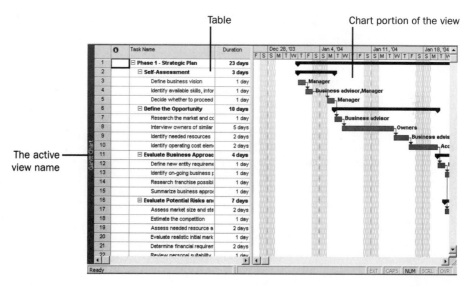

Table

Chart portion of the view

The active
view name

In general, views focus on either task or resource details. The Gantt Chart view, for example, lists task details in a table on the left side of the view and graphically represents each task as a bar in the chart on the right side of the view. The Gantt Chart view is a common way to represent a project plan, especially when presenting it to others. It is also useful for entering and fine-tuning task details and for analyzing your project.

In this exercise, you'll start at the Gantt Chart view and then switch to other views that highlight different aspects of a project plan. Finally, you'll explore combination views that let you focus on specific project details more easily.

1 On the **View** menu, click **Resource Sheet**.

The Resource Sheet view replaces the Gantt Chart view. The Project Guide is updated to display a list of activities specific to resources:

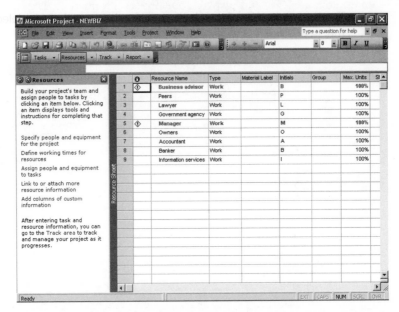

The Resource Sheet view displays details about resources in a row-and-column for-mat (called a *table*), with one resource per row. This view is called a sheet view. There is one other sheet view, the Task Sheet view, which lists the task details. Note that Resource Sheet view doesn't tell you anything about the tasks to which resources might be assigned. To see that type of information, you'll switch to a dif-ferent view.

2 On the **View** menu, click **Resource Usage**.

The Resource Usage view replaces the Resource Sheet view, and the Project Guide is updated again.

This usage view groups the tasks to which each resource is assigned. Another usage view, the Task Usage view, flips this around to display all the resources assigned to each task. Usage views also show you work assignments per resource on a timescale such as daily or weekly. Next you'll switch to the Task Usage view.

3   On the **View** menu, click **Task Usage**.

The Task Usage view replaces the Resource Usage view, and the Project Guide is updated again.

4   In the table portion of the view on the left, click **Define business vision**, the name of task 3.

5   On the Standard toolbar, click the **Go To Selected Task** button.

Go To
Selected Task

The timescale side of the view scrolls to show you the scheduled work values for this task, shown below.

Timescale

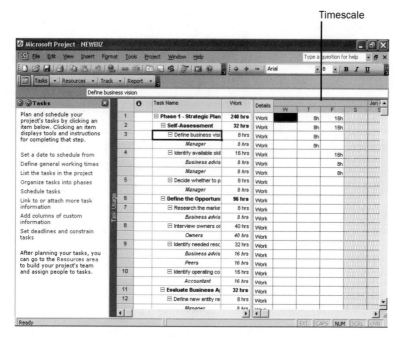

A usage view is a fairly sophisticated way of viewing project details. Next you'll switch to a simpler view.

6   On the **View** menu, click **Calendar**.

The Calendar view appears as shown here:

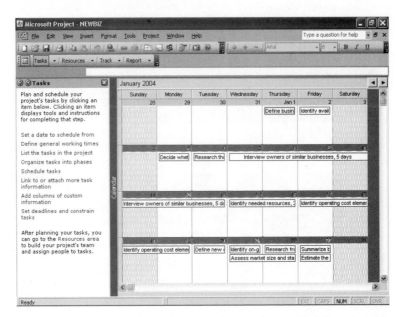

This simple month-at-a-glance view lacks the table structure, timescale, or chart elements you've seen in previous views. Task names appear on the days they're scheduled to start, and if a task's duration is longer than one day, its name will span multiple days.

Another common view used in project management is the Network Diagram. You'll look at this next.

7   On the **View** menu, click **Network Diagram**.

The Network Diagram view appears. Use the scroll bars to view different parts of the Network Diagram view.

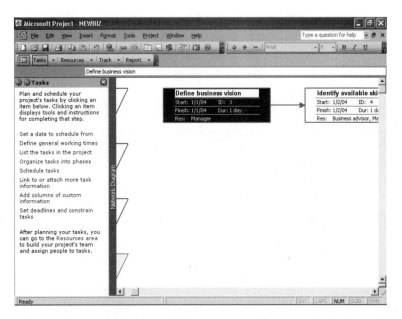

This view focuses on task relationships. Each box or node in the Network Diagram displays details about a task, and lines between boxes indicate task relationships. Like the Calendar view, the Network Diagram view lacks a table structure; the entire view is a chart.

To conclude this exercise, you'll look at combination views. These *split* the project plan window into two panes, each pane containing a different view. The views are synchronized, so selecting a specific task or resource in one view causes the other view to display details about that task or resource.

8   On the **View** menu, click **More Views**.

The **More Views** dialog box appears. This dialog box lists all the predefined views available in Project.

9 In the **Views** box, click **Task Entry**, and then click the **Apply** button.

The Task Entry view appears:

Gantt Chart view in upper pane

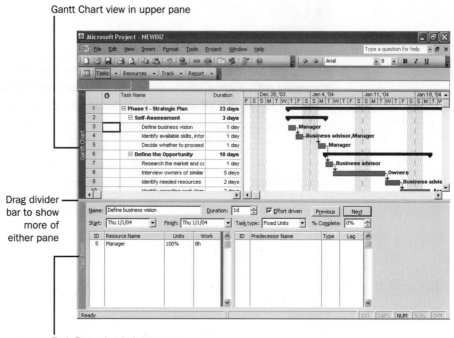

Drag divider
bar to show
more of
either pane

Task Form view in lower pane

Show/Hide
Project Guide

Tip Depending on your screen resolution, you might need to close the Project Guide to see the full width of this view. To do this, click the **Show/Hide Project Guide** button on the **Project Guide** toolbar. You can also make the Project Guide pane narrower by dragging its right edge to the left.

This view is a predefined split-screen or combination view, with the Gantt Chart in the upper pane and the Task Form in the lower pane. A form is the final element of a view you'll see in this chapter. A form displays details about the selected task or resource, much like a dialog box. You can enter, change, or review these details in the form.

10 In the Gantt Chart portion of the view, if the selection is not on task 3, *Define business vision*, click that task's name.

The details about task 3 appear in the Task Form portion of the view.

11 In the Gantt Chart portion of the view, click the name of task 4, *Identify available skills, information, and support*.

The details about task 4 appear in the Task Form.

Tip   Besides using the predefined combination views, you can display two views of your choice by clicking **Split** on the **Window** menu. After the Project window is split into two panes, click in the upper or lower pane, and then choose the view you want to appear there. To return to a single view, on the **Window** menu, click **Remove Split.**

It is important to understand that in all these views, as well as all the other views in Project, you are looking at different aspects of the same set of details about a single project plan. Even a simple project plan can contain too much data to display all at once. You can use views to help you focus on the specific details you want.

In later exercises you'll do more with views to further focus on the most relevant project details.

Exploring Reports

Reports are predefined formats intended for printing Project data. Unlike views, which you can either print or work with on the screen, reports are designed to be printed. You don't enter data directly into a report. Project includes several predefined task and resource reports you can manipulate to get the information you want.

In this exercise, you view a report in the Print Preview window.

1   On the **View** menu, click **Reports.**

The **Reports** dialog box appears, showing the six broad categories of reports available in Project.

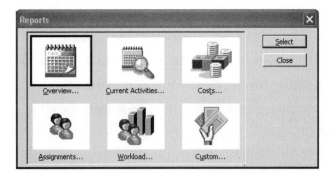

2   Click **Custom,** and then click the **Select** button.

The **Custom Reports** dialog box appears, listing all predefined reports in Project and any custom reports that have been added.

3   In the **Reports** list, click **Task**, and then click the **Preview** button.

Project displays the Task report in the Print Preview window. Your screen should look similar to the following illustration:

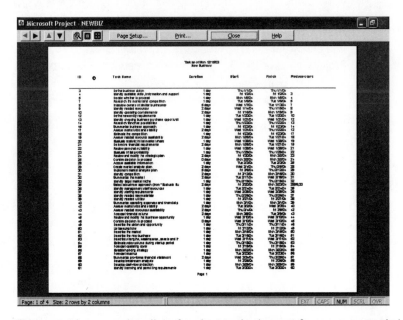

This report is a complete list of project tasks (except for summary tasks), similar to what you'd see in the *Entry table* of the Gantt Chart view. If you want to zoom in, move the mouse pointer (shaped like a magnifying glass) to a portion of the report, and click. Click again to toggle back to the full page preview.

4   On the **Print Preview** toolbar, click the **Close** button.

The Print Preview window closes, and the **Custom Reports** dialog box reappears.

5   In the **Custom Reports** dialog box, click the **Close** button.

6   Click the **Close** button again to close the **Reports** dialog box.

> **Tip**   We've frequently seen Project users go to a lot of trouble to customize the Gantt Chart view to include specific information they want in the format they want. Before you do that, check the predefined views (for online work or printing) or reports (for printing). There's a good chance the Project designers have anticipated your needs and provided a predefined solution for you.

To conclude this exercise, you'll close the file you've been using to explore views and reports.

7   On the **File** menu, click **Close** to close the New Business plan. When prompted to save changes, click the **No** button.

Creating a New Project Plan

Now that you've had a brief look at the major parts of the Project interface, you are ready to create the project plan you will use in Parts 1 through 3 of this book.

A project plan is essentially a model you construct of some aspects of the real project you anticipate—what you think will happen, or what you want to happen (it's usually best if these are not too different). This model focuses on some but not all aspects of the real project—tasks, resources, time frames, and possibly their associated costs.

Project Management Focus: Project Is Part of a Larger Picture

Depending on your needs and the information to which you have access, the project plans you develop might not deal with other important aspects of real projects. Many large projects, for example, are carried out in organizations that have a formal change management process. Before a major change to the scope of a project is allowed, it must first be evaluated and approved by the people managing and implementing the project. This is an important project management activity, but not something done directly within Project.

In this exercise, you create a new plan using the Project Guide.

1   On the **File** menu, click the **New** command.

The New Project task pane appears.

2   Under **New**, click the **Blank Project** link.

Project creates a new project, and the New Project task pane is replaced by the Tasks pane of the Project Guide:

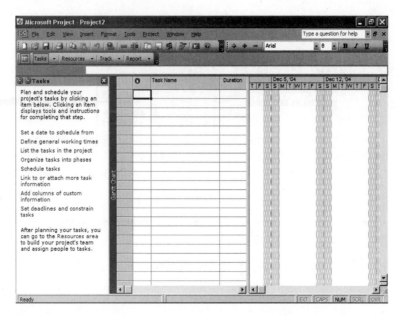

Take a moment to look over the Tasks pane. This pane contains links to several activities, all focused on tasks. (You'll see other types of activities in later chapters.) Each activity in the Project Guide consists of a series of numbered steps. Each step appears in its own pane, like pages in a book.

3   In the Tasks pane, click the **Set a date to schedule from** link (in Project Standard) or the **Define the project** link (in Project Professional).

The *Set a date to schedule from* (in Project Standard) or *Define the project* (Project Professional) pane appears.

4   In the next pane that appears, in the **Date** box click the down arrow.

A small monthly calendar appears. By default, Project uses the current date as the project start date. However, in this exercise, you change the project start date to January 3, 2005.

5   Click the left or right arrow until January 2005 is displayed.

6   Click **3**, as shown next.

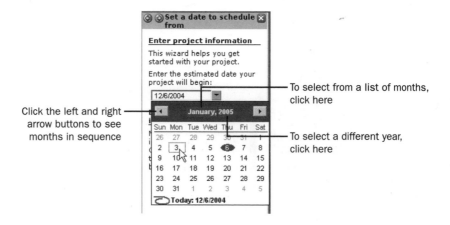

To select from a list of months, click here

Click the left and right arrow buttons to see months in sequence

To select a different year, click here

Tip   You use this type of calendar in several places in Project. Here is a handy shortcut for quickly picking a date with the calendar: Click the name of the month to display a shortcut menu of all months, and then select the month you want. Next click the year to display up and down arrows, and then type or select the year you want.

7   At the bottom of the pane, click **Done** (in Project Standard) or the **Save and go to Step 2** link (in Project Professional).

8   If you have Project Professional, you'll see additional panes that relate to Project Server. In the Step 2 pane, click **No**, then go to Step 3. In Step 3, click **Save and Finish**.

The Tasks activity list reappears in the Project Guide pane. You've completed the Define the Project activity.

Save

9   On the Standard toolbar, click the **Save** button. You can also click the **Save** link or button in the pane.

Because this project plan has not previously been saved, the **Save As** dialog box appears.

10   Locate the Chapter 1 Getting Started folder in the Project 2003 Step by Step folder on your hard disk. The default location for the Project 2003 Step by Step folder is \My Documents\Microsoft Press.

11   In the **File name** box, type Wingtip Toys Commercial 1.

12   Click the **Save** button to close the **Save As** dialog box.

Project saves the project plan as *Wingtip Toys Commercial 1*.

> **Tip**   You can instruct Project to automatically save the active project plan at pre-defined intervals, such as every 10 minutes. On the **Tools** menu, click **Options**. In the **Options** dialog box, click the **Save** tab, select the **Save Every** check box, and then specify the time interval you want.

Setting Nonworking Days

This exercise introduces *calendars*, the primary means by which you control when tasks and resources can be scheduled for work in Project. In later chapters you will work with other types of calendars; in this chapter you will work only with the *project calendar*.

The project calendar defines the general working and nonworking time for tasks. Think of the project calendar as your organization's normal working times. This might be, for example, Monday through Friday, 8 A.M. through 5 P.M. with an hour off for lunch. Your organization or specific resources might have exceptions to this normal working time, such as holidays or vacation. In a later chapter you'll address resource vacations, but here you'll address a holiday in the project calendar.

1   In the Tasks pane, click the **Define general working times** link.

The Project Working Times pane appears. Your screen should look similar to the following illustration:

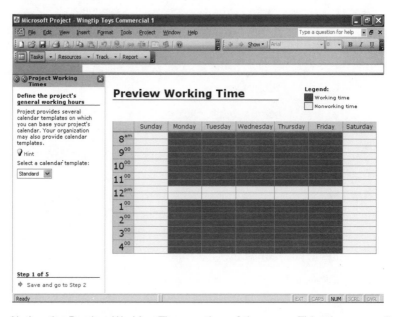

Notice the Preview Working Time portion of the pane. This shows you (in blue) the times at which Project can schedule tasks and resources and (in yellow) when it cannot, based on the settings in the project calendar.

Tip   Click the **Hint** link in the Project Working Times pane. The hint appears in place, without navigating away from the pane. Click it again to collapse it. You will see many such hints throughout the Project Guide.

2   In the **Select a calendar template** box, click the down arrow.

The list that appears contains the three *base calendars* included with Project. These are as follows:

- ■   Standard: the traditional working day, Monday through Friday from 8 A.M. to 5 P.M., with an hour off for lunch.

- ■   24 Hours: has no nonworking time.

- ■   Night Shift: covers a "graveyard" shift schedule of Monday night through Saturday morning, 11 P.M. to 8 A.M., with a one-hour break.

Just one of the base calendars serves as the project calendar. For this project you'll use the Standard base calendar as the project calendar, so leave it selected.

Tip   To learn more about calendars, type **About calendars** into the box labeled *Type a question for help*.

3   At the bottom of the pane, click the **Save and go to Step 2** link.

The second pane appears. This pane gives you the option of changing the project calendar's working time for a specific day of every week. For example, you could choose to end the workday every Wednesday at 3 P.M. instead of 5 P.M. For this project, however, you'll use the default work week.

4   At the bottom of the pane, click the **Save and go to Step 3** link.

The third pane appears. Here you'll specify some specific nonworking days for the project calendar.

5   Click the **Change working time** link in the pane.

The Project Guide displays the **Change Working Time** dialog box. This is the same dialog box you would see if you clicked the **Change Working Time** command on the **Tools** menu.

6   In the calendar below the **Select Date(s)** label, scroll up or down to January 2005 (unfortunately you can't use the date picking shortcut mentioned previously with this particular calendar). You know that the entire staff will be at a morale event January 28, and no work should be scheduled that day.

7   Select the date **January 28**.

8   Under **Set selected date(s) to**, click **Nonworking time**:

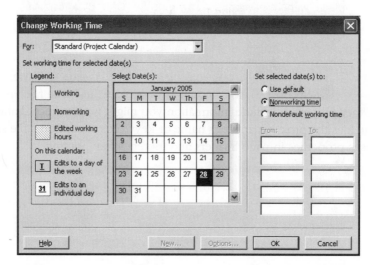

This date is now nonworking time for the project. In the dialog box, the date appears underlined, and it is formatted gray to indicate nonworking time.

9   Click **OK** to close the **Change Working Time** dialog box.

10   To verify the change to the project calendar, scroll the chart portion of the Gantt Chart view (the portion on the right) to the right until Friday, January 28, is visible. Like the weekends, January 28 is formatted gray to indicate nonworking time:

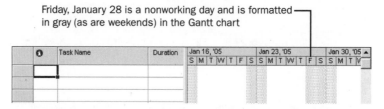

11   At the bottom of the pane, click the **Save and go to Step 4** link.

Take a moment to read the text in the Define Time Units pane, because this is a common source of confusion among Project users. Because you did not change the default working times for the project calendar, you should not change these time units.

12   At the bottom of the pane, click the **Save and go to Step 5** link.

The final pane of the Project Working Times activity appears.

13   At the bottom of the pane, click the **Save and Finish** link.

The Tasks activity list reappears in the Project Guide pane. You've completed the Define General Working Times activity.

Entering Project Properties

Like other Office programs, Project keeps track of several file properties. Some of these properties are statistics, such as how many times the file has been revised. Other properties include information you might want to record about a project plan, such as the project manager's name or keywords to support a file search. Project also uses properties in page headers and footers when printing.

In this exercise, you enter some properties that you will use later when printing project information and for other purposes.

1   On the **File** menu, click **Properties**.

The **Properties** dialog box appears.

2   Click the **Summary** tab.

3   In the **Subject** box, type Video Production Schedule.

4   In the **Author** box, type your name.

5   In the **Manager** box, type your name, type your manager's name, or leave the box blank.

6   In the **Company** box, type Southridge Video.

7   Select the **Save preview picture** check box.

8   The next time this file appears in the **Open** dialog box with the **Preview** view option selected, a small image showing the first few tasks of the project will be displayed.

9   Click **OK** to close the dialog box.

"A Database That Knows About Time"

The project plans you create in Project are files that have many things in common with database files, like those you might work with in Access. If you were to peek inside a Microsoft Project Plan (MPP) file, you'd find it has much in common with a database file format. Data is stored in a set of tables, and relationships connect information in different tables. In fact it's not uncommon for Project users in large organizations to save project plans in a database format, sometimes to a central database on a network server.

What Project provides that a regular database application can't, however, is the active scheduling engine mentioned earlier. One Project expert we know describes it as "a database that knows about time."

CLOSE: the Wingtip Toys Commercial 1 file.

Key Points

- The Project product family includes Project Standard, Project Professional, Project Server, and Project Web Access. Normally you would use Project Standard on the desktop, or the latter three in combination to form an enterprise project management solution.

- One of the key distinguishing factors that separates Project from other list-keeping tools like Excel is that Project has a scheduling engine that can work with time.

- Project includes several sophisticated templates that may provide you with a good start to a new project plan.

- The main working space in Project is a view. Normally you have one or sometimes two views displayed at a time. The Gantt Chart view is the default and probably best known view in Project.

- Project includes a large number of built-in reports. These are intended for viewing (but not editing) Project data.

- You use calendars in Project to control when work can be scheduled to occur.

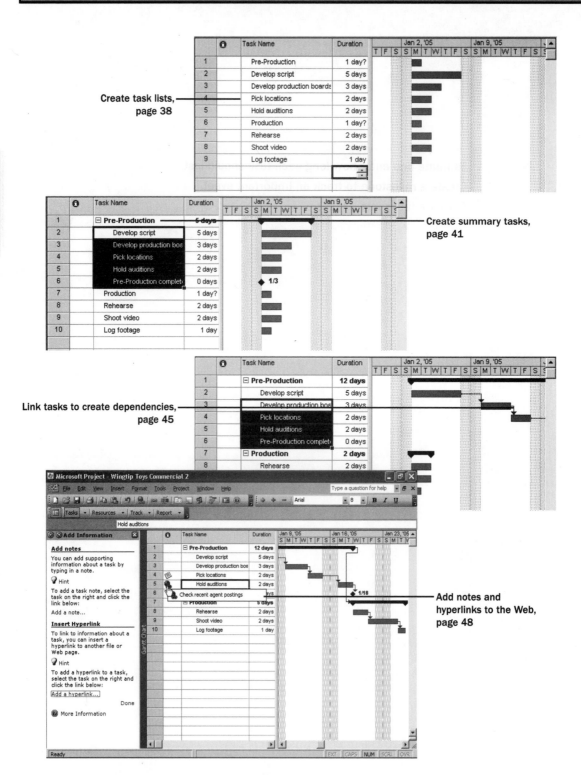

Create task lists, page 38

Create summary tasks, page 41

Link tasks to create dependencies, page 45

Add notes and hyperlinks to the Web, page 48

2 Creating a Task List

In this chapter you will learn to:

✓ Enter task information.

✓ Estimate and enter how long each task should last.

✓ Create a milestone to track an important event.

✓ Organize tasks into phases.

✓ Create task relationships by linking tasks.

✓ Record task details in notes and insert a hyperlink to content on the World Wide Web.

✓ Check a project plan's overall duration.

See Also Do you need a quick refresher on the topics in this chapter? See the quick reference entries on pages xx–xxi.

Important Before you can use the practice files in this chapter, be sure you install them from the book's companion CD to their default location. See "Using the Book's CD-ROM," on page xiii, for more information.

Entering Tasks

Tasks are the most basic building blocks of any project—tasks represent the work to be done to accomplish the goals of the project. Tasks describe project work in terms of sequence, duration, and resource requirements. Later in this chapter, you will work with two special types of tasks: summary tasks (which summarize or "roll up" the durations, costs, and so on of subtasks) and milestones (which indicate a significant event in the life of a project).

In this exercise, you enter the first tasks required in the video project:

BE SURE TO: Start Microsoft Office Project 2003, if it's not already open.

Important If you are running Project Professional, you may need to make a one-time adjustment to use the My Computer account and to work offline. This helps ensure that the practice files you work with in this chapter don't affect your Project Server data. For more information, see "Starting Project Professional," on page 10.

OPEN: Wingtip Toys Commercial 2a from the *My Documents\Microsoft Press\Project 2003 Step by Step\Chapter 2 Simple Tasks* folder. You can also access the practice files for this book by clicking **Start**, **All Programs**, **Microsoft Press**, **Project 2003 Step by Step**, and then selecting the chapter folder of the file you want to open.

1   On the **File** menu, click **Save As**.

The **Save As** dialog box appears.

2   In the **File name** box, type **Wingtip Toys Commercial 2**, and then click **Save**.

3   If the Tasks pane is not already displayed in the Project Guide, on the **Project Guide** toolbar, click **Tasks**.

4   In the Tasks pane, click the **List the tasks in the project** link.

The List Tasks pane appears. Take a moment to read the information in the pane. Later you'll use this pane to create a milestone task.

5   Click the cell directly below the **Task Name** column heading.

6   Type **Pre-Production**, and then press ⌞Enter⌟.

7   Click the name of the new task 1, **Pre-Production**.

Your screen should look similar to the following illustration:

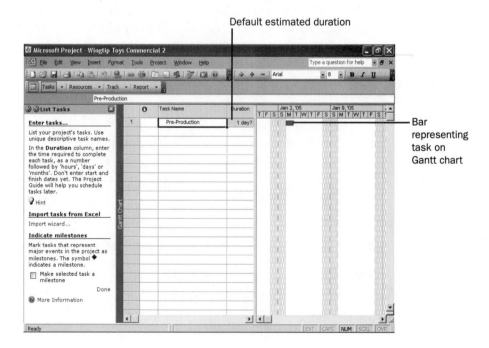

The task you entered is given an ID number. Each task has a unique ID number, but it does not necessarily represent the order in which tasks occur.

Project assigns a duration of one day to the new task, and the question mark indicates that this is an estimated duration. A corresponding task bar of one day's length appears in the Gantt chart. By default the task start date is the same as the project start date.

8 Enter the following task names below the Pre-Production task name, pressing `Enter` after each task name:

Develop script
Develop production boards
Pick locations
Hold auditions
Production
Rehearse
Shoot video
Log footage

Your screen should look similar to the following illustration:

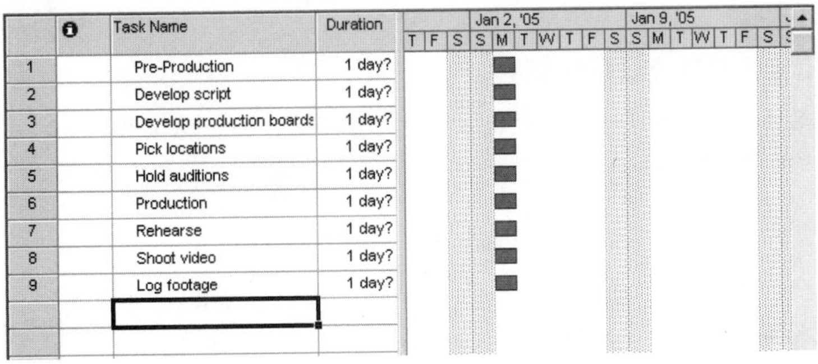

	❶	Task Name	Duration	Jan 2, '05	Jan 9, '05
				T F S S M T W T F S	S M T W T F S S
1		Pre-Production	1 day?		
2		Develop script	1 day?		
3		Develop production boards	1 day?		
4		Pick locations	1 day?		
5		Hold auditions	1 day?		
6		Production	1 day?		
7		Rehearse	1 day?		
8		Shoot video	1 day?		
9		Log footage	1 day?		

Tip In addition to typing task information directly into Project, you can develop task lists in other applications and then import them into Project. For example, Project installs an Excel template named Microsoft Project Task List Import Template, which you or others can complete and then import into Project with the proper structure. In Excel, this template appears on the **Spreadsheet Solutions** tab of the **Templates** dialog box. You can also import your Outlook task list into a project plan. In Project, click **Import Outlook Tasks** on the **Tools** menu.

Project Management Focus:
Defining the Right Tasks for the Right Deliverable

Every project has an ultimate goal or intent: the reason that the project was started. This is called the project *deliverable*. This deliverable is usually a product, such as a TV commercial, or a service or event, such as a software training session. Defining the right tasks to create the right deliverable is an essential skill for a project manager. The task lists you create in Project should describe all the work required, and only the work required, to complete the project successfully.

In developing your task lists, you might find it helpful to distinguish product scope from project scope. *Product scope* describes the quality, features, and functions of the deliverable of the project. In the scenario used in Part 1 of this book, for example, the deliverable is a TV commercial, and the product scope might include its length, subject, and audience. *Project scope*, on the other hand, describes the work required to deliver such a product or service. In our scenario, the project scope includes detailed tasks relating to the creation of a TV commercial, such as holding auditions, shooting the video, editing it, and so on.

Estimating Durations

A task's *duration* is the amount of time you expect it will take to complete the task. Project can work with task durations that range from minutes to months. Depending on the scope of your project, you'll probably want to work with task durations on the scale of hours, days, and weeks.

For example, a project might have a *project calendar* with working time defined as 8 A.M. through 5 P.M. with an hour off for lunch Monday through Friday, leaving nonworking time defined as evenings and weekends. If you estimate that a task will take 16 hours of working time, you could enter its duration as **2d** to schedule work over two eight-hour workdays. You should then expect that starting the task at 8 A.M. on a Friday means that it wouldn't be completed until 5 P.M. on the following Monday. No work would be scheduled over the weekend, because Saturday and Sunday have been defined as nonworking time.

Tip You determine the overall duration of a project by calculating the difference between the earliest start date and the latest finish date of the tasks that compose it. The project duration is also affected by other factors, such as task relationships, which are discussed in the topic "Linking Tasks," on page 43. Because Project distinguishes between working and nonworking time, a task's duration doesn't necessarily correlate to elapsed time.

When working in Project, you can use abbreviations for durations.

If you enter this abbreviation	It appears like this	And means
m	min	minute
h	hr	hour
d	day	day
w	wk	week
mo	mon	month

Tip You can schedule tasks to occur during working and nonworking time. To do this, assign an *elapsed duration* to a task. You enter elapsed duration by preceding the duration abbreviation with an *e*. For example, type **3ed** to indicate three elapsed days. You might use an elapsed duration for a task that you don't directly control but that nonetheless is critical to your project. For instance, you might have the tasks *Pour foundation concrete* and *Remove foundation forms* in a construction project. If so, you might also want a task called *Wait for concrete to cure,* because you don't want to remove the forms until the concrete has cured. The task *Wait for concrete to cure* should have an elapsed duration, because the concrete will cure over a contiguous range of days, whether they are working or nonworking days. If the concrete takes 48 hours to cure, you can enter the duration for that task as **2ed**, schedule the task to start on Friday at 9 A.M., and expect it to be complete by Sunday at 9 A.M. In most cases, however, you'll work with nonelapsed durations in Project.

Project uses standard values for minutes and hours for durations: one minute equals 60 seconds, and one hour equals 60 minutes. However, you can define nonstandard durations for days, weeks, and months for your project. To do this, on the **Tools** menu, click the **Options** command, and in the **Options** dialog box, click the **Calendar** tab, illustrated here:

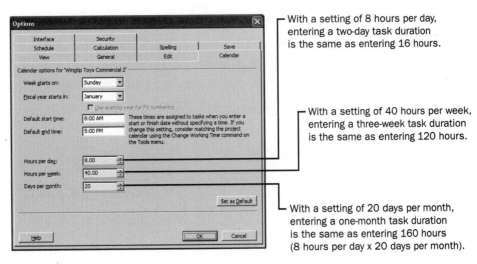

With a setting of 8 hours per day, entering a two-day task duration is the same as entering 16 hours.

With a setting of 40 hours per week, entering a three-week task duration is the same as entering 120 hours.

With a setting of 20 days per month, entering a one-month task duration is the same as entering 160 hours (8 hours per day x 20 days per month).

The exercises in this chapter use the default values: 8 hours per day, 40 hours per week, and 20 days per month.

Tip   Although it's beyond the scope of this book, Program Evaluation and Review Technique (PERT) analysis can be a useful tool for estimating task durations. For more information, type **Estimate task durations by using PERT analysis** into the **Search** box in the upper right corner of the Project window. The **Search** box initially contains the text *Type a question for help*.

In this exercise, you enter durations for the tasks you've created. When you created those tasks, Project entered an estimated duration of one day for each. (The question mark in the **Duration** field indicates that the duration is an explicit estimate, although really you should consider all task durations to be estimates until the task is completed.) To enter durations:

1   Click the cell below the **Duration** column heading for task 2, *Develop script*.

The **Duration** field for task 2 is selected.

2   Type 5d, and then press Enter .

The value *5 days* appears in the **Duration** field.

3   Enter the following durations for the remaining tasks:

Task ID	Task name	Duration
3	Develop production boards	3d
4	Pick locations	2d
5	Hold auditions	2d
6	Production	(Press Enter to skip this task for now)
7	Rehearse	2d
8	Shoot video	2d
9	Log footage	1d

Your screen should look similar to the following illustration:

	❶	Task Name	Duration	Jan 2, '05	Jan 9, '05
1		Pre-Production	1 day?		
2		Develop script	5 days		
3		Develop production boards	3 days		
4		Pick locations	2 days		
5		Hold auditions	2 days		
6		Production	1 day?		
7		Rehearse	2 days		
8		Shoot video	2 days		
9		Log footage	1 day		

Project Management Focus:
How Do You Come Up with Accurate Task Durations?

You should consider two general rules when estimating task durations:

■ Project duration often correlates to task duration; long projects tend to have tasks with longer durations than do tasks in short projects.

■ If you track progress against your project plan (described in Chapter 6, "Tracking Progress on Tasks," and in Part 2, "Advanced Project Scheduling"), you need to think about the level of detail you want to apply to your project's tasks. If you have a multi-year project, for example, it might not be practical or even possible to track tasks that are measured in minutes or hours. In general, you should measure task durations at the lowest level of detail or control you care about, but no lower.

For the projects you work on in this book, the durations are supplied for you. For your real-world projects, you will often have to estimate task durations. Good sources of task duration estimates include:

■ Historical information from previous, similar projects.

■ Estimates from the people who will complete the tasks.

■ The expert judgment of people who have managed similar projects.

■ The standards of professional or industry organizations that carry out projects similar to yours.

For complex projects, you probably would combine these and other sources to estimate task durations. Because inaccurate task duration estimates are a major source of *risk* in any project, making good estimates is well worth the effort.

Entering a Milestone

In addition to tracking tasks to be completed, you might want to track an important event for your project, such as when the pre-production *phase* of the project will end. To do this, you will create a *milestone*.

Milestones are significant events that are either reached within the project (completion of a phase of work, for example) or imposed upon the project (a deadline by which to apply for funding, for example). Because the milestone itself doesn't normally include any work, milestones are represented as tasks with zero duration.

In this exercise, you create a milestone.

1   Click the name of task 6, **Production**.

2   On the **Insert** menu, click **New Task**.

Project inserts a row for a new task and renumbers the subsequent tasks.

Tip   You can also press the ⌤Insert key to insert a new task above the selected task. To insert multiple new tasks, select multiple tasks first, and then press ⌤Insert. Project will insert the same number of new tasks.

3   Type **Pre-Production complete!**, and then press the → key to move to the **Duration** field.

4   Either type **0d** in the **Duration** field, or in the List Tasks pane select the **Make selected task a milestone** check box.

The milestone is added to your plan. Your screen should look similar to the following illustration:

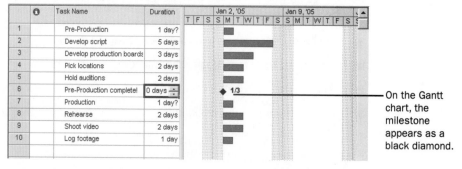

On the Gantt chart, the milestone appears as a black diamond.

5   At the bottom of the List Tasks pane, click the **Done** link.

The Tasks pane appears.

> **Tip** You can also mark a task of any duration as a milestone. Double-click the task name to display the **Task Information** dialog box, and then click the **Advanced** tab. Select the **Mark task as milestone** option.

Organizing Tasks into Phases

It is helpful to organize groups of closely related tasks into *phases*. Seeing phases of tasks helps you and anyone else reviewing a project plan to think in terms of major work items and detailed work items. For example, it is common to divide a film or video project into major phases of work such as pre-production, production, and post-production. You create phases by indenting and outdenting tasks. You can also collapse a task list into phases, much as you can work with an outline in Word. In Project, phases are represented by *summary tasks*.

A summary task behaves differently from other tasks. You can't edit its duration, start date, or other calculated values directly, because this information is derived or "rolled up" from the detail tasks, called subtasks (these appear indented under the summary tasks). Summary tasks are useful for getting information about phases of project work.

Project Management Focus: Top-Down and Bottom-Up Planning

The two most common approaches to developing tasks and phases are top-down and bottom-up planning.

Top-down planning identifies major phases or products of the project before filling in the tasks required to complete those phases. Complex projects can have several layers of phases. This approach works from general to specific.

Bottom-up planning identifies as many of the bottom-level detailed tasks as possible before organizing them into logical groups, called phases or summary tasks. This approach works from specific to general.

Creating accurate tasks and phases for most complex projects requires a combination of top-down and bottom-up planning. For some project work, you will already know the low-level tasks; for others, you might initially know only the broader project goals.

In this exercise, you create two summary tasks by indenting tasks.

1   In the Tasks pane, click the **Organize tasks into phases** link.

The Organize Tasks pane appears.

2   Select the names of tasks 2 through 6. Your screen should look similar to the following illustration:

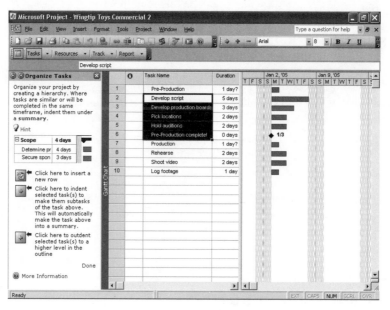

3   In the Organize Tasks pane, click the **Indent Tasks** button. (You can also click this button on the Formatting toolbar.)

Indent Tasks

Task 1 becomes a summary task, and a summary task bar for it appears in the Gantt chart. The summary task name is also formatted in bold type. Your screen should look similar to the following illustration:

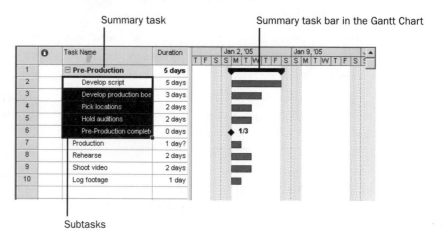

Summary task   Summary task bar in the Gantt Chart

Subtasks

4   Next select the names of tasks 8 through 10.

5   In the Organize Tasks pane, click the **Indent Tasks** button.

Task 7 becomes a summary task, and a summary task bar for it appears in the Gantt chart. Your screen should look similar to the following illustration:

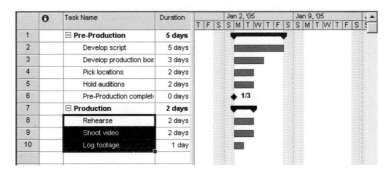

6   At the bottom of the Organize Tasks pane, click the **Done** link.

The Tasks pane reappears.

Tip   If your organization uses a work breakdown structure (WBS) process in the project-planning phase, you may find it helpful to view WBS codes in Project. For information about using WBS codes with Project, type **View WBS codes** into the **Search** box.

Linking Tasks

Projects require tasks to be done in a specific order. For example, the task of filming a scene must be completed before the task of editing the filmed scene can occur. These two tasks have a finish-to-start *relationship* (also called a link or a dependency), which has two aspects:

■   The second task must occur after the first task; this is a *sequence*.

■   The second task can occur only if the first task is completed; this is a *dependency*.

In Project, the first task ("film the scene") is called the *predecessor* because it precedes tasks that depend on it. The second task ("edit the filmed scene") is called the *successor* because it succeeds tasks on which it is dependent. Any task can be a predecessor for one or more successor tasks. Likewise, any task can be a successor to one or more predecessor tasks.

This might sound complicated, but it turns out tasks can have one of only four types of task relationships:

This task relationship	Means	Looks like this in the Gantt chart	Example
Finish-to-start (FS)	The finish date of the predecessor task determines the start date of the successor task.		A film scene must be shot before it can be edited.
Start-to-start (SS)	The start date of the predecessor task determines the start date of the successor task.		Reviewing a script and developing the script breakdown and schedule are closely related, and they should occur simultaneously.
Finish-to-finish (FF)	The finish date of the predecessor task determines the finish date of the successor task.		Tasks that require specific equipment must end when the equipment rental ends.
Start-to-finish (SF)	The start date of the predecessor task determines the finish date of the successor task.		The time when the editing lab becomes available determines when a pre-editing task must end. (This type of relationship is rarely used.)

Representing task relationships and handling changes to scheduled start and finish dates is one area where using a scheduling engine like Project really pays off. For example, you can change task durations or add or remove tasks from a chain of linked tasks, and Project will reschedule tasks accordingly.

Task relationships appear in several ways in Project. For example:

- In the Gantt Chart and Network Diagram views, task relationships appear as the lines connecting tasks.

- In tables, such as the Entry table, task ID numbers of predecessor tasks appear in the Predecessor fields of successor tasks.

You create task relationships by creating *links* between tasks. Currently, all the tasks in the project plan are scheduled to start on the same day—the project start date. In this exercise, you use different methods to create links between several tasks, creating finish-to-start relationships.

1 In the Tasks pane, click **Schedule tasks**.

The Schedule Tasks pane appears. First you'll create a finish-to-start dependency between two tasks.

2 Select the names of tasks 2 and 3. Your screen should look similar to the following illustration:

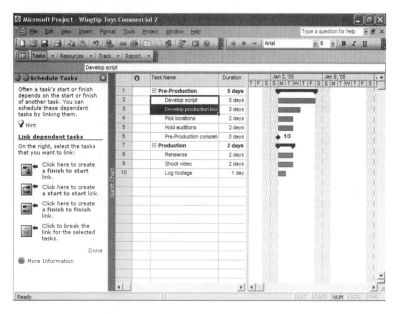

3 In the Schedule Tasks pane, click the **Finish-to-Start Link** button.

Finish-to-Start
Link

Link Tasks

Note To create a finish-to-start dependency, you can also click the **Link Tasks** button on the Standard toolbar, or click **Link Tasks** on the **Edit** menu.

Tasks 2 and 3 are linked with a finish-to-start relationship. Note that Project changed the start date of task 3 to the next working day following the completion of task 2 (skipping over the weekend), and the duration of the Pre-Production summary task grew correspondingly. Your screen should look similar to the illustration on the next page.

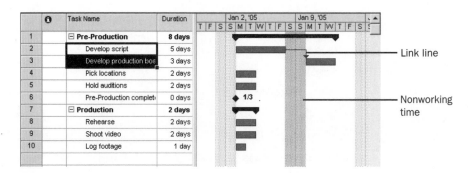

Link line

Nonworking time

Unlink Tasks

Tip   To unlink tasks, select the tasks you want to unlink, and then click the **Unlink Tasks** button on the Standard toolbar (you can also click **Unlink Tasks** on the **Edit** menu). If you unlink a single task that is part of a chain of linked tasks with finish-to-start relationships, Project reestablishes links between the remaining tasks.

Next you will link several tasks at once.

4 Select the names of tasks 3 through 6.

5 In the Schedule Tasks pane, click the **Finish-to-Start Link** button.

Tasks 3 through 6 are linked with a finish-to-start relationship. Your screen should look similar to the following illustration:

Next you will link two tasks in a different way. You will make task 8 the predecessor of task 9.

6 Select the name of task 9.

Task Information

7 On the Standard toolbar, click the **Task Information** button.

The **Task Information** dialog box appears.

8   Click the **Predecessors** tab.

9   Click the empty cell below the **Task Name** column heading, and then click the down arrow that appears.

10   In the **Task Name** list, click **Rehearse**, and press ⌷Enter⌷. Your screen should look similar to the following illustration:

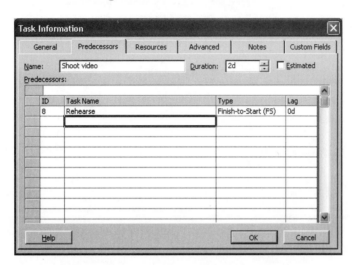

11   Click **OK** to close the **Task Information** dialog box.

Tasks 8 and 9 are linked with a finish-to-start relationship.

To wrap up this exercise, you'll link the remaining production tasks and then link the two summary tasks.

12   Select the names of tasks 9 and 10.

Finish-to-Start
Link

13   In the Schedule Tasks pane, click the **Finish-to-Start Link** button.

14   Now select the name of task 1, and while holding down the ⌷Ctrl⌷ key, select the name of task 7. This is how you make a nonadjacent selection in a table in Project.

15   In the Schedule Tasks pane, click the **Finish-to-Start Link** button to link the two summary tasks.

> **Tip**   When working with summary tasks, you can either link summary tasks directly (as you did above), or link the latest task in the first phase with the earliest task in the second phase. The scheduling end result is the same either way, but it's preferable to link the summary tasks to better reflect the sequential nature of the two phases. Under no circumstances, however, can you link a summary task to one of its own subtasks. Doing so would create a circular scheduling problem, so Project doesn't allow it.

16 Scroll the chart portion of the Gantt Chart view to the right until the second phase of the project plan is visible.

Your screen should look similar to the following illustration:

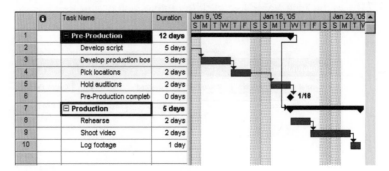

17 Click **Done** in the Schedule Tasks pane.

Tip You can also create a finish-to-start relationship between tasks right in the Gantt chart. Point to the task bar of the predecessor task until the pointer changes to a four-pointed star. Then drag the mouse pointer up or down to the task bar of the successor task. While you're dragging the mouse pointer to create a task relationship, the pointer image changes to a chain link.

Documenting Tasks

You can record additional information about a task in a *note*. For example, you might have detailed descriptions of a task and still want to keep the task's name succinct. You can add such details to a task note. That way, the information resides in the Project file and can be easily viewed or printed.

There are three types of notes: task notes, resource notes, and assignment notes. You enter and review task notes on the **Notes** tab in the **Task Information** dialog box. (You can open the **Task Information** dialog box by clicking the **Task Information** command on the **Project** menu.) Notes in Project support a wide range of text formatting options; you can even link to or store graphic images and other types of files in notes.

Hyperlinks enable you to connect a specific task to additional information that resides outside of the project plan—such as another file, a specific location in a file, a page on the World Wide Web, or a page on an intranet.

In this exercise, you enter task notes and hyperlinks to document important information about some tasks.

1 In the Tasks pane, click the **Link to or attach more task information** link.

The Add Information pane appears. Take a moment to read the information in the pane.

2 Select the name of task 4, *Pick locations*.

3   In the Add Information pane, click the **Add a note** link.

Task Notes

Tip   You can also click the **Task Notes** button on the Standard toolbar, or right-click on the task name and in the shortcut menu that appears click **Task Notes**.

Project displays the **Task Information** dialog box with the **Notes** tab visible.

4   In the **Notes** box, type Includes exterior street scene and indoor studio scenes.

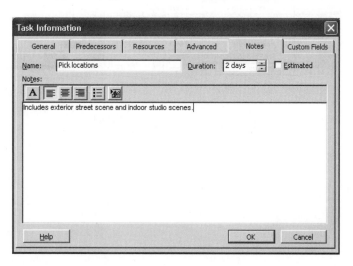

5   Click **OK**.

A note icon appears in the Indicators column.

6   Point to the note icon as shown here:

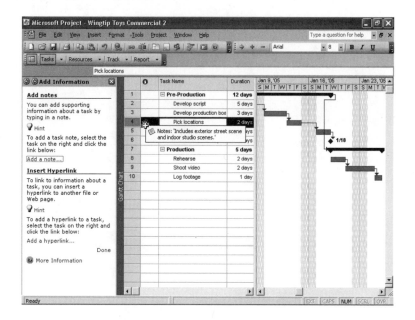

The note appears in a *ScreenTip*. For notes that are too long to appear in a ScreenTip, you can double-click the note icon to display the full text of the note.

To conclude this exercise, you create a hyperlink.

7   Select the name of task 5, *Hold auditions*.

8   In the Add Information pane, click the **Add a hyperlink** link.

Insert
Hyperlink

> **Tip**   You can also click the **Insert Hyperlink** button on the Standard toolbar.

The **Insert Hyperlink** dialog box appears.

9   In the **Text to display** box, type Check recent agent postings.

10   In the **Address** box, type http://www.southridgevideo.com

11   Click **OK**.

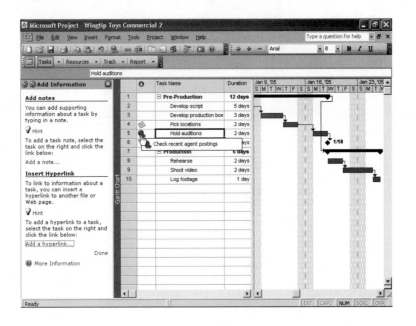

A hyperlink icon appears in the Indicators column. Pointing to the icon displays the descriptive text you typed above. Clicking the icon opens the Web page in your browser.

12 Click **Done** in the Add Information pane.

Checking the Plan's Duration

At this point, you might want to know how long the project is expected to take. You haven't directly entered a total project duration or finish date, but Project has calculated these values, based on individual task durations and task relationships. An easy way to see the project's scheduled finish date is via the **Project Information** dialog box.

In this exercise, you see the current total duration and scheduled finish date of the project, based on the task durations and relationships you've entered.

1 On the **Project** menu, click **Project Information**.

The **Project Information** dialog box appears.

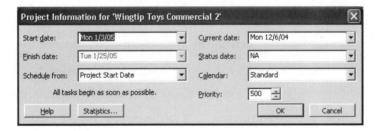

Note the Finish date: 1/25/05.

Tip *This tip describes enterprise project management (EPM) functionality.* If you are running Project Professional, you will see a slightly different dialog box. The **Project Information** dialog box in Project Professional includes an **Enterprise Custom Fields** section. Enterprise custom fields are used only with Project Server. For more information about Project Server, see Part 4, "Introducing Project Server."

You can't edit the finish date directly because this project is set to be scheduled from the start date. Project calculates the project's finish date based on the total number of working days required to complete the tasks, starting at the project's start date. As this project plan is now built, any change to the start date will cause Project to recalculate the finish date.

Next let's look at the duration information in more detail.

2   Click the **Statistics** button.

The **Project Statistics** dialog box appears:

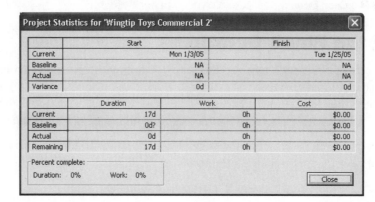

You don't need to pay attention to all these numbers yet, but the current finish date and the current duration are worth noting. The duration is the number of working days in the project calendar between the project's start date and finish date.

You can visually verify these numbers on the Gantt chart.

3   Click the **Close** button to close the **Project Statistics** dialog box.

Show/Hide
Project Guide

4   Click the **Show/Hide Project Guide** button on the **Project Guide** toolbar.

The Project Guide closes. Next you will look at the complete project by changing the timescale in the Gantt Chart view.

5   On the **View** menu, click **Zoom**.

The **Zoom** dialog box appears.

6   Click **Entire project**, and then click **OK**.

The entire project appears on the screen. Your screen should look similar to the following illustration:

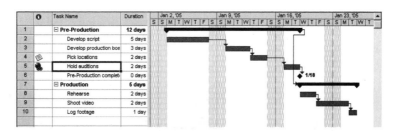

You can see the project's overall duration in the Gantt Chart view.

Tip   You can also click the **Zoom In** and **Zoom Out** buttons to change the time-scale of the Gantt Chart view.

Zoom   Zoom
In   Out

CLOSE: the Wingtip Toys Commercial 2 file.

Key Points

■   Essential aspects of tasks in a project plan include their duration and order of occurrence.

■   The Project Guide can help you develop a good initial task list.

■   Task links, or relationships, cause the start or end of one task to affect the start or end of another task. A common task relationship is a finish-to-start relationship, where the completion of one task controls the start of another task.

■   In Project, phases of a schedule are represented as summary tasks.

■   The **Project Information** dialog box (**Project** menu) is an excellent way to see the key values of a project plan, such as its scheduled finish date and duration.

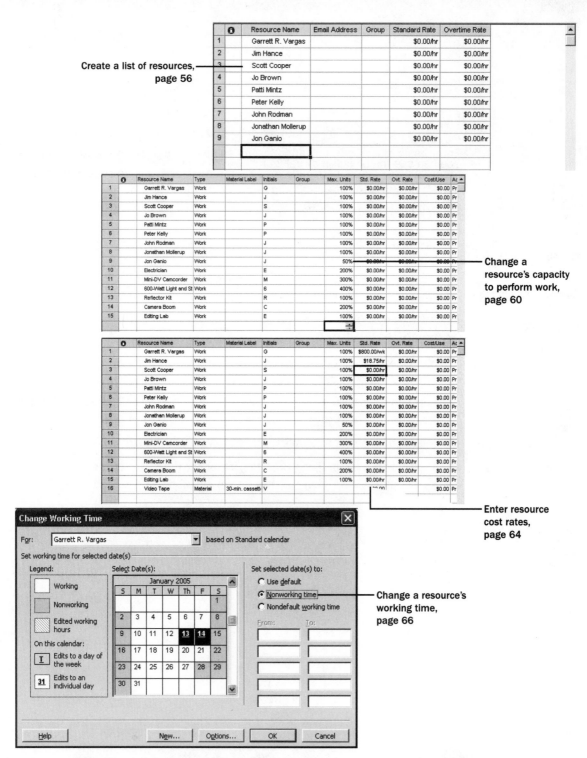

Create a list of resources, page 56

Change a resource's capacity to perform work, page 60

Enter resource cost rates, page 64

Change a resource's working time, page 66

Chapter 3 at a Glance

3 Setting Up Resources

In this chapter you will learn to:

✔ Set up basic resource information for the people who work on projects.

✔ Enter basic resource information for the equipment that will be used in projects.

✔ Enter basic resource information for the materials that will be consumed as the project progresses.

✔ Set up cost information for resources.

✔ Change a resource's availability for work.

✔ Record additional information about a resource in a note.

See Also   Do you need a quick refresher on the topics in this chapter? See the quick reference entries on pages xxi–xxii.

Resources are the people, equipment, and material needed to complete the tasks in a project. Microsoft Office Project 2003 focuses on two aspects of resources: their availability and and their costs. Availability determines when specific resources can work on tasks and how much work they can do, and costs refer to how much money will be required to pay for those resources.

In this chapter, you will set up the resources you need to complete the TV commercial project. Effective resource management is one of the most powerful advantages of using Project over task-focused planning tools, such as paper-based organizers. You do not need to set up resources and assign them to tasks in Project; however, without this information, you might have less control over who does what work, when, and at what cost. Setting up resource information in Project takes a little effort, but the time is well spent if your project is primarily driven by time or cost *constraints*. (And nearly all complex projects are driven by one, if not both, of these factors.)

 Important   Before you can use the practice files in this chapter, be sure you install them from the book's companion CD to their default location. See "Using the Book's CD-ROM," on page xiii, for more information.

Setting Up People Resources

Project works with two types of resources: work resources and material resources. *Work resources* are the people and equipment that do the work of the project. You will learn about material resources later in this chapter.

Some examples of work resources are listed below.

Work resource	Example
Individual people identified by name	Jon Ganio; Jim Hance
Individual people identified by job title or function	Director; camera operator
Groups of people who have common skills (When assigning such interchangeable resources to a task, you do not care who the individual resource is, as long as the resource has the right skills.)	Electricians; carpenters; extras
Equipment	Video camera; 600-watt light

Equipment resources don't need to be portable; a fixed location or piece of machinery (for example, a video editing studio) can also be considered equipment.

All projects require some people resources, and some projects require only people resources. Project can help you make smarter decisions about how to manage work resources and monitor financial costs.

Tip *This tip describes enterprise project management (EPM) functionality.* The combination of Project Professional and Project Server provides substantial, enterprise-level resource management capabilities, such as skills-based resource assignments and a centralized enterprise resource pool. For more information, see Part 4, "Introducing Project Server."

In this exercise, you set up resource information for several people resources.

BE SURE TO: Start Project if it's not already running.

Important If you are running Project Professional, you may need to make a one-time adjustment to use the My Computer account and to work offline. This helps ensure that the practice files you work with in this chapter don't affect your Project Server data. For more information, see "Starting Project Professional," on page 1xxx.

OPEN: Wingtip Toys Commercial 3a from the *My Documents**Microsoft Press**Project 2003 Step by Step*\\ *Chapter 3 Simple Resources* folder. You can also access the practice files for this book by clicking **Start**, **All Programs**, **Microsoft Press**, **Project 2003 Step by Step**, and then selecting the chapter folder of the file you want to open.

1 On the **File** menu, click **Save As**.

The **Save As** dialog box appears.

2 In the **File name** box, type Wingtip Toys Commercial 3, and then click **Save**.

3   On the **Project Guide** toolbar, click **Resources**.

You will use the Project Guide to help set up the initial list of resources for the toy commercial project.

4   In the Resources pane, click the **Specify people and equipment for the project** link.

The Specify Resources pane appears, and the Project Guide: Simple Resource Sheet view replaces the Gantt Chart view.

5   Select the **Enter resources manually** option.

Tip   For your own projects, if your resource information resides in the right source on your network, such as a Microsoft Exchange address book or Active Directory, you can quickly import the resource information into Project. This saves you the effort of retyping the information and reduces the chance of making a data-entry error.

6   In the Simple Resource Sheet view, click the cell directly below the **Resource Name** column heading.

7   Type Garrett R. Vargas, and press [Enter].

Project creates a new resource.

8   Widen the **Resource Name** column by moving the mouse pointer to the vertical divider line between the **Resource Name** and **Email Address** columns and double-clicking. Your screen should look like the following illustration:

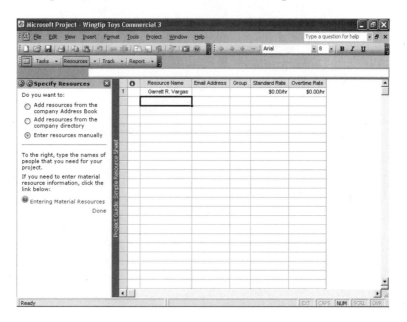

9 Enter the remaining resource information into the Simple Resource Sheet.

Jim Hance

Scott Cooper

Jo Brown

Patti Mintz

Peter Kelly

John Rodman

Jonathan Mollerup

Jon Ganio

Your screen should look similar to the following illustration:

	❶	Resource Name	Email Address	Group	Standard Rate	Overtime Rate	
1		Garrett R. Vargas			$0.00/hr	$0.00/hr	
2		Jim Hance			$0.00/hr	$0.00/hr	
3		Scott Cooper			$0.00/hr	$0.00/hr	
4		Jo Brown			$0.00/hr	$0.00/hr	
5		Patti Mintz			$0.00/hr	$0.00/hr	
6		Peter Kelly			$0.00/hr	$0.00/hr	
7		John Rodman			$0.00/hr	$0.00/hr	
8		Jonathan Mollerup			$0.00/hr	$0.00/hr	
9		Jon Ganio			$0.00/hr	$0.00/hr	

10 Click the **Close** button in the upper right corner of the Project Guide pane to close the Project Guide.

You can also have a resource that represents multiple people. Next you will switch to a different view to set up such a resource.

11 On the **View** menu, click **Resource Sheet**.

The Resource Sheet view appears. This sheet contains more resource-related fields than the Simple Resource Sheet does.

12 In the **Resource Name** field below the last resource, type Electrician, and then press ⌷Tab⌷.

13 In the **Type** field, make sure that **Work** is selected, and then press ⌷Tab⌷ several times to move to the **Max. Units** field.

The **Max. Units** field represents the maximum capacity of a resource to accomplish any task. Specifying that a resource such as Garrett R. Vargas, for example, has 100 percent maximum units means that 100 percent of Garrett's time is available to work on the tasks to which you assign him. Project will alert you if you assign Garrett to more tasks than he can accomplish at 100 percent maximum units (or, in other words, if Garrett becomes overallocated).

14 In the **Max. Units** field for the electrician, type or select 200%, and then press ⬚.

Tip When you click a numeric field, up and down arrows appear. You can click these to display the number you want, or just type the number in the field.

The resource named Electrician does not represent a single person; instead, it represents a category of interchangeable people called electricians. Because the Electrician resource has a maximum units setting of 200 percent, you can plan on two electricians being available to work full time every workday. At this point in the planning phase, you do not know exactly who these electricians will be, and that's OK. You can still proceed with more general planning.

Now you'll update the maximum units value for Jon Ganio to indicate that he works half time.

15 Click the **Max. Units** field for Jon Ganio, type or select 50%, and then press ⬚.

Your screen should look similar to the following illustration:

	ⓘ	Resource Name	Type	Material Label	Initials	Group	Max. Units	Std. Rate	Ovt. Rate	Cost/Use	Ac
1		Garrett R. Vargas	Work		G		100%	$0.00/hr	$0.00/hr	$0.00	Pr
2		Jim Hance	Work		J		100%	$0.00/hr	$0.00/hr	$0.00	Pr
3		Scott Cooper	Work		S		100%	$0.00/hr	$0.00/hr	$0.00	Pr
4		Jo Brown	Work		J		100%	$0.00/hr	$0.00/hr	$0.00	Pr
5		Patti Mintz	Work		P		100%	$0.00/hr	$0.00/hr	$0.00	Pr
6		Peter Kelly	Work		P		100%	$0.00/hr	$0.00/hr	$0.00	Pr
7		John Rodman	Work		J		100%	$0.00/hr	$0.00/hr	$0.00	Pr
8		Jonathan Mollerup	Work		J		100%	$0.00/hr	$0.00/hr	$0.00	Pr
9		Jon Ganio	Work		J		50%	$0.00/hr	$0.00/hr	$0.00	Pr
10		Electrician	Work		E		200%	$0.00/hr	$0.00/hr	$0.00	Pr

When you create a new resource, Project assigns it 100% Max. Units by default. You change the resource's Max. Units here.

What Is the Best Way to Enter Resource Names?

In Project, resource names can refer to specific people (for example, Jon Ganio or Jim Hance) or to specific job titles (for example, Camera Operator or Actor). Use whatever makes the most sense to you and those who will see the project plan information you publish. The important questions are Who will see these resource names? and How will they identify the resources? The resource names you choose will appear both in Project and in information published from Project. For example, in the default Gantt Chart view, the name of the resource, as you enter it in the **Resource Name** field, appears next to the bars of the tasks to which that resource is assigned.

A resource might refer to somebody already on staff or to a position to be filled later. If you have not yet filled all the resource positions required, you might not have real people's names yet. In that case, use placeholder names or job titles when setting up resources in Project.

Tip If you prefer, you can enter maximum units as partial or whole numbers (for example, .5, 1, 2) rather than as percentages (50%, 100%, or 200%). To use this format, on the **Tools** menu, click **Options**, and then click the **Schedule** tab. In the **Show assignment units as a** box, click **Decimal**.

Setting Up Equipment Resources

You set up people and equipment resources exactly the same way in Project. However, you should be aware of important differences in how you can schedule these two types of resources. For example, most people resources have a working day of no more than 12 hours, but equipment resources might work around the clock. Moreover, people resources might be flexible in the tasks they can perform, but equipment resources tend to be more specialized. For example, a director of photography for a film or video project might also act as a camera operator in a pinch, but a video camera cannot replace an editing studio.

You do not need to track every piece of equipment that will be used in your project, but you might want to set up equipment resources when

- Multiple teams or people might need a piece of equipment to do different tasks simultaneously, and the equipment might be overbooked.

- You want to plan and track costs associated with the equipment.

In this exercise, you enter information about equipment resources in the **Resource Information** dialog box.

1 In the Resource Sheet, click the next empty cell in the **Resource Name** column.

Resource
Information

2 On the Standard toolbar, click the **Resource Information** button.

The **Resource Information** dialog box appears.

Tip You can also double-click a resource name or an empty cell in the **Resource Name** column to display the **Resource Information** dialog box.

3 Click the **General** tab if it is not already displayed.

In the upper portion of the **General** tab, you might recognize the fields you saw in the Resource Sheet view. As with many types of information in Project, you can usually work in at least two ways: a table or a dialog box.

4 In the **Resource name** field, type Mini-DV Camcorder.

5 In the **Type** field, click **Work**.

Your screen should look similar to the following illustration:

The Resource Information dialog box contains many of the
same fields you see in the Resource Sheet view.

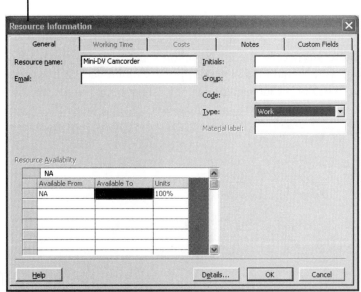

Tip   The **Resource Information** dialog box contains a button labeled **Details**. If you
have an e-mail program that complies with the Messaging Application Programming
Interface (MAPI) and the program is installed on the same computer as Project, you
can click **Details** to see contact information about the selected resource. MAPI-
compliant programs include Outlook and Outlook Express.

6   Click **OK** to close the **Resource Information** dialog box and return to the Resource
Sheet.

The **Max. Units** field shows 100% for this resource; next you will change this.

Tip   You can also double-click on an empty cell in the **Resource Name** column to
create a new resource using the **Resource Information** dialog box. Note that when
creating a resource in this way, you cannot enter a Max. Units value. However, you
can edit this value in the dialog box, as well as in the Resource Sheet, after you create the resource.

7 In the **Max. Units** field for the Mini-DV Camcorder, type or click the arrows until the value shown is **300%** and press ⎋.

This means that you plan to have three camcorders available every workday.

8 Enter the following information about equipment resources directly in the Resource Sheet or in the **Resource Information** dialog box, whichever you prefer. In either case, make sure **Work** is selected in the **Type** field.

Resource name	Max. Units
600-Watt Light and Stand	400%
Reflector Kit	100%
Camera Boom	200%
Editing Lab	100%

Your screen should look similar to the following illustration:

	❶	Resource Name	Type	Material Label	Initials	Group	Max. Units	Std. Rate	Ovt. Rate	Cost/Use	A↑
1		Garrett R. Vargas	Work		G		100%	$0.00/hr	$0.00/hr	$0.00	Pr
2		Jim Hance	Work		J		100%	$0.00/hr	$0.00/hr	$0.00	Pr
3		Scott Cooper	Work		S		100%	$0.00/hr	$0.00/hr	$0.00	Pr
4		Jo Brown	Work		J		100%	$0.00/hr	$0.00/hr	$0.00	Pr
5		Patti Mintz	Work		P		100%	$0.00/hr	$0.00/hr	$0.00	Pr
6		Peter Kelly	Work		P		100%	$0.00/hr	$0.00/hr	$0.00	Pr
7		John Rodman	Work		J		100%	$0.00/hr	$0.00/hr	$0.00	Pr
8		Jonathan Mollerup	Work		J		100%	$0.00/hr	$0.00/hr	$0.00	Pr
9		Jon Ganio	Work		J		50%	$0.00/hr	$0.00/hr	$0.00	Pr
10		Electrician	Work		E		200%	$0.00/hr	$0.00/hr	$0.00	Pr
11		Mini-DV Camcorder	Work		M		300%	$0.00/hr	$0.00/hr	$0.00	Pr
12		600-Watt Light and St	Work		6		400%	$0.00/hr	$0.00/hr	$0.00	Pr
13		Reflector Kit	Work		R		100%	$0.00/hr	$0.00/hr	$0.00	Pr
14		Camera Boom	Work		C		200%	$0.00/hr	$0.00/hr	$0.00	Pr
15		Editing Lab	Work		E		100%	$0.00/hr	$0.00/hr	$0.00	Pr

Setting Up Material Resources

Material resources are consumables that you use up as the project proceeds. On a construction project, material resources might include nails, lumber, and concrete. For the toy commercial project, video tape is the consumable resource that interests you most. You work with material resources in Project mainly to track the rate of consumption and the associated cost. Although Project is not a complete system for tracking inventory, it can help you stay better informed about how quickly you are consuming your material resources.

Comparing Work and Material Resources

Following are some ways material resources are similar to and different from work resources.

For both material and work resources, you can edit and *contour* resource *assignments*, set up multiple pay rates, specify different pay rates to apply at different times, and share resources through a *resource pool*. (You will work with these subjects in later chapters.) In addition, cost calculations for material resources work just about the same way as they do for work resources.

Unlike work resources, however, material resources do not use overtime cost rates, resource calendars, or maximum units.

In this exercise, you enter information about a material resource.

1   In the Resource Sheet, click the next empty cell in the **Resource Name** column.

2   Type Video Tape and press ⟨Tab⟩.

3   In the **Type** field, click the down arrow and select **Material**, and press ⟨Tab⟩.

4   In the **Material Label** field, type 30-min. cassette and press ⟨Enter⟩.

You will use 30-minute cassettes as the unit of measure to track video tape consumption during the project. Your screen should look similar to the following illustration:

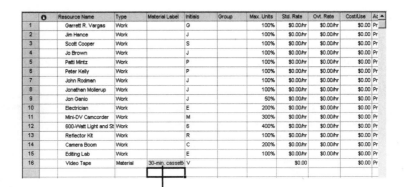

	0	Resource Name	Type	Material Label	Initials	Group	Max. Units	Std. Rate	Ovt. Rate	Cost/Use	Ac
1		Garrett R. Vargas	Work		G		100%	$0.00/hr	$0.00/hr	$0.00	Pr
2		Jim Hance	Work		J		100%	$0.00/hr	$0.00/hr	$0.00	Pr
3		Scott Cooper	Work		S		100%	$0.00/hr	$0.00/hr	$0.00	Pr
4		Jo Brown	Work		J		100%	$0.00/hr	$0.00/hr	$0.00	Pr
5		Patti Mintz	Work		P		100%	$0.00/hr	$0.00/hr	$0.00	Pr
6		Peter Kelly	Work		P		100%	$0.00/hr	$0.00/hr	$0.00	Pr
7		John Rodman	Work		J		100%	$0.00/hr	$0.00/hr	$0.00	Pr
8		Jonathan Mollerup	Work		J		100%	$0.00/hr	$0.00/hr	$0.00	Pr
9		Jon Ganio	Work		J		50%	$0.00/hr	$0.00/hr	$0.00	Pr
10		Electrician	Work		E		200%	$0.00/hr	$0.00/hr	$0.00	Pr
11		Mini-DV Camcorder	Work		M		300%	$0.00/hr	$0.00/hr	$0.00	Pr
12		600-Watt Light and St	Work		6		400%	$0.00/hr	$0.00/hr	$0.00	Pr
13		Reflector Kit	Work		R		100%	$0.00/hr	$0.00/hr	$0.00	Pr
14		Camera Boom	Work		C		200%	$0.00/hr	$0.00/hr	$0.00	Pr
15		Editing Lab	Work		E		100%	$0.00/hr	$0.00/hr	$0.00	Pr
16		Video Tape	Material	30-min. cassett	V			$0.00		$0.00	Pr

The Material Label field only applies to material resources.

Entering Resource Pay Rates

Almost all projects have some financial aspect, and cost limits drive the scope of many projects. Tracking and managing cost information allows the project manager to answer such important questions as

■ What is the expected total cost of the project, based on our task duration and resource estimates?

■ Are we using expensive resources to do work that less expensive resources could do?

■ How much money will a specific type of resource or task cost over the life of the project?

■ Are we spending money at a rate that we can sustain for the planned duration of the project?

For the TV commercial project, you have been entrusted with pay rate information for all people resources used in the project. In the information below, note that the fees for the camcorders, the lights, and the editing lab are rental fees. Because the Southridge Video company already owns the reflector kit and camera booms, you will not bill yourself for them.

In this exercise, you enter cost information for each resource.

1 In the Resource Sheet, click the **Std. Rate** field for resource 1, *Garrett R. Vargas*.

2 Type 800/w and press [Enter].

Garrett's standard weekly rate of $800 per week appears in the **Std. Rate** column.

3 In the **Std. Rate** field for resource 2, *Jim Hance*, type 18.75/h, and press [Enter].

Jim's standard hourly rate appears in the **Std. Rate** column. Your screen should look similar to the following illustration:

	❶	Resource Name	Type	Material Label	Initials	Group	Max. Units	Std. Rate	Ovt. Rate	Cost/Use	Ac
1		Garrett R. Vargas	Work		G		100%	$800.00/wk	$0.00/hr	$0.00	Pr
2		Jim Hance	Work		J		100%	$18.75/hr	$0.00/hr	$0.00	Pr
3		Scott Cooper	Work		S		100%	$0.00/hr	$0.00/hr	$0.00	Pr
4		Jo Brown	Work		J		100%	$0.00/hr	$0.00/hr	$0.00	Pr
5		Patti Mintz	Work		P		100%	$0.00/hr	$0.00/hr	$0.00	Pr
6		Peter Kelly	Work		P		100%	$0.00/hr	$0.00/hr	$0.00	Pr
7		John Rodman	Work		J		100%	$0.00/hr	$0.00/hr	$0.00	Pr
8		Jonathan Mollerup	Work		J		100%	$0.00/hr	$0.00/hr	$0.00	Pr
9		Jon Ganio	Work		J		50%	$0.00/hr	$0.00/hr	$0.00	Pr
10		Electrician	Work		E		200%	$0.00/hr	$0.00/hr	$0.00	Pr
11		Mini-DV Camcorder	Work		M		300%	$0.00/hr	$0.00/hr	$0.00	Pr
12		600-Watt Light and St	Work		6		400%	$0.00/hr	$0.00/hr	$0.00	Pr
13		Reflector Kit	Work		R		100%	$0.00/hr	$0.00/hr	$0.00	Pr
14		Camera Boom	Work		C		200%	$0.00/hr	$0.00/hr	$0.00	Pr
15		Editing Lab	Work		E		100%	$0.00/hr	$0.00/hr	$0.00	Pr
16		Video Tape	Material	30-min. cassett	V			$0.00		$0.00	Pr

4   Enter the following standard pay rates for the given resources:

Resource name	Standard rate	Resource name	Standard rate
Scott Cooper	775/w	Electrician	22/h
Jo Brown	18.75/h	Mini-DV Camcorder	250/w
Patti Mintz	9.40/h	600-Watt Light and Stand	100/w
Peter Kelly	16.75/h	Reflector Kit	0/h
John Rodman	22/h	Camera Boom	0/h
Jonathan Mollerup	10/h	Editing Lab	200/d
Jon Ganio	15.50/h	Video Tape	5

Your screen should look similar to the following illustration:

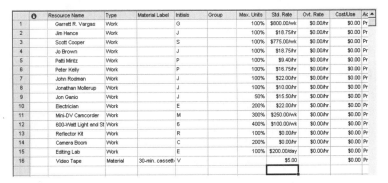

	ⓘ	Resource Name	Type	Material Label	Initials	Group	Max. Units	Std. Rate	Ovt. Rate	Cost/Use	Ac
1		Garrett R. Vargas	Work		G		100%	$800.00/wk	$0.00/hr	$0.00	Pr
2		Jim Hance	Work		J		100%	$18.75/hr	$0.00/hr	$0.00	Pr
3		Scott Cooper	Work		S		100%	$775.00/wk	$0.00/hr	$0.00	Pr
4		Jo Brown	Work		J		100%	$18.75/hr	$0.00/hr	$0.00	Pr
5		Patti Mintz	Work		P		100%	$9.40/hr	$0.00/hr	$0.00	Pr
6		Peter Kelly	Work		P		100%	$16.75/hr	$0.00/hr	$0.00	Pr
7		John Rodman	Work		J		100%	$22.00/hr	$0.00/hr	$0.00	Pr
8		Jonathan Mollerup	Work		J		100%	$10.00/hr	$0.00/hr	$0.00	Pr
9		Jon Ganio	Work		J		50%	$15.50/hr	$0.00/hr	$0.00	Pr
10		Electrician	Work		E		200%	$22.00/hr	$0.00/hr	$0.00	Pr
11		Mini-DV Camcorder	Work		M		300%	$250.00/wk	$0.00/hr	$0.00	Pr
12		600-Watt Light and St	Work		6		400%	$100.00/wk	$0.00/hr	$0.00	Pr
13		Reflector Kit	Work		R		100%	$0.00/hr	$0.00/hr	$0.00	Pr
14		Camera Boom	Work		C		200%	$0.00/hr	$0.00/hr	$0.00	Pr
15		Editing Lab	Work		E		100%	$200.00/day	$0.00/hr	$0.00	Pr
16		Video Tape	Material	30-min. cassett	V			$5.00		$0.00	Pr

Note that you don't enter a rate (hourly, daily, or weekly) for the video tape's cost. For material resources, the standard rate value is per unit of consumption—in our case, 30-minute cassettes.

Project Management Focus: Getting Resource Cost Information

Work and material resources account for the majority of costs in many projects. To take full advantage of the extensive cost management features in Project, the project manager should know the costs associated with each work and material resource. For people resources, it might be difficult to get such information. In many organizations, only senior management and human resource specialists know the pay rates of all resources working on a project, and they might consider this information confidential. Depending on your organizational policies and project priorities, you might not be able to track resource pay rates. If you cannot track this information, your effectiveness as a project manager might be reduced, and the *sponsors* of your projects should understand this.

Adjusting Working Time for Individual Resources

Project uses different types of calendars for different purposes. In this exercise, we will focus on the *resource calendar*. A resource calendar controls the working and nonworking times of a resource. Project uses resource calendars to determine when work for a specific resource can be scheduled. Resource calendars apply only to work resources (people and equipment) and not to material resources.

When you initially create resources in a project plan, Project creates a resource calendar for each resource. The initial working time settings for resource calendars exactly match those of the *Standard base calendar*. (This is a calendar built into Project that accommodates an 8 A.M. to 5 P.M., Monday through Friday work schedule.) If all the working times of your resource match the working time of the Standard base calendar, you do not need to edit any resource calendars. However, chances are that some of your resources will need exceptions to the working time in the Standard base calendar—such as

- A flex-time work schedule

- Vacation time

- Other times when a resource is not available to work on the project, such as time spent training or attending a conference

Any changes you make to the Standard base calendar are automatically reflected in all resource calendars that are based on the Standard base calendar. Any specific changes you have made to the working time of a resource are not changed, however.

Tip   If you have a resource who is available to work on your project only part-time, you might be tempted to set the working time of the resource in your project to reflect a part-time schedule—for example, 8 A.M. to 12 P.M. daily. However, a better approach would be to adjust the availability of the resource as recorded in the **Max. Units** field to 50%. Changing the unit availability of the resource keeps the focus on the capacity of the resource to work on the project, rather than on the specific times of the day when that work might occur. You set the maximum units for a resource in the Resource Sheet view, which you display by selecting the resource and then clicking **Resource Sheet** on the **View** menu. For more information about resource units, see "Setting Up People Resources," on page 55.

In this exercise, you specify the working and nonworking times for individual work resources.

1   On the **Tools** menu, click **Change Working Time.**

         The **Change Working Time** dialog box appears.

2 In the **For** box, click **Garrett R. Vargas**.

Garrett R. Vargas's resource calendar appears in the **Change Working Time** dialog box. Garrett, the producer of the TV commercial, has told you he will not be available to work on Thursday and Friday, January 13 and 14.

3 In the calendar below **Select Date(s)**, drag the vertical scroll bar or click the up or down arrow buttons until **January 2005** appears.

4 Select the dates January 13 and 14.

Tip To quickly select this date range, drag from **13** through **14**.

5 Under **Set selected date(s) to,** click **Nonworking time**.

Your screen should look similar to the following illustration:

Every resource calendar is based on the Standard base calendar unless you pick a different base calendar.

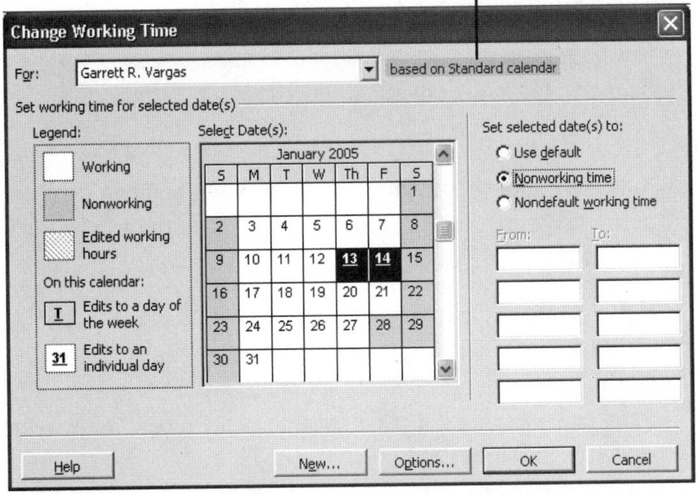

Project will not schedule work for Garrett on these dates.

Tip If your team uses the calendar module in Outlook and Project Web Access, resources can automatically report to you times they are not available to work on project activities. These times are based on calendar items marked as busy or out of office in Outlook. Once the times are reported, you can easily update the resource's working time in the project plan without retyping anything. For more information, see Part 4, "Introducing Project Server."

To conclude this exercise, you will set up a "4 by 10" work schedule (that is, 4 days per week, 10 hours per day) for a resource.

6   In the **For** box, click **John Rodman**.

7   When prompted to save the resource calendar changes you made for Garrett, click **Yes**.

8   Select the Monday through Thursday column headings in the calendar.

> **Tip**   To quickly select the Monday through Thursday column headings, drag from the **M** through the **Th**.

Although you can see only one month at a time in the dialog box, selecting a column heading for a day of the week selects every occurrence of that day—past, present, and future.

9   In the lower **To** box, click **5:00 PM** and replace it with 7:00 PM.

10   Click the **Friday** column heading.

11   Under **Set selected date(s) to**, click **Nonworking time**.

Now Project can schedule work for John as late as 7 P.M. every Monday through Thursday, but it will not schedule work for him on Fridays.

12   Click **OK** to close the **Change Working Time** dialog box.

Because you have not yet assigned these resources to tasks, you don't see the scheduling effect of their nonworking time settings. You will in Chapter 4, "Assigning Resources to Tasks."

> **Tip**   If you find that you must edit several resource calendars in a similar way (to handle a night shift, for example), it may be easier to assign a different base calendar to a resource or collection of resources. This is more efficient than editing individual calendars, and it allows you to make project-wide adjustments to a single base calendar if needed.

For example, if your project includes a day shift and a *night shift*, you can apply the Night Shift base calendar to those resources who work the night shift. You change a resource's base calendar in Step 2 of the Resource Working Times Project Guide, or in the **Base Calendar** box on the **Working Time** tab of the **Resource Information** dialog box. You can open this dialog box by clicking **Resource Information** on the **Project** menu when in a resource view. For collections of resources, you can make these changes directly in the **Base Calendar** column on the Entry table in the Resource Sheet view.

Documenting Resources

You might recall from Chapter 2, "Creating a Task List," that you can record any additional information that you want about a task, resource, or assignment in a *note*. For example, if a resource is not available to work on a specific date range, it is a good idea to record why in a note. That way, the note resides in the project plan and can be easily viewed or printed.

In this exercise, you enter resource notes to document why a resource is not available to work on certain dates.

1   In the **Resource Name** column, click the name of resource 1, **Garrett R. Vargas.**

2   On the Standard toolbar, click the **Resource Notes** button.

Resource
Notes

Project displays the **Resource Information** dialog box with the **Notes** tab visible.

3   In the **Notes** box, type Garrett attending West Coast film festival January 13 and 14; unavailable to work on project. Then click **OK.**

A note icon appears in the Indicators column.

4   Point to the note icon, as shown here:

	ⓘ	Resource Name	Type	Material Label	Initials	Group	Max. Units	Std. Rate	Ovt. Rate	Cost/Use	Ac
1		Notes: 'Garrett attending West Coast film festival January 13 and 14; unavailable to work on project. '			G		100%	$800.00/wk	$0.00/hr	$0.00	Pr
2					J		100%	$18.75/hr	$0.00/hr	$0.00	Pr
3					S		100%	$775.00/wk	$0.00/hr	$0.00	Pr
4		Jo Brown	Work		J		100%	$18.75/hr	$0.00/hr	$0.00	Pr
5		Patti Mintz	Work		P		100%	$9.40/hr	$0.00/hr	$0.00	Pr

The note appears in a ScreenTip. For notes that are too long to appear in a ScreenTip, you can double-click the note icon to display the full text of the note.

CLOSE: the Wingtip Toys Commercial 3 file.

Key Points

■   Recording resource information in your project plans helps you better control who does what work when, and at what cost.

■   People and equipment resources perform the work in a project.

■   Material resources are consumed during a project.

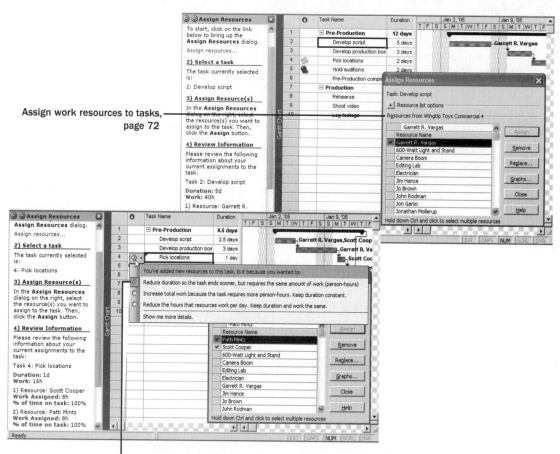

Assign work resources to tasks,
page 72

Control how effort-driven
scheduling affects task durations,
page 78

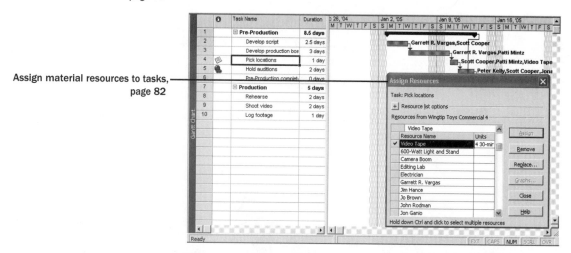

Assign material resources to tasks,
page 82

Chapter 4 at a Glance

4 Assigning Resources to Tasks

In this chapter you will learn to:

✔ Assign resources to tasks.

✔ Control how Microsoft Office Project 2003 schedules additional resource assignments.

✔ Assign material resources to tasks.

See Also Do you need a quick refresher on the topics in this chapter? See the quick reference entries on pages xxii–xxiii.

If you completed Chapter 2, "Creating a Task List," and Chapter 3, "Setting Up Resources," you have already created *tasks* and *resources*. Now you are ready to assign resources to tasks. An *assignment* is the matching of a resource to a task to do *work*. From the perspective of tasks, you might call the process of assigning a resource a task assignment; from the perspective of resources, you might call it a resource assignment. It is the same thing either way: a task plus a resource equals an assignment.

You do not have to assign resources to tasks in Project; you could work with just tasks. But there are several good reasons to assign resources in your project plan. If you assign resources to tasks, you can answer questions such as

■ Who should be working on what tasks and when?

■ Do you have the right number of resources to do the scope of work your project requires?

■ Are you expecting a resource to work on a task at a time when that resource will not be available to work (for example, when the resource will be on vacation)?

■ Have you assigned a resource to so many tasks that you have exceeded the capacity of the resource to work—in other words, have you *overallocated* the resource?

In this chapter, you assign resources to tasks. You assign work resources (people and equipment) and material resources to tasks, and you see where resource assignments should affect task duration and where they should not.

Important   Before you can use the practice files in this chapter, be sure you install them from the book's companion CD to their default location. See "Using the Book's CD-ROM," on page xiii, for more information.

Assigning Resources to Tasks

Assigning a resource to a task enables you to track the progress of the resource's work on the task. If you enter cost information, Project also calculates resource and task costs for you.

You might recall from Chapter 3 that the capacity of a resource to work is measured in *units* and recorded in the **Max. Units** field. Unless you specify otherwise, Project assigns 100 percent of the units for the resource to the task—that is, Project assumes that all the resource's work time can be allotted to the task. If the resource has less than 100 percent maximum units, Project assigns the resource's maximum units value.

In this exercise, you make the initial resource assignments to tasks in the project plan.

BE SURE TO: Start Project if it's not already running.

Important   If you are running Project Professional, you may need to make a one-time adjustment to use the My Computer account and to work offline. This helps ensure that the practice files you work with in this chapter don't affect your Project Server data. For more information, see "Starting Project Professional" on page 10.

OPEN: Wingtip Toys Commercial 4a from the *My Documents**Microsoft Press**Project 2003 Step by Step*\ *Chapter 4 Simple Assignments* **folder. You can also access the practice files for this book by clicking Start, All Programs, Microsoft Press, Project 2003 Step by Step, and then selecting the chapter folder of the file you want to open.**

1   On the **File** menu, click **Save As**.

The **Save As** dialog box appears.

2   In the **File name** box, type Wingtip Toys Commercial 4, and then click the **Save** button.

3   On the **Project Guide** toolbar, click **Resources**.

4   In the Resources pane, click the **Assign people and equipment to tasks** link.

The Assign Resources Project Guide pane and the Gantt Chart view appear.

5   In the Assign Resources Project Guide pane, click the **Assign Resources** link.

The **Assign Resources** dialog box appears. In it you see resource names you entered in Chapter 3. If the **Assign Resources** dialog box obscures the **Task Name** column, drag the dialog box to the lower right corner of the screen. Your screen should look similar to the following illustration:

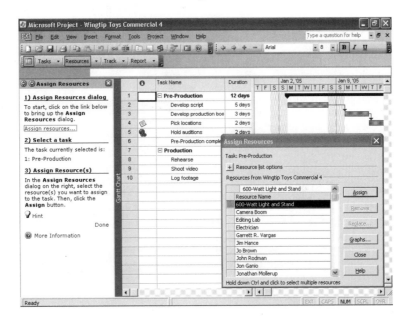

Tip   When you display the **Assign Resources** dialog box from the Project Guide, you see a slightly simplified version of the dialog box. You'll see the more complete version of it later in this chapter.

6   In the **Task Name** column, click task 2, **Develop script**.

7   In the **Resource Name** column in the **Assign Resources** dialog box, click **Garrett R. Vargas**, and then click the **Assign** button.

A check mark appears next to Garrett's name, indicating that you have assigned him to the task of developing the script.

Tip   Except for assigned resources, which appear at the top of the list, resources are sorted alphabetically in the **Assign Resources** dialog box.

8   If necessary, scroll the Assign Resources pane down to see the information under step 4, **Review Information**. Your screen should look similar to the following illustration:

The names of assigned resources appear next to the Gantt bars.

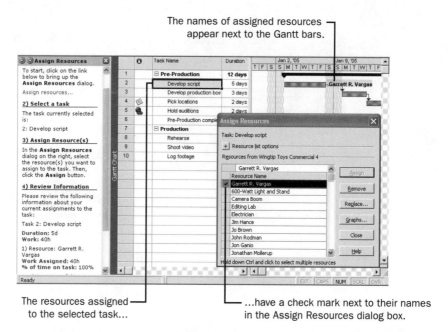

The resources assigned to the selected task...   ...have a check mark next to their names in the Assign Resources dialog box.

Here you can see the essential scheduling values for this task: *duration*, *work*, and assignment *units* (units are reported here as *% of time on task*). In the next exercise, you will look at these values more closely to understand the basic scheduling logic that Project follows.

Next you assign two resources simultaneously to a task.

9   In the **Task Name** column, click task 3, **Develop production boards**.

10   In the **Assign Resources** dialog box, click **Garrett R. Vargas**, hold down the Ctrl key, click **Patti Mintz**, and then click the **Assign** button.

Check marks appear next to Garrett's and Patti's names, indicating that you have assigned both to task 3.

Troubleshooting   If you should accidentally assign just a single resource when you intended to assign multiple resources, you can undo the assignment. On the **Edit** menu click **Undo Assignment**. You must do this before you perform another action, however, as Project can undo only the most recent action you've performed.

To conclude this exercise, you will make initial resource assignments for remaining pre-production tasks.

11 In the **Task Name** column, click the name of task 4, **Pick locations**.

12 In the **Assign Resources** dialog box, click **Scott Cooper**, and then click the **Assign** button.

A check mark appears next to Scott's name, indicating that you have assigned him to task 4.

Tip   To remove or unassign a resource from the selected task, in the **Assign Resources** dialog box, click the resource name, and then click the **Remove** button.

13 In the **Task Name** column, click the name of task 5, **Hold auditions**.

14 In the **Assign Resources** dialog box, click **Peter Kelly**, hold down the ⌃Ctrl⌃ key, click **Scott Cooper**, and then click the **Assign** button.

Check marks appear next to Peter's and Scott's names, indicating that you have assigned both to task 5. Your screen should look similar to the following illustration:

The name of the selected task also appears here. ⌐

Assigned resources appear at the top of the list.

Tip   In Part 2 you will work more with assignments, but if you want to read more about assignments now, type **About assignments** into the **Search** box in the upper right corner of the Project window.

The Scheduling Formula: Duration, Units, and Work

After you create a task but before you assign a resource to it, the task has duration but no work associated with it. Why no work? Work represents the amount of effort a resource or resources will spend to complete a task. For example, if you have one person working full-time, the amount of time measured as work is the same as the amount of time measured as duration. In general, the amount of work will match the duration unless you assign more than one resource to a task or the one resource you assign is not working full-time.

Project calculates work using what is sometimes called the *scheduling formula*:

Duration × Units = Work

Let's look at a specific example. The duration of task 2 is five days. For our TV commercial project, five days equals 40 hours. When you assigned Garrett R. Vargas to task 2, Project applied 100 percent of Garrett's working time to this task. The scheduling formula for task 2 looks like this:

40 hours task duration × 100% assignment units = 40 hours work

In other words, with Garrett assigned to task 2 at 100 percent units, the task should require 40 hours of work.

Here's a more complex example. You assigned two resources, each at 100 percent assignment units, to task 5. The scheduling formula for task 5 looks like this:

16 hours task duration × 200% assignment units = 32 hours work

The 32 hours of work is the sum of Peter's 16 hours of work plus Scott's 16 hours of work. In other words, both resources will work on the task in parallel.

Assigning Additional Resources to a Task

Now you will assign additional resources to some of the pre-production tasks to see the effect on the overall duration of the tasks. By default, Project uses a scheduling method called *effort-driven scheduling*. This means that the task's initial work value remains constant, regardless of the number of additional resources you assign. The most visible effect of effort-driven scheduling is that as you assign additional resources to a task, that task's duration decreases. Project applies effort-driven scheduling only when you assign resources to or remove resources from tasks.

As you saw previously, you define the amount of work a task represents when you initially assign a resource or resources to it. With effort-driven scheduling turned on, if you later add resources to that task, the amount of work for the task does not change but the task's duration decreases. Or you might initially assign more than one resource to a task and later remove one of those resources from the task. With effort-driven scheduling on, the amount of work for the task stays constant. The duration, or time it takes the remaining resource to complete that task, increases.

Tip By default, effort-driven scheduling is enabled for all tasks you create in Project. To change the default setting for all new tasks in a project plan, on the **Tools** menu, click **Options**, and in the **Options** dialog box, click the **Schedule** tab. Select or clear the **New tasks are effort-driven** check box. To control effort-driven scheduling for a specific task or tasks, first select the task or tasks. Then on the **Project** menu, click **Task Information**, and on the **Advanced** tab of the **Task Information** dialog box, select or clear the **Effort driven** check box.

In this exercise, you assign additional resources to tasks and see how this affects task durations.

1 In the Gantt Chart view, click the name of task 2, **Develop script**.

Currently, Garrett R. Vargas is assigned to this task. A quick check of the scheduling formula looks like this:

40 hours (the same as 5 days) task duration × 100% of Garrett's assignment units = 40 hours work.

If you want, you can scroll the Assign Resources pane down to see these values. Next you will assign a second resource to the task.

2 In the **Resource Name** column in the **Assign Resources** dialog box, click **Scott Cooper,** and click the **Assign** button.

Scott Cooper is assigned to task 2. Your screen should look similar to the following illustration:

The duration of this task decreases as additional resources are assigned to it.

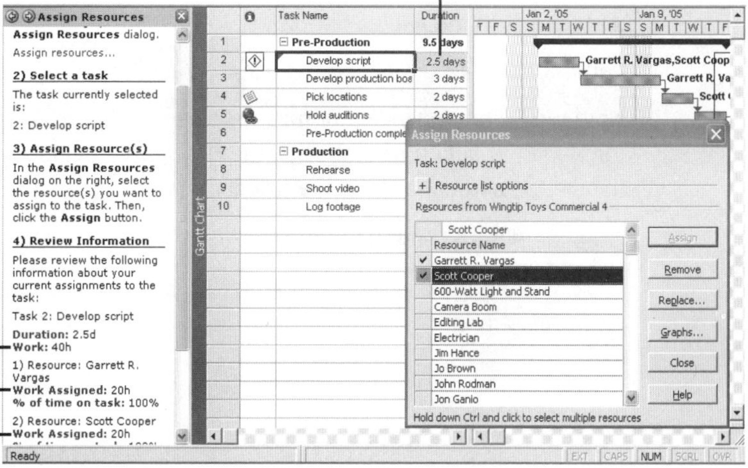

The 40 hours total task work is divided between the two assigned resources.

As you can see in the Gantt Chart view, Project reduced the duration of task 2 from 5 days to 2.5 days.

The total work required is still 40 hours, as it was when only Garrett was assigned to the task, but now the work is distributed evenly between Garrett and Scott. This shows how effort-driven scheduling works. If, after an initial assignment, you add resources to a task, the total work remains constant but is distributed among the assigned resources. Further, the task's duration decreases accordingly.

The scheduling formula now looks like this:

20 hours (the same as 2.5 days) task duration × 200% assignment units
= 40 hours work

The 200 percent assignment units is the sum of Garrett's 100 percent plus Scott's 100 percent, and the 40 work hours is the sum of Garrett's 20 hours plus Scott's 20 hours.

The other important effect of reducing the duration of task 2 is that the start dates of all successor tasks have changed as well. In Chapter 2, you created finish-to-start task relationships for these tasks. In this example, you see the benefit of creating task relationships rather than entering fixed start and finish dates. Project adjusts the start dates of successor tasks that do not have a constraint, such as a fixed start date or finish date.

Next you assign multiple resources to other tasks, using a Smart Tag to control how Project schedules the work on the tasks.

3   In the Gantt Chart view, click the name of task 4, **Pick locations**.

Currently, only Scott Cooper is assigned to this two-day task. You'd like to assign an additional resource and reduce the task's duration to one day.

4   In the **Resource Name** column of the **Assign Resources** dialog box, click **Patti Mintz**, and then click the **Assign** button.

Patti Mintz is also assigned to task 4.

Note the Smart Tag indicator that appears next to the name of task 4. Until you perform another action, you can use the Smart Tag to choose how you want Project to handle the additional resource assignment.

Smart Tag
Actions

5   Click the **Smart Tag Actions** button.

Look over the options in the list that appears. Your screen should look like the following illustration:

Clicking the Smart Tag Actions button displays a list of options, but it is available only until you perform another action in Project.

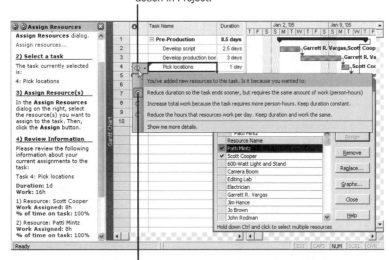

In the Actions list, the selected option describes the result of your most recent action; if this is not the result you want, pick another option.

These options let you choose the scheduling result you want, should it differ from the effort-driven scheduling result. You can adjust the task's duration, the resource's work, or the assignment units.

For this task, you want the additional resource assignment to reduce the task's duration. Because this is the default setting in the Smart Tag Actions list, you don't need to make any changes.

6   Click the **Smart Tag Actions** button again to close the list.

Tip   You will see other SmartTags while using Project. They generally appear when you might otherwise ask yourself, "Hmm, why did Project just do that?" (for example, when a task's duration changes after you assign an additional resource). The Smart Tag Actions list gives you the chance to change how Project responds to your actions.

To conclude this exercise, you will assign additional resources to a task and change how Project schedules the work on the task.

7   In the Gantt Chart view, click the name of task 5, **Hold auditions**.

8   In the **Resource Name** column of the **Assign Resources** dialog box, click **Jonathan Mollerup**, hold down the ⌃Ctrl key, click **Patti Mintz**, and then click the **Assign** button.

Project assigns Jonathan and Patti to the task. Because effort-driven scheduling is on for this task, Project reduces the duration of the task and adjusts the start dates of all successor tasks. Your screen should look similar to the following illustration:

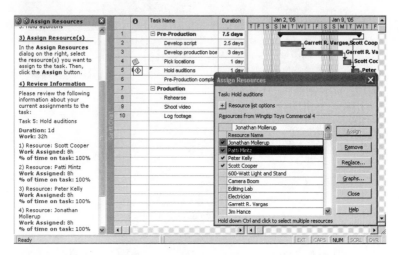

However, this time you do not want the additional resource assignments to change the task's duration. Jonathan and Patti will perform additional work on the task, beyond the scope of the task's previous work, which was assigned to Peter and Scott.

9   Click the **Smart Tag Actions** button.

10   In the **Smart Tag Actions** list, select the option **Increase total work because the task requires more person-hours. Keep duration constant.**

Project changes the task's duration back to two days and adjusts the start dates of all successor tasks. The additional resources get the same work values that the initially assigned resources had, so the total work on the task increases. Your screen should look similar to the following illustration:

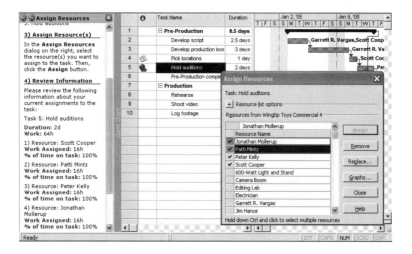

Tip   If you initially assign two resources to a task with a duration of three days (the same as 24 hours), Project schedules each resource to work 24 hours, for a total of 48 hours of work on the task. However, you might initially assign one resource to a task with a duration of 24 hours and later add a second resource. In this case, effort-driven scheduling will cause Project to schedule each resource to work 12 hours in parallel, for a total of 24 hours of work on the task. Remember that effort-driven scheduling adjusts task duration only if you add or delete resources from a task.

Project Management Focus:
When Should Effort-Driven Scheduling Apply?

You should think through the extent to which effort-driven scheduling should apply to the tasks in your projects. For example, if one resource should take 10 hours to complete a task, could 10 resources complete the task in one hour? How about 20 resources in 30 minutes? Probably not; the resources would likely get in each other's way and require additional coordination to complete the task. If the task is very complicated, it might require significant ramp-up time before a resource could contribute fully. Overall productivity might even decrease if you assign more resources to the task.

No single rule exists about when you should apply effort-driven scheduling and when you should not. As the project manager, you should analyze the nature of the work required for each task in your project and use your best judgment.

Assigning Material Resources to Tasks

In Chapter 3, you created the material resource named Video Tape. In our TV commercial project, we are interested in tracking the use of video cassettes and their cost. When assigning a material resource, you can handle consumptions and cost in one of two ways:

■ Assign a fixed-unit quantity of the material resource to the task. Project will multiply the unit cost of this resource by the number of units assigned to determine the total cost. (You'll use this method in the following exercise.)

■ Assign a variable-rate quantity of the material resource to the task. Project will adjust the quantity and cost of the resource as the task's duration changes. (You'll use this method in Chapter 9, "Fine-Tuning the Project Plan.")

In this exercise, you assign the material resource Video Tape to a task and enter a fixed-unit quantity of consumption. You will also work with the more complete version of the **Assign Resources** dialog box.

1   In the **Assign Resources** dialog box, click the **Close** button.

Show/Hide Project Guide

2   Click the **Show/Hide Project Guide** button on the **Project Guide** toolbar.

The Project Guide closes.

Assign Resources

3   On the **Standard** toolbar, click the **Assign Resources** button.

The **Assign Resources** dialog box appears. Unlike the version of this dialog box you saw using the Project Guide, this version includes the **Units** column. *Units* here refers to assignment units.

> **Tip**   If you are using Project Professional, you also see the **R/D** (request or demand) column in the **Assign Resources** dialog box. This relates to setting a priority for a resource assignment when using a Project Server feature called resource substitution. For more information, see Part 4, "Introducing Project Server."

4   In the **Task Name** column, click the name of task 4, **Pick locations**.

You plan to use up to four tapes while picking locations.

5   In the **Assign Resources** dialog box, select the **Units** field for the Video Tape resource.

6   Type 4, and then click the **Assign** button.

Project assigns the video tape to the task. Your screen should look like the following illustration:

When you assign a material resource to a task, ——
its label value appears in the Units column...

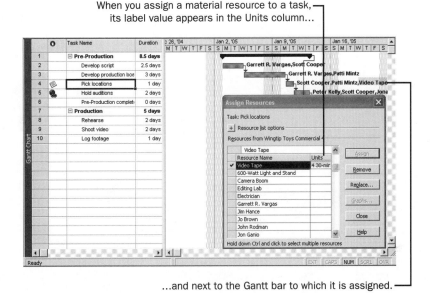

...and next to the Gantt bar to which it is assigned. ——

Because video tape is a material resource, it cannot do work. Therefore, assigning a material resource does not affect the duration of a task.

CLOSE: the Wingtip Toys Commercial 4 file.

Key Points

- In Project, a task normally has work associated with it after a work resource (people or equipment) has been assigned to the task.

- When resources are assigned more work than they can complete in a specific period of time, they are said to be overallocated during that time period.

- You must assign resources to tasks before you can track their progress or cost.

- Project follows the scheduling formula: duration times units equals work.

- Effort-driven scheduling is a task-level setting. It determines whether work remains constant when you assign additional resources to the task.

- The easiest way to understand effort-driven scheduling is to ask yourself, "If one person can do this task in 10 days, could two people do it in five days?" If so, then effort-driven scheduling should be turned on for the task.

- Smart tags appear after you perform certain actions in Project. They allow you to quickly change the effect of your action to something other than the default effect.

- Assigning material resources to tasks allows you to track consumables.

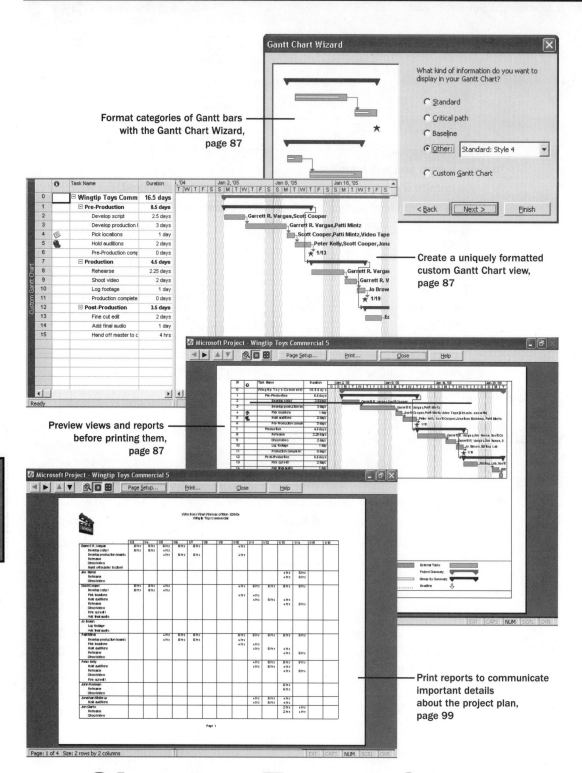

Format categories of Gantt bars with the Gantt Chart Wizard, page 87

Create a uniquely formatted custom Gantt Chart view, page 87

Preview views and reports before printing them, page 87

Print reports to communicate important details about the project plan, page 99

Chapter 5 at a Glance

5 Formatting and Printing Your Plan

In this chapter you will learn to:

✔ Customize a view and preview the way it will look when printed.

✔ Draw on the chart portion of a Gantt Chart view.

✔ Change the formatting of text in a project plan.

✔ Edit and print reports.

See Also Do you need a quick refresher on the topics in this chapter? See the quick reference entries on pages xxiii–xxiv.

In this chapter, you use some of the formatting features in Microsoft Office Project 2003 to change the way your data appears, and then you preview the results in the Print Preview window. As you might recall from Chapter 1, "Getting Started with Project," a Project plan is really a database of information, not unlike a Microsoft Office Access 2003 database file. You don't normally see all the data in a project plan at one time. Instead, you focus on the aspect of the plan that you're currently interested in. *Views* and *reports* are the most common ways to see or print a project plan's data. In both cases (especially with views), you can substantially format the data to meet your needs.

The primary way Project represents tasks graphically is as bars on the chart portion of a Gantt Chart view. These are called Gantt bars. On a Gantt chart, tasks, summary tasks, and milestones all appear as Gantt bars, and each type of bar has its own format. Whenever you work with Gantt bars, keep in mind that they represent tasks in a project plan.

Tip This chapter introduces you to some of the simpler view and report formatting features in Project. You'll find quite a bit more material about formatting, printing, and publishing your project plans in Chapters 10, 11, 12, and 17. To find more information about available views and reports in Project's online Help, type **About printing views and reports** into the **Search** box in the upper right corner of the Project window. The **Search** box initially contains the text *Type a question for help*.

Important   Before you can use the practice files in this chapter, be sure you install them from the book's companion CD to their default location. See "Using the Book's CD-ROM," on page xiii, for more information.

Creating a Custom Gantt Chart View

The Gantt chart became a standard way of visualizing project plans when, in the early twentieth century, American engineer Henry Gantt developed a bar chart showing the use of resources over time. For many people, a Gantt chart is synonymous with a project plan. In Project, the default view is the Gantt Chart view. You are likely to spend a lot of your time in Project in this view.

The Gantt Chart view consists of two parts: a *table* on the left and a *timescaled* bar chart on the right. The bars on the chart graphically represent the tasks in the table in terms of start and finish dates, duration, and status (for example, whether work on the task has started or not). Other elements on the chart, such as link lines, represent *relationships* between tasks. The Gantt chart is a popular and widely understood representation of project information throughout the project management world.

Tip   By default, Project displays the Gantt Chart view when you start it. However, you can change this to display any view you want at startup. On the **Tools** menu, click **Options**. In the **Options** dialog box, click the **View** tab. In the **Default View** box, click the view you want. The next time you start Project, that view will appear.

The default formatting applied to the Gantt Chart view works well for onscreen viewing, sharing with other programs, and printing. However, you can change the formatting of just about any element on the Gantt chart. In this exercise, we will focus on Gantt bars.

There are three distinct ways to format Gantt bars:

- Format whole categories of Gantt bars in the **Bar Styles** dialog box, which you can open by clicking the **Bar Styles** command on the **Format** menu. In this case, the formatting changes you make to a type of Gantt bar (a *summary task*, for example) apply to all such Gantt bars in the Gantt chart.

- Format whole categories of Gantt bars using the Gantt Chart Wizard, which you can start by clicking the **Gantt Chart Wizard** command on the **Format** menu. This wizard contains a series of pages in which you select formatting options for the most-used Gantt bars on the Gantt chart. Use the Gantt Chart Wizard to step you through some of the formatting actions that you can perform in the **Bar Styles** dialog box.

■   Format individual Gantt bars directly. The formatting changes you make have no effect on other bars in the Gantt chart. You can double-click a Gantt bar on the Gantt chart to see its formatting options.

In this exercise, you create a custom Gantt chart and apply predefined formatting to it with the Gantt Chart Wizard. You then preview the results for printing.

Important   If you are running Project Professional, you may need to make a one-time adjustment to use the My Computer account and to work offline. This helps ensure that the practice files you work with in this chapter don't affect your Project Server data. For more information, see "Starting Project Professional," on page 10.

OPEN: Wingtip Toys Commercial 5a from the *My Documents**Microsoft Press**Project 2003 Step by Step*\ *Chapter 5 Simple Formatting* folder. You can also access the practice files for this book by clicking **Start**, **All Programs**, **Microsoft Press**, **Project 2003 Step by Step**, and then selecting the chapter folder of the file you want to open.

1   On the **File** menu, click **Save As**.

The **Save As** dialog box appears.

2   In the **File name** box, type Wingtip Toys Commercial 5, and then click the **Save** button.

Next you will display the project summary task to see the top-level or rolled-up details of the project. Project automatically generates the *project summary task* but doesn't display it by default.

3   On the **Tools** menu, click **Options**.

4   In the **Options** dialog box, click the **View** tab.

5   Under the **Outline options for** label, select the **Show project summary task** check box, and then click **OK**.

Project displays the project summary task at the top of the Gantt Chart view. You might see pound signs (##) in the project summary task's duration field. If so, complete steps 6 and 7.

6   Drag the vertical divider bar between the table and chart to the right until you can see the right edge of the **Duration** column.

Tip   Double-clicking the divider bar will snap the divider to the nearest column edge.

7   Double-click the right edge of the **Duration** column, in the column heading, to expand the column so that you can see the entire value.

Tip   You can also double-click anywhere in a column heading, and in the **Column Definition** dialog box that appears, click the **Best Fit** button.

The **Duration** column widens to show the widest value in the column. In this case, that value is the duration for the project summary task. Your screen should look similar to the following illustration:

Double-click the right edge of a column heading to widen that column.

Drag the divider bar to show more or less of the table and chart portions of the Gantt Chart view.

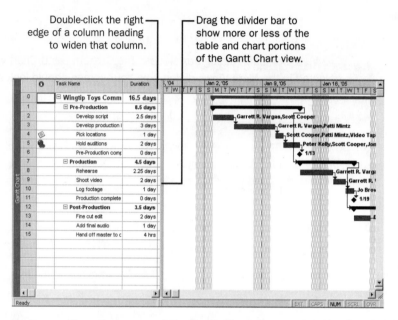

Next you will create a copy of the Gantt Chart view so that the formatting changes you make won't affect the original Gantt Chart view.

8   On the **View** menu, click **More Views**.

The **More Views** dialog box appears, with the current view (the Gantt Chart view) selected.

9   Click the **Copy** button.

The **View Definition** dialog box appears. Your screen should look similar to the following illustration:

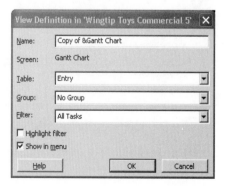

The **Name** field contains the proposed name of the new view, as it will appear in the **More Views** dialog box and, if you specify, on the **View** menu. Note the ampersand (&) in the **Name** field. This is a code that indicates the keyboard shortcut character of the new view name, should you wish to include one.

10   In the **Name** field, type Custom Gantt Chart, and then click **OK**.

The **View Definition** dialog box closes. The Custom Gantt Chart view appears and is selected in the **More Views** dialog box. Your screen should look similar to the following illustration:

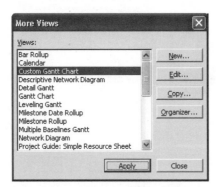

11   In the **More Views** dialog box, click the **Apply** button.

At this point, the Custom Gantt Chart view is an exact copy of the original Gantt Chart view, so the two views look alike. Note, however, that the view title on the left edge of the view is updated.

Next you will use the Gantt Chart Wizard to format the Gantt bars and milestones in the chart portion of the Custom Gantt Chart view.

12   On the **Format** menu, click **Gantt Chart Wizard**.

The welcome page of the Gantt Chart Wizard appears. Your screen should look similar to the following illustration:

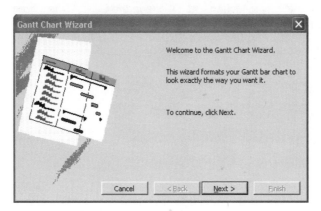

Tip   You can also start the Gantt Chart Wizard, and several other formatting features, using the items in the Report pane of the Project Guide.

13 Click **Next**.

The next screen of the Gantt Chart Wizard appears.

14 Click the **Other** button, and in the drop-down list next to the **Other** option, click **Standard: Style 4**.

Your screen should look similar to the following illustration:

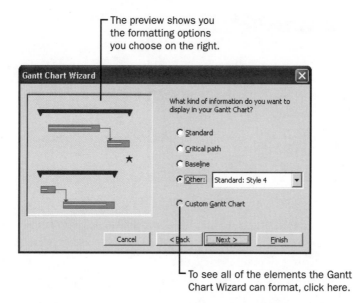

The preview shows you the formatting options you choose on the right.

To see all of the elements the Gantt Chart Wizard can format, click here.

Tip   If you want to see the other built-in Gantt chart formats available in the wizard, click them in the **Other** box to see the preview on the left side of the wizard's window. When you are done, make sure that **Standard: Style 4** is selected.

15 This is the only selection you'll make in the Gantt Chart Wizard for now, so click the **Finish** button.

The final page of the Gantt Chart Wizard appears.

16 Click the **Format It** button, and then click the **Exit Wizard** button.

The Gantt Chart Wizard applies the Standard: Style 4 formatting to the Custom Gantt Chart view and then closes. Your screen should look similar to the following illustration:

The reformatted Gantt bars (summary, task, and milestone) appear in the chart portion of the view.

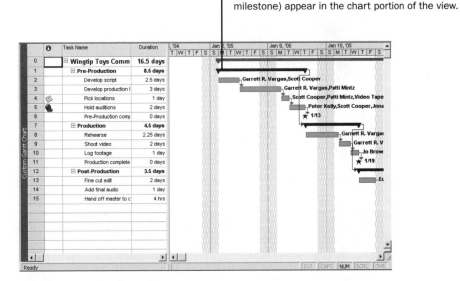

Here you can see the effects of the Standard: Style 4 formatting applied to the project plan. Note that none of the data in the project plan has changed; only the way it is formatted has changed. These formatting changes affect only the Custom Gantt Chart view; all the other views in Project are unaffected.

To conclude this exercise, you will preview the Custom Gantt Chart view. What you see on the screen closely approximates what you'd see on the printed page, and you'll verify this now.

17 On the **File** menu, click **Print Preview**.

Project displays the Custom Gantt Chart view in the Print Preview window. You will do more work in the Print Preview window later in this chapter and in Chapter 11, "Printing Project Information." Your screen should look similar to the following illustration:

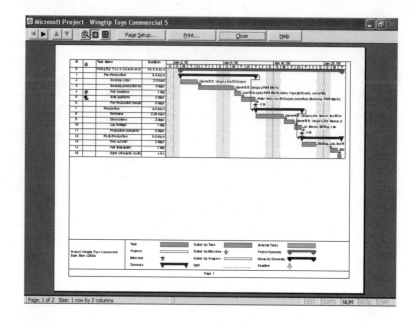

Note If you have a plotter (a device used to draw charts, diagrams, and other line-based graphics) selected as your default printer, or you have a different page size selected for your default printer, what you see in the Print Preview window might differ from what you see here.

18 On the **Print Preview** toolbar, click the **Close** button.

You can print the project plan now if you want, but previewing it is adequate for the purposes of this chapter. When printing in Project, you have additional options in the **Print** dialog box, which you can open by clicking the **Print** command on the **File** menu. For example, you can choose to print a specific date range of a timescaled view such as the Gantt Chart view, or you can print a specific page range.

Drawing on a Gantt Chart

Project includes a **Drawing** toolbar with which you can draw objects directly on the chart portion of a Gantt chart. For example, if you would like to note a particular event or graphically call out a specific item, you can draw objects such as text boxes, arrows, and other items directly on a Gantt chart. If you want, you can link a drawn object to either end of a Gantt bar or to a specific date on the timescale. Here's how to choose the kind of link you need:

■ Link objects to a Gantt bar when the object is specific to the task the Gantt bar represents. The object will move with the Gantt bar, if it is rescheduled.

■ Link objects to a date when the information the object refers to is date-sensitive. The object will remain in the same position relative to the timescale, no matter which part of the timescale is displayed.

Tip   If the **Drawing** toolbar does not have the type of item you would like to add, you can add bitmap images or documents using the **Object** command on the **Insert** menu.

In this exercise, you display the **Drawing** toolbar and add a text box to the Custom Gantt Chart view.

1   On the **View** menu, point to **Toolbars**, and then click **Drawing**.

The **Drawing** toolbar appears.

Tip   You can also right-click any toolbar to see the **Toolbars** shortcut menu, and then display or hide a toolbar listed on that menu.

Text Box

2   On the **Drawing** toolbar, click the **Text Box** button, and then drag a small square anywhere on the chart portion of the Custom Gantt Chart view.

3   In the square you just drew, type Film festival January 13 and 14.

4   On the **Format** menu, point to **Drawing**, and then click **Properties**.

The **Format Drawing** dialog box appears.

Tip   You can also double-click the border of the text box to view its properties.

5   Click the **Line & Fill** tab if it is not already selected.

6   In the **Color** box under the **Fill** label, click **Yellow**.

Next, you'll attach the text box to a specific date on the timescale.

7   Click the **Size & Position** tab.

8   Make sure that **Attach To Timescale** is selected, and in the **Date** box, type or click 1/13/05.

9   In the **Vertical** box under **Attach To Timescale**, type 2.75, (this is the number of inches below the timescale where the top of the box will be positioned) and then click **OK** to close the **Format Drawing** dialog box.

Project colors the text box yellow and positions it below the timescale near the date you specified. Your screen should look similar to the following illustration:

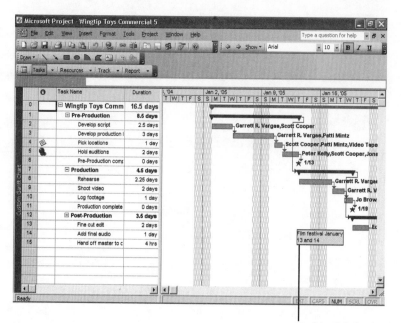

Double-click the border of a drawn object to change its formatting or other properties.

10 Because you attached the text box to a specific date on the timescale, it will always appear near this date, even if you zoom the timescale in or out, or scroll the chart left or right. Had you attached the text box to a Gantt bar, it would move with the Gantt bar if the task were rescheduled. To conclude this exercise, you will hide the **Drawing** toolbar.

11 On the **View** menu point to **Toolbars**, and then click **Drawing**.

The **Drawing** toolbar is hidden.

Formatting Text in a View

You can format text in tables, such as task names in a Gantt Chart view. There are two distinct ways to format text:

■ Format whole categories of text in the **Text Styles** dialog box, which you can open by clicking the **Text Styles** command on the **Format** menu. The formatting changes you make to a category (milestones or summary tasks, for example) apply to all cases of that category in the active view. You can see the categories for which you can change text formatting in the **Item to Change** box in the **Text Styles** dialog box.

■ Format individual selections of text directly. The formatting changes you make have no effect on other text in the view.

Tip   You might notice some similarities between Project and Word in how you can format text. In Project, style-based formatting (available through the **Text Styles** command on the **Format** menu) is similar to applying paragraph styles in Word. Likewise, the direct formatting of text (available through the **Font** command on the **Format** menu) is similar to direct text formatting in Word.

As with all formatting options in Project, the formatting changes you make to any view or report affect only that view or report, and only for the active project plan. Later chapters will introduce ways of copying custom views or reports between project plans.

In this exercise, you switch to a different view and then use text styles and direct formatting to change the appearance of the text in that view.

1   On the **View** menu, click **More Views**.

The **More Views** dialog box appears, with the current view (the Custom Gantt Chart view) selected.

2   In the **Views** box, click **Task Sheet**, and then click the **Apply** button.

The Task Sheet view appears. Unlike Gantt Chart views, this view does not include a chart component; it consists of a single table. Next you will change the table displayed in the Task Sheet view.

3   On the **View** menu, point to **Table: Entry**, and then click **Summary**.

The Summary table appears in the Task Sheet view. Like the Entry table, this table focuses on task details, but it includes a different set of *fields*. The field we're most interested in now is the **Cost** field. Your screen should look similar to the following illustration:

	Task Name	Duration	Start	Finish	% Comp.	Cost	Work
0	⊟ Wingtip Toys Comm	16.5 days	Mon 1/3/05	Tue 1/25/05	0%	$8,671.40	700 hrs
1	⊟ Pre-Production	8.5 days	Mon 1/3/05	Thu 1/13/05	0%	$2,831.70	168 hrs
2	Develop script	2.5 days	Mon 1/3/05	Wed 1/5/05	0%	$787.50	40 hrs
3	Develop production	3 days	Wed 1/5/05	Mon 1/10/05	0%	$705.60	48 hrs
4	Pick locations	1 day	Mon 1/10/05	Tue 1/11/05	0%	$250.20	16 hrs
5	Hold auditions	2 days	Tue 1/11/05	Thu 1/13/05	0%	$888.40	64 hrs
6	Pre-Production comp	0 days	Thu 1/13/05	Thu 1/13/05	0%	$0.00	0 hrs
7	⊟ Production	4.5 days	Thu 1/13/05	Wed 1/19/05	0%	$4,476.70	456 hrs
8	Rehearse	2.25 days	Thu 1/13/05	Mon 1/17/05	0%	$1,717.40	214 hrs
9	Shoot video	2 days	Mon 1/17/05	Tue 1/18/05	0%	$2,409.30	226 hrs
10	Log footage	1 day	Wed 1/19/05	Wed 1/19/05	0%	$350.00	16 hrs
11	Production complete	0 days	Wed 1/19/05	Wed 1/19/05	0%	$0.00	0 hrs
12	⊟ Post-Production	3.5 days	Thu 1/20/05	Tue 1/25/05	0%	$1,563.00	76 hrs
13	Fine cut edit	2 days	Thu 1/20/05	Fri 1/21/05	0%	$978.00	48 hrs
14	Add final audio	1 day	Mon 1/24/05	Mon 1/24/05	0%	$505.00	24 hrs
15	Hand off master to c	4 hrs	Tue 1/25/05	Tue 1/25/05	0%	$80.00	4 hrs

Next you'll change how Project formats an entire category of information—in this case, summary tasks.

4   On the **Format** menu, click **Text Styles**.

The **Text Styles** dialog box appears.

Tip   Text styles in Project are similar to styles in Word. The **Item to Change** list displays all the types of information in a project plan that you can consistently format.

5   In the **Item to Change** list, click **Summary Tasks**.

The current format settings of summary tasks appear in the dialog box, and a preview appears in the **Sample** box. Next you will change the formatting so that the summary tasks appear larger and in color.

6   In the **Size** box, click **10**.

7   In the **Color** box, click **Blue**.

Your screen should look similar to the following illustration:

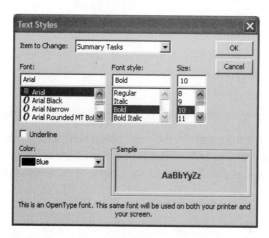

8   Click **OK**.

Project applies the new format settings to all summary tasks in the project (except for the project summary task, which appears separately in the **Item to Change** list). Any new summary tasks added to the project plan will also appear with the new formatting.

9 Double-click between the text in the column labels to widen any columns that display pound signs (##).

Your screen should look similar to the following illustration:

After applying the text style formatting change, all summary tasks are reformatted.

If you see pound signs (##), double-click here to widen the column to the right.

	Task Name	Duration	Start	Finish	% Comp.	Cost	Work
0	Wingtip Toys Comm	16.5 days	Mon 1/3/05	Tue 1/25/05	0%	$8,671.40	700 hrs
1	Pre-Production	8.5 days	Mon 1/3/05	Thu 1/13/05	0%	$2,631.70	168 hrs
2	Develop script	2.5 days	Mon 1/3/05	Wed 1/5/05	0%	$787.50	40 hrs
3	Develop production I	3 days	Wed 1/5/05	Mon 1/10/05	0%	$705.60	48 hrs
4	Pick locations	1 day	Mon 1/10/05	Tue 1/11/05	0%	$250.20	16 hrs
5	Hold auditions	2 days	Tue 1/11/05	Thu 1/13/05	0%	$888.40	64 hrs
6	Pre-Production comp	0 days	Thu 1/13/05	Thu 1/13/05	0%	$0.00	0 hrs
7	Production	4.5 days	Thu 1/13/05	Wed 1/19/05	0%	$4,476.70	456 hrs
8	Rehearse	2.25 days	Thu 1/13/05	Mon 1/17/05	0%	$1,717.40	214 hrs
9	Shoot video	2 days	Mon 1/17/05	Tue 1/18/05	0%	$2,409.30	226 hrs
10	Log footage	1 day	Wed 1/19/05	Wed 1/19/05	0%	$350.00	16 hrs
11	Production complete	0 days	Wed 1/19/05	Wed 1/19/05	0%	$0.00	0 hrs
12	Post-Production	3.5 days	Thu 1/20/05	Tue 1/25/05	0%	$1,563.00	76 hrs
13	Fine cut edit	2 days	Thu 1/20/05	Fri 1/21/05	0%	$978.00	48 hrs
14	Add final audio	1 day	Mon 1/24/05	Mon 1/24/05	0%	$505.00	24 hrs
15	Hand off master to c	4 hrs	Tue 1/25/05	Tue 1/25/05	0%	$80.00	4 hrs

The format changes you've made to summary tasks apply to all tables that you can display in the Task Sheet view, but only in the Task Sheet view. If you displayed the Summary table in the Gantt Chart view, for example, these format changes would not appear there.

To conclude this exercise, you will apply direct formatting to a specific item in a view. As with styles in Word, you can use direct formatting in conjunction with text style formatting. In this project plan, you'll apply italic formatting to the production phase's cost.

10 In the **Summary** table, click the **Cost** field for task 7, the Production summary task.

11 On the **Format** menu, click **Font**.

The **Font** dialog box appears. This is similar to the **Text Styles** dialog box you worked with earlier. However, the options you choose here apply only to the selected text.

Troubleshooting The **Font** command on the **Format** menu applies only to selections of text; you can't use this command to affect the formatting of empty rows in a table. To set the default formatting of rows, use the **Text Styles** command (**Format** menu) instead.

12 In the **Font Style** box, click **Bold Italic**.

Your screen should look similar to the following illustration:

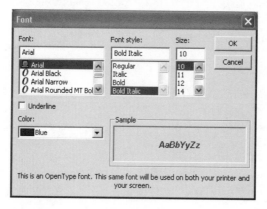

13 Click **OK**.

Project applies bold italic formatting to task 7's **Cost** field. Your screen should look similar to the following illustration:

After applying direct formatting, only this value is formatted.

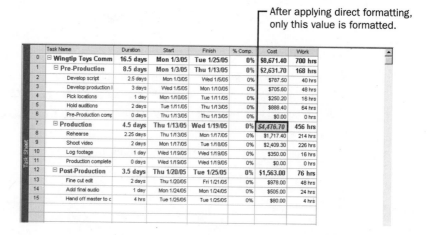

Troubleshooting   You can remove direct formatting that's been applied to text and restore that text to the formatting defined by the **Text Styles** dialog box (**Format** menu). First select the cell containing the formatted text. Next, on the **Edit** menu point to **Clear**, and click **Formats**.

To sum up, use the **Text Styles** command (on the **Format** menu) to change the formatting of entire categories of information, such as all summary tasks. When you want to reformat a specific item (such as one task's cost value) to draw attention to it, use the **Font** command (on the **Format** menu). Note that the **Font** command is not available in some views, such as the Calendar view.

Note Some buttons on the Formatting toolbar correspond to the options available with the **Font** command (on the **Format** menu). These options control direct formatting, not the style-based formatting you might apply with the **Text Styles** dialog box.

Formatting and Printing Reports

Reports are predefined formats intended for printing Project data. Unlike views, which you can either print or work with on the screen, reports are designed only for printing or for viewing in the Print Preview window. You do not enter data directly into a report. Project includes several predefined task, resource, and assignment reports you can edit to get the information you want.

In this exercise, you view a report in the Print Preview window, and then you edit its format to include additional information.

1 On the **View** menu, click **Reports**.

The **Reports** dialog box appears, showing the six broad categories of reports available in Project. Your screen should look similar to the following illustration:

2 Click **Overview**, and then click the **Select** button.

The **Overview Reports** dialog box appears, listing the five predefined reports in Project that provide project-wide overview information.

3 In the **Overview Reports** dialog box, click **Project Summary**, and then click the **Select** button.

Project displays the Project Summary report in the Print Preview window. This is a handy summary of the project plan's tasks, resources, costs, and current status. You could use this report, for example, as a recurring status report that you share with the clients or other *stakeholders* of the project.

Depending on your screen resolution, the text in the report might not be readable when you view a full page.

Tip   Here's a quick way to see vital project statistics on the screen: Click the **Project Information** command on the **Project** menu, and then click **Statistics**.

4   In the Print Preview window, click the upper half of the page with the mouse pointer.

Project zooms in to show the page at a legible resolution. Your screen should look similar to the following illustration:

The project title and company name come from the values entered in the Properties dialog box (File menu).

Click to zoom out.

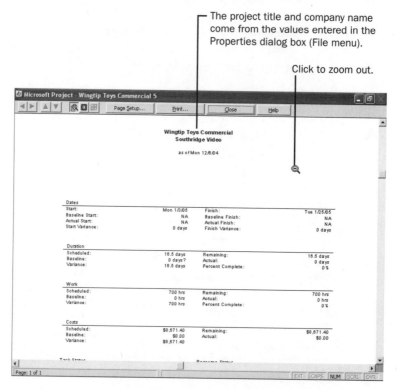

At this point in the project life cycle, the most pertinent pieces of information in the report are the planned start and finish dates and the total cost. If any of these values did not fit within the expectations of the project *sponsor* or other stakeholders, now would be a good time to find out.

5   On the **Print Preview** toolbar, click the **Close** button.

The Print Preview window closes, and the **Reports** dialog box reappears. Next you will preview and edit a different report.

For a small, simple project such as the TV commercial, a report is a simple way to communicate assignments to the resources involved. To do this, you will work with the Who Does What When report.

Tip *This tip describes enterprise project management (EPM) functionality.* For more detailed projects, communicating resource assignments (and subsequent changes) and other project details can be a significant responsibility for a project manager. Project Server offers an intranet-based solution for communicating such project details in conjunction with Project Professional. For more information, see Part 4, "Introducing Project Server."

6 Click **Assignments**, and then click the **Select** button.

The **Assignment Reports** dialog box appears, listing four predefined reports in Project that provide resource assignment information.

7 In the **Assignment Reports** dialog box, click **Who Does What When**, and then click the **Select** button.

Project displays the first page of the Who Does What When report in the Print Preview window. Your screen should look similar to the following illustration:

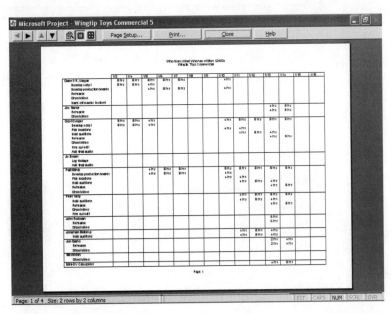

Note that the status bar message tells you this report spans four pages. To get a broader view of the output, you will switch to a multipage view.

8 On the **Print Preview** toolbar, click the **Multiple Pages** button.

Multiple Pages

The entire report appears in the Print Preview window. Your screen should look similar to the following illustration:

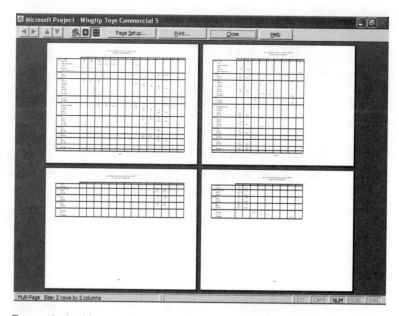

To conclude this exercise, you will customize the header that appears at the top of each printed page so that it includes a logo graphic.

9   On the **Print Preview** toolbar, click the **Page Setup** button.

The **Page Setup** dialog box for the Who Does What When report appears.

10   Click the **Header** tab.

Your screen should look similar to the following illustration:

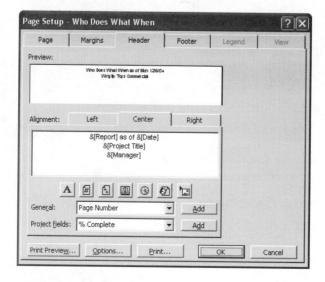

As you can see in the **Preview** and **Alignment** boxes, codes such as &[Date] determine the specific text that appears in the header. You will add a logo to the left side of the header.

11 Next to **Alignment**, click the **Left** tab.

As with all regions of the header and footer, you can insert standard elements, such as page numbers, as well as any Project field. In this exercise, you'll insert a logo graphic that's supplied for you.

Insert Picture

12 Click the **Insert Picture** button.

13 Navigate to the *Chapter 5 Simple Formatting* folder and double-click the Logo file.

The logo image appears on the left side of the header in the **Page Setup** dialog box.

14 Click **OK** to close the **Page Setup** dialog box.

The updated header appears on each page in the Print Preview window.

One Page

15 To get a closer look at the updated header, on the **Print Preview** toolbar, click the **One Page** button.

Project displays the first page of the report. Your screen should look similar to the following illustration:

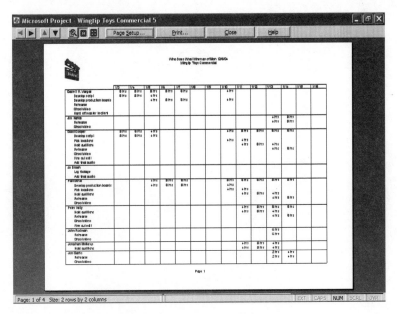

16 On the **Print Preview** toolbar, click the **Close** button.

17 Click **Close** again to close the **Reports** dialog box. The Task Sheet view reappears.

Tip You can change the headers and footers of views in the same way you do in reports. Keep in mind that changes you make to the page setup of any view or report apply only to that view or report. However, the general way you customize the page setup is the same for any report or view.

CLOSE: the Wingtip Toys Commercial 5 file.

Key Points

- To format whole categories of Gantt bars you can use either the **Bar Styles** dialog box (**Format** menu) or the Gantt Chart Wizard (**Format** menu). To format individual Gantt bars, use the **Bar** command (**Format** menu).

- You can redefine the formatting of a built-in view, or copy a view first and then reformat it.

- You can draw or insert graphic objects on the chart portion of a Gantt chart view, but not on the table portion.

- Reports are intended for print-previewing or printing only; you cannot enter or edit data directly in a report. You can, however, edit some elements of reports such as the text that appears in the header or footer of the page.

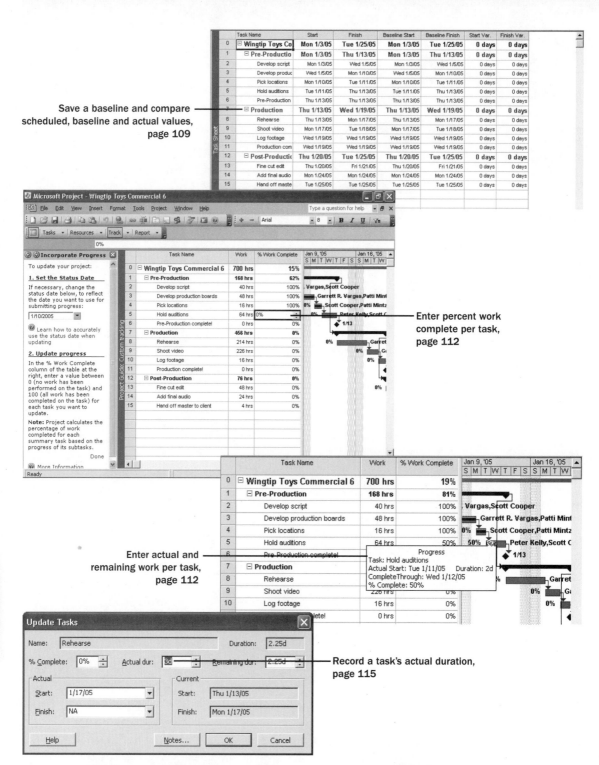

Save a baseline and compare scheduled, baseline and actual values, page 109

Enter percent work complete per task, page 112

Enter actual and remaining work per task, page 112

Record a task's actual duration, page 115

Chapter 6 at a Glance

6 Tracking Progress on Tasks

In this chapter you will learn to:

✔ Save current values in a schedule as a baseline.

✔ Record progress on tasks through a specific date.

✔ Record a task's percentage of completion.

✔ Enter actual start, finish, work, and duration values for tasks.

See Also   Do you need a quick refresher on the topics in this chapter? See the quick reference entries on pages xxiv–xxv.

Until now, you have focused on project *planning*—developing and communicating the details of a project before actual work begins. When work begins, so does the next phase of project management: tracking progress. *Tracking* means recording project details such as who did what work, when the work was done, and at what cost. These details are often called *actuals*.

Tracking actuals is essential to properly managing, as opposed to just planning, a project. The project manager must know how well the project team is performing and when to take corrective action. Properly tracking project performance and comparing it to the original plan lets you answer such questions as these:

■ Are tasks starting and finishing as planned, and, if not, what will be the impact on the project's finish date?

■ Are resources spending more or less time than planned to complete tasks?

■ Are higher-than-anticipated task costs driving up the overall cost of the project?

Microsoft Office Project 2003 supports several ways to track progress. Your choice of a tracking method should depend on the level of detail or control required by you, your project *sponsor*, and other *stakeholders*. Tracking the fine details of a project requires more work from you and possibly from the resources working on the project. So before you begin tracking progress, you should determine the level of detail you need. The different levels of tracking detail include the following:

■ Record project work as scheduled. This works best if everything in the project occurs exactly as planned. Hey, it could happen!

- Record each task's percentage of completion, either at precise values or at increments such as 25, 50, 75, or 100 percent.

- Record the actual start, actual finish, actual work, and actual and remaining duration for each task or assignment.

- Track assignment-level work by time period. This is the most detailed level of tracking. Here you record actual work values per day, week, or another interval.

Because different portions of a project might have different tracking needs, you might need to apply a combination of these approaches within a single project. For example, you might want to track high-risk tasks more closely than low-risk ones. In this chapter, you will perform the first three actions in the preceding list; the fourth (tracking assignment-level work by time period) is addressed in Part 2, "Advanced Project Scheduling." For users of Project Professional and Project Server, enterprise-level tracking is addressed in Part 4, "Introducing Project Server."

Important   Before you can use the practice files in this chapter, be sure you install them from the book's companion CD to their default location. See "Using the Book's CD-ROM," on page xiii, for more information.

Saving a Project Baseline

One of a project manager's most important activities, after developing a project plan, is to record actuals and evaluate project performance. To judge project performance properly, you will need to compare it to your original plan. This original plan is called the baseline plan, or just the *baseline*. A baseline is a collection of important values in a project plan, such as the planned start dates, finish dates, and the costs of the tasks, resources, and assignments. When you save a baseline, Project takes a "snapshot" of the existing values and saves it in your Project plan for future comparison.

The specific values saved in a baseline include the task, resource, and assignment fields, and *timephased fields* in the following list.

Task fields	Resource fields	Assignment fields
Start	Work and timephased work	Start
Finish	Cost and timephased cost	Finish
Duration		Work and timephased work
Work and timephased work		Cost and timephased cost
Cost and timephased cost		

Tip   Timephased fields show task, resource, and assignment values distributed over time. For example, you can look at a task with five days of work planned at the weekly, daily, or hourly level and see the specific baseline work values per time increment. In Part 2 you will work with timephased values.

You should save the baseline when

■   You have developed the project plan as fully as possible. (However, this does not mean you cannot add tasks, resources, or assignments to the project after work has started. Usually this is unavoidable.)

■   You have not yet started entering actual values, such as a task's percentage of completion.

The TV commercial project plan is now fully developed, and actual work on the project will soon begin. In this exercise, you save the baseline for the TV commercial project and then view the baseline task values.

Important   If you are running Project Professional, you may need to make a one-time adjustment to use the My Computer account and to work offline. This helps ensure that the practice files you work with in this chapter don't affect your Project Server data. For more information, see "Starting Project Professional," on page 10.

OPEN: Wingtip Toys Commercial 6a from the *My Documents\\Microsoft Press\\Project 2003 Step by Step* *Chapter 6 Simple Tracking* folder. You can also access the practice files for this book by clicking **Start**, **All Programs**, **Microsoft Press**, **Project 2003 Step by Step**, and then selecting the chapter folder of the file you want to open.

1   On the **File** menu, click **Save As**.

The **Save As** dialog box appears.

2   In the **File name** box, type Wingtip Toys Commercial 6, and then click the **Save** button.

3   On the **Project Guide** toolbar, click the **Track** button.

The Track pane appears.

4   In the Track pane, click the **Save a baseline plan to compare with later versions** link.

The Save Baseline pane appears.

5   Click the **Save Baseline** button.

Project saves the baseline, even though there's no indication in the Gantt Chart view that anything has changed. You will now see some of the changes caused by saving the baseline.

Tip   To save a baseline, you can also click the **Save Baseline** command. (On the **Tools** menu, point to **Tracking** and click **Save Baseline**.)

Show/Hide
Project Guide

6   Click the **Show/Hide Project Guide** button on the **Project Guide** toolbar.

The Project Guide closes.

Tip   You can save up to 11 baselines in a single plan. (The first one is called Baseline, and the rest are Baseline 1 through Baseline 10.) Saving multiple baselines can be useful for projects with exceptionally long planning phases, where you might want to compare different sets of baseline values. For example, you might want to save and compare the baseline plans every month as the planning details change. To learn more about baselines in Project's online Help, type **About baselines** into the **Search** box in the upper right corner of the Project window. The **Search** box initially contains the text *Type a question for help.*

7   On the **View** menu, click **More Views**.

The **More Views** dialog box appears.

8   In the **Views** box, click **Task Sheet**, and then click the **Apply** button.

Because the Task Sheet view does not include the Gantt chart, you have more room to see the fields in the table. Now you'll switch to a different table in the Task Sheet view.

9   On the **View** menu, point to **Table: Summary**, and click **Variance**.

The Variance table appears. This table includes both the scheduled and baseline starts and finish columns, shown side by side for easy comparison.

Tip   If any column contains pound signs (###), double-click between the column titles to widen that column.

Your screen should look similar to the following illustration:

	Task Name	Start	Finish	Baseline Start	Baseline Finish	Start Var.	Finish Var.
0	⊟ Wingtip Toys Co	**Mon 1/3/05**	**Tue 1/25/05**	**Mon 1/3/05**	**Tue 1/25/05**	**0 days**	**0 days**
1	⊟ Pre-Productio	**Mon 1/3/05**	**Thu 1/13/05**	**Mon 1/3/05**	**Thu 1/13/05**	**0 days**	**0 days**
2	Develop script	Mon 1/3/05	Wed 1/5/05	Mon 1/3/05	Wed 1/5/05	0 days	0 days
3	Develop produc	Wed 1/5/05	Mon 1/10/05	Wed 1/5/05	Mon 1/10/05	0 days	0 days
4	Pick locations	Mon 1/10/05	Tue 1/11/05	Mon 1/10/05	Tue 1/11/05	0 days	0 days
5	Hold auditions	Tue 1/11/05	Thu 1/13/05	Tue 1/11/05	Thu 1/13/05	0 days	0 days
6	Pre-Production	Thu 1/13/05	Thu 1/13/05	Thu 1/13/05	Thu 1/13/05	0 days	0 days
7	⊟ Production	**Thu 1/13/05**	**Wed 1/19/05**	**Thu 1/13/05**	**Wed 1/19/05**	**0 days**	**0 days**
8	Rehearse	Thu 1/13/05	Mon 1/17/05	Thu 1/13/05	Mon 1/17/05	0 days	0 days
9	Shoot video	Mon 1/17/05	Tue 1/18/05	Mon 1/17/05	Tue 1/18/05	0 days	0 days
10	Log footage	Wed 1/19/05	Wed 1/19/05	Wed 1/19/05	Wed 1/19/05	0 days	0 days
11	Production com	Wed 1/19/05	Wed 1/19/05	Wed 1/19/05	Wed 1/19/05	0 days	0 days
12	⊟ Post-Productio	**Thu 1/20/05**	**Tue 1/25/05**	**Thu 1/20/05**	**Tue 1/25/05**	**0 days**	**0 days**
13	Fine cut edit	Thu 1/20/05	Fri 1/21/05	Thu 1/20/05	Fri 1/21/05	0 days	0 days
14	Add final audio	Mon 1/24/05	Mon 1/24/05	Mon 1/24/05	Mon 1/24/05	0 days	0 days
15	Hand off maste	Tue 1/25/05	Tue 1/25/05	Tue 1/25/05	Tue 1/25/05	0 days	0 days

At this point, because no actual work has occurred yet and no changes to the scheduled work have been made, the values in the **Start** and **Baseline Start** fields are identical, as are the values in the **Finish** and **Baseline Finish** fields. After actual work is recorded or later schedule adjustments are made, the scheduled start and finish values might differ from the baseline values. You would then see the differences displayed in the variance columns.

Now that you have had a look at some baseline fields, it is time to enter some actuals!

Tracking a Project as Scheduled

The simplest approach to tracking progress is to report that the actual work is proceeding exactly as planned. For example, if the first month of a five-month project has elapsed and all of its tasks have started and finished as scheduled, you can quickly record this in the **Update Project** dialog box.

In the TV commercial project, suppose that some time has now passed since saving the baseline. Work has started, and so far, so good. In this exercise, you record project actuals by updating work to the current date.

1 On the **View** menu, click **Gantt Chart**.

The Gantt Chart view appears.

2 On the **Tools** menu, point to **Tracking**, and click **Update Project**.

The **Update Project** dialog box appears.

3 Make sure the **Update work as complete through** option is selected. In the adjacent date list, type or select 1/10/05, and click the **OK** button, as shown next:

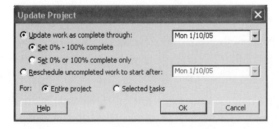

Tip You can also click the down arrow in the **Update work as complete through** box, and in the calendar that appears, select **January 10, 2005**.

Project records the completion percentage for the tasks that were scheduled to start before January 10. Then it displays that progress by drawing *progress bars* in the Gantt bars for those tasks. Your screen should look similar to the following illustration:

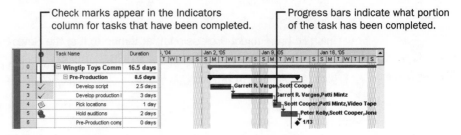

Check marks appear in the Indicators column for tasks that have been completed.

Progress bars indicate what portion of the task has been completed.

In the Gantt Chart view, the progress bar shows how much of each task has been completed. Because tasks 2 and 3 have been completed, a check mark appears in the Indicators column for those tasks, and the progress bars extend through the full length of the tasks' Gantt bars.

Entering a Task's Completion Percentage

After work has begun on a task, you can quickly record progress on it as a percentage. When you enter a completion percentage other than 0, Project changes the task's actual start date to match its scheduled start date. It then calculates actual duration, remaining duration, actual costs, and other values, based on the percentage you enter. For example, if you specify that a four-day task is 50 percent complete, Project calculates that it has had two days of actual duration and has two days of remaining duration.

Here are some ways of entering completion percentages:

■ Use the **Tracking** toolbar (on the **View** menu, point to **Toolbars**, and then click **Tracking**). This toolbar contains buttons for quickly recording that a task is 0, 25, 50, 75, or 100 percent complete.

■ Enter any percentage value you want in the **Update Tasks** dialog box (on the **Tools** menu, point to **Tracking**, and then click **Update Tasks**).

■ Use the Project Guide (as you will do in this exercise).

In this exercise, you record completion percentages of tasks via the Project Guide.

1 On the **Project Guide** toolbar, click the **Track** button.

The Track pane appears.

2 In the Track pane, click the **Prepare to track the progress of your project** link.

3 If you have Project Professional, you'll see an additional pane that relates to using Project Server to collect actuals from resources. In the step 1 pane, click **No**, and then click **Save and go to Step 2**. If you have Project Standard, you won't see this pane.

4 In the Setup Tracking pane, select the **Always track by entering the Percent of Work Complete** option, and then click the **Done** link (in Project Standard) or the **Save and Finish** link (in Project Professional) at the bottom of the SetupTracking pane.

Project updates the Project Guide: Custom Tracking view to the right. In the **% Work Complete** column in the Custom Tracking view, you will enter the completion percentage of the next few tasks.

5 In the Track pane, click the **Incorporate progress information into the project** link.

The Incorporate Progress pane appears. Here you can set the *status date*. In this chapter, you won't change the status date directly. The status date and other calculation options can help you control how Project schedules actual and remaining work. You will work with the status date in Part 2.

6 In the **% Work Complete** field for task 4, type or select **100**, and then press [Enter].

Project records the actual work for the task as scheduled and extends a progress bar through the length of the Gantt bar. Next you'll get a better look at the task's Gantt bar.

Go To
Selected Task

7 On the Standard toolbar, click the **Go To Selected Task** button.

Your screen should look similar to the following illustration:

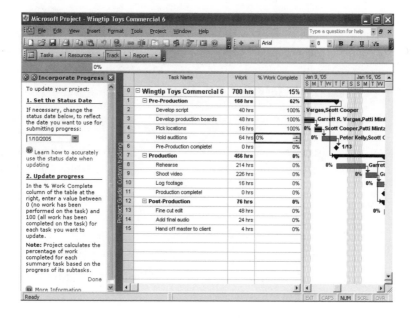

Next you will enter a completion percentage value for a different task.

8   In the **% Work Complete** field for task 5, type or select 50, and then press Enter.

Project records the actual work for the task as scheduled, and then it draws a progress bar through 50 percent of the Gantt bar.

9   In the chart portion (on the right) in the Gantt Chart view, hold the mouse pointer over the progress bar in task 5's Gantt bar.

Your screen should look similar to the following illustration:

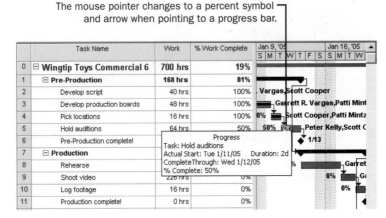

The mouse pointer changes to a percent symbol and arrow when pointing to a progress bar.

The ScreenTip tells you the task's completion percentage and other tracking values.

10   At the bottom of the Incorporate Progress pane, click the **Done** link.

So far, you have recorded actual work that started and finished on schedule. While this might prove true for some tasks, often you need to record actuals for tasks that lasted longer or shorter than planned. This is the subject of the next topic.

Entering Actual Values for Tasks

One way to keep your schedule up to date is to record what actually happens for each task in your project. You can record each task's actual start, finish, work, and duration values. When you enter these values, Project updates the schedule and calculates the task's completion percentage. Project uses the following rules:

■   When you enter a task's actual start date, Project moves the scheduled start date to match the actual start date.

■   When you enter a task's actual finish date, Project moves the scheduled finish date to match the actual finish date and sets the task to 100 percent complete.

■   When you enter a task's actual work value, Project recalculates the task's remaining work values.

- When you enter a task's actual duration, if it is less than the scheduled duration, Project subtracts the actual duration from the scheduled duration to determine the remaining duration.

- When you enter a task's actual duration, if it is equal to the scheduled duration, Project sets the task to 100 percent complete.

- When you enter a task's actual duration, if it is longer than the scheduled duration, Project adjusts the scheduled duration to match the actual duration and sets the task to 100 percent complete.

Suppose that a few more days have passed and work on the TV commercial has progressed. In this exercise, you record actual work values for some tasks, and start dates and durations for other tasks.

1 In the Track pane, click the **Prepare to track the progress of your project** link.

2 If you have Project Professional, you'll see an additional pane that relates to using Project Server to collect actuals from resources. In the Step 1 pane, click **No**, and then click **Save and go to Step 2**. If you have Project Standard, you won't see this pane.

3 Select the **Always track by entering the Actual Work Done and Work Remaining** option, and then click the **Done** link (in Project Standard) or the **Save and Finish** link (in Project Professional).

Project updates the Project Guide: Custom Tracking view to the right. In the **Actual Work** and **Remaining Work** columns in the Project Guide: Custom Tracking view, you will enter actual and remaining work values of the next few tasks.

In the chart portion of the Custom Tracking view, you can see that task 5 is currently 50 percent complete, and in the table portion of the view, you can see the resulting hour values of work that this percentage corresponds to. You want to record that the task is now complete but required more work than expected.

4 In the Track pane, click the **Incorporate progress information into the project** link.

The Incorporate Progress pane appears. Here you can set the status date and read about how to enter values in the **Actual Work** or **Remaining Work** fields. In this chapter, you won't change the status date directly.

Show/Hide
Project Guide

5 Click the **Show/Hide Project Guide** button on the **Project Guide** toolbar.

The Project Guide closes.

6 In the **Actual Work** field for task 5, type or select 80, and then press Enter.

Project records that 80 hours of work have been completed on task 5. It extends the Gantt bar of the task to indicate its longer duration and reschedules subsequent tasks.

Your screen should look similar to the following illustration:

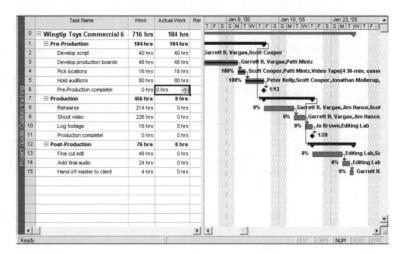

Now suppose that more time has passed. To conclude this exercise, you will enter actual start dates and durations of tasks.

7 In the **Task Name** column, click task 8, **Rehearse**.

This task started one working day behind schedule (the Monday after its scheduled start date) and took a total of three days to complete. You will record this information in fields that are not in the Project Guide: Custom Tracking view by default. You could insert the fields, switch to a different table that includes them, or (as you will do now) enter the values in the **Update Tasks** dialog box.

8 On the **Tools** menu, point to **Tracking**, and then click **Update Tasks**.

The **Update Tasks** dialog box appears. This dialog box shows both the actual and scheduled values for the task's duration, start, and finish, as well as its remaining duration. In it, you can update the actual and remaining values.

9 In the **Start** field in the **Actual** box on the left side of the dialog box, type or select 1/17/05.

10 In the **Actual dur** field, type or select **3d**.

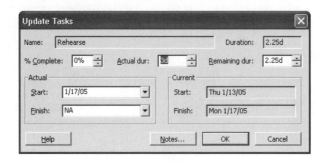

11   Click the **OK** button.

Project records the actual start date and duration of the task. Your screen should look similar to the following illustration:

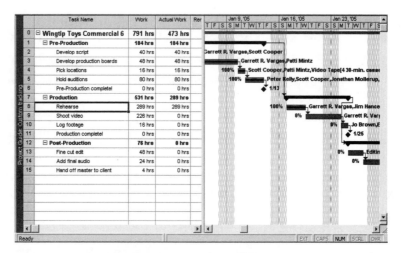

To conclude this exercise, you will record that task 9 started on time but took longer than planned to complete.

12   In the **Task Name** column, click task 9, **Shoot Video**.

13   On the **Tools** menu, point to **Tracking**, and then click **Update Tasks**.

The **Update Tasks** dialog box appears.

14   In the **Actual dur** field, type or select **3d**, and then click the **OK** button.

Project records the actual duration of the task. Your screen should look similar to the following illustration:

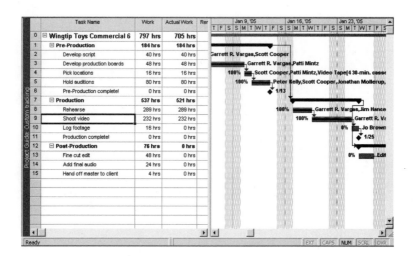

Because you did not specify an actual start date, Project assumes that the task started as scheduled, but the actual duration you entered causes Project to calculate an actual finish date that is later than the originally scheduled finish date.

Project Management Focus: Is the Project on Track?

Properly evaluating a project's status can be tricky. Consider the following issues:

- For many tasks, it is very difficult to evaluate a completion percentage. When is an engineer's design for a new motor assembly 50 percent complete? Or when is a programmer's code for a software module 50 percent complete? Reporting work in progress is in many cases a "best guess" effort and inherently risky.

- The elapsed portion of a task's duration is not always equal to the amount of work accomplished. For example, a task might require relatively little effort initially, but require more work as time passes. (This is referred to as a back-loaded task.) When 50 percent of its duration has elapsed, far less than 50 percent of its total work will have been completed.

- The resources assigned to a task might have different criteria for what constitutes the task's completion than the project manager or the resources assigned to successor tasks might.

Good project planning and communication can avoid or mitigate these and other problems that arise in project execution. For example, developing proper task durations and status-reporting periods should help you identify tasks that have substantially varied from the baseline early enough to make adjustments. Having well-documented and well-communicated task completion criteria should help prevent "downstream" surprises. Nevertheless, large, complex projects will almost always vary from the baseline.

CLOSE: the Wingtip Toys Commercial 6 file.

Key Points

■ Before tracking actual work in a project plan, you should save a baseline. This gives you a "snapshot" of your initial project plan for later comparison against actual progress. This is one way to tell if your project is on track or not.

■ The ability to track actual work in a project plan is a major advantage that a real project management tool like Project has over list-keeping tools like Excel. In Project, you can track actual work at a very broad or very granular level.

■ The Project Guide helps you set up your project plan correctly for the level of tracking you want to do.

■ To properly evaluate a project's status after you begin tracking requires a combination of recording accurate data in Project and using your good judgment when interpreting the results.

II
Advanced Project Scheduling

Change how tasks are related to each other, page 123

	Task Name	Predecessors
7	Paint background scenes	
8	Set up lighting	7FS+1 day
9	Install props	8FS-50%

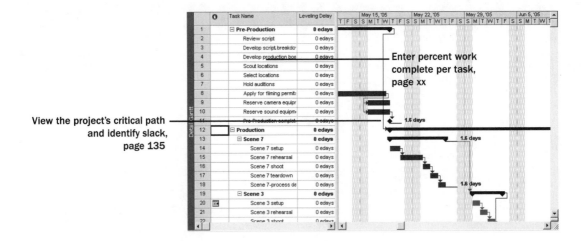

	🛈	Task Name	Duration
19		⊟ Scene 3	4 days
20		Scene 3 setup	1 day
21		This task has a 'Start No Earlier Than' constraint on Mon 5/30/05.	day
22			3 hrs
23		Scene 3 teardown	1 day
24		Scene 3-process de	1 day
25		⊟ Scene 1	6 days

Apply constraints to control when tasks can start or stop, page 131

View the project's critical path and identify slack, page 135

Enter percent work complete per task, page xx

Change a task's duration, work, or assignment units and control how Project handles the change, page 141

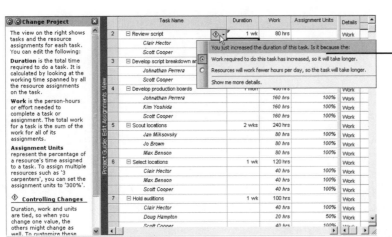

Chapter 7 at a Glance

7 Fine-Tuning Task Details

In this chapter you will learn to:

✔ Adjust task links to have more control over how tasks are related.

✔ Apply a constraint to a task.

✔ Identify the tasks on the critical path.

✔ Split a task to record an interruption in work.

✔ Create a task calendar and apply it to tasks.

✔ Change a task type to control how Project schedules tasks.

✔ Record deadlines for tasks.

✔ Enter a fixed cost and specify how it should accrue.

✔ Set up a recurring task in the project schedule.

See Also Do you need a quick refresher on the topics in this chapter? See the quick reference entries on pages xxvi–xxviii.

In this chapter, you examine and use a variety of advanced features of Microsoft Office Project 2003. These features focus on fine-tuning task details prior to saving a baseline and commencing work on the project with the goal of developing the most accurate schedule representation of the tasks you anticipate for the plan.

 Important Before you can use the practice files in this chapter, be sure you install them from the book's companion CD to their default location. See "Using the Book's CD-ROM," on page xiii, for more information.

Adjusting Task Relationships

You might recall from Chapter 2, "Creating a Task List," that there are four types of task dependencies, or relationships:

- Finish-to-start (FS): The finish date of the predecessor task determines the start date of the successor task.

- Start-to-start (SS): The start date of the predecessor task determines the start date of the successor task.

■ Finish-to-finish (FF): The finish date of the predecessor task determines the finish date of the successor task.

■ Start-to-finish (SF): The start date of the predecessor task determines the finish date of the successor task.

Link Tasks

When you enter tasks in Project and link them by clicking the **Link Tasks** button on the Standard toolbar, the tasks are given a finish-to-start (FS) relationship. This might be fine for most tasks, but you will probably want to change some task relationships. Here are some examples of tasks that require relationships other than finish-to-start:

■ You can start setting up the lighting for a film scene as soon as you start setting up the props (start-to-start relationship). This reduces the overall time required to complete the two tasks, as they are completed in parallel:

■ Planning the filming sequence can begin before the script is complete, but it cannot be finished until after the script is complete. You want the two tasks to finish at about the same time (finish-to-finish relationship):

Task relationships should reflect the sequence in which work should be done. After you have established the correct task relationships, you can fine-tune your schedule by entering overlap (called *lead time*) or delay (called *lag time*) between the finish or start dates of predecessor and successor tasks.

Assuming that two tasks have a finish-to-start relationship:

■ Lead time causes the successor task to begin before its predecessor task concludes.

■ Lag time causes the successor task to begin some time after its predecessor task concludes.

Here is an illustration of how lead and lag time affect task relationships. Let's say you initially planned the following three tasks using finish-to-start relationships:

Initially the tasks are linked with finish-to-start
relationships, so the successor tasks begin
as soon as the predecessor tasks finish.

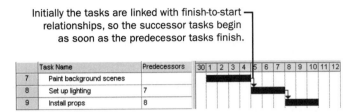

Before task 8 can start, you need to allow an extra day for the paint applied in task 7 to dry. You do not want to add a day to the duration of task 7, because no real work will occur on that day. Instead, you enter a one-day lag between tasks 7 and 8:

This lag time causes a delay in
the start of the successor task.

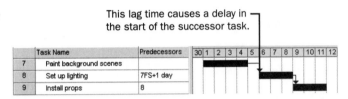

However, task 9 can start as soon as task 8 is halfway completed; to make this happen, enter a 50-percent lead time between tasks 8 and 9:

This lead time causes the successor task to
start before the predecessor task finishes.

You can enter lead and lag time as units of time (for example, two days) or as a percentage of the duration of the predecessor task (for example, 50 percent). Lag time is entered in positive units, lead time in negative units (for example, minus two days or minus 50 percent). You can apply lead or lag time to any type of task relationship: finish-to-start, start-to-start, and so on.

Tip   Some of the places you can enter lead or lag time include the **Task Information** dialog box, and the **Predecessors** column in the Entry table.

In this exercise, you change task relationships and enter lead and lag time between predecessor and successor tasks.

Important   If you are running Project Professional, you may need to make a one-time adjustment to use the My Computer account and to work offline. This helps ensure that the practice files you work with in this chapter don't affect your Project Server data. For more information, see "Starting Project Professional," on page 10.

OPEN: Short Film Project 7a from the *\My Documents\Microsoft Press\Project 2003 Step by Step\ Chapter 7 Advanced Tasks* folder. You can also access the practice files for this book by clicking **Start, All Programs, Microsoft Press, Project 2003 Step by Step,** and then selecting the chapter folder of the file you want to open.

1   On the **File** menu, click **Save As**.

The **Save As** dialog box appears.

2   In the **File name** box, type **Short Film Project 7**, and then click the **Save** button.

3   Double-click the name of task 9, **Reserve camera equipment**.

The **Task Information** dialog box appears.

4   Click the **Predecessors** tab.

Here you can see that task 9 has one predecessor task, task 8.

5   In the **Lag** field for predecessor task 8, type –50%.

To enter lead time against a predecessor task, enter it as negative lag time either in units of time such as days, or as a percentage of the duration of the predecessor task.

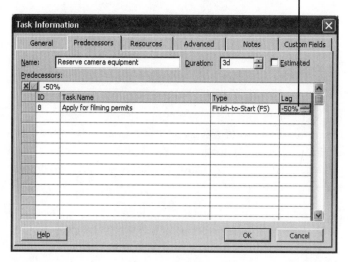

Entering lag time as a negative value produces lead time.

6   Click **OK** to close the **Task Information** dialog box.

> **Tip**   You can also double-click a link line (the lines connecting Gantt bars) on the Gantt chart to enter lead or lag time, change the task relationship, or delete the link.

7   To see how the lag time affects the scheduling of the successor task, on the Standard toolbar, click the **Go To Selected Task** button.

Go To Selected
Task

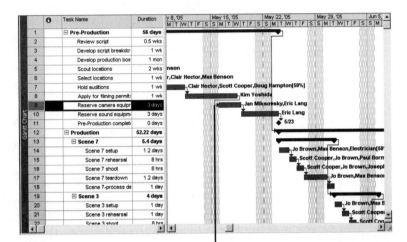

Lead time causes the successor task to start
before the predecessor task has finished,
although the two tasks still have a finish-to-start
relationship.

Project scrolls the Gantt chart to display the Gantt bar for task 9. Task 9 is now scheduled to start when task 8 is 50 percent complete. Should the duration of task 8 change, Project will reschedule the start of task 9 so that it keeps a 50 percent lead time.

Next you will change the task relationship between two tasks.

8   Double-click the name of task 10, **Reserve sound equipment**.

The **Task Information** dialog box appears. The **Predecessors** tab should be visible.

9   Click in the **Type** column for predecessor task 9. Select **Start-to-Start** (SS), and click **OK**.

Project changes the task relationship between tasks 9 and 10 to start-to-start.

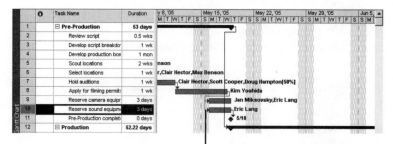

The start-to-start task relationship causes the successor task to start at the same time as the predecessor task. If the start date of the predecessor task changes, then the start date of the successor task will change as well.

Important   Assigning tasks start-to-start relationships and entering lead times where appropriate are both excellent techniques to shorten overall project duration. However, Project cannot automatically make such schedule adjustments for you. As project manager, you must analyze the sequences and relationships of your tasks and make those adjustments where appropriate.

Setting Task Constraints

Every task you enter into Project has some type of constraint applied to it. A constraint controls the start or finish date of a task and the degree to which that task can be rescheduled. There are three categories of constraints:

■ *Flexible constraints.* Project can change the start and finish dates of a task. For example, the task *Select locations to film* can start as soon as possible. This type of flexible constraint is called As Soon As Possible, or ASAP for short, and is the default constraint type in Project. No constraint date is associated with flexible constraints.

■ *Inflexible constraints.* A task must begin or end on a certain date. For example, a task such as *Set up lighting* must end on April 8, 2005. Inflexible constraints are sometimes called hard constraints.

■ *Semi-flexible constraints.* A task has a start or finish date boundary. However, within that boundary, Project has the scheduling flexibility to change start and finish dates of a task. For example, a task such as *Install props* must finish no later than March 25, 2005. However, the task could finish before this date. Semi-flexible constraints are sometimes called soft or moderate constraints.

In all, there are eight types of task constraints:

This constraint category	Includes these constraint types	And means
Flexible	As Soon As Possible (ASAP)	Project will schedule a task to occur as soon as it can occur. This is the default constraint type applied to all new tasks when scheduling from the project start date.
	As Late As Possible (ALAP)	Project will schedule a task to occur as late as it can occur. This is the default constraint type applied to all new tasks when scheduling from the project finish date.
Semi-flexible	Start No Earlier Than (SNET)	Project will schedule a task to start on or after the constraint date you specify. Use this constraint type to ensure that a task will not start before a specific date.
	Start No Later Than (SNLT)	Project will schedule a task to start on or before the constraint date you specify. Use this constraint type to ensure that a task will not start after a specific date.
	Finish No Earlier Than (FNET)	Project will schedule a task to finish on or after the constraint date you specify. Use this constraint type to ensure that a task will not finish before a specific date.
	Finish No Later Than (FNLT)	Project will schedule a task to finish on or before the constraint date you specify. Use this constraint type to ensure that a task will not finish after a specific date.
Inflexible	Must Start On (MSO)	Project will schedule a task to start on the constraint date you specify. Use this constraint type to ensure that a task will start on an exact date.
	Must Finish On (MFO)	Project will schedule a task to finish on the constraint date you specify. Use this constraint type to ensure that a task will finish on an exact date.

Important   Beginning Project users are often tempted to enter start or finish dates for tasks. However, doing so applies semi-flexible constraints such as Start No Earlier Than or Finish No Earlier Than. This essentially prevents users from taking full advantage of the Project scheduling engine. Although this is one of the most common scheduling problems people have with Project, it is usually avoidable.

These three categories of constraints have very different effects on the scheduling of tasks:

■   Flexible constraints, such as As Soon As Possible, allow tasks to be scheduled without any limitations other than their predecessor and successor relationships. No fixed start or end dates are imposed by these constraint types. Use these constraint types whenever possible:

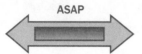

■   Semi-flexible constraints, such as Start No Earlier Than or Start No Later Than, limit the rescheduling of a task within the date boundary you specify:

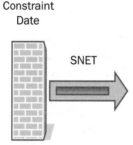

■   Inflexible constraints, such as Must Start On, completely prevent the rescheduling of a task. Use these constraint types only when absolutely necessary:

The type of constraint you apply to the tasks in your projects depends on what you need from Project. You should use inflexible constraints only if the start or finish date of a task is fixed by factors beyond the control of the project team. Examples of such tasks include handoffs to clients and the end of a funding period. For tasks without such limitations, you should use flexible constraints. Flexible constraints give you the most discretion in adjusting start and finish dates, and they allow Project to adjust dates if your project plan changes. For example, if you have used ASAP constraints and the duration of a predecessor task changes from four days to two days, Project adjusts or "pulls in" the start and finish dates of all successor tasks. However, if a successor task had an inflexible constraint applied, Project could not adjust its start or finish dates.

In this exercise, you apply a Start No Earlier Than constraint to a task.

Tasks

1   On the **Project Guide** toolbar, click **Tasks**.

The Tasks pane appears.

2   In the Tasks pane, click the **Set deadlines and constrain tasks** link.

The Deadlines and Constraints pane appears.

3   Select task 20, **Scene 3 setup**.

This scene must be shot at a location that is not available to the film crew until May 30, 2005.

4   Under **Constrain a task** in the Deadlines and Constraints pane, select **Start No Earlier Than**.

5   In the date box below it, type or select **5/30/05**. Your screen should look like the following illustration:

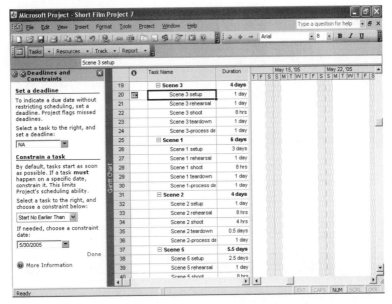

6   At the bottom of the Deadlines and Constraints pane, click the **Done** link.

Project applies an SNET constraint to the task, and a constraint icon appears in the Indicators column.

You can point to the icon to see the constraint details in a ScreenTip.

Position your mouse pointer over a constraint indicator
(or any icon in the Indicators column) to see a ScreenTip.

	ⓘ	Task Name	Duration
19		⊟ **Scene 3**	**4 days**
20		Scene 3 setup	1 day
21		This task has a 'Start No Earlier Than'	day
22		constraint on Mon 5/30/05.	3 hrs
23		Scene 3 teardown	1 day
24		Scene 3-process de	1 day
25		⊟ **Scene 1**	**6 days**

Task 20 is rescheduled to start on May 30 instead of May 26. All tasks that depend on task 20 are also rescheduled.

Show/Hide
Project Guide

7 Click the **Show/Hide Project Guide** button on the **Project Guide** toolbar.

The Project Guide closes.

Here are a few more things to keep in mind when applying constraints to tasks:

■ Entering a Finish date for a task (for example, in the **Finish** column) applies an FNET constraint to the task.

■ Entering a Start date for a task (for example, in the **Start** column) or dragging a Gantt bar directly on the Gantt chart applies a SNET constraint to the task.

■ In many cases, entering a deadline date is a preferable alternative to entering a semi-flexible or inflexible constraint. You will work with deadline dates later in this chapter.

■ Unless you specify a time, Project schedules a constraint date's start or finish time using the Default Start Time or Default End Time values on the **Calendar** tab (**Tools** menu, **Options** command). In this project, the default start time is 8 A.M. If you want a constrained task to be scheduled to start at a different time, enter that time along with the start date. For example, if you want to schedule a task to start at 10 A.M. on May 30, enter **5/30/05 10AM** in the **Start** field.

■ To remove a constraint, on the Project menu, click **Task Information**, and in the **Task Information** dialog box, click the **Advanced** tab. In the **Constraint Type** box, select **As Soon As Possible** or (if scheduling from the project finish date) **As Late As Possible**.

■ If you need to apply semi-flexible or inflexible constraints to tasks in addition to task relationships, you might create what is called *negative slack*. For example, you have a successor task that has a finish-to-start relationship with its predecessor task. If you entered a Must Start On constraint on the successor task earlier than the finish date of the predecessor task, this would result in negative slack and a scheduling conflict. By default, the constraint date applied to the successor task will override the relationship. However, if you prefer, you can set Project to honor relationships over constraints. On the **Tools** menu, click **Options**, and in the **Options** dialog box, click the **Schedule** tab. Clear the **Tasks will always honor their constraint dates** check box. This setting applies only to the current project file.

■ If you must schedule a project from a finish date rather than a start date, some constraint behaviors change. For example, the ALAP (rather than the ASAP) constraint type becomes the default for new tasks. You should pay close attention to constraints when scheduling from a finish date to make sure they have the effects you intend.

Viewing the Project's Critical Path

A *critical path* is the series of tasks that will push out the project's end date if the tasks are delayed. The word *critical* has nothing to do with how important these tasks are to the overall project. It refers only to how their scheduling will affect the project's finish date. However, the project finish date is of great importance in most projects. If you want to shorten the duration of a project to bring in the finish date, you must begin by shortening the critical path.

Over the life of a project, the project's critical path is likely to change from time to time as tasks are completed ahead of or behind schedule. Schedule changes, such as assigning resources to tasks, can also change the critical path. After a task on the critical path is completed, it is no longer critical, because it cannot affect the project finish date. In Chapter 16, "Getting Your Project Back on Track," you will work with a variety of techniques to shorten a project's overall duration.

A key to understanding the critical path is to understand slack, also known as float. There are two types of slack: free and total. *Free slack* is the amount of time a task can be delayed before it delays another task. *Total slack* is the amount of time a task can be delayed before it delays the completion of the project.

A task is on the critical path if its total slack is less than a certain amount—normally, if it is zero. In contrast, *noncritical tasks* have slack, meaning they can start or finish earlier or later within their slack time without affecting the completion date of a project.

In this exercise, you view the project's critical path. One way to see the critical path is to switch to the Detail Gantt view.

1 On the **View** menu, click **More Views.**

2 In the **More Views** dialog box, select **Detail Gantt,** and then click the **Apply** button.

The project appears in the Detail Gantt view.

3   On the **Edit** menu, click **Go To**.

Tip   Ctrl+G is the keyboard shortcut for Go To.

4   In the **ID** box, type **12**, and then click **OK**.

Project displays task 12, the production summary task.

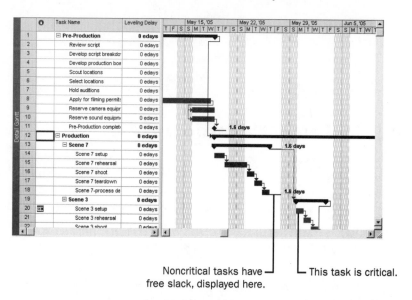

Noncritical tasks have free slack, displayed here.   This task is critical.

The Scene 3 tasks and later tasks are critical tasks. In the Detail Gantt view, Project distinguishes between critical and noncritical tasks. Critical task bars are red, but noncritical task bars are blue. In this view, you can also see tasks with free slack.

Notice the Gantt bar of task 18, Scene 7–process dailies. The blue bar represents the duration of the task. The thin teal line and the number next to it represent free slack for this task. As you can see, this particular task has some slack and is therefore a noncritical task. (Remember that the term *critical* in this sense has nothing to do with the task's importance, only with how much or little total slack the task has.) The slack on task 18 was caused by the Start No Earlier Than constraint applied to task 20.

5   On the **View** menu, click **Gantt Chart**.

Working with the critical path is the most important way to manage a project's overall duration. In later exercises, you will make adjustments that might extend the project's duration. Checking the project's critical path and, when necessary, shortening the overall project duration are important project management skills.

Tip　*Critical path* is a frequently misused phrase on many projects. Just listen for references to critical path work on your current projects to see how frequently the phrase is used correctly. Remember that *critical* has nothing to do with the relative importance of a task, only with its effect on the project finish date.

Here are a few more things to keep in mind when working with the critical path:

■　By default, Project defines a task as critical if it has zero slack. However, you can change the amount of slack required for a task to be critical. On the **Tools** menu, click **Options**, and in the **Options** dialog box, click the **Calculation** tab. In the **Tasks are critical if slack is less than or equal to** box, enter the number of days you want.

■　Project constantly recalculates the critical path, even if you never display it.

■　You see free slack represented in the chart portion of the Detail Gantt view, and you can also see the values of free and total slack in the Schedule table. You can apply the Schedule table to any Gantt or Task Sheet view.

Tip　To learn more about managing a critical path, type **About the critical path** into the **Search** box in the upper right corner of the Project window. The **Search** box initially contains the text *Type a question for help*.

Interrupting Work on a Task

When initially planning project tasks, you might know that work on a certain task will be interrupted. You can split the task to indicate times when the work will be interrupted and when it can resume. Here are some reasons why you might want to split a task:

■　You anticipate an interruption in a task. For example, a resource might be assigned to a week-long task but needs to attend an event on Wednesday that is unrelated to the task.

■　A task is unexpectedly interrupted. After a task is under way, a resource might have to stop work on the task because another task has taken priority. After the second task is completed, the resource can resume work on the first task.

In this exercise, you split a task.

1　On the **Edit** menu, click **Go To**.

2　In the **ID** box, type 4, and then click **OK**.

Project displays task 4, *Develop production boards*.

You know that work on this task will be interrupted for two days starting March 21.

The timescale is divided into tiers. The time setting of the lowest tier determines how you can split tasks. In this example, you can split tasks into one-day increments.

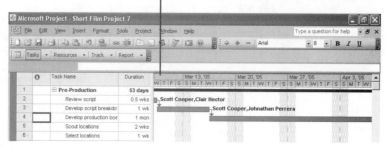

		Split Task
	Split Task	

3   On the Standard toolbar, click the **Split Task** button.

A ScreenTip appears, and the mouse pointer changes.

	Split Task mouse pointer

4   Move the mouse pointer over the Gantt bar of task 4.

This ScreenTip is essential for accurately splitting a task; it contains the date at which you would start the second segment of the task if you dragged the mouse pointer from its current location on the Gantt bar. As you move the mouse pointer along the Gantt bar, you will see the start date in the ScreenTip change.

Use this ScreenTip to help you accurately split tasks. This information will change as you move the Split Task mouse pointer.

Split Task mouse pointer

5   Move (but don't click) the mouse pointer over the Gantt bar of task 4 until the start date of Monday, 3/21/05, appears in the ScreenTip.

6   Drag the mouse pointer to the right until the start date of Wednesday, 3/23/05, appears in the ScreenTip, and then release the mouse button.

Project inserts a task split, represented in the Gantt chart as a dotted line, between the two segments of the task.

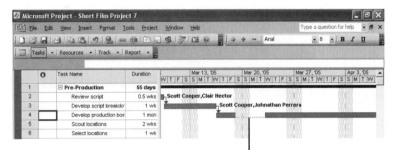

The split appears as a dotted line connecting the segments —┘
of the task. It indicates interruption of work on a task.

Four-headed
arrow mouse
pointer

Tip   Splitting tasks with the mouse might take a little practice. If you didn't split task 4 so that the second segment starts on 3/23/05, just point to it again. When the mouse pointer changes to a four-headed arrow, drag the segment to the correct start date.

Here are a few more things to keep in mind when splitting tasks:

- Adjusting the bottom tier of the timescale is important for splitting tasks: the calibration of the bottom tier determines the smallest time increment into which you can split a task. With the bottom tier set at the Days level, you must split a task by at least a day. If you wanted to split a task at the hourly level, you would have to adjust the bottom tier further (through the **Timescale** command on the **Format** menu).

- You can split a task into as many segments as you want.

- You can drag a segment of a split task left or right to reschedule the split.

- The time of the task split itself, represented by the dotted line, is not counted in the duration of the task unless the task type is Fixed Duration. No work occurs during the split.

- If the duration of a split task changes, the last segment of the task is increased or decreased.

- If a split task is rescheduled (for example, if its start date changes), the entire task, splits and all, is rescheduled. The task keeps the same pattern of segments and splits.

- Resource leveling or manually contouring assignments over time can cause tasks to split. You will level resources in Chapter 8, "Fine-Tuning Resource and Assignment Details," and contour assignments in Chapter 9, "Fine-Tuning the Project Plan."

- To rejoin two segments of a split task, drag one segment of the task until it touches the other segment.

- If you do not want to display splits as a dotted line, you can remove them. On the **Format** menu, click **Layout**, and in the **Layout** dialog box, clear the **Show Bar Splits** check box.

Adjusting Working Time for Individual Tasks

Sometimes you want specific tasks to occur at times that are outside of the project calendar's (or for assigned resources, the resource calendar's) working time. To accomplish this, you apply a *task calendar* to these tasks. As with the project calendar, you specify which base calendar to use as a task calendar. Here are some examples of when you might need a task calendar:

- You are using the Standard base calendar as your project calendar, and you have a task that must run overnight.

- You have a task that must occur on a specific weekday.

- You have a task that must occur over the weekend.

Unlike resources and resource calendars, Project does not create task calendars as you create tasks. When you need a custom task calendar, you assign one of the base calendars provided with Project (or more likely a new base calendar you have created) to the task.

For example, if you assign the 24 Hours base calendar to a task, Project will schedule that task according to a 24-hour workday rather than the working time specified in the project calendar.

For tasks that have both a task calendar and resource assignments, Project schedules work in the working times that are common between the task calendar and resource calendar(s). If there is no common working time, Project alerts you when you apply the task calendar or assign a resource to the task.

Tip   When you assign a base calendar to a task, you can choose to ignore resource calendars for all resources assigned to the task. Doing so causes Project to schedule the resources to work on the task according to the task calendar and not their own resource calendars (for example, to work 24 hours per day). If this would result in resources working in what would otherwise be their nonworking time, you might want to first discuss this with the affected resources.

In the film project, one of the scenes must be filmed at night. However, the project calendar does not include working time late enough to cover the filming of this scene. Because this task is really an exception to the normal working time of the project, you do not want to change the project calendar. In this exercise, you create a new base calendar and apply it to the appropriate task.

1   On the **Tools** menu, click **Change Working Time**.

2   In the **Change Working Time** dialog box, click the **New** button.

     The **Create New Base Calendar** dialog box appears.

3   In the **Name** box, type Evening Shoot.

4   Click the **Make a copy of** option if it is not selected, click **Standard** in the corresponding drop-down menu, and then click **OK**.

5   In the calendar below the **Select Date(s)** label, select the column headings **M** through **F**, for Monday through Friday.

6   In the upper row of the **From** and **To** boxes, enter 5:00 PM and 11:00 PM, and then delete the values in the second row. Your **Change Working Time** dialog box should look like the following illustration:

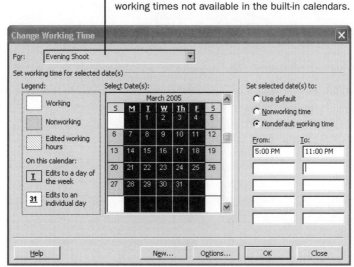

This custom base calendar contains the unique working times not available in the built-in calendars.

7   Click **OK** to close the dialog box.

     Next you will apply the Evening Shoot calendar to a task that must be filmed in the evening.

8   Select the name of task 34, **Scene 2 shoot**.

9   To see the Gantt bar of this task, on the Standard toolbar, click the **Go To Selected Task** button.

Go To Selected
Task

139

Task
Information

10 On the Standard toolbar, click the **Task Information** button.

The **Task Information** dialog box appears.

11 Click the **Advanced** tab.

12 In the **Calendar** box, select **Evening Shoot** from the list.

13 Click the **Scheduling ignores resource calendars** check box, and then click **OK** to close the dialog box.

Project applies the Evening Shoot calendar to task 34. A calendar icon appears in the Indicators column, reminding you that this task has a task calendar applied to it. Because you chose to ignore resource calendars in the previous step, the resources assigned to these tasks will be scheduled at times that would otherwise be nonworking times for them.

Tip To remove a task calendar from a task, on the **Advanced** tab of the **Task Information** dialog box, click **None** in the **Calendar** box.

Changing Task Types

You might recall from Chapter 4, "Assigning Resources to Tasks," that Project uses the following formula, called the scheduling formula, to calculate a task's work value:

Work = Duration × Units

Remember also that a task has work when it has at least one work resource assigned to it. Each value in the scheduling formula corresponds to a task type. A *task type* determines which of the three scheduling formula values remains fixed if the other two values change.

The default task type is *fixed units*: when you change a task's duration, Project recalculates work. Likewise, if you change a task's work, Project recalculates the duration. In either case, the units value is unchanged. The two other task types are *fixed duration* and *fixed work*.

For a fixed-duration task, you can change the task's units or work value, and Project will recalculate the other value. For a fixed-work task, you can change the units or duration value, and Project will recalculate the other value. Note that you cannot turn off effort-driven scheduling for a fixed-work task.

Which is the right task type to apply to each of your tasks? It depends on how you want Project to schedule that task. The following table summarizes the effects of changing any value for any task type. You read it like a multiplication table.

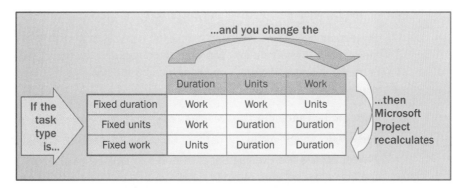

Task
Information

To see the task type of the selected task, on the Standard toolbar, click the **Task Information** button, and in the **Task Information** dialog box, click the **Advanced** tab. You can also see the task type in the Task Form. (When in the Gantt Chart view, you can display the Task Form by clicking the **Split** command on the **Window** menu.) You can change a task type at any time. Note that characterizing a task type as *fixed* does not mean that its duration, units, or work values are unchangeable. You can change any value for any task type.

In this exercise, you change scheduling formula values and task types.

Track

1   On the **Project Guide** toolbar, click **Track**.

The Track pane appears.

2   In the Track pane, click the **Make changes to the project** link.

The Change Project pane appears, and the Project Guide: Edit Assignments view replaces the Gantt Chart view. This type of view is called a usage view. This view groups the assigned resources below each task and shows you, among other things, each task's and assignment's duration, work, and assignment units values—the three variables of the scheduling formula.

3   On the **Edit** menu, click **Go To**.

4   In the **ID** box, type 2, and then click **OK**.

Project displays task 2, *Review script*, and its assignments.

You can see that task 2 has a total work value of 40 hours (that is, 20 hours each for two resources), resource units of 100 percent each, and a duration of one-half of a week. Next you will change the task's duration to see the effects on the other values.

After a discussion among all the resources who will review the script, all agree that the task's duration should double but the work required to complete the task should remain the same.

5   In the **Duration** field for task 2, type or select 1w, and press ⌷Enter⌷.

Project changes the duration of task 2 to one week and increases the work per resource to 40 hours each. You want the duration to double (it did) but the work to remain the same (it didn't), so you will use the Smart Tag to adjust the results of the new task duration.

Smart Tag Actions

6   Point at the **Duration** field and then click the **Smart Tag Actions** button.

Look over the options in the list that appears. Your screen should look like the following illustration:

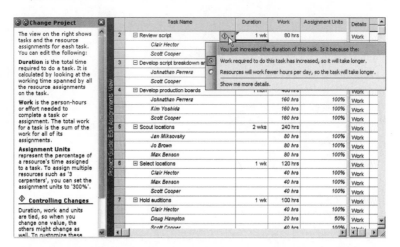

Because task 2's task type is fixed units (the default task type), the Smart Tag's default selection is to increase work as the duration increased. However, you'd like to keep the work value the same and decrease assignment units for the task's new duration.

7   In the **Smart Tag Actions** list, click **Resources will work fewer hours per day, so the task will take longer**.

The assignment units value of each resource decreases to 50 percent, and the total work on the task remains fixed at 40 hours (that is, 20 hours per each assigned resource).

	Task Name	Duration	Work	Assignment Units	Details
2	⊟ Review script	1 wk	40 hrs		Work
	Clair Hector		20 hrs	50%	Work
	Scott Cooper		20 hrs	50%	Work

Next you will change a task type using the **Task Information** dialog box.

8   On the **Edit** menu, click **Go To**.

9   In the **ID** box, type 67, and then click **OK**.

Project displays task 67, *Hold formal approval showing*.

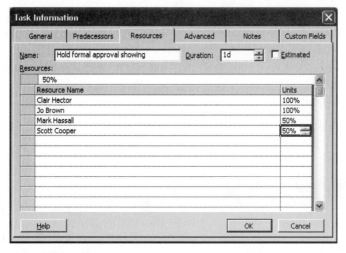

Task
Information

10   On the Standard toolbar, click the **Task Information** button.

The **Task Information** dialog box appears.

11   Click the **Advanced** tab if it is not already selected.

The selected task describes the formal screening of the film for the financial backers of the project. You can see in the **Task Type** box that this task currently has a fixed-units task type.

The task is scheduled for a full day, although a few of the assigned resources will work for the equivalent of half a day. To reflect this (and properly manage resource costs for the task), you will make this a fixed-duration task and adjust the assignment unit values for some of the assigned resources.

12   In the **Task Type** box, select **Fixed Duration**.

13   Click the **Resources** tab.

14   In the **Units** column, set the units values for Mark Hassall and Scott Cooper to 50% each.

15   Click **OK** to close the **Task Information** dialog box.

You can see the updated work values of the two resources in the Project Guide: Edit Assignments view. Note that the duration value remains unchanged.

16   On the **View** menu, click **Gantt Chart**.

Tip A summary task always has a fixed-duration task type, and you cannot change it. Because a summary task is based on the earliest start date and the latest finish date of its subtasks, its duration is calculated based on its subtasks and is not directly editable. If you want to confirm this, double-click **Summary Task 1, Pre-Production**—or another summary task—and view the **Advanced** tab in the **Task Information** dialog box.

Task Types and Effort-Driven Scheduling

Many people misunderstand task types and effort-driven scheduling and conclude that these two issues are more closely related than they really are. Both settings can affect your schedule. But whereas the effect of a task type applies whenever you edit a task's work, duration, or unit values, effort-driven scheduling affects your schedule only when you're assigning or removing resources from tasks. For more information about effort-driven scheduling, see Chapter 4, "Assigning Resources to Tasks."

Entering Deadline Dates

One common mistake new Project users make is to place semi-flexible or inflexible constraints on too many tasks in their projects. Such constraints severely limit your scheduling flexibility.

Yet if you know that a specific task must be completed by a certain date, why not enter a Must Finish On constraint? Here is why not: let's say you have a five-day task that you want to see completed by October 14, and today is October 3. If you enter a Must Finish On constraint on the task and set it to October 14, Project will move it out so that it will, indeed, end on October 14.

This task has a Must Finish On constraint, so Project schedules it to finish on the specified date, but no earlier.

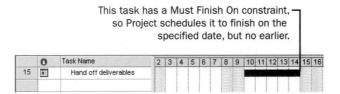

Now, even if the task could be completed earlier, Project will not reschedule it to start earlier. In fact, by applying that constraint, you have increased the risk for this task. If the task is delayed for even one day for any reason (a required resource is out sick, for example), the task will miss its planned finish date.

A better approach to scheduling this task is to use the default As Soon As Possible (ASAP) constraint and enter a deadline of October 14. A deadline is a date value you enter for a task that indicates the latest date by which you want the task to be completed, but the deadline date itself does not constrain the task.

With an As Soon As Possible constraint applied,
the task starts earlier and leaves slack between
the finish date and the deadline date.

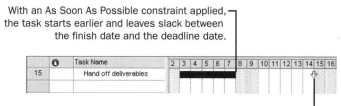

The deadline marker appears on the Gantt chart.

Now the task has the greatest scheduling flexibility. It might be completed well before its deadline, depending on resource availability, predecessor tasks, and whatever other scheduling issues apply.

Deadline
Indicator

Entering a deadline date causes Project to display a deadline indicator on the chart portion of the Gantt Chart view. If the task's finish date moves past its deadline, Project displays a missed deadline indicator in the Indicator field for that task.

Missed
Deadline
Indicator

In this exercise, you enter deadline dates for some tasks.

1   On the **Edit** menu, click **Go To.**

2   In the **ID** box, type **11** and click **OK.**

Project displays task 11. This task is a milestone marking the scheduled finish date of the pre-production phase of the project. You want to make sure that the pre-production tasks conclude by May 27, 2005, so you will enter a deadline date for this milestone.

3   If the Tasks pane is not already displayed, on the **Project Guide** toolbar, click **Tasks.**

The Tasks pane appears.

4   In the Tasks pane, click the **Set deadlines and constrain tasks** link.

The Deadlines and Constraints pane appears.

5   In the **Date** box under **Set a deadline**, type or select **5/27/05**, and then press Tab.

Project inserts a deadline indicator in the chart portion of the Gantt Chart view. Your screen should look like the following illustration:

Deadline indicator ⎯

	ⓘ	Task Name	Duration	May 22, '05	May 29, '05	Jun 5
				S M T W T F S	S M T W T F S	S M
1		⊟ Pre-Production	57.5 days	▼		
2		Review script	1 wk			
3		Develop script breakdo	1 wk			
4		Develop production bos	1 mon			
5		Scout locations	2 wks			
6		Select locations	1 wk	ax Benson		
7		Hold auditions	1 wk	ctor,Scott Cooper,Doug Hampton[50%]		
8		Apply for filming permit:	1 wk	Kim Yoshida		
9		Reserve camera equipr	3 days	Jan Miksovsky,Eric Lang		
10		Reserve sound equipm	3 days	Eric Lang		
11		Pre-Production complet	0 days	◆ 5/25 ⸝		
12		⊟ Production	51.82 days			
13		⊟ Scene 7	5.4 days			
14		Scene 7 setup	1.2 days	Jo Brown,Max Benson,Electricia		
15		Scene 7 rehearsal	8 hrs	Scott Cooper,Jo Brown,Paul		
16		Scene 7 shoot	8 hrs	Scott Cooper,Jo Bro		
17		Scene 7 teardown	1.2 days	Jo Brown,Max Be		
18		Scene 7-process de	1 day			
19		⊟ Scene 3	4 days			
20	🖩	Scene 3 setup	1 day	Jo Brown,I		
21		Scene 3 rehearsal	1 day	Scott Cc		
22		Scene 3 shoot	8 hrs			

Deadlines and Constraints pane (left):

Set a deadline

To indicate a due date without restricting scheduling, set a deadline. Project flags missed deadlines.

Select a task to the right, and set a deadline:

5/27/2005 ▾

Constrain a task

By default, tasks start as soon as possible. If a task **must** happen on a specific date, constrain it. This limits Project's scheduling ability.

Select a task to the right, and choose a constraint below:

As Soon As Possible ▾

If needed, choose a constraint date:

NA ▾

Done

More Information

Now you can see at a glance how close the pre-production phase is to meeting or missing its deadline. If the scheduled completion of the pre-production phase moves past 5/27/05, Project will display a missed deadline indicator in the Indicators column.

Next you will enter a deadline date for a summary task.

6 Select the name of task 12, **Production**.

This task is the Production Summary task. You want to conclude filming by mid-August 2005.

7 In the **Date** box under **Set a deadline**, type or select **8/19/05**, and then press ⌨Tab.

Project inserts a deadline date marker for the summary task. If you wish to see it, scroll the chart portion of the Gantt Chart view to the right.

8 At the bottom of the Deadlines and Constraints pane, click the **Done** link.

9 Click the **Show/Hide Project Guide** button on the **Project Guide** toolbar.

The Project Guide closes.

Show/Hide
Project Guide

Tip You can also enter a deadline date for the selected task on the **Advanced** tab in the **Task Information** dialog box. On the **Project** menu, click **Task Information**.

Except for one situation, entering a deadline date has no effect on the scheduling of a summary or subtask. However, a deadline date will cause Project to alert you if the scheduled completion of a task exceeds its deadline date.

The one situation in which the deadline date can affect the scheduling of a task involves slack. When a task is given a deadline date, its slack does not extend beyond the deadline date.

Tip   To remove a deadline from a task, clear the **Date** field in the Deadlines and Constraints pane of the Project Guide, or clear the **Deadline** field on the **Advanced** tab of the **Task Information** dialog box (available by clicking **Task Information** on the **Project** menu).

Entering Fixed Costs

For most projects, financial costs are derived mainly from resource costs. Typically, you set up hourly, weekly, or monthly cost rates for resources. However, in addition to (or sometimes instead of) the resource costs associated with a task, a task might have a *fixed cost*. A fixed cost is a specific monetary amount budgeted for a task. It remains the same regardless of how much time or effort resources expend to complete the task. Here are some common examples of fixed costs in projects:

■   Travel expenses for a consultant, paid in addition to an hourly or a daily fee.

■   A setup fee, charged in addition to a per-day rental fee, for a piece of equipment.

■   A permit to film in a public location.

If you enter both resource costs and fixed costs for a task, Project adds the two to determine the task's total cost. If you do not enter resource cost information into a project plan (perhaps because you do not know how much your resources will be paid), you can still gain some control over the project's total cost by entering fixed costs per task.

You can specify when fixed costs should accrue:

■   Start. The entire fixed cost is scheduled for the start of the task. When you track progress, the entire fixed cost of the task is incurred as soon as the task starts.

■   End. The entire fixed cost is scheduled for the end of the task. When you track progress, the entire fixed cost of the task is incurred only after the task is completed.

■   Prorated. The fixed cost is distributed evenly over the duration of the task. When you track progress, the project incurs the cost of the task at the rate at which the task is completed. For example, if a task has a $100 fixed cost and is 75 percent complete, the project has incurred $75 against that task.

When you plan a project, the *accrual* method you choose for fixed costs determines how these costs are scheduled over time. This can be important in anticipating budget and cash-flow needs. By default, Project assigns the prorated accrual method for fixed costs, but you can change that to match your organization's cost accounting practices.

For the film project, you know from past experience that the filming permits will cost $500, payable when you apply for the permits. In this exercise, you assign a fixed cost to a task and specify its accrual method.

1   On the **View** menu, click **More Views**.

2   In the **More Views** dialog box, click **Task Sheet**, and then click the **Apply** button.

     The Task Sheet view appears.

3   On the **View** menu, point to **Table: Entry**, and click **Cost**.

     The Cost table appears, replacing the Entry table.

4   In the **Fixed Cost** field for task 8, *Apply for filming permits*, type 500, and press ⎇Tab⎇.

5   In the **Fixed Cost Accrual** field, select **Start**, and press ⎇Tab⎇.

	Task Name	Fixed Cost	Fixed Cost Accrual	Total Cost	Baseline	Variance	Actual	Remaining
1	⊟ Pre-Production	**$0.00**	Prorated	**$21,926.50**	**$0.00**	**$21,926.50**	**$0.00**	**$21,926.50**
2	Review script	$0.00	Prorated	$787.50	$0.00	$787.50	$0.00	$787.50
3	Develop script breakdo	$0.00	Prorated	$1,655.00	$0.00	$1,655.00	$0.00	$1,655.00
4	Develop production boa	$0.00	Prorated	$8,124.00	$0.00	$8,124.00	$0.00	$8,124.00
5	Scout locations	$0.00	Prorated	$4,920.00	$0.00	$4,920.00	$0.00	$4,920.00
6	Select locations	$0.00	Prorated	$2,535.00	$0.00	$2,535.00	$0.00	$2,535.00
7	Hold auditions	$0.00	Prorated	$1,835.00	$0.00	$1,835.00	$0.00	$1,835.00
8	Apply for filming permit:	$500.00	Start	$876.00	$0.00	$876.00	$0.00	$876.00
9	Reserve camera equipr	$0.00	Prorated	$822.00	$0.00	$822.00	$0.00	$822.00

                     └ A fixed cost value is either accrued at the start or finish of a task or prorated over the duration of the task, depending on the option you choose.

Now Project will schedule a $500 cost against the task *Apply for filming permits* at the task's start date, and the project will incur this cost when the task starts. This cost is independent of the task's duration and of the costs of resources assigned to it. In fact, the task's total cost (visible in the **Total Cost** column) includes both the $500 fixed cost and the cost of the resources assigned to the task.

Setting Up a Recurring Task

Many projects require repetitive tasks, such as attending project status meetings, creating and publishing status reports, or running quality control inspections. Although it is easy to overlook the scheduling of such events, you should account for them in your project plan. After all, status meetings and similar events that indirectly support the project require time from resources. And such events take time away from your resources' other assignments.

To help account for such events in your project plan, create a *recurring task*. As the name suggests, a recurring task is repeated at a specified frequency, such as daily, weekly, monthly, or yearly. When you create a recurring task, Project creates a series of tasks with Start No Earlier Than constraints, no task relationships, and effort-driven scheduling turned off.

In this exercise, you create a recurring task.

1   On the **View** menu, click **Gantt Chart**.

The Gantt Chart view appears.

2   Select the name of task 12, **Production**.

You want the recurring tasks to be inserted into the project as the last items in the pre-production phase, directly above task 12.

3   On the **Insert** menu, click **Recurring Task**.

The **Recurring Task Information** dialog box appears.

4   In the **Task Name** box, type Staff planning meeting.

5   In the **Duration** box, type 2h.

6   Under **Recurrence pattern**, make sure **Weekly** is selected, and then select the **Monday** check box.

Next you will specify the date of its first occurrence. By default, it is the project start date. However, you want the weekly status meetings to begin a week later.

7   In the **Start** box, type or select 3/14/05.

Next you will specify the number of recurrences. You do this by entering either an exact number of recurrences or a date by which the task should end.

8   Select **End after**, and type or select 10 occurrences.

9   Click **OK** to create the recurring task.

Project inserts the recurring tasks, nested within the Pre-Production phase. Initially the summary task is collapsed. A recurring task icon appears in the Indicators column.

Go To Selected Task

10 To see the first occurrences of the recurring meeting's Gantt bars, on the Standard toolbar, click the **Go To Selected Task** button.

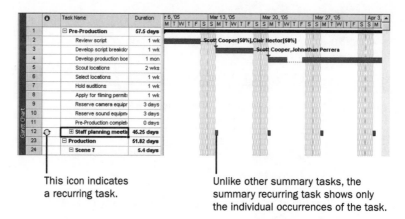

This icon indicates a recurring task.

Unlike other summary tasks, the summary recurring task shows only the individual occurrences of the task.

Note that the summary Gantt bar for the recurring task does not look like the other summary Gantt bars in the Gantt chart. A summary Gantt bar for a recurring task shows only the occurrences or roll-ups of the individual occurrences of the task. For example, contrast the summary Gantt bar for the recurring task with that of task 1, Pre-Production.

Next you will assign resources to the recurring task.

11 Verify that task 12 is selected, then on the Standard toolbar, click **Assign Resources**.

Assign Resources

12 In the **Assign Resources** dialog box, click **Clair Hector**. Then hold down the ⌨Ctrl key while clicking **Johnathan Perrera** and **Scott Cooper**.

13 Click the **Assign** button, and then click **Close**.

The **Assign Resources** dialog box closes, and Project assigns the selected resources to the recurring task. Next you will view the individual occurrences of the recurring task.

14 Click the **plus sign** next to the summary recurring task's title, **Staff planning meeting**. Your screen should look similar to the following illustration:

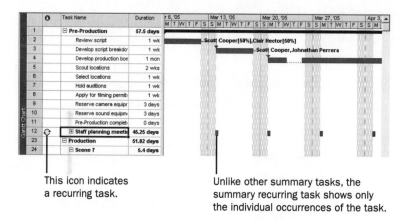

The names of recurring tasks are
automatically numbered sequentially.

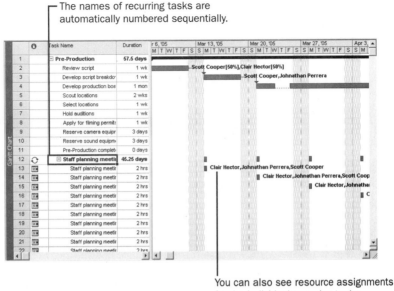

You can also see resource assignments
for the individual recurring tasks.

Each occurrence of the summary task is sequentially numbered (if you wish to verify this, widen the **Task Name** column), and the resource assignments appear for the subtasks.

15 Click the **minus sign** next to the summary recurring task's title, **Staff planning meeting**, to hide the subtasks.

Here are a few more things to keep in mind when creating recurring tasks:

■ By default, Project schedules a recurring task to start at the Default Start Time value entered on the **Calendar** tab (on the **Tools** menu, click **Options**). In this project, that is 8 A.M. If you want to schedule a recurring task to start at a different time, enter that time along with the start date in the **Start** box of the **Recurring Task Information** dialog box. For example, if you had wanted the recurring staff meeting to be scheduled for 10 A.M. starting on October 3, you would enter **10/3/05 10AM** in the **Start** box.

■ When you schedule a recurring task to end on a specific date, Project suggests the current project end date. If you use this date, be sure to manually change it if the project end date changes later.

- Project alerts you if you create a recurring task that would occur during non-working time (a holiday, for example). You can then choose not to create that occurrence or to schedule it for the next working day.

- You should always assign resources to recurring tasks with the **Assign Resources** dialog box. Entering resource names in the **Resource Name** field of the summary recurring task assigns the resources to the summary task, not to the individual occurrences.

CLOSE: the Short Film Project 7 file.

Key Points

- By using a combination of task relationships, and lead and lag time, you can more accurately model how work should be done.

- When entering lead time between a predecessor and successor task, entering a percentage lead time value offers more flexibility because Project recalculates the lead time value whenever the predecessor task's duration changes.

- The constraint options in Project enable you to fully take advantage of the scheduling engine in Project, or to effectively turn it off. Think through the effects of semi-flexible and inflexible constraints on your schedules, and use them sparingly.

- You can often set a deadline date for a task instead of applying a hard constraint like Must Finish On.

- The critical path indicates the series of tasks that determine the project's finish date. Project constantly recalculates the critical path, which may change as the details of your project plan change.

- For tasks that must be completed outside of the project's normal working time (as specified by the project calendar), you can create a new calendar and apply it to the task.

- Project supports three different task types; fixed units is the default. A task's type determines how Project reschedules a task when you change work, duration, or assignment units values.

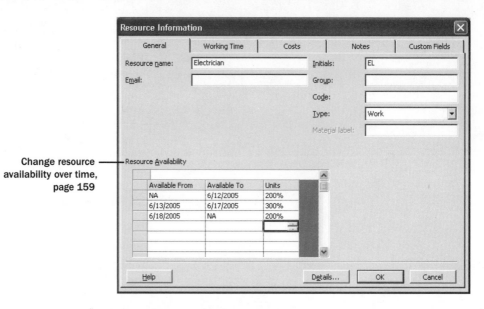

Change resource availability over time, page 159

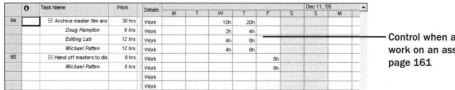

Control when a resource starts work on an assignment, page 161

Contour resource assignments manually or with built-in contour patterns, page 163

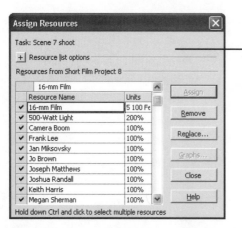

Assign material resources to tasks using variable consumption rates, page 168

Fine-Tuning Resource and Assignment Details

In this chapter you will learn to:

✔ Set up different pay rates for resources.

✔ Set up pay rates that will change over time for a resource.

✔ Set resource availability to change over time.

✔ Delay the start of a resource assignment.

✔ Control how a resource's work on a task is scheduled over time by using work contours.

✔ Apply different cost rates for a resource assigned to different kinds of tasks.

✔ Enter variable consumption rates for material resources.

See Also   Do you need a quick refresher on the topics in this chapter? See the quick reference entries on pages xxviii–xxix.

Because people and equipment resources are often the most expensive part of a project, understanding how to make the best use of resources' time is an important project planning skill. In this chapter, you examine and use a variety of advanced Microsoft Office Project 2003 features relating to *resources* and their *assignments* to *tasks*.

Important   Before you can use the practice files in this chapter, be sure you install them from the book's companion CD to their default location. See "Using the Book's CD-ROM," on page xiii, for more information.

Entering Multiple Pay Rates for a Resource

Some *work resources* might perform different tasks with different pay rates. For example, in the short film project, the director of photography could also serve as a camera operator. Because the pay rates for director of photography and camera operator are different, you can enter two *cost rate tables* for the resource. Then, after you assign the resource to tasks, you specify which rate table should apply. Each resource can have up to five cost rate tables.

In this exercise, you create a second cost rate table for a resource.

Important   If you are running Project Professional, you may need to make a one-time adjustment to use the My Computer account and to work offline. This helps ensure that the practice files you work with in this chapter don't affect your Project Server data. For more information, see "Starting Project Professional," on page 10.

OPEN: Short Film Project 8a from the *My Documents\Microsoft Press\Project 2003 Step by Step\Chapter 8 Advanced Resources and Assignments* folder. You can also access the practice files for this book by clicking **Start**, **All Programs**, **Microsoft Press**, **Project 2003 Step by Step**, and then selecting the chapter folder of the file you want to open.

1   On the **File** menu, click the **Save As** button.

The **Save As** dialog box appears.

2   In the **File name** box, type Short Film Project 8, and then click the **Save** button.

3   On the **View** menu, click **Resource Sheet**.

The Resource Sheet view replaces the Gantt Chart view.

4   In the Resource Sheet view, click the name of resource 18, **Jan Miksovsky**.

Your screen should look similar to the following illustration:

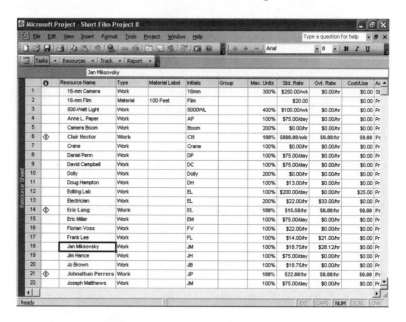

Resource
Information

5   On the Standard toolbar, click the **Resource Information** button.

The **Resource Information** dialog box appears.

Tip   You can also double-click the **Resource Name** field to display the **Resource Information** dialog box.

6   Click the **Costs** tab.

You see Jan's default pay rate of $18.75 per hour on rate table A. Each tab (labeled A, B, and so on) corresponds to one of the five pay rates a resource can have.

7   Under **Cost rate tables**, click the **B** tab.

8   Select the default entry of **$0.00/h** in the field directly below the column heading **Standard Rate**, and then type 14/h.

9   In the **Overtime Rate** field in the same row, type 21/h, and then press the ⌷Enter⌷ key:

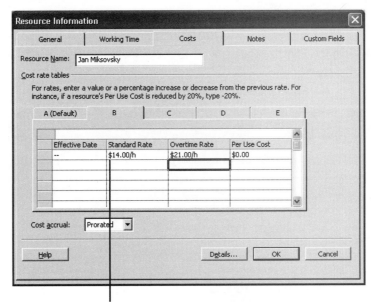

When you enter a pay rate, Project supplies
the currency symbol if you do not.

10   Click **OK** to close the **Resource Information** dialog box.

Notice that on the Resource Sheet, Jan's standard pay rate is still $18.75 per hour. (This is recorded in the **Std. Rate** column.) This matches the value in her rate table A, the default rate table. This rate table will be used for all of Jan's task assignments unless you specify a different rate table. You will do this in a later section.

Setting Up Pay Rates to Apply at Different Times

Resources can have both standard and overtime pay rates. By default, Project uses these rates for the duration of the project. However, you can change a resource's pay rates to be effective as of the date you choose. For example, you could initially set up a resource on January 1 with a standard rate of $10 per hour, planning to raise the resource's standard rate to $13 per hour on July 1.

Project uses these pay rates when calculating resource costs, based on when the resource's work is scheduled. You can assign up to 25 pay rates to be applied at different times to each of a resource's five cost rate tables.

In this exercise, you enter different pay rates for a resource to be applied at a later date.

1   In the **Resource Name** column, select the name of resource 11, **Doug Hampton**.

2   On the Standard toolbar, click the **Resource Information** button.

Resource
Information

The **Resource Information** dialog box appears.

3   Click the **Costs** tab.

You'll enter a pay rate increase in cost rate table A.

4   In the **Effective Date** cell in the second row of cost rate table A, type or select 7/1/05.

5   In the **Standard Rate** cell in the second row, type 20%, and then press the `Enter` key:

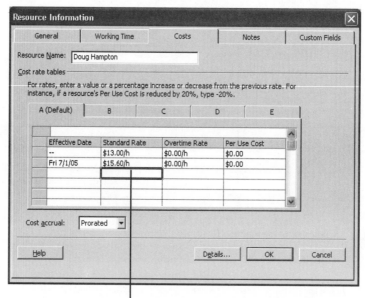

If you enter a positive or negative percentage value here, Project automatically calculates the new rate value based on the previous rate value.

Note that Project calculates the 20 percent increase to produce a rate of $15.60 per hour. The previous rate of $13 per hour plus 20 percent equals $15.60 per hour. You can enter a specific value or a percentage increase or decrease from the

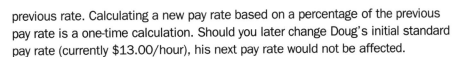

previous rate. Calculating a new pay rate based on a percentage of the previous pay rate is a one-time calculation. Should you later change Doug's initial standard pay rate (currently $13.00/hour), his next pay rate would not be affected.

Tip   In addition to or instead of standard and overtime pay rates that can change over time, a resource can also have a cost per use that can change over time.

6   Click **OK** to close the **Resource Information** dialog box.

Note that Doug Hampton's initial rate, $13.00/hr, appears in his **Std. Rate** field. This field will display $13 per hour until the current date changes to 7/1/05 or later. Then it will display his new standard rate of $15.60 per hour.

Setting Up Resource Availability to Apply at Different Times

One of the values Project stores for each work resource is the resource's Max. Units value. This is the maximum capacity of a resource to accomplish tasks. A resource's working time settings (recorded in the individual resource calendars) determine when work assigned to a resource can be scheduled. However, the resource's capacity to work (measured in *units*, and limited by the resource's Max. Units value) determines the extent to which the resource can work within those hours without becoming *overallocated*.

You can specify different Max. Units values to be applied at different time periods for any resource. Setting a resource's availability over time enables you to control exactly what a resource's Max. Units value is at any time. For example, you might have two electricians available for the first eight weeks, three for the next six weeks, and then two for the remainder of the project. You set resource availability over time in the **Resource Availability** grid on the **General** tab of the **Resource Information** dialog box. (You can open this dialog box by clicking the **Resource Information** command on the **Project** menu when in a resource view.)

Important   Setting the Max. Units values for different times will not prevent a resource from becoming overallocated, but Project will indicate when the resource's assignments exceed their Max. Units capacity.

In this exercise, you customize a resource's availability over time.

1   In the **Resource Name** column, click the name of resource 13, **Electrician**.

2   On the Standard toolbar, click the **Resource Information** button.

Resource
Information

3   Click the **General** tab.

You expect to have two electricians available to work on this project from the start of the project through June 12, 2005, three electricians from June 13 through June 17, and then just two for the remainder of the project.

4   Under **Resource Availability**, in the first row of the **Available From** column, leave **NA** (for Not Applicable).

5   In the **Available To** cell in the first row, type or select 6/12/05.

6   In the **Available From** cell in the second row, type or select 6/13/05.

7   In the **Available To** cell in the second row, type or select 6/17/05.

8   In the **Units** cell in the second row, type or select 300%.

9   In the **Available From** cell in the third row, type or select 6/18/05.

10   Leave the **Available To** cell in the third row blank. (Project will insert *NA* for you after you complete the next step.)

11   In the **Units** cell in the third row, type or select 200%, and then press the [Enter] key:

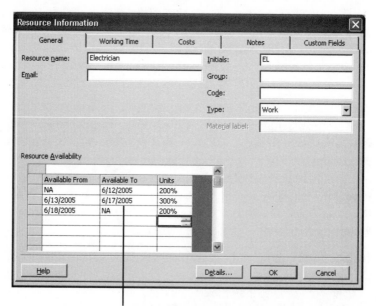

When you enter dates in an abbreviated format, such as 6/12/05, Project converts them to this expanded format.

Tip   *This tip describes enterprise project management (EPM) functionality.* If you have Project Professional, you'll see additional items in the **Resource Information** dialog box that relate to enterprise resource features enabled by Project Server. For more information, see Part 4, "Introducing Project Server."

Now, for the period between June 13 through June 17, you can schedule up to three electricians without overallocating them. Before and after this period, you have just two electricians to schedule.

12 Click **OK** to close the **Resource Information** dialog box.

Note   The Max. Units field for the Electricians resource will display 300% only when the current date (based on your computer's system clock) is within the June 13 through June 17 range. At other times it will display 200%.

Delaying the Start of Assignments

If more than one resource is assigned to a task, you might not want all the resources to start working on the task at the same time. You can delay the start of work for one or more resources assigned to a task.

For example, let's say a task has four resources assigned. Three of the resources initially work on the task, and the fourth later inspects the quality of the work. The inspector should start work on the task later than the other resources.

Tip   If you need to delay the start of all resources assigned to a task rather than adjusting each resource's assignment, you should reschedule the start date of the task.

In this exercise, you delay the start of one resource's assignment on a task.

1 On the **View** menu, click **Task Usage**.

The Task Usage view appears. In this view, the assigned resources are listed under each task.

2 On the **Edit** menu, click **Go To**, enter **84** in the **ID** box, and then click **OK**.

Tip   Remember that [Ctrl]+[G] is a shortcut for displaying the **Go To** dialog box.

Project displays task 84, *Archive master film and audio tape*:

	O	Task Name	Work	Details	M	T	W	T	F	S	Dec 11, '05 S	M
84		⊟ Archive master film anc	30 hrs	Work			10h	20h				
		Doug Hampton	6 hrs	Work			2h	4h				
		Editing Lab	12 hrs	Work			4h	8h				
		Michael Patten	12 hrs	Work			4h	8h				
85		⊟ Hand off masters to dis	8 hrs	Work					8h			
		Michael Patten	8 hrs	Work					8h			
				Work								
				Work								

As you can see, this task currently has three resources (two people and the editing lab) assigned to it. You want to delay the start of Doug Hampton's work on this task until Monday, December 12.

3   Under task 84 in the **Task Name** column, select the name of the resource **Doug Hampton**.

Assignment
Information

4   On the Standard toolbar, click the **Assignment Information** button.

The **Assignment Information** dialog box appears.

Note   You may have noticed that the same toolbar button is used for the **Resource Information** and **Assignment Information** buttons that you've used in this chapter, as well as the **Task Information** button. Which Information dialog box you get (Task, Resource, or Assignment) depends on what you have selected when you click the button.

5   Click the **General** tab.

6   In the **Start** box, type or select **12/12/05**, and then click **OK** to close the **Assignment Information** dialog box:

The total work for the
task does not change.

After delaying the start of the
resource's assignment, work
is shifted to the next workday.

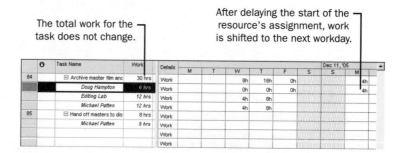

Note   If you want an assignment to start at a specific time as well as on a specific date, you can specify the time in the **Start** box. For example, if you want Doug Hampton's assignment to start at 1 P.M. on December 12, type **12/12/04 1:00 PM**. Otherwise, Project uses the default start time as specified in the **Default start time** box on the **Calendar** tab of the **Options** dialog box.

Project adjusts Doug Hampton's assignment on this task so that he works no hours on it Wednesday through Friday but four hours on the following Monday and two on Tuesday. The other resources assigned to the task are not affected. Note that the total work of this task did not change, but its duration did—the work was spread from two days (Wednesday and Thursday) to five days (Wednesday through Tuesday).

Tip   You can also delay or make other changes to individual resource assignments by using the Project Guide. Click the **Track** button on the **Project Guide** toolbar, and then click the **Make changes to the project** link. In the Project Guide's Edit Assignments view, change the assignment-level details you want.

Applying Contours to Assignments

In the Resource Usage and Task Usage views, you can see exactly how long each resource is scheduled to work on each task. In addition to viewing assignment details, you can change the amount of time a resource works on a task in any given time period. There are two ways to do this:

- Apply a predefined work *contour* to an assignment. Predefined contours generally describe how work is distributed over time in terms of graphical patterns. For example, the Bell predefined contour distributes less work to the beginning and end of the assignment, and distributes more work toward the middle. If you were to graph the work over time, the graph's shape would resemble a bell.

- Edit the assignment details directly. For example, in the Resource Usage or Task Usage view, you can change the assignment values directly in the time-scaled grid.

How you contour or edit an assignment depends on what you need to accomplish. Predefined contours work best for assignments in which you can predict a likely pattern of effort—a task that requires considerable ramp-up time might benefit from a back-loaded contour, for example, to reflect the likelihood that the resource will be most productive toward the end of the assignment.

In this exercise, you apply a predefined contour to one task's assignments, and you manually edit another assignment.

1   On the **Edit** menu, click **Go To**, enter **79** in the **ID** box, and then click **OK**.

Project scrolls to task 79, *Record final narration*. This task has three resources assigned to it:

	❶	Task Name	Work	Details	M	T	W	T	F	S	Oct 9, '05 S	M	
79		⊟ Record final narration	216 hrs	Work			12h	24h	24h			24h	
		David Campbell	72 hrs	Work			4h	8h	8h			8h	
		Michael Patten	72 hrs	Work			4h	8h	8h			8h	
		Scott Cooper	72 hrs	Work			4h	8h	8h			8h	
80		⊟ Add head and tail titles	120 hrs	Work									
		Editing Lab	40 hrs	Work									
		Jo Brown	40 hrs	Work									
		Michael Patten	40 hrs	Work									

As you can see in the timescaled data at the right, all three resources are scheduled to work on this task at a regular rate of eight hours per day—except for the first and last days of the task. These assignments have a flat contour. This is the default work contour type Project uses when scheduling work.

You want to change Michael Patten's assignment on this task so that although the other assigned resources work full-time, he starts with a brief daily assignment and increases his work time as the task progresses. He should continue working on the task after the other resources have finished their assignments. To accomplish this, you will apply a back-loaded contour to the assignment.

Note The reason each resource assigned to task 79 has just four hours of work on the task's first and last day is that the task is scheduled to start halfway through the workday (at 1 P.M.) on Wednesday, and finish in the middle of the workday on Tuesday.

2 In the **Task Name** column, select **Michael Patten**, the second resource assigned to task 79.

Assignment
Information

3 On the Standard toolbar, click the **Assignment Information** button.

Project displays the **Assignment Information** dialog box.

4 Click the **General** tab.

5 In the **Work Contour** box, select **Back Loaded**, and then click **OK** to close the **Assignment Information** dialog box.

Project applies the contour to this resource's assignment and reschedules his work on the task:

The back-loaded contour causes Project to assign very little ⌐
work to the resource initially and then add more work each day.

	❶	Task Name	Work	Details	M	T	W	T	F	S	Oct 9, '05 S	M	
79		⊟ Record final narration	216 hrs	Work			8.4h	16.8h	17.2h			17.6h	
		David Campbell	72 hrs	Work			4h	8h	8h			8h	
	⊞|| *Michael Patten*	*72 hrs*	Work			0.4h	0.8h	1.2h			1.6h	
		Scott Cooper	72 hrs	Work			4h	8h	8h			8h	
80		⊟ Add head and tail titles	120 hrs	Work									
		Editing Lab	40 hrs	Work									
		Jo Brown	40 hrs	Work									
		Michael Patten	40 hrs	Work									

└ The contour indicator matches the type of
contour applied—back-loaded in this case.

If you scroll the timescaled data to the right, you see that in each successive day of the task's duration, Michael Patten is assigned slightly more time to work on the assignment. You also see a contour indicator in the Indicators column, showing the type of contour that is applied to the assignment.

6 Point to the indicator:

	ⓘ	Task Name	Work
79		⊟ Record final narration	216 hrs
		David Campbell	72 hrs
		Michael Patten	72 hrs
		This assignment dynamically schedules work using a back loaded pattern.	hrs
80			hrs

Project displays a ScreenTip describing the type of contour applied to this assignment.

Because Michael Patten's assignment to this task finishes later than the assignments of the other resources, Michael Patten determines the finish date of the task. One common way to phrase this is that Michael Patten is the *driving resource* of this task; his assignment determines, or drives, the finish date of the task.

Next you will directly edit another task's assignment values.

Tip   Applying a contour to this assignment caused the overall duration of the task to be extended. If you do not want a contour to extend a task's duration, change the task type (on the **Advanced** tab of the **Task Information** dialog box) to **Fixed Duration** before applying the contour. Applying a contour to a fixed-duration task will cause Project to recalculate the resource's work value so that he or she works less in the same time period.

7   On the **Edit** menu, click **Go To**, enter **2** in the **ID** box, and then click **OK**.

Project scrolls vertically to task 2, *Review script*:

	ⓘ	Task Name	Work	Details		Mar 6, '05							Me ▲
					S	S	M	T	W	T	F	S	
2		⊟ Review script	40 hrs	Work			8h	8h	8h	8h	8h		
		Clair Hector	20 hrs	Work			4h	4h	4h	4h	4h		
		Scott Cooper	20 hrs	Work			4h	4h	4h	4h	4h		
3		⊟ Develop script breakdo	80 hrs	Work									
		Johnathan Perrera	40 hrs	Work									
		Scott Cooper	40 hrs	Work									

Note that Clair Hector is currently assigned four hours per day for each day of the assignment's duration. Why four hours? Clair normally has eight working hours per day on these days (as determined by her resource calendar). She was assigned to this task at 50 percent assignment units, however, so the resulting scheduled work is just four hours per day.

You want to change Clair Hector's assignment on the last two days of this task so that she will work full-time on it. To accomplish this, you will manually edit her assignment values.

8   Select Clair Hector's four-hour assignment for Thursday, March 10.

9   Type **8h**, and then press the ⟨Tab⟩ key.

10 In Clair's assignment for Friday, type **8h**, and then press `Enter`:

Here are Clair Hector's assigned work values
for Thursday and Friday, after you edited them.

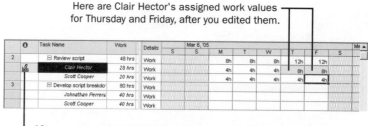

After you manually edit Clair's assignment, this indicator appears.

Now Clair is assigned eight hours per day on these days. Project displays a contour indicator in the Indicators column, this time showing that a manually edited contour has been applied to the assignment.

Assignment Notes

Tip   If you want to document details about contouring an assignment, or anything about an assignment, you can record the details in an assignment note. In Task Usage or Resource Usage view, select the assignment, and then click the **Assignment Notes** button on the Standard toolbar. Assignment notes are similar to task and resource notes.

Applying Different Cost Rates to Assignments

You can set as many as five pay rates per resource. This enables you to apply different pay rates to different assignments for a resource, for example, depending on the skills required for each assignment. For each assignment, Project initially uses rate table A by default, but you can specify that another rate table should be used.

In a previous section, you set up a second rate table for Jan Miksovsky to be applied for any assignments where she is functioning as a camera operator. Jan is currently assigned to task 27, *Scene 7 shoot*, as a camera operator, but her assignment still reflects her default pay rate as director of photography. In this exercise, you change the pay rate table to be applied to Jan for her assignment to task 27.

1 On the **Edit** menu, click **Go To**, enter **27** in the **ID** box, and then click **OK**.

Project scrolls the Task Usage view to display task 27, *Scene 7 shoot*.

2 On the **View** menu, point to **Table: Usage**, and click **Cost**.

Project displays the Cost table.

3 Click the row heading directly to the left of *Jan Miksovsky* so that the entire assignment is selected.

4 Scroll the table portion (on the left) of the Task Usage view to the right until the **Total Cost** column is visible:

┌ In the Cost table you can see the task's and each assignment's total cost.
To see other assignment cost values such as actual cost or variance, scroll
the table to the right.

	Fixed Cost Accrual	Total Cost	Baseli	Details					May 29, '05				
					W	T	F	S	S	M	T	W	T
27	Prorated	$1,483.00		Work			102h			34h			
		$150.00	$	Work			18h			6h			
		$40.00	$	Work			12h			4h			
		$0.00	$	Work			6h			2h			
		$112.00	$	Work			6h			2h			
		$150.00	$	Work			6h			2h			
		$150.00	$	Work			6h			2h			
		$75.00	$	Work			6h			2h			
		$96.00	$	Work			6h			2h			
		$112.00	$	Work			6h			2h			
		$144.00	$	Work			6h			2h			
		$155.00	$	Work			6h			2h			
		$75.00	$	Work			6h			2h			
		$112.00	$	Work			6h			2h			
		$112.00	$	Work			6h			2h			
28	Prorated	$430.00		Work						15h	5h		
		$88.00	$	Work						3h	1h		
		$150.00	$	Work						6h	2h		

Note the current cost of Jan's assignment to this task: $150.00.

Assignment Information

5   On the Standard toolbar, click the **Assignment Information** button.

The **Assignment Information** dialog box appears.

6   Click the **General** tab.

7   In the **Cost Rate Table** box, type or select **B**, and then click **OK** to close the **Assignment Information** dialog box.

Project applies Jan's cost rate table B to the assignment. The new cost of the assignment, $112.00, appears in the **Total Cost** column.

Tip   If you frequently change cost rate tables for assignments, you will find it quicker to display the **Cost Rate Table** field directly in the Resource Usage or Task Usage view. Select a column heading, and on the **Insert** menu, click **Column**. In the **Field Name** box, select **Cost Rate Table** in the drop-down list, and then click **OK**.

Entering Material Resource Consumption Rates

The short film project includes one *material resource*: 16-mm film. If you completed Chapter 4, "Assigning Resources to Tasks," you assigned a material resource with a fixed amount, or *fixed consumption rate*, to a task. Another way to use material resources is to assign them with a *variable consumption rate*. Here is the difference between the two rates:

■   A fixed consumption rate means that regardless of the duration of the task to which the material resource is assigned, an absolute quantity of the resource will be used. For example, pouring concrete for a house foundation requires a fixed amount of concrete, no matter how long it takes to pour it.

■ A variable consumption rate means that the quantity of the material resource consumed depends on the duration of the task. When shooting film, for example, you will shoot more film in four hours than in two, and you can determine an hourly rate at which you shoot (or consume) film. After you enter a variable consumption rate for a material resource's assignment, Project calculates the total quantity of the material resource consumed, based on the task's duration. The advantage of using a variable rate of consumption is that the rate is tied to the task's duration. If the duration changes, the calculated quantity and cost of the material resource will change as well.

In either case, after you enter a standard pay rate for one unit of the material resource, Project calculates the total cost of the assignment. For example, we will assume that a 100-foot spool of 16-mm film costs $20 to purchase and process.

In this exercise, you enter an hourly variable consumption rate for a task that requires shooting (or consuming) film. Then you look at the resulting quantity or number of units of film required by the duration of the task, as well as the cost of the material resource assignment.

1　On the **View** menu, click **Gantt Chart**.

The Gantt Chart view appears.

2　On the **Edit** menu, click **Go To**, enter **27** in the **ID** box, and then click **OK**.

Project displays task 27, *Scene 7 shoot*. This is the first of several tasks that require film to be shot. Next you will assign the material resource 16-mm Film to this task.

Assign
Resources

3　On the Standard toolbar, click the **Assign Resources** button.

The **Assign Resources** dialog box appears.

4　In the **Units** field for **16-mm Film** in the **Assign Resources** dialog box, type **5/h** and then click the **Assign** button.

Note　Be sure to select **16-mm Film** and not *16-mm Camera* in the **Assign Resources** dialog box.

Project assigns the film to the task, at a consumption rate of five 100-foot spools per hour:

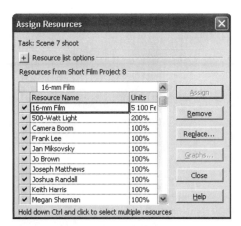

Because this task currently has an eight-hour duration, the total film assignment should be 40 spools of film. To verify this and see the resulting cost of the material resource assignment, you will change views.

5   In the **Assign Resources** dialog box, click the **Close** button.

6   On the **View** menu, click **Task Usage**.

Next you will view the cost and work values of the 16-mm Film assignment to task 27 via the **Assignment Information** dialog box.

7   Click the **16-mm Film** assignment under task 27, *Scene 7 shoot*.

Assignment
Information

8   On the Standard toolbar, click the **Assignment Information** button.

The **Assignment Information** dialog box appears.

9   If the **General** tab is not already active, select it.

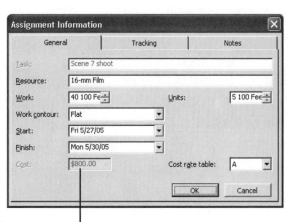

Because the cost of the assignment is calculated,
you can't edit it directly.

Here you can see the cost and work values of the 16-mm Film assignment. The calculated cost of the assignment, $800, is the 40 units of this material resource for this assignment multiplied by the $20 per unit cost entered for this material resource. (This value is recorded in the **Std. Rate** field for the resource.) Should the duration of the task change, the number of units of film consumed and its total cost would change correspondingly. In the **Work** box, you can see that the 16-mm Film assignment to task 27 is currently 40 100-foot spools of film.

CLOSE: the Short Film Project 8 file.

Key Points

- When working with resource costs, you can specify different cost rates for different assignments and apply different cost rates at different times.

- You can account for variable resource availability over time (via a resource's Max. Units value), which allows you to more finely control when a resource will appear to be overallocated.

- In a usage view you can edit the scheduled work values of resource assignments over time. For example, you can delay the start of one resource on an assignment without affecting the other resources assigned to the same task.

- Material resources, when assigned to a task, can have a fixed or variable consumption rate.

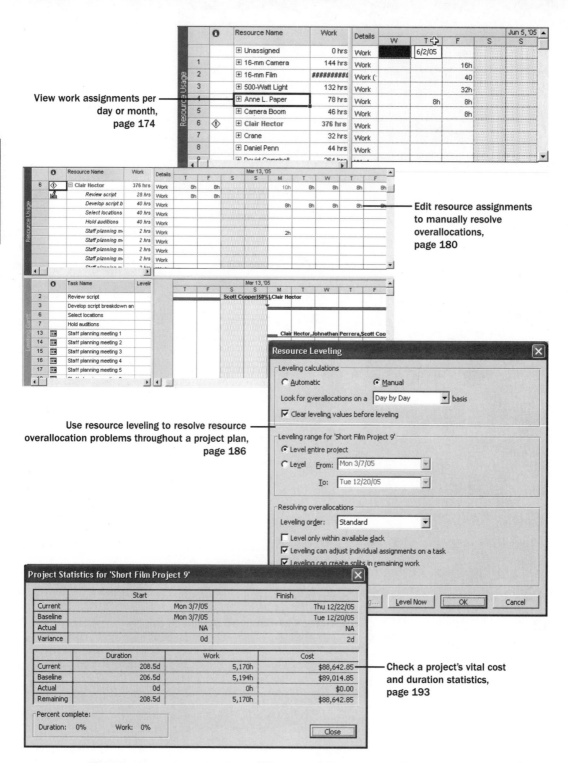

View work assignments per day or month, page 174

Edit resource assignments to manually resolve overallocations, page 180

Use resource leveling to resolve resource overallocation problems throughout a project plan, page 186

Check a project's vital cost and duration statistics, page 193

Chapter 9 at a Glance

9 Fine-Tuning the Project Plan

In this chapter you will learn to:

✔ Look at how resources are scheduled to work over the duration of a project.

✔ Edit a resource assignment to resolve a resource overallocation.

✔ Resolve resource overallocations automatically.

✔ See detailed and overall project costs.

✔ See tasks on the critical path that determines a project's finish date.

See Also Do you need a quick refresher on the topics in this chapter? See the quick reference entries on page xxx.

Up to now you have worked with tasks, resources, and assignments separately. Now you will fine-tune some settings that affect all three elements. When you build a project plan, you work with tasks, resources, and assignments together. Changes you make to tasks, for example, affect the resources assigned to those tasks.

Important Before you can use the practice files in this chapter, be sure you install them from the book's companion CD to their default location. See "Using the Book's CD-ROM," on page xiii, for more information.

Examining Resource Allocations over Time

In this exercise, you will focus on resource allocation—how the task assignments you've made affect the workloads of the people and equipment resources of a project. The relationship between a resource's capacity and his or her task assignments is called *allocation*. Each resource is in one of three states of allocation:

■ *Underallocated*. The resource's assignments do not fill his or her maximum capacity. For example, a full-time resource who has only 25 hours of work assigned in a 40-hour work week is underallocated.

■ *Fully allocated*. The resource's assignments fill his or her maximum capacity. For example, a full-time resource who has 40 hours of work assigned in a 40-hour work week is fully allocated.

■   *Overallocated*. The resource's assignments exceed his or her maximum capacity. For example, a full-time resource who has 65 hours of work assigned in a 40-hour work week is overallocated.

In Microsoft Office Project 2003, a resource's capacity to work is measured in units; the maximum capacity of a given resource is called *maximum units*. Units are measured either as numbers (for example, three units) or as a percentage (for example, 300 percent units).

Project Management Focus: Evaluating Resource Allocation

It is tempting to say that fully allocating all resources all the time is every project manager's goal—but that would be an oversimplification. Depending on the nature of your project and the resources working on it, some underallocations might be perfectly fine. Overallocation might not always be a problem either, depending on the amount of overallocation. If one resource is overallocated for just a half hour, Project can alert you, but such a minor overallocation might not be a problem you need to solve, depending on the resource involved and the nature of the assignment. Severe overallocation—for example, a resource being assigned twice the work he or she could possibly accomplish in one day—is always a problem, however, and you should know how to identify it and have strategies for addressing it. This chapter helps you identify and remedy resource overallocation.

In this exercise, you look at resource allocations and focus on two resources who are overallocated.

Important   If you are running Project Professional, you may need to make a one-time adjustment to use the My Computer account and to work offline. This helps ensure that the practice files you work with in this chapter don't affect your Project Server data. For more information, see "Starting Project Professional," on page 10.

OPEN: Short Film Project 9a from the *My Documents**Microsoft Press**Project 2003 Step by Step*\ *Chapter 9 Advanced Plan* folder. You can also access the practice files for this book by clicking **Start**, **All Programs**, **Microsoft Press**, **Project 2003 Step by Step**, and selecting the chapter folder of the file you want to open.

1   On the **File** menu, click **Save As**.

     The **Save As** dialog box appears.

2   In the **File name** box, type **Short Film Project 9**, and then click the **Save** button.

     Next you will use the Project Guide to view resource usage.

3   On the **Project Guide** toolbar, click the **Report** button.

4   In the Report pane, click the **See how resources' time is allocated** link.

A split view, with the Resource Usage view on top and the Gantt Chart view on the bottom, appears:

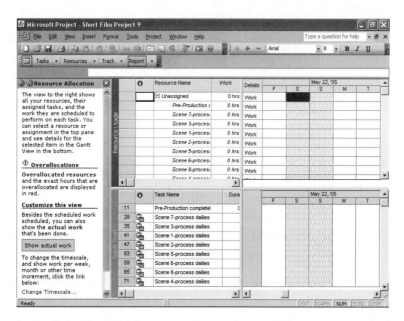

On the left side of the Resource Usage view is a table (the Usage table, by default) that shows assignments grouped per resource, the total work assigned to each resource, and each assignment's work. This information is organized into an *outline* that you can expand or collapse.

The right side of the view contains assignment details (work, by default) arranged on a timescale. You can scroll the timescale horizontally to see different time periods. You can also change the tiers of the timescale to display data in units of weeks, days, hours, and so on.

Next you will collapse the outline in the table to see total work per resource over time.

5   In the upper pane, click the **Resource Name** column heading.

6   On the Formatting toolbar, click the **Hide Subtasks** button.

Hide Subtasks

Project collapses the Resource Usage view. Resource assignments are hidden in the Usage table, and the resources' total work values over time appear in the timescaled grid on the right, as shown in the following illustration:

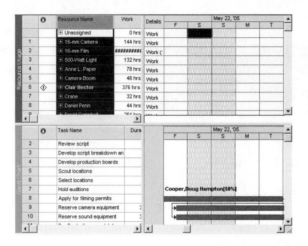

Tip Notice the name of the first resource, *Unassigned*. This resource lists all tasks to which no specific resources are assigned.

Next you will look at two people resources and their allocations.

7 In the **Resource Name** column, click the name of resource 4, **Anne L. Paper**.

Go To Selected
Task

8 On the Standard toolbar, click the **Go To Selected Task** button.

Project scrolls the timescaled grid to show Anne L. Paper's earliest assignment: eight hours on a Thursday. Below the Resource Usage view, the Gantt Chart view shows the tasks to which Anne is assigned.

9 Point to the **T** column heading (for Thursday) at the top of the timescaled grid:

In any timescaled view, you can get details about dates
by hovering your mouse pointer over the timescale.

A ScreenTip appears with the date of the assignment: 6/2/05. Such ScreenTips are handy in any timescaled view, such as the Resource Usage view or the Gantt Chart view.

Currently the timescale is set to display weeks in the middle tier and days in the bottom tier. Now you'll change the timescale to see the work data summarized more broadly.

10 At the bottom of the Resource Allocation pane in the Project Guide, click the **Change Timescale** link.

The **Timescale** dialog box appears.

Tip   You can also click **Timescale** on the **Format** menu.

The timescale can display up to three tiers, typically in descending order of detail, such as years, months, and days. However, the top tier is disabled by default.

11 Make sure that the **Middle Tier** tab is selected, and in the **Units** box under **Middle tier formatting**, click **Months**.

12 In the **Show** box under **Timescale options**, click **One tier (Middle)**. Your screen should look similar to the following illustration:

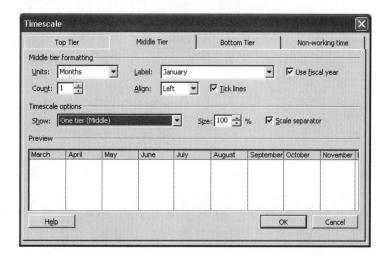

13 Click **OK** to close the **Timescale** dialog box.

Project changes the timescaled grid to show work values per month:

	ⓘ	Resource Name	Work	Details	May	June	July	August	Sep
		⊞ Unassigned	0 hrs	Work					
1		⊞ 16-mm Camera	144 hrs	Work	24h	64h	56h		
2		⊞ 16-mm Film	#########	Work (	40	140	110		
3		⊞ 500-Watt Light	132 hrs	Work	16h	68h	48h		
4		⊞ Anne L. Paper	78 hrs	Work		44h	34h		
5		⊞ Camera Boom	46 hrs	Work	8h	28h	10h		
6	◇	⊞ Clair Hector	376 hrs	Work	86h			12h	
7		⊞ Crane	32 hrs	Work		12h	20h		
8		⊞ Daniel Penn	44 hrs	Work		16h	28h		
9		⊞ David Campbell	264 hrs	Work		44h	52h	96h	

As you can see in the timescaled grid, Anne L. Paper is underallocated in each of the two months in which she has assignments in the project: June and July. Anne is one of the actors assigned to the scenes in which her character is needed, so this underallocation is really not a problem you need to address.

Notice that the names of Clair Hector and other resources appear in red. The red formatting means that these resources are overallocated: at one or more points in the schedule their assigned tasks exceed their capacity to work. You will focus on Clair Hector, first by changing the timescale settings.

14 At the bottom of the Resource Allocation pane, click the **Change Timescale** link.

The **Timescale** dialog box appears.

15 Make sure that the **Middle Tier** tab is selected, and in the **Units** box, click **Weeks**.

16 In the **Show** box under **Timescale options**, click **Two tiers (Middle, Bottom)**, and then click **OK** to close the **Timescale** dialog box.

17 In the **Resource Name** column, click the name of resource 6, **Clair Hector**.

18 On the Standard toolbar, click the **Go To Selected Task** button.

Project scrolls the timescaled grid to show Clair Hector's earliest assignments. For the week of March 6, Clair has no overallocations.

19 Scroll the Resource Usage view so that Clair Hector appears at the top of the view, and then scroll the timescaled portion of the view (using the scroll bars at the bottom of the screen) to display the week of March 13, 2005. Your screen should look similar to the following illustration:

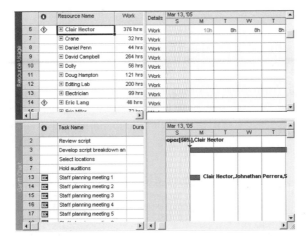

Monday, March 14, shows Clair's first overallocation: 10 hours. In the Gantt Chart view below, you can see the two tasks to which Clair is assigned on Monday.

20 Click the plus sign next to Clair Hector's name in the **Resource Name** column.

Project expands the Resource Usage view to show Clair Hector's individual assignments.

21 Scroll the Resource Usage view down to see both of Clair's assignments on Monday, March 14.

Clair has two assignments on March 14: the two-hour task *Staff planning meeting 1* and the eight-hour task *Develop script breakdown and schedule*. These two tasks have been scheduled at times that overlap between the hours of 8 A.M. and 10 A.M. (If you want to see this, format the timescale to display days in the middle tier and hours in the bottom tier.) This is a real overallocation: Clair probably cannot complete both tasks simultaneously. However, it is a relatively minor overallocation given the scope of the project, and you don't need to be too concerned about resolving this level of overallocation.

There are other, more serious overallocations in the schedule, however, which you will remedy later in this chapter.

Here are a few more things to keep in mind when viewing resource allocation:

■ By default, the Resource Usage view displays the Usage table. You can display different tables, however. On the **View** menu, click **Table: Usage**, and then click the table you want displayed.

■ By default, the Resource Usage view displays work values in the timescaled grid. However, you can display additional assignment values, such as cost and remaining availability. On the **Format** menu, click **Details**, and then click the value you want displayed.

Zoom Zoom
In   Out

■ Instead of using the **Timescale** command on the **Format** menu to change the tiers of the timescale, you can click the **Zoom In** and **Zoom Out** buttons on the Standard toolbar. However, this method might not produce the exact level of detail you want. If it does not, use the **Timescale** command on the **Format** menu.

■ To see allocations for each resource graphed against a timescale, you can display the Resource Graph view by clicking the **Resource Graph** command on the **View** menu. Use the arrow keys or horizontal scroll bar to switch between resources in this view.

Manually Resolving Resource Overallocations

In this exercise and the next, you will continue to focus on resource allocation—how the task assignments you have made affect the workloads of the people and equipment resources of the project. In this exercise, you will manually edit an assignment to resolve a resource overallocation. In the next exercise, you will automatically resolve resource overallocations.

Manually editing an assignment is just one way to resolve a resource overallocation. Other solutions include the following:

■ Replace the overallocated resource with another resource using the **Replace** button in the **Assign Resources** dialog box.

■ Reduce the value in the **Units** field in the **Assignment Information** or **Assign Resources** dialog box.

If the overallocation is not too severe (for example, 10 hours of work assigned in a normal eight-hour workday), you can often leave the overallocation in the schedule.

Tip To learn more about resolving resource overallocation problems, type **Resolving resource overallocation** into the **Search** box in the upper right corner of the Project window. The **Search** box initially contains the text *Type a question for help*.

In this exercise, you will use the Resource Allocation view to examine one overallocated resource's assignments and edit the assignment to eliminate the overallocation.

1 On the **Window** menu, click **Remove Split**.

Show/Hide
Project Guide

2 Click the **Show/Hide Project Guide** button on the **Project Guide** toolbar.

The Project Guide closes, leaving the Resource Usage view visible.

3 On the **View** menu, click **More Views**, click **Resource Allocation**, and then click the **Apply** button:

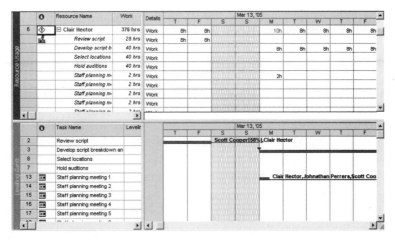

Project switches to the Resource Allocation view. This view is a combination view that displays the Resource Usage view in the top pane and the Leveling Gantt view in the bottom pane.

4 In the Resource Usage view, scroll vertically through the **Resource Name** column.

Note that several names appear in red. These are overallocated resources.

5 In the **Resource Name** column, click the name of resource 14, **Eric Lang**.

6 Click the plus sign next to Eric Lang's name to display his assignments.

Go To Selected
Task

7 On the Standard toolbar, click the **Go To Selected Task** button.

Your screen should look similar to the following illustration:

Even though this resource's assignments on
this day don't exceed his daily work capacity,
they have been scheduled at times that overlap,
resulting in an hour-by-hour overallocation.

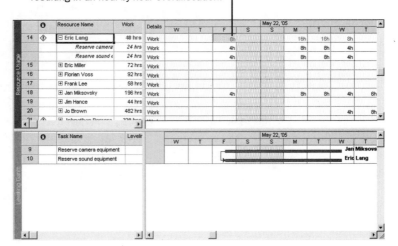

In the upper pane you see that Eric is assigned full-time to two tasks that both start on Friday, May 20. He is overallocated for the duration of both tasks. In the lower pane, you see the Gantt bars for the specific tasks that have caused Eric to be overallocated on these days. For tasks 9 and 10, Eric is assigned eight hours of work on each task Monday and Tuesday. This results in 16 hours of work per day, which is beyond Eric's capacity to work.

You might also notice that Eric is assigned a total of eight hours of work on Friday, and then again on the following Wednesday. These values also appear in red, indicating that Eric is overallocated on those days as well. This is because the two tasks are scheduled to start at the same time Friday and end at the same time Wednesday. So even though Eric has a total of eight hours of work assigned on Friday and Wednesday, he really has two four-hour assignments in parallel. This is an overallocation.

Next you will manually resolve this overallocation.

8   In the **Resource Name** column, click Eric's first assignment, **Reserve camera equipment**.

Assignment
Information

9   On the Standard toolbar, click the **Assignment Information** button.

The **Assignment Information** dialog box appears.

10   Click the **General** tab.

11   In the **Units** box next to Eric's name, type or click 50%, and then click **OK** to close the **Assignment Information** dialog box:

Eric's daily work assignments on this task are reduced to two or four hours per day, but the task duration increased. You'd like to reduce the work but not extend the duration of the task. Note the Smart Tag indicator that appears next to the name of the assignment. You will use the Smart Tag to change the scheduling effect of the new assignment units.

12 Click the **Smart Tag Actions** button.

Look over the options in the list that appears. Your screen should look like the following illustration:

13 In the **Smart Tag Actions** list, click **Change the task's total work (person-hours) to match the units and duration**.

Project reduces Eric's work assignments on the task and restores the task to its original duration.

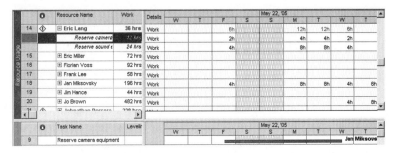

However, Eric is still overallocated. To remedy this, you will reduce his assignment units on his second task.

14 In the **Resource Name** column, click Eric's second assignment, **Reserve sound equipment**.

15 On the Standard toolbar, click the **Assignment Information** button.

The **Assignment Information** dialog box appears.

16 Click the **General** tab if it is not already visible.

17 In the **Units** box next to Eric's name, type or click **50%**, and then click **OK** to close the **Assignment Information** dialog box.

18 Click the **Smart Tag Actions** button.

19   In the **Smart Tag Actions** list, click **Change the task's total work (person-hours) to match the units and duration**.

Your screen should look like the following illustration:

Eric's total assignments on Monday and Tuesday are now reduced to eight hours each day. He is fully allocated on these days. By manually editing Eric's assignments to reduce his work on these days, you have resolved his overallocation. There are other resource overallocations in the short film project that you can resolve automatically with resource leveling, however. You will do this in the next section.

Leveling Overallocated Resources

In the previous section, you read about resource allocation, learned what causes overallocation, and manually resolved an overallocation. *Resource leveling* is the process of delaying or splitting a resource's work on a task to resolve an overallocation. The options in the **Level Resources** dialog box enable you to set parameters about how you want Project to resolve resource overallocations. Project will attempt to resolve such overallocations when you choose to level resources. Depending on the options you choose, this might involve delaying the start date of an assignment or task or splitting the work on the task.

Note   Although the effects of resource leveling on a schedule might be significant, resource leveling never changes who is assigned to tasks, or the total work or assignment unit values of those assignments.

For example, consider the following tasks, all of which have the same full-time resource assigned:

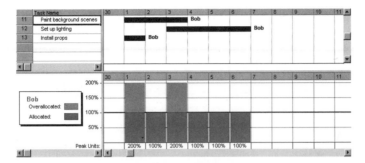

In this split view, the Resource Graph view appears below the Gantt Chart view. On day 1, the resource is overallocated at 200 percent. On day 2, the resource is fully allocated at 100 percent. On day 3, he is overallocated at 200 percent again. After day 3, the resource is fully allocated at 100 percent.

When you perform resource leveling, Project delays the start dates of the second and third tasks so that the resource is not overallocated, as shown in the following figure:

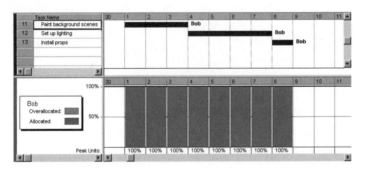

Note that the finish date of the latest task has moved from day 6 to day 8. This is common with resource leveling, which often pushes out the project finish date. Before leveling, there was a total of eight days of work, but two of those days overlapped, causing the resource to be overallocated on those days. After leveling, all eight days of work are still there, but the resource is no longer overallocated.

Resource leveling is a powerful tool, but it does only a few basic things: it delays tasks, splits tasks, and delays resource assignments. It does this following a fairly complex set of rules and options you specify in the **Resource Leveling** dialog box. (These options are explained in the following exercise.) Resource leveling is a great fine-tuning tool, but it cannot replace your good judgment about resource availability, task durations, relationships, and constraints. Resource leveling will work with all this information as it is entered into your project plan, but it might not be possible to fully resolve all resource overallocations within the time frame you want unless you change some of the basic task and resource information.

Tip   To learn more about resource leveling, type **About resource leveling** into the **Search** box in the upper right corner of the Project window.

In this exercise, you level resources and look at the effects on assignments and the project finish date.

1   On the **Window** menu, click **Remove Split**.

2   On the **View** menu, click **Resource Sheet**.

The Resource Sheet view appears. Note that several resource names appear in red and display the Overallocated icon in the Indicators column.

Overallocated

Troubleshooting   If you do not see the Overallocated icon for any resources, try the following: On the **Tools** menu, click **Level Resources**. In the **Resource Leveling** dialog box, make sure that **Day By Day** is selected in the **Look for overallocations on a … basis** box and then click OK.

3   On the **Tools** menu, click **Level Resources**.

The **Resource Leveling** dialog box appears. In the next several steps, you will walk through the options in this dialog box.

4   Under **Leveling calculations**, make sure that **Manual** is selected.

These settings determine whether Project levels resources constantly (Automatic) or only when you tell it to (Manual). Automatic leveling occurs as soon as a resource becomes overallocated.

Tip   All settings in the **Resource Leveling** dialog box apply to all project plans you work with in Project, not to just the active project plan. Using automatic leveling might sound tempting, but it will cause frequent adjustments to project plans whether you want them or not. For that reason, we recommend you keep this setting on Manual.

5   In the **Look for overallocations on a … basis** box, make sure that **Day by Day** is selected.

This setting determines the time frame in which Project will look for overallocations. If a resource is overallocated at all, its name will be formatted in red. If it's overallocated at the level you choose here, Project will also show the Overallocated indicator next to its name.

Tip   On most projects, leveling in finer detail than day by day can result in unrealistically precise adjustments to assignments.

6   Make sure that the **Clear leveling values before leveling** check box is selected.

Sometimes you will need to level resources repeatedly to get the results you want. For example, you might initially attempt to level week by week, and then switch to day by day. If the **Clear leveling values before leveling** check box is selected, Project removes any existing leveling delays from all tasks and assignments before leveling. If, for example, you previously leveled the project plan and then added more assignments, you might clear this check box before leveling again so that you wouldn't lose the previous leveling results.

7   Under **Leveling range for 'Short Film Project 9'** make sure that **Level entire project** is selected.

Here you choose to level either the entire project or only those assignments that fall within a date range you specify. Leveling within a date range is most useful after you have started tracking actual work and you want to level only the remaining assignments in a project.

8   In the **Leveling order** box, make sure that **Standard** is selected.

You control the priority Project uses to determine which tasks it should delay to resolve a resource conflict. The **ID Only** option delays tasks only according to their ID numbers: numerically higher ID numbers will be delayed before numerically lower ID numbers. You might want to use this option when your project plan has no task relationships or constraints. The **Standard** option delays tasks according to predecessor relationships, start dates, task constraints, *slack*, priority, and IDs. The **Priority, Standard** option looks at the *task priority* value before the other standard criteria. (Task priority is a numeric ranking between 0 and 1000 that indicates the task's appropriateness for leveling. Tasks with the lowest priority are delayed or split first.)

9   Make sure that the **Level only within available slack** check box is cleared.

Tip   Remember that to *clear* a check box means to remove a check from the check box, and to *select* a check box means to put a check in it. You can toggle the selection state of a check box by clicking it.

Clearing this check box allows Project to extend the project's finish date, if necessary, to resolve resource allocations.

Selecting this check box would prevent Project from extending the project's finish date in order to resolve resource overallocations. Instead, Project would use only the free slack within the existing schedule. Depending on the project, this might not be adequate to fully resolve resource overallocations.

10   Make sure that the **Leveling can adjust individual assignments on a task** check box is selected.

This allows Project to add leveling delay (or split work on assignments if **Leveling can create splits in remaining work** is also selected) independently of any other resources assigned to the same task. This might cause resources to start and finish work on a task at different times.

11   Make sure that the **Leveling can create splits in remaining work** check box is selected.

This allows Project to split work on a task (or on an assignment if **Leveling can adjust individual assignments on a task** is also selected) as a way of resolving an overallocation. Your screen should look similar to the following illustration:

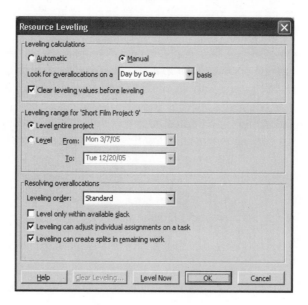

Part II: Advanced Project Scheduling
Fine-Tuning the Project Plan **9**

> **Tip** *This tip describes enterprise project management (EPM) functionality.* If you have Project Professional, you'll see additional items in the **Level Resources** dialog box that relate to enterprise resource features enabled by Project Server. For more information, see Part 4, "Introducing Project Server."

12 Click the **Level Now** button.

13 Project asks whether you want to level the entire pool or only selected resources. Leave **Entire Pool** selected, and click **OK**.

Project levels the overallocated resources.

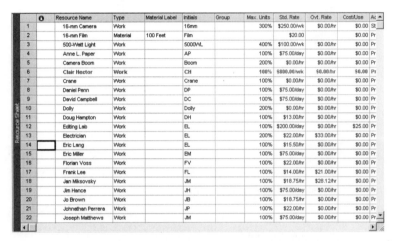

	ⓘ	Resource Name	Type	Material Label	Initials	Group	Max. Units	Std. Rate	Ovt. Rate	Cost/Use	Ac
1		16-mm Camera	Work		16mm		300%	$250.00/wk	$0.00/hr	$0.00	St
2		16-mm Film	Material	100 Feet	Film			$20.00		$0.00	Pr
3		500-Watt Light	Work		5000VVL		400%	$100.00/wk	$0.00/hr	$0.00	Pr
4		Anne L. Paper	Work		AP		100%	$75.00/day	$0.00/hr	$0.00	Pr
5		Camera Boom	Work		Boom		200%	$0.00/hr	$0.00/hr	$0.00	Pr
6		Clair Hector	Work		CH		100%	$800.00/wk	$0.00/hr	$0.00	Pr
7		Crane	Work		Crane		100%	$0.00/hr	$0.00/hr	$0.00	Pr
8		Daniel Penn	Work		DP		100%	$75.00/day	$0.00/hr	$0.00	Pr
9		David Campbell	Work		DC		100%	$75.00/day	$0.00/hr	$0.00	Pr
10		Dolly	Work		Dolly		200%	$0.00/hr	$0.00/hr	$0.00	Pr
11		Doug Hampton	Work		DH		100%	$13.00/hr	$0.00/hr	$0.00	Pr
12		Editing Lab	Work		EL		100%	$200.00/day	$0.00/hr	$25.00	Pr
13		Electrician	Work		EL		200%	$22.00/hr	$33.00/hr	$0.00	Pr
14		Eric Lang	Work		EL		100%	$15.50/hr	$0.00/hr	$0.00	Pr
15		Eric Miller	Work		EM		100%	$75.00/day	$0.00/hr	$0.00	Pr
16		Florian Voss	Work		FV		100%	$22.00/hr	$0.00/hr	$0.00	Pr
17		Frank Lee	Work		FL		100%	$14.00/hr	$21.00/hr	$0.00	Pr
18		Jan Miksovsky	Work		JM		100%	$18.75/hr	$28.12/hr	$0.00	Pr
19		Jim Hance	Work		JH		100%	$75.00/day	$0.00/hr	$0.00	Pr
20		Jo Brown	Work		JB		100%	$18.75/hr	$0.00/hr	$0.00	Pr
21		Johnathan Perrera	Work		JP		100%	$22.00/hr	$0.00/hr	$0.00	Pr
22		Joseph Matthews	Work		JM		100%	$75.00/day	$0.00/hr	$0.00	Pr

Notice that the Overallocated indicators are gone, although some resource names still appear in red. This means that some resources are still overallocated hour by hour (or minute by minute) but not day by day.

Next you will look at the project plan before and after leveling, using the Leveling Gantt view.

14 On the **View** menu, click **More Views**, click **Leveling Gantt**, and then click the **Apply** button.

Project switches to the Leveling Gantt view.

15 Click the name of task 8, **Apply for filming permits**.

189

Go To Selected
Task

16 On the Standard toolbar, click the **Go To Selected Task** button.

This view gives you a better look at some of the tasks that were affected by leveling:

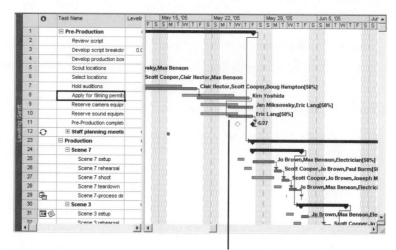

In the Leveling Gantt view, the bar on top represents the prelevel schedule of the task. The bar below represents the schedule after leveling.

Notice that each task now has two bars. The green bar on top represents the preleveled task. You can see a task's preleveled start, finish, and duration by pointing to a green bar. The blue bar on the bottom represents the leveled task.

Project was able to resolve the resource overallocations. For this particular project, leveling pushed out the project finish date by two days.

Examining Project Costs

Not all project plans include cost information, but for those that do, keeping track of project costs can be as important as or more important than keeping track of the scheduled finish date. Two factors to consider when examining project costs are the specific types of costs you want to see and how you can best see them.

The types of costs you might have over the life of a project include the following:

■ Baseline costs: The original planned task, resource, or assignment costs saved as part of a baseline plan.

■ Current (or scheduled) costs: The calculated costs of tasks, resources, and assignments in a project plan. As you make adjustments in a project plan, such as assigning or removing resources, Project recalculates current costs, just as it recalculates task start and finish dates. After you start incurring actual costs (normally by tracking actual work), the current cost equals the actual cost plus remaining cost per task, resource, or assignment. Current costs are the values you see in fields labeled *Cost* or *Total Cost*.

- Actual costs: The costs that have been incurred for tasks, resources, or assignments.

- Remaining costs: The difference between the current or scheduled costs and the actual costs for tasks, resources, or assignments.

You might need to compare these costs (baseline vs. actual, for example), or examine them individually per task, resource, or assignment. Or you might need to examine cost values for summary tasks or for an entire project plan. Some common ways to see these types of costs include the following:

- You can see the entire project's current, baseline, actual, and remaining costs in the **Project Statistics** dialog box (on the **Project** menu, click **Project Information**, and then click **Statistics**).

- You can see or print formatted reports that include cash flow, budget, overbudget tasks or resources, and earned value (on the **View** menu, click **Reports**, and then click the **Costs** button).

See Also   Earned value is a powerful schedule analysis tool that relies on cost information in a project plan. For more information, see Chapter 19, "Measuring Performance with Earned Value Analysis."

- You can see task, resource, or assignment-level cost information in usage views by displaying the Cost table (on the **View** menu, point to **Table: Entry**, and then click **Cost**).

Tip   When printing usage views, you can include cost totals. You can include row totals when printing date ranges from a usage view (on the **File** menu, click **Page Setup**, and in the **Page Setup** dialog box, click the **View** tab, and select the **Print row totals for values within print date range** check box). You can also include column totals in usage views (on the **File** menu, click **Page Setup**; in the **Page Setup** dialog box, click the **View** tab, and select the **Print column totals** check box).

In this exercise, you look at the overall project costs and at individual task costs.

1   On the **View** menu, click **More Views**, click **Task Sheet**, and then click the **Apply** button.

Project switches to the Task Sheet view. Next you will display the project summary task to see the top-level or rolled-up values of the project.

2   On the **Tools** menu, click **Options**.

3   In the **Options** dialog box, click the **View** tab.

4 Under the **Outline options for** label, select the **Show project summary task** check box, and then click the **OK** button.

Project displays the project summary task at the top of the Task Sheet view. Next you will switch to the Cost table.

5 On the **View** menu, point to **Table: Entry**, and click **Cost**.

The Cost table appears.

6 Double-click between the text in the column labels to widen any columns that display pound signs (##).

Your screen should look like the following illustration:

	Task Name	Fixed Cost	Fixed Cost Accrual	Total Cost	Baseline	Variance	Actual	Remaining
0	⊟ **Short Film Project**	**$0.00**	**Prorated**	**$88,642.85**	**$89,014.85**	**($372.00)**	**$0.00**	**$88,642.85**
1	⊟ **Pre-Production**	**$0.00**	**Prorated**	**$23,794.00**	**$24,166.00**	**($372.00)**	**$0.00**	**$23,794.00**
2	Review script	$0.00	Prorated	$947.50	$947.50	$0.00	$0.00	$947.50
3	Develop script break	$0.00	Prorated	$2,455.00	$2,455.00	$0.00	$0.00	$2,455.00
4	Develop production l	$0.00	Prorated	$8,124.00	$8,124.00	$0.00	$0.00	$8,124.00
5	Scout locations	$0.00	Prorated	$4,920.00	$4,920.00	$0.00	$0.00	$4,920.00
6	Select locations	$0.00	Prorated	$2,535.00	$2,535.00	$0.00	$0.00	$2,535.00
7	Hold auditions	$0.00	Prorated	$1,887.00	$1,887.00	$0.00	$0.00	$1,887.00
8	Apply for filming per	$500.00	Start	$876.00	$876.00	$0.00	$0.00	$876.00
9	Reserve camera equ	$0.00	Prorated	$636.00	$822.00	($186.00)	$0.00	$636.00
10	Reserve sound equi	$0.00	Prorated	$186.00	$372.00	($186.00)	$0.00	$186.00
11	Pre-Production comp	$0.00	Prorated	$0.00	$0.00	$0.00	$0.00	$0.00
12	⊞ **Staff planning me**	**$0.00**	**Prorated**	**$1,227.50**	**$1,227.50**	**$0.00**	**$0.00**	**$1,227.50**
23	⊟ **Production**	**$0.00**	**Prorated**	**$36,380.95**	**$36,380.95**	**$0.00**	**$0.00**	**$36,380.95**
24	⊟ **Scene 7**	**$0.00**	**Prorated**	**$3,702.50**	**$3,702.50**	**$0.00**	**$0.00**	**$3,702.50**
25	Scene 7 setup	$0.00	Prorated	$322.50	$322.50	$0.00	$0.00	$322.50
26	Scene 7 rehears:	$0.00	Prorated	$705.00	$705.00	$0.00	$0.00	$705.00
27	Scene 7 shoot	$0.00	Prorated	$2,245.00	$2,245.00	$0.00	$0.00	$2,245.00
28	Scene 7 teardov	$0.00	Prorated	$430.00	$430.00	$0.00	$0.00	$430.00
29	Scene 7-process	$0.00	Prorated	$0.00	$0.00	$0.00	$0.00	$0.00
30	⊟ **Scene 3**	**$0.00**	**Prorated**	**$4,180.40**	**$4,180.40**	**$0.00**	**$0.00**	**$4,180.40**
31	Scene 3 setup	$0.00	Prorated	$518.00	$518.00	$0.00	$0.00	$518.00

Here you can see many types of cost values for the overall project, project phases (summary tasks), and individual tasks. At this point in the project life cycle, the project plan includes a baseline, so you see values in the **Baseline** column; some assignment adjustments were made earlier in this chapter, so you see some values in the **Variance** column; but it does not yet contain any actual progress, so the **Actual** column contains only zero values.

Checking the Project's Finish Date

A project's finish date is a function of its duration and start date. Most projects have a desired, or *soft,* finish date, and many projects have a "must hit," or hard, finish date. When managing projects like these, it is essential that you know the project's current or scheduled finish date and understand how the adjustments you make in the planning stage affect the finish date.

In the language of project management, a project's finish date is determined by its *critical path*. The critical path is the series of tasks that will push out the project's end date if the tasks are delayed. For this reason, when evaluating the duration of a project, you should focus mainly on the tasks on the critical path, called critical tasks.

Tip   Remember that the word *critical* has nothing to do with how important these tasks are to the overall project. The word refers only to how their scheduling will affect the project's finish date.

In this exercise, you look at the project's critical path and finish date.

1   On the **Project** menu, click **Project Information**.

The **Project Information** dialog box appears.

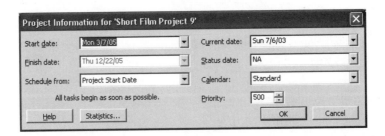

Tip   *This tip describes enterprise project management (EPM) functionality.* If you are running Project Professional, you will see a slightly different dialog box. The **Project Information** dialog box in Project Professional includes an **Enterprise Custom Fields** section. Enterprise custom fields are used only with Project Server. For more information about Project Server, see Part 4, "Introducing Project Server."

In the **Project Information** dialog box you can see the current or scheduled finish date for the project: December 22, 2005. Note that you can edit the start date of the project here, but not its finish date. Project has calculated this finish date based on the start date plus the overall duration of the project. This project is scheduled from the start date, as the **Schedule from** box indicates. In some cases you might want to schedule a project from a finish date, in which case you enter the finish date and task information and Project calculates the start date.

Tip   It might sound tempting to schedule a project from a finish date, especially if it has a hard "must-hit" deadline. However, in nearly all cases you should resist this temptation and instead schedule from a start date. To learn more about the effects of scheduling from a finish date, type **About scheduling a project from a finish date** into the **Search** box in the upper right corner of the Project window.

Next you will look at the duration values for this project.

2   In the **Project Information** dialog box, click the **Statistics** button.

The **Project Statistics** dialog box appears:

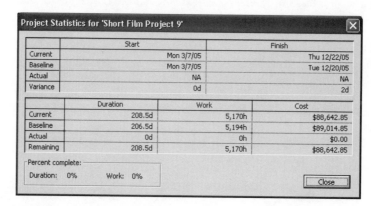

Project Statistics for 'Short Film Project 9'			✕

	Start		Finish
Current	Mon 3/7/05		Thu 12/22/05
Baseline	Mon 3/7/05		Tue 12/20/05
Actual	NA		NA
Variance	0d		2d

	Duration	Work	Cost
Current	208.5d	5,170h	$88,642.85
Baseline	206.5d	5,194h	$89,014.85
Actual	0d	0h	$0.00
Remaining	208.5d	5,170h	$88,642.85

Percent complete:
Duration: 0%   Work: 0%

Close

Here you can see the project's current, baseline, and actual start and finish dates, as well as its schedule variance.

This project currently has no actual work reported, so you see *NA* in the **Actual Start** and **Actual Finish** fields, and zero values in the **Actual Duration** and **Actual Work** fields.

3   Click the **Close** button to close the **Project Statistics** dialog box. To conclude this exercise, you will look at the critical path.

4   On the **Project Guide** toolbar, click the **Report** button.

5   In the Report pane, click the **See the project's critical tasks** link.

The Project Guide: Critical Tasks view replaces the Task Sheet view. In the Critical Path pane, you can see the current scheduled finish date and apply a *filter* to the view.

6   Click the **Show/Hide Project Guide** button on the **Project Guide** toolbar.

Show/Hide
Project Guide

The Project Guide closes.

7   On the **Edit** menu, click **Go To**.

8   In the **ID** box, type 30, and then click **OK**.

Project scrolls the view to show task 30, the Scene 3 summary task. Your screen should look like the following illustration:

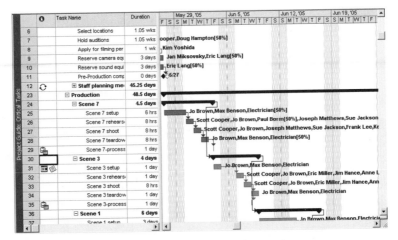

Here you can see both critical tasks (their Gantt bars are red) and noncritical tasks (blue). Any changes to the durations of critical tasks will affect the project finish date. However, changes to the noncritical tasks won't necessarily affect the project finish date, depending on available slack. When you make adjustments to the project plan, and especially after you start tracking actual work, the specific tasks on the critical path are likely to change. For this reason you should frequently check the project finish date and the critical tasks that determine it.

CLOSE: the Short Film Project 9 file.

Key Points

- A resource's maximum units (Max. Units) value determines when the resource becomes overallocated.

- The Resource Usage view enables you to see the details of assignments that cause resource overallocation.

- You can manually or automatically resolve resource overallocations.

- When editing a resource assignment value (such as assignment units), you can use a Smart Tag to change the scheduling effect of your action.

- You can view cost details from the individual assignment level all the way to the entire project level.

- The tasks on the critical path determine the project finish date.

Sort task or resource data,
page 198

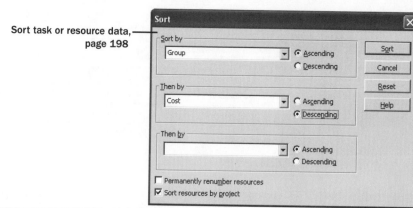

Group tasks or resources
and show summary or
"roll-up" values per grouping,
page 202

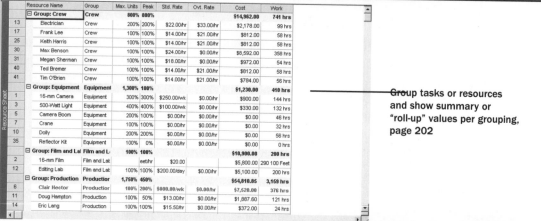

Apply custom filters to show just
the data you want to see,
page 207

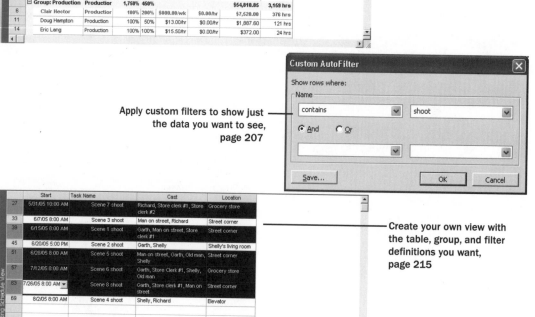

Create your own view with
the table, group, and filter
definitions you want,
page 215

10 Organizing and Formatting Project Details

In this chapter you will learn to:

✔ Sort task and resource data.

✔ Display task and resource data in groups.

✔ Filter or highlight task and resource data.

✔ Create a custom table.

✔ Create a custom view.

See Also Do you need a quick refresher on the topics in this chapter? See the quick reference entries on pages xxxi–xxxii.

After you've built a project plan, chances are you will need to examine specific aspects of it for your own analysis or to share with other *stakeholders*. Although the built-in views, tables, and reports in Microsoft Office Project 2003 provide many ways to examine a project plan, you might need to organize information to suit your own specific needs.

In this chapter, you use some of the formatting tools in Project to change the way your data appears. Project includes powerful features that enable you to organize and analyze data that otherwise would require separate tools, such as a spreadsheet application.

Important Before you can use the practice files in this chapter, be sure you install them from the book's companion CD to their default location. See "Using the Book's CD-ROM," on page xiii, for more information.

Sorting Project Details

Sorting is the simplest way to reorganize task or resource data in Project. You can sort tasks or resources by predefined criteria, or you can create your own sort order with up to three levels of nesting. For example, you can sort resources by resource group and then sort by cost within each resource group.

Like grouping and filtering, which you will work with in later sections, sorting does not (with one exception) change the underlying data of your project plan; it simply reorders the data you have. The one exception is the option it offers to renumber task or resource IDs after sorting. After tasks or resources are renumbered, you cannot restore their original numbered sequence.

However, it's fine to permanently renumber tasks or resources if that's what you intend to do. For example, when building a resource list, you might enter resource names in the order in which the resources join your project. Later, when the list is complete, you might want to sort them alphabetically by name and permanently renumber them.

Each resource in the Short Film Project plan is assigned to one of several resource groups. These groups have names like *Crew, Production, Talent,* and other names that make sense in a film production company. For your project plans, you might use resource groups to represent functional teams, departments, or whatever most logically describes collections of similar resources.

Sorting all resources by resource group enables you to see more easily the costs associated with each resource group. This can help you plan your project's budget. You can also sort resources within each group by cost from most to least expensive.

In this exercise, you sort a resource view.

Important   If you are running Project Professional, you may need to make a one-time adjustment to use the My Computer account and to work offline. This helps ensure that the practice files you work with in this chapter don't affect your Project Server data. For more information, see "Starting Project Professional," on page 10.

OPEN: Short Film Project 10a from the *My Documents**Microsoft Press**Project 2003 Step by Step**Chapter 10 Advanced Formatting* folder. You can also access the practice files for this book by clicking **Start**, **All Programs**, **Microsoft Press**, **Project 2003 Step by Step**, and then selecting the chapter folder of the file you want to open.

1   On the **File** menu, click **Save As**.

     The **Save As** dialog box appears.

2   In the **File name** box, type Short Film Project 10, and then click the **Save** button.

3   On the **View** menu, click **Resource Sheet**.

     The Resource Sheet view appears. By default, the Entry table appears in the Resource Sheet view; however, the Entry table does not display the cost field per resource. You will switch to the Summary table instead.

4   On the **View** menu, point to **Table: Entry**, and then click **Summary**.

     The Summary table appears. Your screen should look similar to the following illustration:

	Resource Name	Group	Max. Units	Peak	Std. Rate	Ovt. Rate	Cost	Work
1	16-mm Camera	Equipment	300%	300%	$250.00/wk	$0.00/hr	$900.00	144 hrs
2	16-mm Film	Film and Lat		eet/hr	$20.00		$5,800.00	290 100 Feet
3	500-Watt Light	Equipment	400%	400%	$100.00/wk	$0.00/hr	$330.00	132 hrs
4	Anne L. Paper	Talent	100%	100%	$75.00/day	$0.00/hr	$731.25	78 hrs
5	Camera Boom	Equipment	200%	100%	$0.00/hr	$0.00/hr	$0.00	46 hrs
6	Clair Hector	Production	100%	200%	$800.00/wk	$0.00/hr	$7,520.00	376 hrs
7	Crane	Equipment	100%	100%	$0.00/hr	$0.00/hr	$0.00	32 hrs
8	Daniel Penn	Talent	100%	100%	$75.00/day	$0.00/hr	$412.50	44 hrs
9	David Campbell	Talent	100%	100%	$75.00/day	$0.00/hr	$2,475.00	264 hrs
10	Dolly	Equipment	200%	200%	$0.00/hr	$0.00/hr	$0.00	56 hrs
11	Doug Hampton	Production	100%	50%	$13.00/hr	$0.00/hr	$1,887.60	121 hrs
12	Editing Lab	Film and Lat	100%	100%	$200.00/day	$0.00/hr	$5,100.00	200 hrs
13	Electrician	Crew	200%	200%	$22.00/hr	$33.00/hr	$2,178.00	99 hrs
14	Eric Lang	Production	100%	100%	$15.50/hr	$0.00/hr	$372.00	24 hrs
15	Eric Miller	Talent	100%	100%	$75.00/day	$0.00/hr	$675.00	72 hrs
16	Florian Voss	Production	100%	100%	$22.00/hr	$0.00/hr	$2,024.00	92 hrs
17	Frank Lee	Crew	100%	100%	$14.00/hr	$21.00/hr	$812.00	58 hrs
18	Jan Miksovsky	Production	100%	100%	$18.75/hr	$28.12/hr	$3,637.00	196 hrs
19	Jim Hance	Talent	100%	100%	$75.00/day	$0.00/hr	$412.50	44 hrs
20	Jo Brown	Production	100%	100%	$18.75/hr	$0.00/hr	$9,037.50	482 hrs
21	Johnathan Perrera	Production	100%	100%	$22.00/hr	$0.00/hr	$4,840.00	220 hrs
22	Joseph Matthews	Talent	100%	100%	$75.00/day	$0.00/hr	$356.25	38 hrs

Now you are ready to sort the Resource Sheet view.

5   On the **Project** menu, point to **Sort**, and click **Sort By**.

The **Sort** dialog box appears.

6   Under **Sort By**, click **Cost** in the drop-down list, and next to that, click **Descending**.

7   Make sure that the **Permanently renumber resources** check box is cleared:

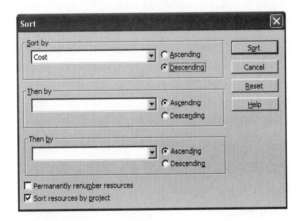

Important   The **Permanently renumber resources** (or when in a task view, the **Permanently renumber tasks**) check box in the **Sort** dialog box is a Project-level (that is, application) setting; if selected, it permanently renumbers resources or tasks in any Project plan in which you sort. Because you might not want to permanently renumber resources or tasks every time you sort, it's a good idea to clear this check box.

8   Click the **Sort** button.

The Summary table in the Resource Sheet view is sorted by the **Cost** column, in descending order. Your screen should look similar to the following illustration:

The Resource Sheet view is now ─┐
sorted by cost, in descending order.

	Resource Name	Group	Max. Units	Peak	Std. Rate	Ovt. Rate	Cost	Work
38	Scott Cooper	Production	100%	200%	$775.00/wk	$0.00/hr	$10,268.75	538 hrs
20	Jo Brown	Production	100%	100%	$18.75/hr	$0.00/hr	$9,037.50	482 hrs
30	Max Benson	Crew	100%	100%	$24.00/hr	$0.00/hr	$8,592.00	358 hrs
6	Clair Hector	Production	100%	200%	$800.00/wk	$0.00/hr	$7,520.00	376 hrs
32	Michael Patten	Production	100%	100%	$700.00/wk	$0.00/hr	$6,230.00	356 hrs
2	16-mm Film	Film and Lab		eet/hr	$20.00		$5,800.00	290 100 Feet
12	Editing Lab	Film and Lab	100%	100%	$200.00/day	$0.00/hr	$5,100.00	200 hrs
21	Johnathan Perrera	Production	100%	100%	$22.00/hr	$0.00/hr	$4,840.00	220 hrs
18	Jan Miksovsky	Production	100%	100%	$18.75/hr	$28.12/hr	$3,637.00	196 hrs
26	Kim Yoshida	Production	100%	100%	$9.40/hr	$0.00/hr	$3,384.00	360 hrs
36	Richard Lum	Production	100%	100%	$625.00/wk	$0.00/hr	$3,125.00	200 hrs
9	David Campbell	Talent	100%	100%	$75.00/day	$0.00/hr	$2,475.00	264 hrs
13	Electrician	Crew	200%	200%	$22.00/hr	$33.00/hr	$2,178.00	99 hrs
16	Florian Voss	Production	100%	100%	$22.00/hr	$0.00/hr	$2,024.00	92 hrs
11	Doug Hampton	Production	100%	50%	$13.00/hr	$0.00/hr	$1,887.60	121 hrs
28	Lisa Garmaise	Production	100%	100%	$9.00/hr	$0.00/hr	$1,440.00	160 hrs
31	Megan Sherman	Crew	100%	100%	$18.00/hr	$0.00/hr	$972.00	54 hrs
34	Paul Borm	Production	50%	50%	$200.00/day	$0.00/hr	$950.00	38 hrs
39	Sue Jackson	Talent	100%	100%	$75.00/day	$0.00/hr	$937.50	100 hrs
1	16-mm Camera	Equipment	300%	300%	$250.00/wk	$0.00/hr	$900.00	144 hrs
17	Frank Lee	Crew	100%	100%	$14.00/hr	$21.00/hr	$812.00	58 hrs
25	Keith Harris	Crew	100%	100%	$14.00/hr	$21.00/hr	$812.00	58 hrs

This arrangement is fine for looking at resource costs in the entire project, but per-haps you'd like to see this data organized by resource group. To see this, you'll apply a two-level sort order.

Tip   When you sort data, the sort order applies to the active view, regardless of the specific table currently displayed in the view. For example, if you sort the Gantt Chart view by start date while displaying the Entry table and then switch to the Cost table, you'll see the tasks sorted by start date in the Cost table.

9   On the **Project** menu, point to **Sort**, and then click **Sort By**.

The **Sort** dialog box appears. In it, you can apply up to three nested levels of sort criteria.

10   Under **Sort By**, click **Group** in the drop-down list, and next to that, click **Ascending**.

Tip   You can sort by any field, not just the fields visible in the active view.

11   Under **Then By** (in the center of the dialog box), click **Cost** in the drop-down list, and next to that, click **Descending**.

12   Make sure that the **Permanently renumber resources** check box is cleared.

Your screen should look similar to the following illustration:

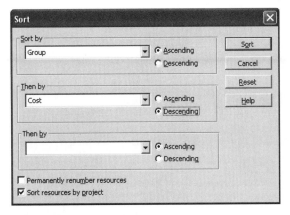

13   Click the **Sort** button.

Project sorts the Resource Sheet view to display resources by group (Crew, Equipment, and so on) and then by cost within each group. Your screen should look similar to the following illustration:

— Now the Resource Sheet view is sorted first by resource group and then within each group by cost.

	Resource Name	Group	Max. Units	Peak	Std. Rate	Ovt. Rate	Cost	Work
30	Max Benson	Crew	100%	100%	$24.00/hr	$0.00/hr	$8,592.00	358 hrs
13	Electrician	Crew	200%	200%	$22.00/hr	$33.00/hr	$2,178.00	99 hrs
31	Megan Sherman	Crew	100%	100%	$18.00/hr	$0.00/hr	$972.00	54 hrs
17	Frank Lee	Crew	100%	100%	$14.00/hr	$21.00/hr	$812.00	58 hrs
25	Keith Harris	Crew	100%	100%	$14.00/hr	$21.00/hr	$812.00	58 hrs
40	Ted Bremer	Crew	100%	100%	$14.00/hr	$21.00/hr	$812.00	58 hrs
41	Tim O'Brien	Crew	100%	100%	$14.00/hr	$21.00/hr	$784.00	56 hrs
1	16-mm Camera	Equipment	300%	300%	$250.00/wk	$0.00/hr	$900.00	144 hrs
3	500-Watt Light	Equipment	400%	400%	$100.00/wk	$0.00/hr	$330.00	132 hrs
5	Camera Boom	Equipment	200%	100%	$0.00/hr	$0.00/hr	$0.00	46 hrs
7	Crane	Equipment	100%	100%	$0.00/hr	$0.00/hr	$0.00	32 hrs
10	Dolly	Equipment	200%	200%	$0.00/hr	$0.00/hr	$0.00	56 hrs
35	Reflector Kit	Equipment	100%	0%	$0.00/hr	$0.00/hr	$0.00	0 hrs
2	16-mm Film	Film and Lab			eet/hr	$20.00	$5,800.00	290 100 Feet
12	Editing Lab	Film and Lab	100%	100%	$200.00/day	$0.00/hr	$5,100.00	200 hrs
38	Scott Cooper	Production	100%	200%	$775.00/wk	$0.00/hr	$10,268.75	530 hrs
20	Jo Brown	Production	100%	100%	$18.75/hr	$0.00/hr	$9,037.50	482 hrs
6	Clair Hector	Production	100%	200%	$800.00/wk	$0.00/hr	$7,520.00	376 hrs
32	Michael Patten	Production	100%	100%	$700.00/wk	$0.00/hr	$6,230.00	356 hrs
21	Johnathan Perrera	Production	100%	100%	$22.00/hr	$0.00/hr	$4,840.00	220 hrs
18	Jan Miksovsky	Production	100%	100%	$18.75/hr	$28.12/hr	$3,637.00	196 hrs
26	Kim Yoshida	Production	100%	100%	$9.40/hr	$0.00/hr	$3,384.00	360 hrs

This sort offers an easy way to identify the most expensive resources in each resource group working on the short film project.

To conclude this exercise, you'll re-sort the resource information to return it to its original order.

14   On the **Project** menu, point to **Sort**, and then click **By ID**.

Project re-sorts the resource list by resource ID.

Note that there is no visual indication that a task or resource view has been sorted other than the order in which the rows of data appear. You cannot save custom sort settings that you have specified, as you can with grouping and filtering. However, the sort order you most recently specified will remain in effect until you re-sort the view.

Grouping Project Details

As you develop a project plan, you can use the default views available in Project to view and analyze your data in several ways. One important way to see the data in task and resource views is by *grouping*. Grouping allows you to organize task or resource information (or, when in a usage view, assignment information) according to criteria you choose. For example, rather than viewing the resource list in the Resource Sheet view sorted by ID, you can view resources sorted by cost. Grouping goes a step beyond just sorting, however. Grouping adds summary values, or "roll-ups," at intervals that you can customize. For example, you can group resources by their cost with a $1,000 interval between groups.

Tip   In some respects, grouping in Project is similar to the Subtotals feature in Excel. In fact, grouping allows you to reorganize and analyze your Project data in ways that would otherwise require you to export your Project data to a spreadsheet program.

Grouping can significantly change the way you view your task or resource data, allowing for a more refined level of data analysis and presentation. Grouping doesn't change the underlying structure of your project plan; it simply reorganizes and summarizes the data. As with sorting, when you group data in a view, the grouping applies to all tables you can display in the view. You can also group the Network Diagram view, which does not contain a table.

Project includes several predefined task and resource groups, such as grouping tasks by duration or resources by standard pay rate. You can also customize any of the built-in groups or create your own.

Tip   You can also use the Project Guide to apply a filter or group to a table or to sort information in a table. On the **Project Guide** toolbar, click **Report**. In the Reports pane, click the **Change the content or order of information in a view** link.

In this exercise, you group resources by their Group name (this is the value in the *Group field—Crew, Equipment,* and so on). This is similar to the sorting you did in the previous section, but this time you will see summary cost values for each resource group.

1   On the **Project** menu, point to **Group By: No Group**, and then click **Resource Group.**

Project reorganizes the resource data into resource groups, adds summary cost values per group, and presents the data in an expanded outline form. Your screen should look similar to the following illustration:

After grouping resources by the Group field,
Project adds summary values for each group.

	Resource Name	Group	Max. Units	Peak	Std. Rate	Ovt. Rate	Cost	Work
	⊟ **Group: Crew**	**Crew**	**800%**	**800%**			**$14,962.00**	**741 hrs**
13	Electrician	Crew	200%	200%	$22.00/hr	$33.00/hr	$2,178.00	99 hrs
17	Frank Lee	Crew	100%	100%	$14.00/hr	$21.00/hr	$812.00	58 hrs
25	Keith Harris	Crew	100%	100%	$14.00/hr	$21.00/hr	$812.00	58 hrs
30	Max Benson	Crew	100%	100%	$24.00/hr	$0.00/hr	$8,592.00	358 hrs
31	Megan Sherman	Crew	100%	100%	$18.00/hr	$0.00/hr	$972.00	54 hrs
40	Ted Bremer	Crew	100%	100%	$14.00/hr	$21.00/hr	$812.00	58 hrs
41	Tim O'Brien	Crew	100%	100%	$14.00/hr	$21.00/hr	$784.00	56 hrs
	⊟ **Group: Equipment**	**Equipment**	**1,300%**	**100%**			**$1,230.00**	**410 hrs**
1	16-mm Camera	Equipment	300%	300%	$250.00/wk	$0.00/hr	$900.00	144 hrs
3	500-Watt Light	Equipment	400%	400%	$100.00/wk	$0.00/hr	$330.00	132 hrs
5	Camera Boom	Equipment	200%	100%	$0.00/hr	$0.00/hr	$0.00	46 hrs
7	Crane	Equipment	100%	100%	$0.00/hr	$0.00/hr	$0.00	32 hrs
10	Dolly	Equipment	200%	200%	$0.00/hr	$0.00/hr	$0.00	56 hrs
35	Reflector Kit	Equipment	100%	0%	$0.00/hr	$0.00/hr	$0.00	0 hrs
	⊟ **Group: Film and Lal**	**Film and L:**	**100%**	**100%**			**$10,900.00**	**200 hrs**
2	16-mm Film	Film and Lat			eet/hr	$20.00	$5,800.00	290 100 Feet
12	Editing Lab	Film and Lat	100%	100%	$200.00/day	$0.00/hr	$5,100.00	200 hrs
	⊟ **Group: Production**	**Production**	**1,750%**	**450%**			**$54,810.85**	**3,159 hrs**
6	Clair Hector	Production	100%	200%	$800.00/wk	$0.00/hr	$7,520.00	376 hrs
11	Doug Hampton	Production	100%	50%	$13.00/hr	$0.00/hr	$1,887.60	121 hrs
14	Eric Lang	Production	100%	100%	$15.50/hr	$0.00/hr	$372.00	24 hrs

Project applies colored formatting (in this case, a yellow background) to the summary data rows. Because the summary data is derived from subordinate data, you cannot edit it directly. Displaying these summary values has no effect on the cost or schedule calculations of the project plan.

This arrangement of the resource cost information is similar to the sorting you did in the previous section. To give yourself more control over how Project organizes and presents the data, you'll now create a group.

2   On the **Project** menu, point to **Group By: Resource Group**, and then click **More Groups**.

The **More Groups** dialog box appears:

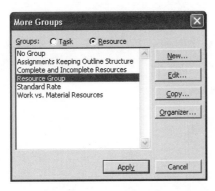

In this dialog box you can see all the available predefined groups for tasks (when in a task view) and resources (when in a resource view). Your new group will be most similar to the Resource Group, so you'll start by copying it.

3   Make sure that **Resource Group** is selected, and then click the **Copy** button.

The **Group Definition in** dialog box appears.

4   In the **Name** box, type Resource Groups by Cost.

5   In the **Field Name** column, click the first empty cell below **Group**.

6   Type or select Cost.

7   In the **Order** column, select **Descending** for the **Cost** field.

The resources will be sorted within their groups by cost from highest to lowest values.

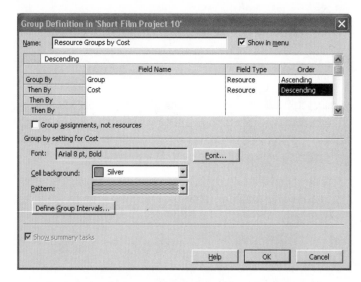

Next you'll fine-tune the cost intervals at which Project will group the resources.

8   Click the **Define Group Intervals** button.

The **Define Group Interval** dialog box appears.

9   In the **Group on** box, select **Interval**.

10   In the **Group interval** box, type 1000.

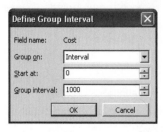

11 Click the **OK** button.

12 Click **OK** again to close the **Group Definition in** dialog box.

 Resource Groups by Cost appears as a new group in the **More Groups** dialog box.

13 Click the **Apply** button.

 Project applies the new group to the Resource Sheet view. To get a better look at the groupings, you'll need to widen the **Resource Name** column.

14 Double-click the **Resource Name** column heading.

 The **Column Definition** dialog box appears.

15 Click the **Best Fit** button.

 Project widens the **Resource Name** column. Your screen should look similar to the following illustration:

After applying a two-level group, information is grouped
first by resource group and then within each group by cost.

	Resource Name	Group	Max. Units	Peak	Std. Rate	Ovt. Rate	Cost	Work
	Group: Crew	**Crew**	**800%**	**800%**			**$14,962.00**	**741 hrs**
	Cost: $8,000.00 - <$9,000.00	**Crew**	**100%**	**100%**			**$8,592.00**	**358 hrs**
30	Max Benson	Crew	100%	100%	$24.00/hr	$0.00/hr	$8,592.00	358 hrs
	Cost: $2,000.00 - <$3,000.00	**Crew**	**200%**	**200%**			**$2,178.00**	**99 hrs**
13	Electrician	Crew	200%	200%	$22.00/hr	$33.00/hr	$2,178.00	99 hrs
	Cost: $0.00 - <$1,000.00	**Crew**	**500%**	**500%**			**$4,192.00**	**284 hrs**
17	Frank Lee	Crew	100%	100%	$14.00/hr	$21.00/hr	$812.00	58 hrs
25	Keith Harris	Crew	100%	100%	$14.00/hr	$21.00/hr	$812.00	58 hrs
31	Megan Sherman	Crew	100%	100%	$18.00/hr	$0.00/hr	$972.00	54 hrs
40	Ted Bremer	Crew	100%	100%	$14.00/hr	$21.00/hr	$812.00	58 hrs
41	Tim O'Brien	Crew	100%	100%	$14.00/hr	$21.00/hr	$784.00	56 hrs
	Group: Equipment	**Equipment**	**1,300%**	**100%**			**$1,230.00**	**410 hrs**
	Cost: $0.00 - <$1,000.00	**Equipment**	**1,300%**	**100%**			**$1,230.00**	**410 hrs**
1	16-mm Camera	Equipment	300%	300%	$250.00/wk	$0.00/hr	$900.00	144 hrs
3	500-Watt Light	Equipment	400%	400%	$100.00/wk	$0.00/hr	$330.00	132 hrs
5	Camera Boom	Equipment	200%	100%	$0.00/hr	$0.00/hr	$0.00	46 hrs
7	Crane	Equipment	100%	100%	$0.00/hr	$0.00/hr	$0.00	32 hrs
10	Dolly	Equipment	200%	200%	$0.00/hr	$0.00/hr	$0.00	56 hrs
35	Reflector Kit	Equipment	100%	0%	$0.00/hr	$0.00/hr	$0.00	0 hrs
	Group: Film and Lab	**Film and L**	**100%**	**100%**			**$10,900.00**	**200 hrs**
	Cost: $5,000.00 - <$6,000.00	**Film and L**	**100%**	**100%**			**$10,900.00**	**200 hrs**
2	16-mm Film	Film and Lab		eet/hr	$20.00		$5,800.00	290 100 Feet

The resources are grouped by their resource group value (the yellow bands that bind together Crew, Equipment, and so on) and within each group by cost values at $1,000 intervals (the gray bands).

To conclude this exercise, you'll remove the grouping.

16 On the **Project** menu, point to **Group By: Resource Groups By Cost**, and click **No Group**.

 Project removes the summary values and outline structure, leaving the original data. Displaying or removing a group has no effect on the data in the project.

No Group ▾

Group By

Tip   All predefined groups and any groups you create are available to you through the **Group By** button on the Standard toolbar. The name of the active group appears on this button, which resembles a box with a drop-down list. Click the arrow in the **Group By** button to see other group names. If no group is applied to the current table, *No Group* appears on the button.

To learn more about using groups, type **Available groups** into the **Search** box in the upper right corner of the Project window. The **Search** box initially contains the text *Type a question for help*.

Filtering Project Details

Another useful way to change the way you view Project task and resource information is by *filtering*. As the name suggests, filtering hides task or resource data that does not meet the criteria you specify, displaying only the data you're interested in. Like grouping, filtering does not change the data in your Project plan; it just changes the way that data appears.

There are two ways to use filters. Either apply predefined filters to a view, or apply an *AutoFilter* to a view:

■   Apply a predefined or custom filter to see or highlight only the task or resource information that meets the criteria of the filter. For example, the Critical Task filter displays only the tasks on the critical path. Some predefined filters, such as the Task Range filter, prompt you to enter specific criteria—for example, a range of task IDs. If a task or resource sheet view has a filter applied, the filter name appears in the **Filter** button on the Formatting toolbar.

■   Use AutoFilters for ad hoc filtering in any table in Project. When the AutoFilter feature is turned on, small arrows appear next to the names of column headings. Click the arrow to display a list of criteria by which you can filter the data. Which criteria you see depends on the type of data contained in the column—for example, AutoFilter criteria in a date column include choices like *Today* and *This month,* as well as a *Custom* option, with which you can specify your own criteria. You use AutoFilter in Project in the same way you might use AutoFilter in Excel.

Both types of filters hide rows in task or resource sheet views that do not meet the criteria you specify. You might see gaps in the task or resource ID numbers. The "missing" data is only hidden and not deleted. As with sorting and grouping, when you filter data in a view, the filtering applies to all tables you can display in the view. Views that do not include tables, such as the Calendar and Network Diagram views, also support filtering (through the **Filtered For** command on the **Project** menu), but not AutoFilters.

A commonly used format for communicating schedule information on a film project is called a *shooting schedule.* In this exercise, you create a filter that displays only the uncompleted film shoot tasks. In later sections, you'll combine this filter with a custom table and a custom view to create a complete shooting schedule for everyone on the film project.

1   On the **View** menu, click **Gantt Chart**.

The Gantt Chart view appears. Before you create a filter, you'll quickly see the tasks you're interested in by applying an AutoFilter.

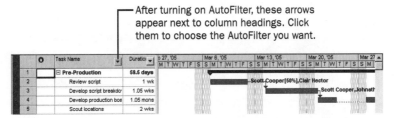

2   On the Formatting toolbar, click the **AutoFilter** button.

Project displays arrows to the right of the column headings. Your screen should look like the following illustration:

3   Click the down arrow in the **Task Name** column heading, and then click (**Custom**).

The **Custom AutoFilter** dialog box appears. You'd like to see just the tasks that contain the word *shoot*.

4   Under **Name**, make sure **contains** appears in the first box.

5   In the adjacent box, type shoot.

6   Click **OK** to close the **Custom AutoFilter** dialog box.

Project filters the task list to show only the tasks that contain the word *shoot* and their summary tasks. Your screen should look similar to the following illustration:

After applying an AutoFilter, the filtered column
name and its AutoFilter arrow are formatted in blue.

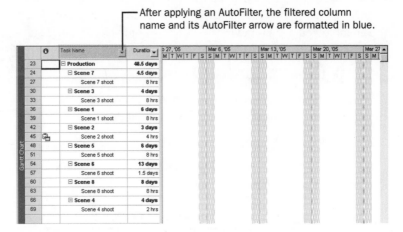

Note that the **Task Name** column heading and arrow appear in blue. These are visual indicators that an AutoFilter has been applied to this view.

Next you turn off the AutoFilter and create a custom filter.

7   On the Formatting toolbar, click the **AutoFilter** button.

Project toggles the AutoFilter off, redisplaying all tasks in the project plan. Now you are ready to create a custom filter.

8   On the **Project** menu, point to **Filtered For: All Tasks**, and then click **More Filters**.

The **More Filters** dialog box appears:

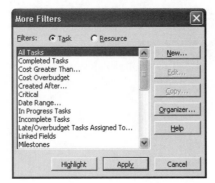

In this dialog box you can see all the predefined filters for tasks (when in a task view) and resources (when in a resource view) available to you.

9   Click the **New** button.

The **Filter Definition in** dialog box appears.

10   In the **Name** box, type Uncompleted Shoots.

11   In the first row in the **Field Name** column, type or select Name.

12   In the first row in the **Test** column, select **contains**.

13   In the first row in the **Value(s)** column, type shoot.

That covers the first criterion for the filter; next you'll add the second criterion.

14   In the second row in the **And/Or** column, select **And**.

15   In the second row in the **Field Name** column, type or select Actual Finish.

16   In the second row in the **Test** column, select **equals**.

17   In the second row in the **Value(s)** column, type NA.

NA means "not applicable" and is the way Project marks some fields that have no value yet. In other words, any shooting task that does not have an actual finish date must be uncompleted.

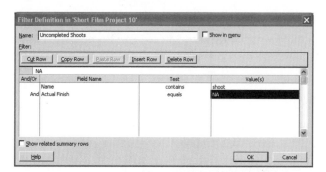

18   Click **OK** to close the **Filter Definition in** dialog box.

The new filter appears in the **More Filters** dialog box.

19   Click the **Apply** button.

Project applies the new filter to the Gantt Chart view. Your screen should look similar to the following illustration:

After applying a filter, Project hides information that does not meet the filter's criteria. Note the gaps in the task IDs; this is one visual clue that a filter has been applied.

Now the tasks are filtered to show only the uncompleted shooting tasks. Because we haven't started tracking actual work yet, all the shooting tasks are uncompleted at this time.

Tip   Rather than hiding tasks that do not meet the filter criteria, you can highlight those that do in blue. Click the **Highlight** button instead of the **Apply** button in the **More Filters** dialog box.

To conclude this exercise, you will remove the filtering.

20   On the **Project** menu, point to **Filtered For: Uncompleted Shoots**, and then click **All Tasks**.

Project removes the filter. As always, displaying or removing a filter has no effect on the original data.

Tip   All filters are also available to you through the **Filter** button on the Formatting toolbar. The name of the active filter appears in this button; click the arrow next to the filter name to see other filters. If no filter is applied to the current view, *All Tasks* or *All Resources* appears on the button, depending on the type of view currently displayed.

To learn more about the filters available in Project, type **About filters** or **Available filters** into the **Search** box in the upper right corner of the Project window.

Customizing Tables

As you might already know, a table is a spreadsheet-like presentation of project data, organized into vertical columns and horizontal rows. Each column represents one of the many fields in Project, and each row represents a single task or resource (or in usage views, an assignment). The intersection of a column and a row can be called a cell (if you're oriented toward spreadsheets) or a field (if you think in database terms).

Project includes several tables that can be applied in views. You've already used some of these tables, such as the Entry table and the Summary table. Chances are that these tables will contain the fields you want most of the time. However, you can modify any predefined table, or you can create a new table that contains only the data you want.

In this exercise, you create a table to display the information found on a shooting schedule, a common format for presenting schedule information in film projects.

1 On the **View** menu, click **More Views**.

The **More Views** dialog box appears.

2 Click **Task Sheet**, and then click the **Apply** button.

Project displays the Task Sheet view.

3 On the **View** menu, point to **Table: Entry**, and then click **More Tables**.

The **More Tables** dialog box appears:

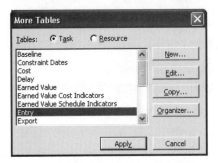

In this dialog box you can see all the available predefined tables for tasks (when in a task view) and resources (when in a resource view).

4 Make sure that **Task** is the active option, and then in the list of tables, make sure that **Entry** is selected.

5 Click the **Copy** button.

The **Table Definition in** dialog box appears.

6 In the **Name** box, type Shooting Schedule Table.

Next you will remove several fields, add others, and then put the remaining fields in the order you want.

7   In the **Field Name** column, click each of the following field names, and then click the **Delete Row** button after clicking each field name:

Indicators

Duration

Finish

Predecessors

Resource Names

After you've deleted these fields, your screen should look similar to the following:

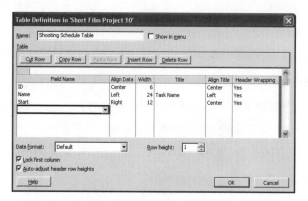

Next you will add some fields to this table definition.

8   In the **Field Name** column, click the down arrow in the next empty cell below **Start**, and then select **Cast (Text9)** from the drop-down list.

9   In the **Align Data** column in the same row, click **Left**.

As soon as you click in the **Align Data** column, Project completes row entries for the **Cast** field name by adding data to the **Width** and **Align Title** columns.

10   In the **Width** column, type or click 25.

11   In the **Field Name** column in the next empty row below **Cast**, click **Location (Text10)** in the drop-down list.

12   In the **Align Data** column, click **Left**.

13   In the **Width** column, type or click 15.

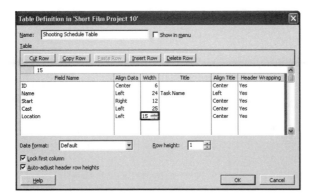

The two customized text fields Cast (Text9) and Location (Text10) contain the character names and film locations for the shooting tasks. These were previously customized in the project plan.

The remaining work to complete this table definition is to reorder the fields to match the order commonly found on a shooting schedule.

14 In the **Field Name** column, click **Start**, and then click the **Cut Row** button.

15 In the **Field Name** column, click **Name**, and then click the **Paste Row** button.

16 In the **Date Format** box, click **1/28/02 12:33PM**.

Your screen should look similar to the following illustration:

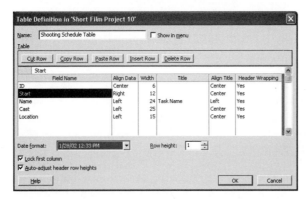

This matches the order in which information is commonly listed on a film-shooting schedule.

17 Click **OK** to close the **Table Definition in** dialog box.

The new table appears in the **More Tables** dialog box.

18 Click the **Apply** button.

Project applies the new table to the Task Sheet view. If the Start column displays pound signs (###), double-click the column heading's right edge to widen it.

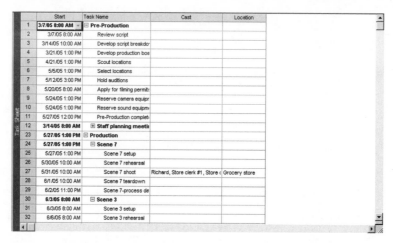

In the next section, you will combine the custom filter with this custom table to create a shooting schedule view for the film project.

Tip To learn more about the tables available in Project, type **Available tables** into the **Search** box in the upper right corner of the Project window.

Customizing Views

Nearly all work you perform in Project occurs in a *view*. A view might contain elements such as tables, groups, and filters. You can combine these with other elements (such as a timescaled grid in a usage view) or with graphic elements (such as the graphic representation of tasks in the chart portion of the Gantt Chart view).

Project includes dozens of views that organize information for specific purposes. You might find that you need to see your project information in some way not available in the predefined views. If Project's available views don't meet your needs, you can edit an existing view or create your own view.

In this exercise, you create a film-shooting schedule view that combines the custom filter and custom table you created in the previous sections. The view you create will more closely match a standard format used in the film industry.

1   On the **View** menu, click **More Views**.

The **More Views** dialog box appears:

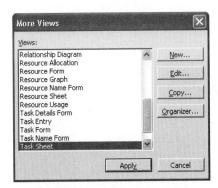

In this dialog box you can see all the predefined views available to you.

2   Click the **New** button.

The **Define New View** dialog box appears. Most views occupy a single pane, but a view can consist of two separate panes.

3   Make sure **Single View** is selected, and then click **OK**.

The **View Definition in** dialog box appears.

4   In the **Name** box, type Shooting Schedule View.

5   In the **Screen** box, select **Task Sheet** from the drop-down list.

6   In the **Table** box, select **Shooting Schedule Table** from the drop-down list.

The specific tables listed in the drop-down list depend on the type of view you selected in step 5: task-related tables or resource-related tables.

7   In the **Group** box, select **No Group** from the drop-down list.

The specific groups listed in the drop-down list depend on the type of view you selected in step 5.

8   In the **Filter** box, select **Uncompleted Shoots** from the drop-down list.

The specific filters listed in the drop-down list depend on the type of view you selected in step 5.

9   Select the **Show in menu** check box.

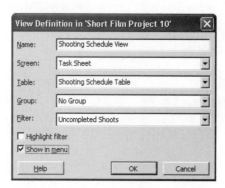

10   Click **OK** to close the **View Definition in** dialog box.

The new view appears and should be selected in the **More Views** dialog box.

11   Click the **Apply** button.

Project applies the new view. Your screen should look similar to the following illustration:

This custom view is arranged like a shooting schedule, a standard format in the film industry.

	Start	Task Name	Cast	Location
27	5/31/05 10:00 A	Scene 7 shoot	Richard, Store clerk #1, Store c	Grocery store
33	6/7/05 8:00 AM	Scene 3 shoot	Man on street, Richard	Street corner
39	6/15/05 8:00 AM	Scene 1 shoot	Garth, Man on street, Store cle	Street corner
45	6/20/05 5:00 PM	Scene 2 shoot	Garth, Shelly	Shelly's living roon
51	6/28/05 8:00 AM	Scene 5 shoot	Man on street, Garth, Old man,	Street corner
57	7/12/05 8:00 AM	Scene 6 shoot	Garth, Store Clerk #1, Shelly, C	Grocery store
63	7/26/05 8:00 AM	Scene 8 shoot	Garth, Store clerk #1, Man on s	Street corner
69	8/2/05 8:00 AM	Scene 4 shoot	Shelly, Richard	Elevator

Now only uncompleted shoots are displayed, and the fields appear in an order consistent with a standard shooting schedule for a film project. Also, Project added the Shooting Schedule view to the **View** menu. This view will be saved with this Project plan, and you can use it whenever you want.

To conclude this exercise, you will adjust row height and column width to display some information that is not currently visible.

12   While holding down the ⌧ key, click the task ID numbers for tasks 27, 39, 51, 57, and 63.

In each of these selected rows, the names in the **Cast** column exceed the width of the column.

13 Drag the bottom edge of the task ID for task 27 down approximately one row.

> **Tip**   While dragging the edge of the task ID, look at the status bar in the lower left corner of the Project window. The status bar indicates the new row height as you drag the edge of the task ID.

Project resizes the selected rows.

14 Double-click the right edge of the **Location** column heading.

Project resizes the column width to accommodate the widest value in the column. Your screen should look similar to the following illustration:

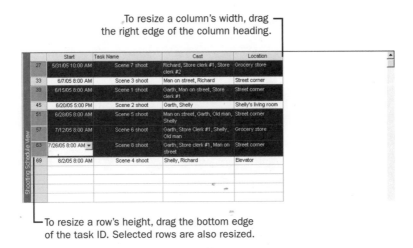

To resize a column's width, drag the right edge of the column heading.

To resize a row's height, drag the bottom edge of the task ID. Selected rows are also resized.

> **Tip**   To learn more about working with views and the views available in Project, type **About views** into the **Search** box in the upper right corner of the Project window.

CLOSE: the Short Film Project 10 file.

Key Points

- Common ways of organizing data in Project include sorting, grouping, and filtering. In all cases Project never deletes the data; it just changes how it is displayed.

- Project includes many built-in sort orders, groupings, and filters, and you can create your own.

■   Whereas sorting and filtering rearrange or selectively show only some data in a project plan, grouping adds summary values or "roll-ups" of values such as costs, based on whatever interval you choose.

■   Tables are the primary elements of most views in Project. Project includes several built-in tables, and you can create your own.

■   You work with data in Project via views. Views may contain tables, groups, filters, and in some cases graphical charts. The Gantt Chart view, for example, consists of a table on the left and a timescaled chart on the right.

■   Project contains many built-in views, and you can create your own.

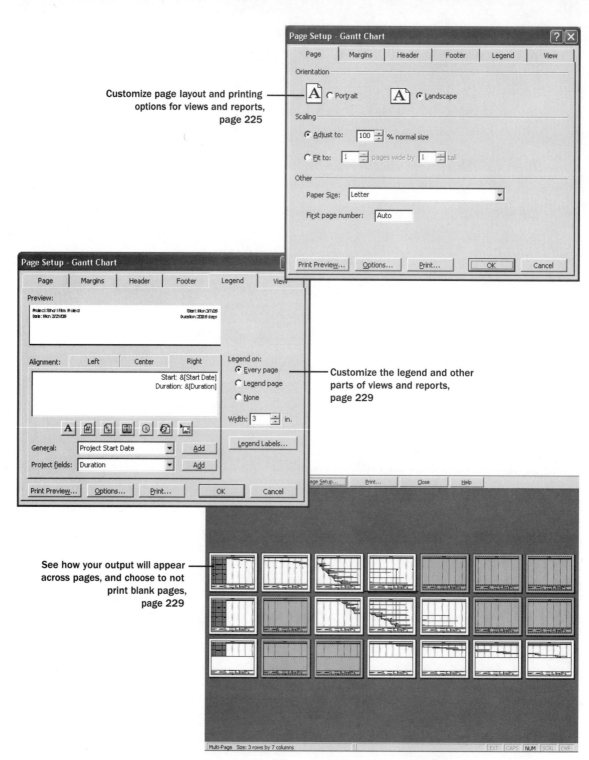

Customize page layout and printing options for views and reports, page 225

Customize the legend and other parts of views and reports, page 229

See how your output will appear across pages, and choose to not print blank pages, page 229

11 Printing Project Information

In this chapter you will learn to:

✔ Change page setup options for views and reports.

✔ Print a view.

✔ Print a report.

See Also Do you need a quick refresher on the topics in this chapter? See the quick reference entries on pages xxxii–xxxiii.

In this chapter, you work with some of the many views and reports in Microsoft Office Project 2003 to print your project plan. One of the most important tasks of any project manager is communicating project information to stakeholders, and that often means printing. To communicate project details in printed form, you can use the predefined views and reports as they are or customize them to better suit your needs.

Tip *This tip describes enterprise project management (EPM) functionality.* Printing information from Project is a common means of communicating with stakeholders. If you are using Project Professional in conjunction with Project Server, you and your stakeholders have many additional options for communicating project information. For more information, see Part 4, "Introducing Project Server."

Important Before you can use the practice files in this chapter, be sure you install them from the book's companion CD to their default location. See "Using the Book's CD-ROM," on page xiii, for more information.

Printing Your Project Plan

Printing information from a project plan to share with stakeholders is a common activity for most project managers. In Project, printing focuses on views and reports.

You've probably already seen several views and a few reports, such as the Gantt Chart view and the Project Summary report. Both views and reports organize details of a project plan into specific formats for specific purposes. In a view you can enter, read, edit, and print information, whereas in a report you can only print information.

Think of views as your general working environment in Project, and think of reports as specific formats for printing.

You can customize the way you print both views and reports; however, Project has fewer options for printing reports. When printing, you have many of the same options with both views and reports, as well as some specific options unique to views or reports. To customize printing for a view or report, you use the **Page Setup** and **Print** dialog boxes.

First let's look at the **Page Setup** dialog box. To see the **Page Setup** dialog box for views, click **Page Setup** on the **File** menu. To see this dialog box for reports, first display a report in the Print Preview window, and then click the **Page Setup** button.

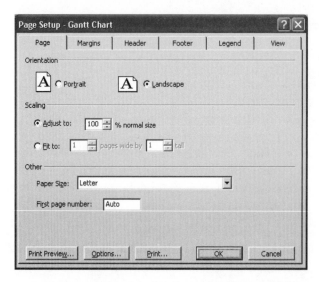

In the **Page Setup** dialog box, the **Page** and **Margins** tabs are available for both views and reports. However, the specific options you choose in the **Page Setup** dialog box for any view or report affect only that view or report; the settings are not shared between views or reports.

Some page setup options are unique to views or reports, and a few options are available to only specific views or reports. Here is a summary of unique page setup options:

- You can use options on the **Header**, **Footer**, and **View** tabs in the **Page Setup** dialog box for all views. The **View** tab in particular includes options that vary depending on which view is currently active. For views that include a legend (such as the Gantt Chart, Network Diagram, and Calendar views), the **Legend** tab is also available.

- You can use options on the **Header** and **Footer** tabs in most reports, but the **View** and **Legend** tabs are not available for any reports.

Project Management Focus: Communicating with Stakeholders

Besides knowing how to print, it's important to know what to print. Most project managers find that they have different stakeholders with different information needs. For example, what the project's financial supporters need to see at the planning stage of a project might be quite different from what the project's resources need to see after work has begun. The built-in views and reports in Project should cover nearly all stakeholder communication needs (at least when printing is the solution). Here is a summary of which views and reports best communicate project plan details to various stakeholders.

If this stakeholder	Is most interested in	Provide this printed view	Or this printed report
Project sponsor or client	Overall project duration information	Gantt Chart with project summary task displayed, filtered for summary tasks	Project Summary
	Overall project cost information	Task Sheet with project summary task displayed and Cost table applied	Budget or other reports in the Cost category
	Schedule status after work has begun	Tracking Gantt with Tracking table applied	Project Summary, Completed Tasks, or Tasks Starting Soon
Resources assigned to tasks in the project	The tasks to which they are assigned	Calendar or Resource Usage, filtered for the specific resource	To-Do List, Who Does What, or Who Does What When
Resource managers in your organization	The scope of work their resources have in the project	Resource Sheet, Resource Graph, or Resource Usage	Resource Usage, Who Does What, or other reports in the Assignments category
Other project managers in your organization	Schedule logic, critical path, and task relationships	Network Diagram, Detail Gantt, or Tracking Gantt	Critical Tasks

This table lists just some of the many built-in views and reports in Project. If you have a specific information need, explore all the views and reports before you attempt to build your own. Chances are, Project has a view or report that will meet your needs or serve as a starting point for customization.

Tip To learn more about which views or reports best convey specific project information, type **About printing views and reports** into the **Search** box in the upper right corner of the Project window. The **Search** box initially contains the text *Type a question for help.*

Next let's look at the **Print** dialog box. To see the **Print** dialog box for views, click **Print** on the **File** menu. To see this dialog box for reports, first display the report in the Print Preview window, and then click the **Print** button.

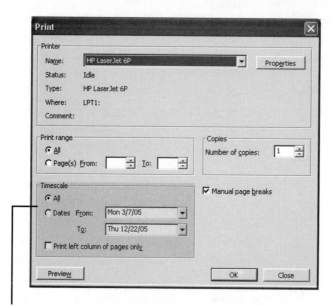

Depending on the active view or report, the Timescale options might not be available.

Tip Depending on the printer or plotter to which you are printing, you might have additional options unique to that device. To set these options, click the **Properties** button for your selected printer in the **Print** dialog box.

In the **Print** dialog box, most options available for views are also available for reports. For example, some views and some reports support timescale options in the **Print** dialog box, but others do not. The Gantt Chart view and the Who Does What When report, for example, both include a timescale. In the **Print** dialog boxes for both, you can print specific ranges from the timescale if you wish.

In this exercise, you compare the page setup options of views and reports.

Important If you are running Project Professional, you may need to make a one-time adjustment to use the My Computer account and to work offline. This helps ensure that the practice files you work with in this chapter don't affect your Project Server data. For more information, see "Starting Project Professional," on page 10.

OPEN: Short Film Project 11a from the *\MyDocuments\Microsoft Press\Project 2003 Step by Step\ Chapter 11 Printing* folder. You can also access the practice files for this book by clicking **Start**, **All Programs**, **Microsoft Press**, **Project 2003 Step by Step**, and then selecting the chapter folder of the file you want to open.

1 On the **File** menu, click **Save As**.

The **Save As** dialog box appears.

2 In the **File name** box, type Short Film Project 11, and then click the **Save** button.

Next you will look at page setup options.

3 On the **File** menu, click **Page Setup**.

The **Page Setup** dialog box appears. Note the title of the dialog box: *Page Setup – Gantt Chart*. Because the **Page Setup** dialog box changes depending on the active view, Project includes the view name in the dialog box title bar.

4 Click the **View** tab.

Your screen should look similar to the following illustration:

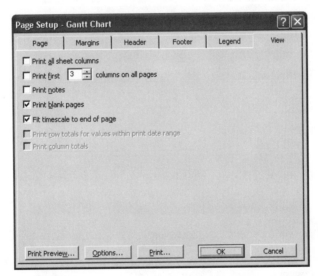

Because the Gantt Chart view includes a table, the **View** tab includes some options relating to columns. The Gantt Chart also includes a timescale, so you see an option relating to the timescale.

5 Click **Cancel**.

The **Page Setup** dialog box closes. Next you'll switch to another view and see how the page setup options differ.

6 On the **View** menu, click **Calendar**.

The Calendar view appears. This view lacks both the table and chart elements you saw in the Gantt Chart view and instead represents tasks in a month-at-a-glance arrangement.

7 On the **File** menu, click **Page Setup**.

The **Page Setup** dialog box appears. Note again the title of the dialog box: *Page Setup – Calendar*.

8 Click the **View** tab if it is not already active.

Your screen should look similar to the following illustration:

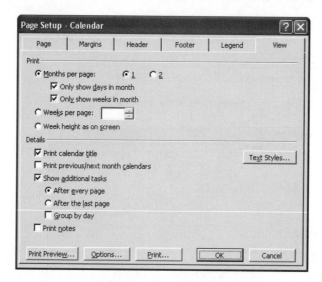

The options available for the Calendar view are quite different from those of the Gantt Chart view. Here you have several options for controlling how details are organized in the Calendar view when printed.

The **Print notes** check box, however, is available for both the Gantt Chart and Calendar views.

9 Click **Cancel**.

The **Page Setup** dialog box closes.

To conclude this exercise, you will see the page setup options for a report.

10 On the **View** menu, click **Reports**.

The **Reports** dialog box appears.

11 Click **Custom**, and then click the **Select** button.

Tip You can also double-click the **Custom** button.

The **Custom Reports** dialog box appears.

12 In the **Custom Reports** box, click **Who Does What**, and then click the **Setup** button.

The **Page Setup** dialog box appears. Note again the title of the dialog box: *Page Setup – Who Does What*. Your screen should look similar to the following illustration:

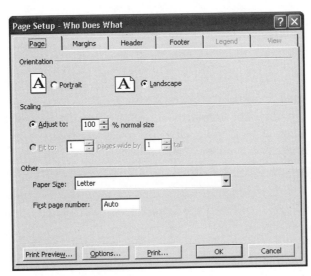

Most of the tabs you've seen for views are also available for reports, but the **Legend** and **View** tabs are not.

13 Click **Cancel** to close the **Page Setup** dialog box, and click **Cancel** again to close the **Custom Reports** dialog box.

14 Click the **Close** button to close the **Reports** dialog box.

15 On the **View** menu, click **Gantt Chart**.

Tip The views available in Project are listed in the **More Views** dialog box. (On the **View** menu, click **More Views**.) Likewise, all available reports are listed in the **Custom Reports** dialog box. (On the **View** menu, click **Reports**, click **Custom**, and then click **Select**.) Another handy way to display a view or report is through the Project Guide. (On the **Project Guide** toolbar, click **Report**, and then click the **Select a view or report** link.)

Printing Views

Printing a view enables you to get on paper just about anything you see on your screen. Any customization you apply to a view, such as applying different tables or *groups*, will be printed as well. With a few exceptions, you can print any view you see in Project. Here are the exceptions:

- You cannot print form views, such as the Task Form and the Relationship Diagram.

- If you have two views displayed in a combination view (one view in the top pane and the other view in the bottom pane), only the view in the active pane will be printed.

Keep in mind that the part of your project plan that you see on your screen at one time might be a relatively small portion of the full project, which could require a large number of pages to print. For example, the Gantt Chart view of a six-month project with 85 tasks can require 14 or more letter-size pages to print in its entirety. Printing Gantt Chart or Network Diagram views can use quite a bit of paper; in fact, some heavy-duty Project users make poster-size printouts of their project plans using plotters.

Whether you have a printer or a plotter, it's a good idea to preview any views you intend to print. By using the **Page Setup** dialog box in conjunction with the Print Preview window, you can control many aspects of the view to be printed. For example, you can control the number of pages on which the view will be printed, apply headers and footers, and determine content that appears in the legend of the Gantt Chart and some other views.

Tip   When printing Gantt Chart views and other views that include a timescale, adjusting the timescale before printing affects the number of pages required. To adjust the timescale so that it shows the largest time span in the smallest number of pages, on the **View** menu, click **Zoom**; then in the **Zoom** dialog box, click **Entire Project**.

Show ▾
Show

To further reduce the number of pages required, you can collapse a project plan's outline to summary tasks. Click the **Show** button on the Formatting toolbar, and then click the outline level you want. A collapsed view showing only summary tasks and milestones might be informative enough for people who simply want an overall sense of the project plan. If you're interested in a specific time period, you can print just that portion of the timescale. Or you might apply a filter to display only the information that's of greatest interest to a particular audience: late or overbudget tasks, for example.

Part II: Advanced Project Scheduling

Printing Project Information 11

In this exercise, you preview the Gantt Chart view and change options in the **Page Setup** dialog box.

1 On the **File** menu, click **Print Preview**.

Project displays the Gantt Chart view in the Print Preview window. Your screen should look similar to the following illustration:

The Print Preview toolbar contains buttons for navigating between pages, zooming in and out, setting Page Setup options, printing, and exiting Print Preview.

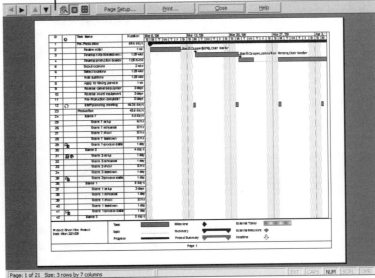

The Print Preview window has several options to explore. Let's start with the page navigation buttons.

Page Right

2 On the **Print Preview** toolbar, click the **Page Right** button several times to display different pages.

Page Down

3 Click the **Page Down** button once.

To get a broader view of the output, you'll switch to a multi-page view.

Multiple Pages

4 Click the **Multiple Pages** button.

The entire Gantt Chart view appears in the Print Preview window. Your screen should look similar to the following illustration.

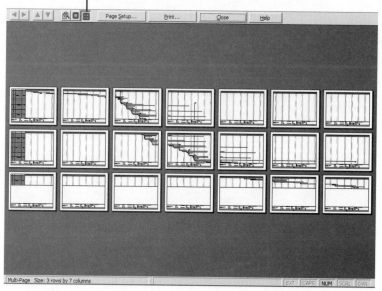

The multiple page Print Preview displays the entire printed output on separate sheets (the paper size is determined by your printer settings).

If you have a plotter selected as your default printer, or you have a different page size selected for your default printer, what you see in the Print Preview window will differ from what's shown here.

The status bar text reads *3 rows by 7 columns*. We refer to rows and columns on the Gantt Chart and in other views; in the Print Preview window, however, these terms denote rows and columns of pages—in this case, three rows of pages by seven columns of pages, for a total of 21 pages. The status bar text can help you quickly determine the size (in pages) of your printed view.

Next you'll change some options in the **Page Setup** dialog box.

One Page

5   On the **Print Preview** toolbar, click the **One Page** button.

Project displays the first page of the Gantt chart.

6   Click the **Page Setup** button.

The **Page Setup** dialog box appears. This is the same dialog box you'd see if you clicked **Page Setup** on the **File** menu. The first change we'll make to the printed Gantt Chart is to add the company name to the header that is printed on every page.

7   Click the **Header** tab.

8   On the **Header** tab are Alignment tabs. Make sure that **Center** is selected.

9 In the **General** box, click **Company Name** in the drop-down list, and then click the **Add** button.

Project inserts the &[Company] code into the header and displays a preview in the Preview window of the **Page Setup** dialog box. The company name comes from the **Properties** dialog box (**File** menu). Next you'll change the content of the Gantt Chart view's legend.

10 Click the **Legend** tab.

11 On the **Legend** tab are Alignment tabs. Click the **Right** tab.

With the current settings, Project will print the project title and the current date on the left side of the legend. You will also print the project start date and duration on the right side of the legend.

12 Click the **Right Alignment** box, and type Start:, followed by a space.

13 In the **General** box, click **Project Start Date** in the drop-down list, and then click the **Add** button.

Project adds the label and code for the project start date to the legend.

14 Press the `Enter` key to add a second line to the legend, and then type Duration:, followed by a space.

15 In the **Project fields** box, click **Duration** in the drop-down list, and then click the **Add** button.

Project adds the label and code for project duration to the legend.

16 In the **Width** box, type or click 3.

This increases the width of the box on the left side of the legend.

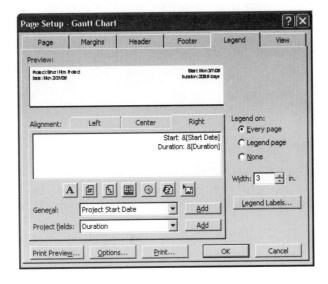

17   Click **OK** to close the **Page Setup** dialog box.

Project applies the changes you specified to the legend. To get a closer look, zoom in on the legend.

18   In the Print Preview window, click the lower left corner of the page with the magnifying-glass pointer.

Project zooms in to show the page at a legible resolution. Your screen should look similar to the following illustration:

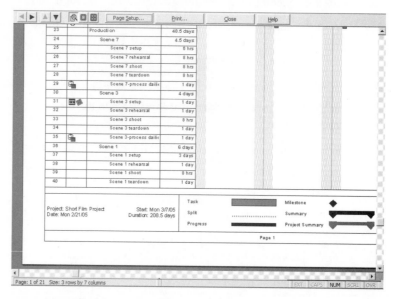

You can see the data you added to the legend, which will be printed on every page of the printed output.

To conclude this exercise, you will choose not to print pages that do not include any Gantt bars.

19   Click the **Multiple Pages** button again.

Note that several of the pages in the lower left and upper right range of the Gantt Chart view do not contain any Gantt bars. If you intend to print a Gantt Chart view and stitch the pages together, these pages don't add any information, so you don't need to print them.

20   Click the **Page Setup** button.

21   In the **Page Setup** dialog box, click the **View** tab.

22 Clear the **Print blank pages** box, and then click **OK**.

Your screen should look similar to the following illustration:

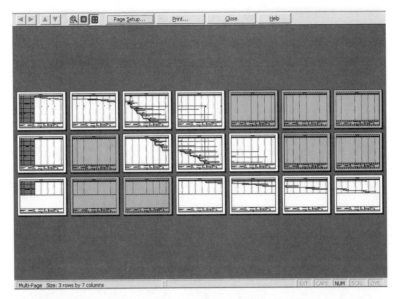

In the Print Preview window, the blank pages are formatted with a gray pattern, indicating that they will not be printed. The two pages in the lower left corner will be printed, however, because they contain the table portion of the Gantt Chart view.

23 On the **Print Preview** toolbar, click the **Close** button.

The Print Preview window closes, and the Gantt Chart view appears. Although you did not print, your changes to the header and the legend will be saved when you save the project file.

Tip   You can print the project plan now if you wish; however, previewing the project plan is adequate for the purposes of the lesson. When printing in Project, you have additional options in the **Print** dialog box, which you can open by clicking the **Print** command on the **File** menu. For example, you can choose to print a specific date range of a timescaled view, such as the Gantt Chart view, or you can print a specific page range.

New in
Office 2003

Tip   In this section you've manually adjusted several print options. The Project Guide includes a wizard-like interface for printing a view that simplifies the printing options. On the **Project Guide** toolbar click **Reports**, and then click the **Print current view as a report** link.

Printing Reports

Reports are predefined formats intended for printing Project data. Unlike views, which you can either print or work with onscreen, reports are designed only for printing. You don't enter data directly into a report. Project includes several pre-defined reports you can edit to display the information you want.

Although reports are distinct from views, some settings you specify for a view might affect certain reports. For example:

■ If subtasks are collapsed or hidden under summary tasks in a view, reports that include task lists will show only the summary tasks and not the subtasks.

■ In usage views, if assignments are collapsed or hidden under tasks or resources, the usage reports (Task Usage or Resource Usage) likewise hide assignment details.

In this exercise, you see a report in the Print Preview window, and then you edit its definition (that is, the set of elements that make up the report) to include additional information.

1 On the **View** menu, click **Reports.**

The **Reports** dialog box appears, showing the broad categories of reports available in Project.

2 Click **Custom**, and then click the **Select** button.

The **Custom Reports** dialog box appears.

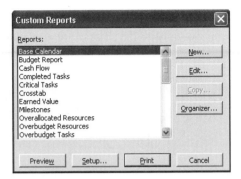

This dialog box lists all predefined reports in Project and any custom reports that have been added.

3 In the **Reports** box, click **Task,** and then click the **Preview** button.

Project displays the Task report in the Print Preview window. Your screen should look similar to the following illustration:

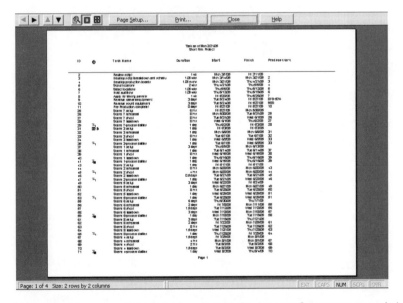

This report is a complete list of project tasks (except for summary tasks), similar to what you'd see in the Entry table of the Gantt Chart view. You'd like to see this data presented in a different way, so you'll edit this report.

4   On the **Print Preview** toolbar, click the **Close** button.

The Print Preview window closes, and the **Custom Reports** dialog box reappears. Next you'll create a copy of a built-in report and modify the copy.

5   In the **Reports** box, make sure that **Task** is still selected, and then click the **Copy** button.

The **Task Report** dialog box appears.

6   In the **Name** box, click the displayed text, and then type Custom Task Report.

7   In the **Period** box, click **Months** in the drop-down list.

Choosing Months here groups tasks by the month in which they occur. Because the report now includes a time period element, the Timescale options in the **Print** dialog box become available, enabling you to print data within a specific date range if you want.

8   In the **Table** box, click **Summary** in the drop-down list.

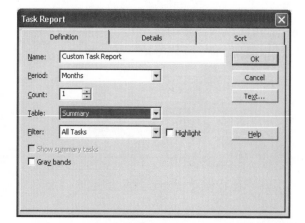

Tip   The tables listed in the **Task Report** dialog box are the same as those you can apply to any view that shows tasks in a table. In fact, if you completed Chapter 10, "Organizing and Formatting Project Details," the Shooting Schedule table you created there appears in the list here. When editing a report format, you can apply predefined or custom tables and filters, choose additional details to include in the report, and apply a sort order to the information—all in the dialog box for the report you're editing.

9   Click **OK** to close the **Task Report** dialog box.

10   In the **Custom Reports** dialog box, make sure that **Custom Task Report** is selected in the **Reports** box, and then click the **Preview** button.

Project applies the custom report settings you chose to the report, and the report appears in the Print Preview window. Next you will zoom in to see the report in more detail.

11   In the Print Preview window, click the upper left corner of the page with the magnifying-glass pointer.

Your screen should look similar to the following illustration:

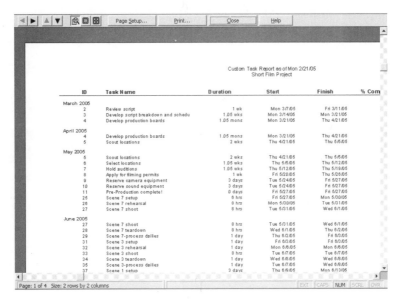

This custom report shows the fields displayed in the Summary Task table but divides the tasks by month.

12   On the **Print Preview** toolbar, click the **Close** button.

13   In the **Custom Reports** dialog box, click the **Close** button.

14   Click the **Close** button again to close the **Reports** dialog box.

The Gantt Chart view reappears.

CLOSE: the Short Film Project 11 file.

Key Points

■   In Project you can print views or reports. Reports are designed only for printing (or print previewing).

■   When printing a view, you generally will get on paper what you see on your screen.

■   With even moderately large project plans, a printed view or report might require more sheets of paper than you expect. For this reason, it's a good idea to always preview your output before printing it.

■   The many reports available in Project are organized into several categories such as Costs and Assignments. These are worth exploring (for example, by previewing) so that you know what's available.

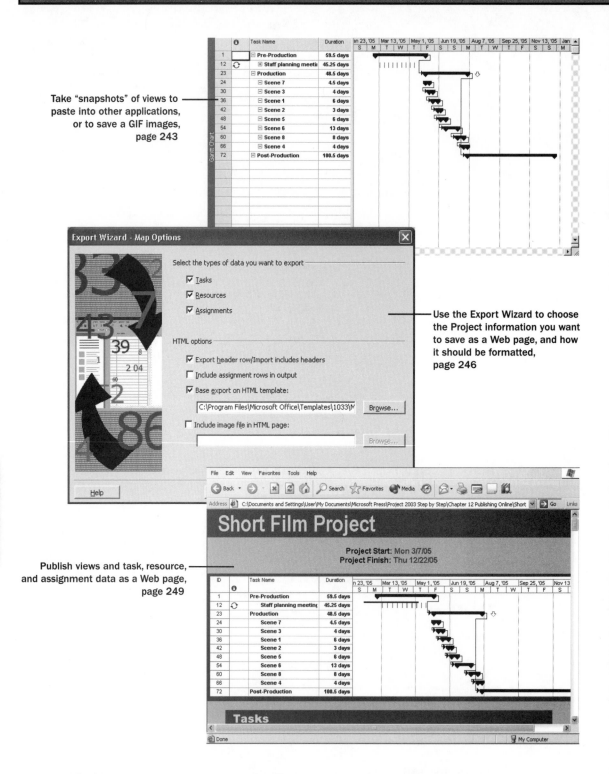

Take "snapshots" of views to paste into other applications, or to save a GIF images, page 243

Use the Export Wizard to choose the Project information you want to save as a Web page, and how it should be formatted, page 246

Publish views and task, resource, and assignment data as a Web page, page 249

12 Publishing Project Information Online

In this chapter you will learn to:

✔ Take a "snapshot" of a Gantt Chart view as a GIF image.

✔ Publish Project information in HTML format.

✔ Control how Project information is saved in HTML format.

See Also   Do you need a quick refresher on the topics in this chapter? See the quick reference entries on pages xxxiii–xxxiv.

Printing Microsoft Office Project 2003 information is a common way to share project details with others, but it has its limitations. Project details can be out of date almost as soon as you commit them to paper. You're also limited to duplicating and distributing copies of the printed output, which has some overhead. Publishing project information online, on the other hand, enables you to more easily update published project details and share them with a wide audience of online viewers.

In this chapter, you work with the Web publishing features of Project. These features include the Copy Picture feature, which enables you to take a "snapshot" of the active view and save it as a GIF image. You also export Project information to HTML format and control how the exported information appears. In many organizations, publishing in HTML format on an intranet is the primary means by which project details are communicated to stakeholders.

Tip   *This tip describes enterprise project management (EPM) functionality.* This chapter describes sharing Project information online by saving it to HTML or GIF format files. Project Professional, when used with Project Server, provides much more sophisticated ways of not only publishing project information online, but collecting information (such as actual work) from resources and other stakeholders online as well. To learn more about the enterprise collaboration tools available with Project Server, see Part 4, "Introducing Project Server."

 Important   Before you can use the practice files in this chapter, be sure you install them from the book's companion CD to their default location. See "Using the Book's CD-ROM," on page xiii, for more information.

Copying Project Information as a GIF Image

When communicating project details to resources, managers, and other stakeholders, chances are you'll need to copy information from Project and paste it into other programs and formats. Project supports the standard copy-and-paste functionality of most Windows programs, and it has an additional feature called *Copy Picture* that takes "snapshots" of a view. You can take these snapshots by choosing the **Copy Picture** command on the **Edit** menu or clicking the **Copy Picture** button on the Standard toolbar.

Copy Picture

With the Copy Picture feature, you have the following options when taking snapshots of the active view:

■   Copy the entire view visible on the screen or selected rows of a table in a view.

■   Copy a range of time that you specify or display on the screen.

Either way, you can save the snapshot to a Graphics Interchange Format (GIF) file in a location you specify. After you save the image as a GIF file, you can use it in any of the many programs that support the GIF format. You can also combine it with HTML content on a Web page, as you'll do later in this chapter. You can even use the Copy Picture feature to copy an image to the Clipboard and later paste it into another program for onscreen viewing (in PowerPoint, for example) or for printing (in Word, for example).

Tip   If you want to copy portions of a table (to paste a task list into a spreadsheet, for example) rather than copying a graphic image, use the **Copy Cell** command on the **Edit** menu.

In this exercise, you change what appears in the Gantt Chart view and then use the Copy Picture feature to save a snapshot of this view as a GIF file. To begin, you filter the Gantt chart to show only summary tasks.

Important   If you are running Project Professional, you may need to make a one-time adjustment to use the My Computer account and to work offline. This helps ensure that the practice files you work with in this chapter don't affect your Project Server data. For more information, see "Starting Project Professional," on page 10.

OPEN: Short Film Project 12a from the *My Documents**Microsoft Press**Project 2003 Step by Step*\\ *Chapter 12 Publishing Online* folder. You can also access the practice files for this book by clicking **Start**, **All Programs**, **Microsoft Press**, **Project 2003 Step by Step**, and then selecting the chapter folder of the file you want to open.

1 On the **File** menu, click **Save As**.

The **Save As** dialog box appears.

2 In the **File name** box, type Short Film Project 12, and then click the **Save** button.

3 On the **Project** menu, point to **Filtered For: All Tasks**, and then click **Summary Tasks**.

Project filters the Gantt chart to display only summary tasks. Next you'll zoom out on the *timescale* to see the entire project.

4 On the **View** menu, click **Zoom**.

The **Zoom** dialog box appears.

5 Click **Entire project**, and then click **OK**.

Project adjusts the timescale in the Gantt Chart view to display the entire project's duration in the window. Your screen should look similar to the following illustration:

		Task Name	Duration	Jan 23, '05	Mar 13, '05	May 1, '05	Jun 19, '05	Aug 7, '05	Sep 25, '05	Nov 13, '05	Jan
1		⊟ Pre-Production	59.5 days								
12	◯	⊞ Staff planning meetii	45.25 days								
23		⊟ Production	48.5 days								
24		⊟ Scene 7	4.5 days								
30		⊟ Scene 3	4 days								
36		⊟ Scene 1	6 days								
42		⊟ Scene 2	3 days								
48		⊟ Scene 5	6 days								
54		⊟ Scene 6	13 days								
60		⊟ Scene 8	8 days								
66		⊟ Scene 4	4 days								
72		⊟ Post-Production	100.5 days								

Copy Picture

6 On the Standard toolbar, click the **Copy Picture** button.

The **Copy Picture** dialog box appears.

> **Tip** You can also click **Copy Picture** on the **Edit** menu.

7 Under **Render image**, click **To GIF image file**.

Project defaults to saving the file in the same location as the practice file and with the same name, except with a .gif extension. Your screen should look similar to the following illustration:

When taking a snapshot of a view, select how you want the image rendered here; the first two options copy the image to the Windows Clipboard, whereas the third enables you to save the image as a GIF file.

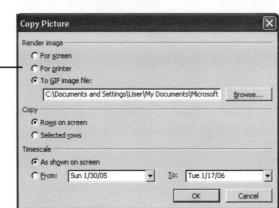

8   Click **OK** to close the **Copy Picture** dialog box.

The GIF image is saved.

You can open your browser or a graphics program to view the GIF image you just saved, but you can also view it from within Project.

9   On the **View** menu, point to **Toolbars**, and then click **Web**.

The **Web** toolbar appears.

Tip   You can also right-click any toolbar to see the **Toolbars** *shortcut menu* and then display or hide a toolbar listed on that menu.

Go

10   On the **Web** toolbar, click the **Go** button, and then click **Open Hyperlink** in the drop-down list.

The **Open Internet Address** dialog box appears.

11   Click the **Browse** button.

The **Browse** dialog box appears.

12   In the **Files of type** box, click **GIF Files** in the drop-down list.

13   Locate the GIF image named Short Film Project 12 in your Chapter 12 Publishing Online folder.

14 Click the GIF image, and then click the **Open** button.

15 In the **Open Internet Address** dialog box, click **OK**.

Project opens the GIF image. If you have Microsoft Internet Explorer as your default program for viewing GIF files, your screen should look similar to the following illustration:

The Gantt Chart view snapshot is saved to a GIF image, which you can view in a browser or graphics editing program.

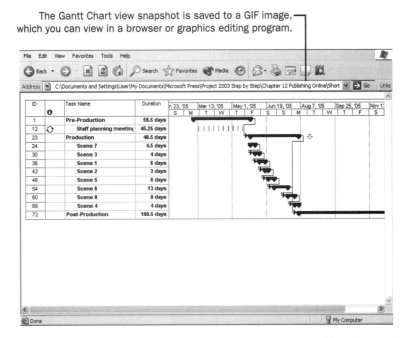

As noted earlier, what you see is a graphic image of the Gantt Chart view. The GIF image shows the view you displayed in Project, almost exactly as you had it set up.

16 Close the program you used to view the GIF file, and then return to Project.

Tip The **Copy Picture** feature is unavailable when a form view, such as the Task Form or Relationship Diagram view, is displayed.

GIF images of views in Project are useful on their own. However, you can also combine them with other Project content and save the results as a Web page for publication to the Web or to an intranet site. You will do this in the following section.

Saving Project Information as a Web Page

Another way to publish Project information is to save it as a Web page. Unlike the Copy Picture feature, the Save As Web Page feature is geared toward publishing text. Project uses maps (also called *export maps* or *data maps*) that specify the exact data to export and how to structure it. Maps organize Project data into HTML tables; the predefined maps resemble some of the predefined tables and reports in Project. You can use maps as they are or customize them to export only the Project data you want.

In this exercise, you save Project data as a Web page using a map, and then you view the results in your browser.

1   On the **File** menu, click **Save As Web Page**.

The **Save As** dialog box appears. Project prompts you to save the information as a Web page in the same location from which you opened the practice file. If you see a different location in the **Save In** box, navigate to the Chapter 12 Publishing Online folder on your hard disk.

2   Click the **Save** button.

The Export Wizard appears. This wizard helps you export the structured data from Project to a different format.

3   Click the **Next** button.

The second page of the Export Wizard appears. Your screen should look similar to the following illustration:

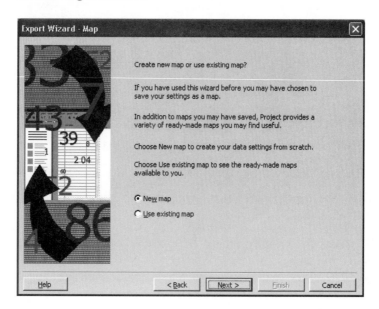

The Export Wizard uses maps to organize the way fields from a Project plan are exported to another file format. For this exercise, you will use one of the maps included with Project.

4   Select the **Use existing map** option, and then click the **Next** button.

5   Under **Choose a map for your data**, click **Export to HTML using standard template**.

Your screen should look similar to the following illustration:

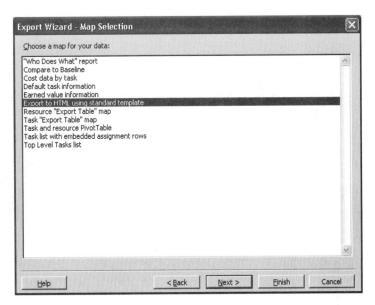

6   Click the **Finish** button.

Project saves the data in HTML format. This particular map produces three tables that contain task, resource, and assignment information from the short film project. All three tables will appear on the single Web page that you saved. Next you will view the Web page.

7   On the **Web** toolbar, click **Go**, and then click **Open Hyperlink** in the drop-down list.

The **Open Internet Address** dialog box appears.

8   Click the **Browse** button.

The **Browse** dialog box appears.

9   Locate the Web page named Short Film Project 12 in the Chapter 12 Publishing Online folder on your hard disk.

10 Click **Short Film Project 12**, and then click the **Open** button.

11 In the **Open Internet Address** dialog box, click **OK**.

Project opens the Web page in your browser. If you have Internet Explorer, your screen should look similar to the following illustration:

This is the result of saving Project data as a — Web page using a standard HTML template.

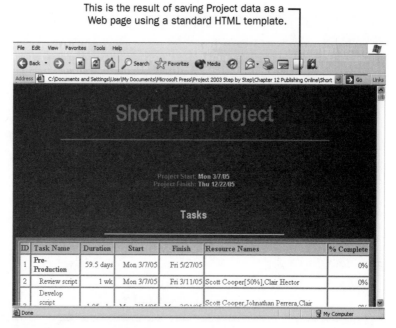

12 Scroll through the Web page. As you can see, it contains the task, resource, and assignment information from the project plan.

13 Close your browser, and return to Project.

Saving information as a Web page enables you to publish large volumes of project information in HTML format.

Important The data you can export when using the **Save As Web Page** command is not tied to the specific view you happen to be in at the time you save. The current view does not affect what data can or can't be exported.

You can do a few things to fine-tune the Web pages you publish from Project:

- You can edit the map. After you select the map in the Export Wizard, click **Next** repeatedly to see the other options in the wizard. You have a great deal of flexibility in choosing the exact task, resource, and assignment fields you want to export and how you want the exported data organized.

- You can apply a different HTML template to the Web page when you save it. This changes the format of the Web page, and it is the subject of the next section.

- If you're HTML-savvy, you can edit the resulting Web page after saving it in Project. For example, you can add several Project-specific tags to a Web page. For a list of those tags, type **Available HTML export templates and tags** into the **Search** box in the upper right corner of the Project window. The **Search** box initially contains the text *Type a question for help*.

Changing the Look of a Project Web Page

Although maps determine which Project data you save as a Web page and how it's organized, *HTML templates* determine how that data is formatted. Project includes several HTML templates that you can apply as you save data as a Web page. You can experiment with different formats to find those you like best.

In this exercise, you save project information as a Web page, apply a different template, and include the GIF image you created earlier.

1 On the **File** menu, click **Save As Web Page**.

The **Save As** dialog box appears. Project prompts you to save the information as a Web page in the same location from which you opened the practice file.

2 In the **File name** box, type Short Film Project 12 With Gantt Chart, and click the **Save** button.

The Export Wizard appears.

3 Click the **Next** button.

4 Select the **Use existing map** option, and then click the **Next** button.

5 Under **Choose a map for your data**, click **Export to HTML using standard template**, and then click the **Next** button.

The Map Options page appears. Your screen should look similar to the following illustration:

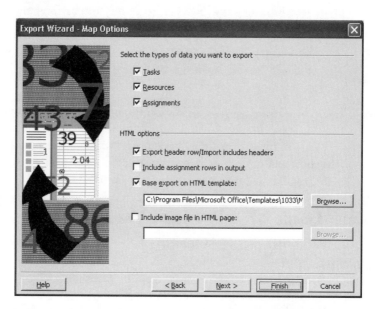

In the previous section, you saw that more information was exported to the Web page than you need, so you'll publish only task and resource information this time.

6   Under **Select the types of data you want to export**, clear the **Assignments** check box.

Next you will pick a different HTML template to use. Under **HTML options**, the **Base export on HTML template** check box is selected by default, and the path to the current template appears.

7   Click the **Browse** button next to the path to the current template.

The **Browse** dialog box appears, displaying all of the HTML templates that are included with Project.

Tip   If you installed Project to the default location, the HTML templates it includes are in the following folder:
C:\Program Files\Microsoft Office\Templates\1033\Microsoft Project Web

8   In the list of templates, click **Stripes Ivy**, and then click **OK**.

There's just one more thing to do before creating the Web page. Earlier in this chapter, you created a GIF image of the Gantt Chart view named Short Film Project 12.gif. You'd like to include this image in the Web page.

9 Select the **Include image file in HTML page** check box.

If the GIF image file has the same name and is in the same folder as the Project file you're saving as a Web page, the path to that image file appears by default. Had you selected a different name or folder when creating the GIF image, you'd need to click the **Browse** button to locate it.

Your screen should look similar to the following illustration:

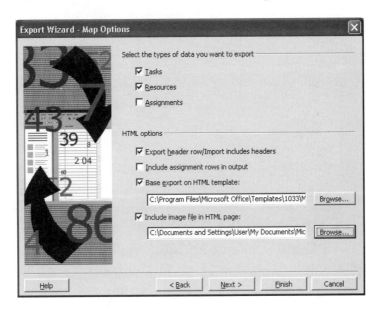

10 Click the **Finish** button.

Project saves your Project data in HTML format. Next you will view the Web page you just created.

Go

11 On the **Web** toolbar, click **Go**, and then click **Open Hyperlink** in the drop-down list.

The **Open Internet Address** dialog box appears.

12 Click the **Browse** button.

The **Browse** dialog box appears.

13 Locate the Web page named Short Film Project 12 With Gantt Chart in your Chapter 12 Publishing Online folder.

14 Click **Short Film Project 12 With Gantt Chart**, and then click the **Open** button.

15 In the **Open Internet Address** dialog box, click **OK**.

The Web page appears in your browser. If you have Internet Explorer, your screen should look similar to the following illustration:

With a different template and the GIF image included,—
this is the result of saving Project data as a Web page.

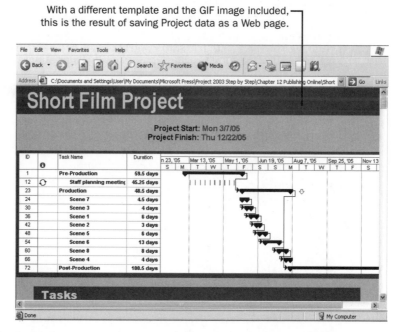

16 Scroll through the Web page to view the Gantt chart image, the Tasks table, and the Resources table. The new Web page doesn't have the Assignments table, and it shows different formatting from the page you created earlier.

17 Close your browser, and return to Project.

18 Right-click any toolbar. In the shortcut menu that appears, click **Web**.

The **Web** toolbar disappears.

You've only scratched the surface of Project's Web publishing capabilities. Depending on the communication needs you have as a project manager, you might use these features extensively. By modifying export maps, applying HTML templates, or editing the resulting Web pages, you can carefully tailor the information you provide over the Web.

CLOSE: the Short Film Project 12 file.

Key Points

■ Project details can change quickly. You may find it more efficient to publish Project plans online, and then update and republish as needed, than to print Project data on paper.

■ The **Copy Picture** command (**Edit** menu) helps you produce a GIF format graphic image you can insert into another document or Web page. You can also copy the image to the Clipboard and later paste to any destination you wish.

■ When saving to a Web page, you use export maps to specify which Project information (or fields) you want to export.

■ When exporting Project data to a Web page, you control the formatting of the exported data by applying one of several built-in HTML templates.

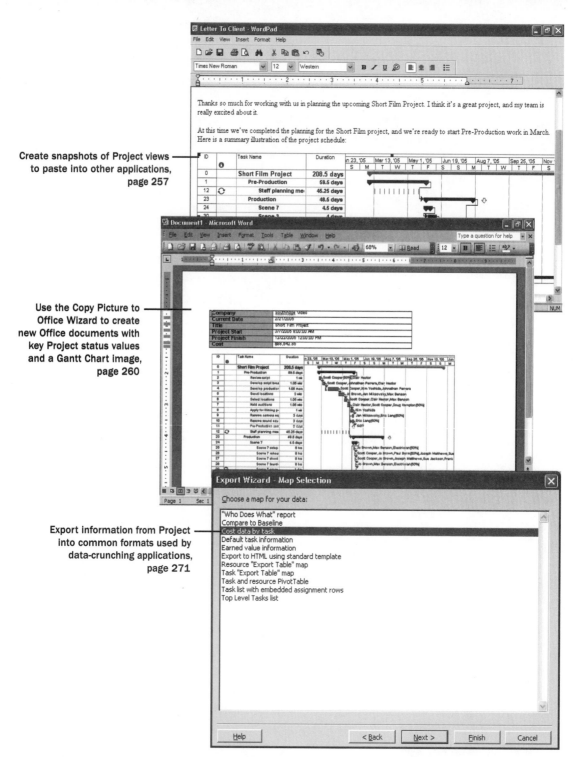

Create snapshots of Project views to paste into other applications, page 257

Use the Copy Picture to Office Wizard to create new Office documents with key Project status values and a Gantt Chart image, page 260

Export information from Project into common formats used by data-crunching applications, page 271

13 Sharing Project Information with Other Programs

In this chapter you will learn to:

✓ Copy and paste data to and from Project.

✓ Generate a new Office document that contains essential project details and an illustration.

✓ Use Project to open a file produced in another program.

✓ Save Project data to other file formats using import/export maps.

See Also Do you need a quick refresher on the topics in this chapter? See the quick reference entries on pages xxxiv–xxxv.

In this chapter, you focus on various ways of getting data into and out of Microsoft Office Project 2003. In addition to the standard Windows copy and paste features with which you might be familiar, Project offers a variety of options for importing and exporting data.

Throughout this chapter, you'll see the following terms:

■ The *source program* is the program from which you copy information.

■ The *destination program* is the program to which you paste information.

Tip *This tip describes enterprise project management (EPM) functionality.* This chapter describes various ways of sharing information between Project and other applications, usually to communicate project details to stakeholders. Project Professional, when used with Project Server, offers much more sophisticated ways of communicating with resources and other stakeholders online. To learn more about the enterprise collaboration tools available with Project Server, see Part 4, "Introducing Project Server."

 Important Before you can use the practice files in this chapter, be sure you install them from the book's companion CD to their default location. See "Using the Book's CD-ROM," on page xiii, for more information.

Copying and Pasting with Project

You can copy and paste data to and from Project by clicking the **Copy Cell**, **Copy Picture**, **Paste**, and **Paste Special** commands on the **Edit** menu (or the corresponding buttons on the Standard toolbar). When copying data from Project, you can choose one of two options, depending on the results you want:

■ You can copy text (such as task names and dates) from a table and paste it as text into a destination program, such as Word.

■ You can copy a graphic image of a view from Project and paste it as a graphic image in the destination program. With the **Copy Picture** command on the **Edit** menu, you can create a graphic image of a view or a selected portion of a view. Use the Copy Picture feature to optimize the image for onscreen viewing (in PowerPoint, for example) or for printing (in Word, for example).

Tip   The **Copy Picture** command also includes an option to save the snapshot to a GIF image file. You can then include the GIF image in a Word document or e-mail message, or post it directly to an intranet site.

There is an important distinction between using Copy and Copy Picture. If you use Copy, you can edit the data in the destination program. However, Copy Picture yields an image that you can edit only with a graphics editing program, such as Microsoft Paint.

Tip   Many Windows programs, such as Word and Excel, have a **Paste Special** command on their **Edit** menu. This command gives you more options for pasting text from Project into the destination program. For example, you can use the **Paste Special** command in Word to paste formatted or unformatted text, a picture, or a Project Document Object (an *OLE* object). You can also choose to paste just the data or paste it with a link to the source data in Project. For more information about using OLE with Project, type **About incorporating text, graphics, or objects** into the **Search** box in the upper right corner of the Project window. The **Search** box initially contains the text *Type a question for help*.

You also have two options when pasting data into Project from other programs:

■ You can paste text (such as a list of task or resource names) into a table in Project. For example, you can paste a range of cells from Excel or a sequence of paragraphs from Word into Project. You might paste a series of task names that are organized in a vertical column from Excel or Word into the **Task Name** column in Project, for instance.

■ You can paste a graphic image or an OLE object from another program into a graphical portion of a Gantt Chart view. You can also paste a graphic image or an OLE object into a task, resource, or assignment note; into a form view, such as the Task or Resource Form views; or into the header, footer, or legend of a view or report.

Important   Pasting text as multiple columns requires some planning. First make sure that the order of the information in the source program matches the order of the columns in the Project table. You can either rearrange the data in the source program to match the column order in the Project table, or vice versa. Second make sure that the columns in the source program support the same types of data—text, numbers, dates, and so on—as do the columns in Project.

For the short film project, you'd like to add a Gantt chart image to a document you've prepared for a stakeholder of the project. In this exercise, you copy a snapshot of a Gantt chart and paste it into Microsoft WordPad (or Word, if you prefer). You copy the same way regardless of the destination program you have in mind. For example, you could paste the snapshot into a word processor file or an e-mail message. To begin, you'll format the Gantt Chart view to show the information you want.

In this exercise, you copy an image of a Gantt Chart view to the Clipboard and then paste it into another document.

Important   If you are running Project Professional, you may need to make a one-time adjustment to use the My Computer account and to work offline. This helps ensure that the practice files you work with in this chapter don't affect your Project Server data. For more information, see "Starting Project Professional," on page 10.

OPEN: Short Film Project 13a from the *My Documents**Microsoft Press**Project 2003 Step by Step*\ *Chapter 13 Sharing* folder. You can also access the practice files for this book by clicking **Start**, **All Programs**, **Microsoft Press**, **Project 2003 Step by Step**, and then selecting the chapter folder of the file you want to open.

1   On the **File** menu, click **Save As**.

The **Save As** dialog box appears.

2   In the **File name** box, type Short Film Project 13, and then click the **Save** button.

3   On the **Project** menu, point to **Filtered For: All Tasks**, and then click **Summary Tasks**.

Project displays only the summary tasks in the project.

4   On the **View** menu, click **Zoom**.

The **Zoom** dialog box appears.

5   In the **Zoom** dialog box, click **Entire project**, and then click **OK**.

Project adjusts the timescale of the Gantt chart to show the entire project. Your screen should look similar to the following illustration:

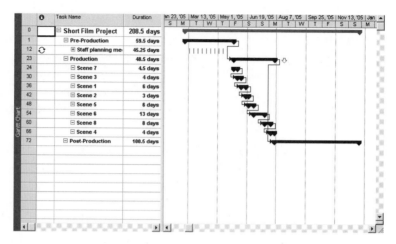

Copy Picture

6   On the Standard toolbar, click the **Copy Picture** button.

The **Copy Picture** dialog box appears.

7   Under the **Render image** label, select **For screen**, and then click **OK**.

Project copies a snapshot of the Gantt Chart view to the Clipboard.

Next you'll open a proposal that's been created in a word processor. You can open this in WordPad or in Word if you have it.

8   Do one of the following:

- ■   If you do not have Word installed, click the Windows **Start** button, point to **All Programs**, point to **Accessories**, and then click **WordPad**.

- ■   If you have Word installed, start it.

9   In WordPad or Word, on the **File** menu, click **Open**.

10   Locate and open the document named Letter To Client in your Chapter 13 Sharing folder (you may have to select **All Files** in the **Files of type** box).

11   Once the document has opened, select the paragraph (**insert Gantt Chart picture here**).

12   On the **Edit** menu, click **Paste**.

Project pastes the snapshot of the Gantt Chart view from the Clipboard to the document. If you are using WordPad, your screen should look similar to the following illustration:

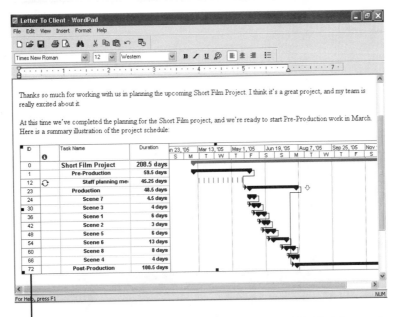

The image of the Gantt Chart view has been pasted into a WordPad document. The Gantt chart cannot be edited in this format except as a graphic image.

Again, note that rather than pasting the image into a Word or WordPad document, you could paste this image into an e-mail message or another type of document.

13 On the WordPad or Word **File** menu, click **Exit**. When prompted to save the document, click **No**.

Generating a Project Summary Report for Word, PowerPoint, or Visio

New in Office 2003   Although the Copy Picture feature is useful for moving an image of the active view to the Clipboard or to a GIF file, Project makes it easy to go a step further and generate a complete document in Word, PowerPoint, or Visio. Project enables this with the Copy Picture to Office Wizard, which steps you through the process of specifying the exact data you want included in the new Office document, and how you want it displayed. This wizard works with most views in Project, but not with the Calendar view, Relationship Diagram view, or form views.

The Copy Picture to Office Wizard generates a new Office document that contains a table of field values that apply to your entire project (such as the project finish date), and a GIF image of the current Project view. The wizard gives you the option of generating a new document in any of the three most common Office formats for project status reporting: PowerPoint, Word, and Visio.

In this exercise you use the Copy Picture to Office Wizard to create a Word document with a GIF image of a Gantt chart.

Important   If the computer on which you are now working does not have PowerPoint, Word, or Visio 2000 or later installed, you cannot complete this example of using the Copy Picture to Office Wizard. If this is the case, go on to the next section.

1   On the **View** menu point to **Toolbars,** and click **Analysis.**

     The **Analysis** toolbar appears.

2   On the **Analysis** toolbar, click the **Copy Picture to Office Wizard** button.

     The Information page of the wizard appears. Your screen should look similar to the following illustration:

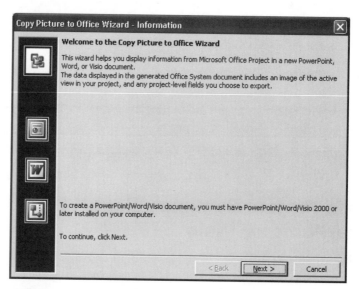

3   Click **Next.**

     Step 1 of the wizard appears. Here you control the outline level of the task list.

4   Make sure that **Keep my original outline level** is selected. Your screen should look similar to the following illustration:

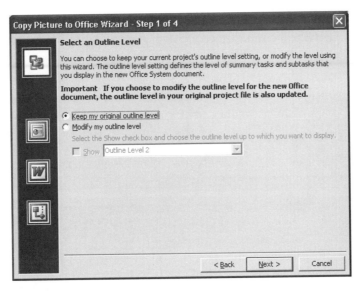

5   Click **Next**.

Step 2 of the wizard appears. Here you specify exactly what you want copied, and at what size.

6   Make sure that, under **Copy, Rows on screen** is selected, under **Timescale, As shown on screen** is selected, and, under **Image Size, Default** is selected. Your screen should look similar to the following illustration:

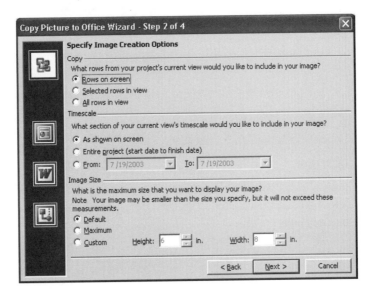

7 Click **Next**.

Step 3 of the wizard appears. Here you specify the Office application for which you want a new document created.

Before you pick an application, however, you'll preview the GIF image the wizard will create. You preview it in your browser, though the wizard eventually inserts the GIF image of the active view into the application format you chose.

8 Click **Preview**.

Project displays the GIF image of your view in your browser. Your screen should look similar to the following illustration:

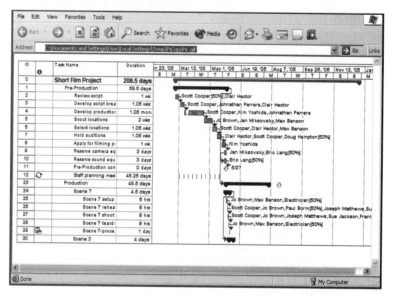

9 Close your browser and return to Step 3 of the wizard in Project.

10 Under **Application**, click **Word**.

11 Under **Orientation**, click **Landscape**.

12 Click **Next**.

Step 4 of the wizard appears. Here you review and, if you wish, modify the project-level fields to be included in the new document. These fields will appear in a table above the GIF image.

13 In the **Microsoft Office Project Fields** box, select **Cost**, and then click the **Add** button.

The Cost field name appears at the bottom of the fields list in the **Fields to Export** box. Your screen should look similar to the following illustration:

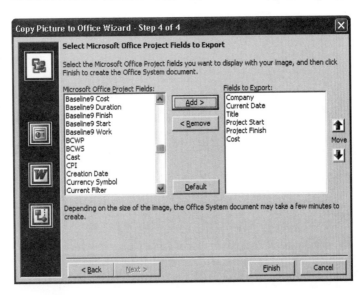

14 Click **Finish**.

Project displays a confirmation message that it completed the new document creation.

15 Click **Close**.

The wizard starts Word, if it is not already running, and creates the new document.

16 If Word is minimized, click the **Word** icon on the taskbar and if necessary switch to the new document in Word.

Your screen should look similar to the following illustration:

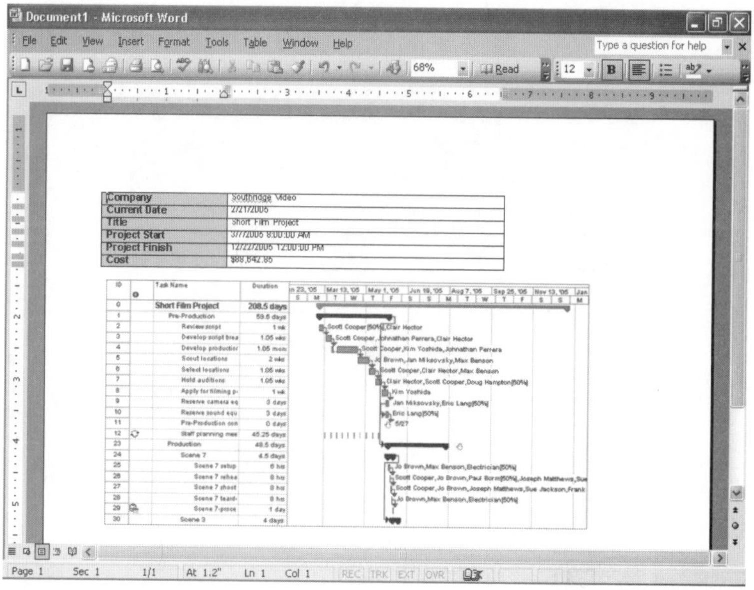

The project-level fields appear in a table above the GIF image of the Gantt Chart view. For your real-world reporting needs you could use such a document as a starting point for a recurring project status report, or for a one-time project write-up.

17 Close the document in Word and switch back to Project.

Opening Other File Formats in Project

Information that you need to incorporate into a Project document can come from a variety of sources. A task list from a spreadsheet or resource costs from a database are two examples. You might want to use the unique features of Project to analyze data from another program. For example, many people keep task lists and simple project schedules in Excel, but accounting for basic scheduling issues like working and non-working time is impractical in Excel.

As you might recall from Chapter 12, "Publishing Project Information Online," Project uses maps when saving data to HTML and other formats. Project also uses maps when opening data from another file format. In fact, the same maps are used for both opening and saving data, so they are known as *import/export maps*. (You might also hear these referred to as *data maps* or just *maps*.) You use import/export maps to specify how you want individual fields in the source program's file to correspond to individual fields in the destination program's file. After you set up an import/export map, you can use it over and over again.

Tip   If you have Excel installed on your computer, open the workbook named Sample Task List in the Chapter 13 Sharing folder. The important things to note about the workbook are the names and the order of the columns, the presence of a header row (the labels at the top of the columns), and that the data is in a worksheet named Tasks. When you're done viewing the workbook, close it without saving changes.

In this exercise, a colleague has sent you an Excel workbook that contains her recommended tasks, durations, and sequence of activities for some work Southridge Video will do in the future. You open the Excel workbook in Project and set up an import/export map to control how the Excel data is imported into Project.

1   In Project, on the **File** menu, click **Open**.

The **Open** dialog box appears.

2   Locate the Chapter 13 Sharing folder in the Project 2003 Step by Step folder on your hard disk.

3   In the **Files of type** box, select **Microsoft Excel Workbooks**.

Tip   While scrolling through the **Files of type** box, you can see the several file formats Project can import. If you work with programs that can save in any of these file formats, you can import their data into Project. For more information, type **File formats supported by Project** into the **Search** box, located in the upper right corner of the Project window.

4   Double-click the **Sample Task List** file.

The Import Wizard appears. This wizard helps you import structured data from a different format to Project.

Tip   If you completed Chapter 12, "Publishing Project Information Online," you will find the Import Wizard to be very similar to the Export Wizard. Remember that Project uses basically the same process and maps for importing as it does for exporting.

5   Click the **Next** button.

The second page of the Import Wizard appears. Your screen should look similar to the following illustration:

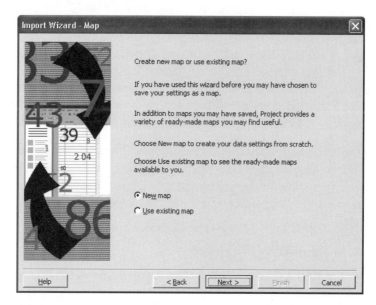

The Import Wizard uses maps to organize the way structured data from another file format is imported into Project. For this exercise, you will create a new map.

6 Make sure that **New map** is selected, and then click the **Next** button.

The Import Mode page of the Import Wizard appears. Your screen should look similar to the following illustration:

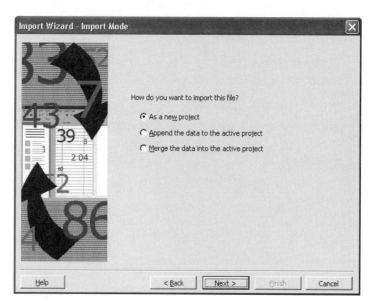

7   Make sure that **As a new project** is selected, and then click the **Next** button.

The Map Options page of the Import Wizard appears.

8   Select the **Tasks** check box, and make sure that **Import includes headers** is selected as well.

Headers here refers to column headings. Your screen should look similar to the following illustration:

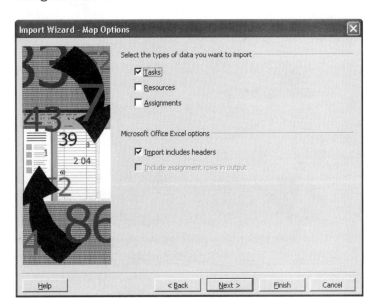

9   Click the **Next** button.

The Task Mapping page of the Import Wizard appears. Here you identify the source workbook and specify how you want to map the data from the source workbook to Project fields.

10 In the **Source worksheet name** list, select **Tasks**.

Project analyzes the header row names from the workbook and suggests the Project field names that are probable matches. Your screen should look similar to the following illustration:

On this page of the Import Wizard you specify how Project should import data for other file formats—in this case an Excel workbook.

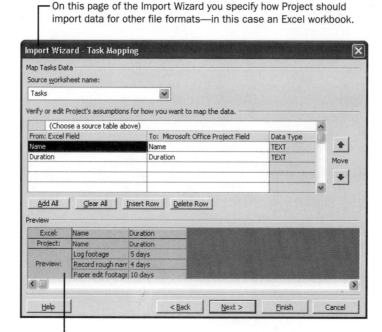

Use the Preview area to see how the data from another file format will be mapped to Project fields, based on the setting you've made above.

11 Click the **Next** button.

The final page of the Import Wizard appears. Here you have the option of saving the settings for the new import map, which is useful when you anticipate importing similar data into Project in the future. This time you'll skip this step.

12 Click the **Finish** button.

Project imports the Excel data into a new Project plan. Your screen should look similar to the illustration shown next. (The dates you see on the timescale will differ from those shown because Project uses the current date as the project start date in the new file.)

After importing the task names and durations, they appear
as an unlinked sequence of tasks, ready for editing.

This task list will become a more fully developed schedule that you'll use in a later
chapter.

13 Close the new file without saving changes.

Tip If you find that others need to give you task lists for creating a plan in Project and
you must reorganize or clean up the lists you get, try using the Microsoft Project Task List
Import Template. Project installs this Excel template. In Excel, this template appears on
the **Spreadsheet Solutions** tab of the **Templates** dialog box. The Excel template is set up
with the proper field headings and column order to make importing a clean task list in
Project easy.

For more complex importing, see the Microsoft Project Plan Import Export Template (also
an Excel template, visible on the **Spreadsheet Solutions** tab of the **Templates** dialog box).
This template contains not only task but also resource and assignment field headings
and column orders for importing more complex information into Project.

Saving to Other File Formats from Project

Pasting Project data into other programs might be fine for one-time or infrequent needs, but this technique might not work as well if you need to export a large volume of data from Project. Instead, you can save Project data in a variety of file formats. You can take one of two approaches to saving Project data in other file formats:

- You can save the entire project as a database. In fact, you can store multiple projects in a single database file for centralized administration or for other purposes. Saving a project in a database format might also help if you need to report or analyze data in ways that Project doesn't support. The supported formats include Project Database (.mpd) and Access Database (.mdb). These two formats are almost identical. One important difference is that the Project Database format requires you to save the entire project, but the Access Database format allows you to save either the entire project or just the data you specify in an export map. You can also save an entire project to Extensible Markup Language (XML) format for structured data exchange with other applications that support it.

- You can save just the data you specify in a different format. The supported formats include Access desktop database, Web page, Excel workbook, Excel Pivot-Table, and tab-delimited or comma-delimited text. If you completed Chapter 12, "Publishing Project Information Online," you worked with an export map when saving Project data to a Web page. You use the same approach when specifying data you want to save in any format. You choose the format in which you want to save, pick a built-in export map (or create your own), and export the data.

Tip Project includes thorough documentation for the Project Database format. If you installed Project in the default location, you'll find the documentation file at *C:\Program Files\Microsoft Office\Office11\1033\Pjdb.htm.*

For more information about the file formats Project can work with, type File formats supported by Project into the Search box in the upper right corner of the Project window.

Although the short film project has not yet started, the project file already contains quite a bit of planned cost data. You'd like to give this data to the financial planner of Southridge Video so she can start work on detailed budgets. However, the financial planner uses a budget program that can't work directly with Project files. You decide to provide her with cost data as tab-delimited text. This will allow her the greatest flexibility in importing the data into her budget program.

Working with Project File Formats

Prior to Project 2000, the Project file format changed significantly with every major release. Starting with Project 2000, however, Microsoft developed a file format that "grows" with each new release of Project but is still usable with previous versions. This means that you can create a project plan in Project 2003 and open it directly in Project 2000 or 2002. Features that are new in the 2003 version will not be visible when the file is opened in the 2000 or 2002 version. Otherwise, you can freely exchange files between the 2003, 2002, and 2000 versions.

Project 2003 can open Project 98 files, as well as save in Project 98 format. Features that were introduced after the 98 version, such as deadline dates and multiple baselines, will not appear when saving a file in 98 format.

Project 2003 can open files in the MPX format, which is supported by a variety of project management programs. Previous versions of Project up to 98 can save in the MPX format. If you need to migrate project plans from versions of Project prior to 98 to Project 2003, use the MPX format. Note that Project 2003 can open, but not save in, MPX format.

Project 2003 can also export files to XML format. XML is an excellent format for exchanging structured data between Project and other applications that support it.

In this exercise, you save project cost data to a text file using a built-in export map. At this point, you should still have Short Film Project 13 open in Project.

1   On the **File** menu, click **Save As**.

The **Save As** dialog box appears. Project suggests saving the file in the same location from which you opened the practice file. If you see anything different in the **Save As** dialog box, locate the Chapter 13 Sharing folder.

2   In the **File name** box, type Short Film Project 13 Costs.

3   In the **Save as type** box, click **Text (Tab delimited)** from the list, and then click the **Save** button.

The Export Wizard appears.

Tip   Remember that when you use import/export maps, it makes no difference what the current view is in Project. The current view does not affect what data can or can't be exported.

4   Click the **Next** button.

The second page of the Export Wizard appears.

5   Click **Use existing map**, and then click the **Next** button.

6   Under **Choose a map for your data**, select **Cost data by task**.

Your screen should look similar to the following illustration:

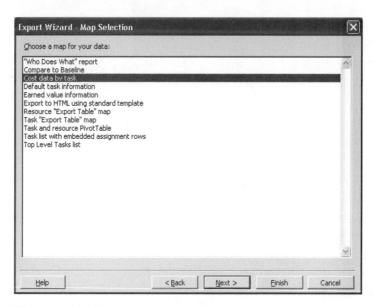

7   Click the **Finish** button.

Project saves the text file. To view it, you will open it in Microsoft Notepad.

8   On the Windows **Start** menu, point to **All Programs**, point to **Accessories**, and click **Notepad**.

Notepad starts.

9   In Notepad, make sure that **Word Wrap** is turned off. (On the **Format** menu, **Word Wrap** should not be selected.)

10   On the **File** menu, click **Open**.

11   Open the document Short Film Project 13 Costs in your Chapter 13 Sharing folder. Your screen should look like the following illustration:

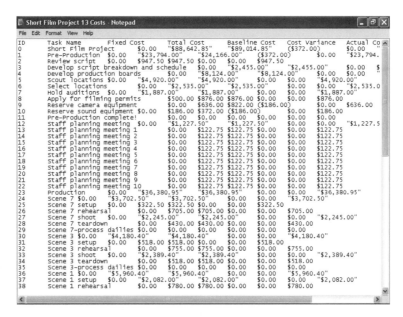

In this file, the fields are separated by tabs. It might not be easy for you to read, but this format is easily imported into virtually any data-crunching program.

12 On the **File** menu, click **Exit**.

Notepad closes, and you return to Project.

Charting Data in Excel with the Analyze Timescaled Data Wizard

You can create charts of *timephased* task or resource information in Excel using a wizard in Project. The wizard is called the Analyze Timescaled Data Wizard. To start it, on the **View** menu, point to **Toolbars**, and then click **Analysis**. On the **Analysis** toolbar, click the **Analyze Timescaled Data In Excel** button. With the Analyze Timescaled Data Wizard, you can see trends of either planned or actual values distributed over time (in daily up to yearly increments) for tasks or resources. You can choose to export the entire project or just selected tasks or resources.

If you have a task view (such as the Gantt Chart) displayed when you start the wizard, you can use the wizard to export any timephased task-related values you want. For example,

(continued)

in the planning stage of a project, you could export and chart the planned Work and Cost totals per month and see the monthly totals charted over time. Here is what such a chart for the Short Film Project 13 file looks like:

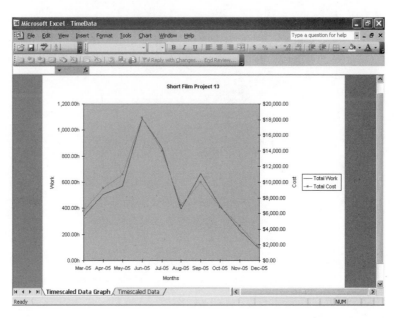

After work has begun, some useful values to chart include Baseline Work with Actual Work and Baseline Cost with Actual Cost.

If you have a resource view (such as the Resource Sheet) displayed when you start the wizard, you can use the wizard to export any timephased resource-related values you want.

You could manually do everything the wizard does for you, but the wizard is faster. The wizard does require that you have Excel installed on the same system as Project, however. In the Excel workbook created by the wizard you also get the detailed, timephased data from which the chart is generated. Here is the timephased data that the chart above is derived from:

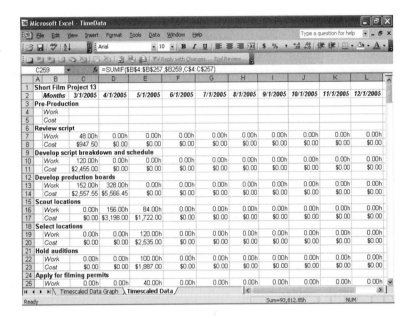

CLOSE: the Short Film Project 13 file.

Key Points

- When sharing Project data with other Office applications, two useful techniques include copying images of the active view and generating a new Office document that includes key Project details and an image of the active view.

- You can both copy from and paste into Project much as you can with other Windows applications. However when pasting data into a table in Project, take care to ensure that the data you want ends up in the correct fields.

- To help import Excel data into Project, Project installs two Excel templates that are properly structured for importing into Project.

- When opening other data formats in Project, Project uses import maps to help organize the imported data into the right structure for a Project table.

- Project supports saving data to common structured data formats such as Access desktop database and XML.

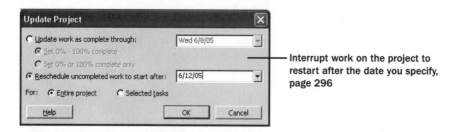

Update a baseline prior to tracking actual work, page 279

		Task Name	Duration
1		⊟ Pre-Production	57.5 days
2		Review script	1 wk
3		Develop script breakdo	1.05 wks
4		Develop production bos	3 wks
5		Review production boa	1 wk
6		Scout locations	2 wks
7		Select locations	1.05 wks

	Task Name	Work	Baseline	Variance	Actual	Remaining	% W. Comp.	Details	S	M	T
1	⊟ Pre-Production	1,204 hrs	1,204 hrs	0 hrs	90 hrs	1,114 hrs	7%	Work		24h	
								Act. W		18h	
2	⊟ Review script	48 hrs	48 hrs	0 hrs	48 hrs	0 hrs	100%	Work			
								Act. W			
	Clair Hector	28 hrs	28 hrs	0 hrs	28 hrs	0 hrs	100%	Work			
								Act. W			
	Scott Cooper	20 hrs	20 hrs	0 hrs	20 hrs	0 hrs	100%	Work			
								Act. W			
3	⊟ Develop script breakdo	120 hrs	120 hrs	0 hrs	42 hrs	78 hrs	35%	Work		18h	
								Act. W		18h	
	Clair Hector	40 hrs	40 hrs	0 hrs	14 hrs	26 hrs	35%	Work		6h	
								Act. W		6h	
	Johnathan Perrers	40 hrs	40 hrs	0 hrs	14 hrs	26 hrs	35%	Work		6h	
								Act. W		6h	
	Scott Cooper	40 hrs	40 hrs	0 hrs	14 hrs	26 hrs	35%	Work		6h	
								Act. W		6h	
4	⊟ Develop production bos	348 hrs	348 hrs	0 hrs	0 hrs	348 hrs	0%	Work			
								Act. W			
	Johnathan Perrers	114 hrs	114 hrs	0 hrs	0 hrs	114 hrs	0%	Work			
								Act. W			
	Kim Yoshida	120 hrs	120 hrs	0 hrs	0 hrs	120 hrs	0%	Work			
								Act. W			
	Scott Cooper	114 hrs	114 hrs	0 hrs	0 hrs	114 hrs	0%	Work			
								Act. W			
5	⊟ Review production boa	80 hrs	80 hrs	0 hrs	0 hrs	80 hrs	0%	Work			

Enter actual work for tasks and assignments, page 283

	Task Name	Work	Details	M	T	W	T	F	S	S	M	T
1	⊞ Pre-Production	1,204 hrs	Work	24h	24h	8h						
			Act. W	24h	24h	8h						
24	⊟ Production	2,188 hrs	Work			10h	38h	113h			49h	5h
			Act. W			10h						
25	⊟ Scene 7	215 hrs	Work			10h	38h	113h			49h	5h
			Act. W			10h						
26	⊟ Scene 7 setup	15 hrs	Work			10h	5h					
			Act. W			10h						
	Electrician	3 hrs	Work			2h	1h					
			Act. W			2h						
	Jo Brown	6 hrs	Work			4h	2h					
			Act. W			4h						
	Max Benson	6 hrs	Work			4h	2h					
			Act. W			4h						
27	⊟ Scene 7 rehearsal	44 hrs	Work				33h	11h				
			Act. W									
	Jan Miksovsky	8 hrs	Work				6h	2h				
			Act. W									
	Jo Brown	8 hrs	Work				6h	2h				
			Act. W									
	Joseph Matthes	8 hrs	Work				6h	2h				
			Act. W									
	Paul Borm	4 hrs	Work				3h	1h				
			Act. W									
	Scott Cooper	8 hrs	Work				6h	2h				

Enter timephased actual work for tasks and assignments, page 291

Update Project

- ○ Update work as complete through: Wed 6/8/05
  - ● Set 0% - 100% complete
  - ○ Set 0% or 100% complete only
- ● Reschedule uncompleted work to start after: 6/12/05

For: ● Entire project   ○ Selected tasks

[Help]   [OK]   [Cancel]

Interrupt work on the project to restart after the date you specify, page 296

Chapter 14 at a Glance

14 Tracking Progress on Tasks and Assignments

In this chapter you will learn to:

✔ Update a previously saved baseline plan.

✔ Record actual work for tasks and assignments.

✔ Record daily actual work values.

✔ Interrupt work on a task and specify the date on which the task should start again.

See Also Do you need a quick refresher on the topics in this chapter? See the quick reference entries on page xxxv.

Building, verifying, and communicating a sound project plan might take much or even most of your time as a project manager. However, planning is only the first phase of managing your projects. After the *planning* is completed, the implementation of the project starts—carrying out the plan that was previously developed. Ideally, projects are implemented just as planned, but this is seldom the case. In general, the more complex the project plan and the longer its planned duration, the more opportunity there is for *variance* to appear. Variance is the difference between what you thought would happen (as recorded in the project plan) and what really happened (as recorded by your tracking method).

Properly *tracking* actual work and comparing it against the plan enables you to identify variance early and adjust the incomplete portion of the plan when necessary. If you completed Chapter 6, "Tracking Progress on Tasks," you were introduced to the simpler ways of tracking *actuals* in a project plan. These include recording the percentage of a task that has been completed as well as its actual start and finish dates. These methods of tracking progress are fine for many projects, but Microsoft Office Project 2003 also supports more detailed ways of tracking.

In this chapter, you track task-level and assignment-level work totals and work per time period, such as work completed per week or per day. Information distributed over time is commonly known as *timephased*, so tracking work by time period is sometimes referred to as *tracking timephased actuals*. This is the most detailed level of tracking progress available in Project.

As with simpler tracking methods, tracking timephased actuals is a way to address the most basic questions of managing a project:

■   Are tasks starting and finishing as planned? If not, what will be the impact on the project's finish date?

■   Are resources spending more or less time than planned to complete tasks?

■   Is it taking more or less money than planned to complete tasks?

As a project manager, you must determine what level of tracking best meets the needs of your project plan and your stakeholders. As you might expect, the more detailed the tracking level, the more effort required from you and the resources assigned to tasks. This chapter exposes you to the most detailed tracking methods available in Project.

In this chapter, you work with different means of tracking work and handling incomplete work. You begin, however, by updating the project baseline.

Tip   *This tip describes enterprise project management (EPM) functionality.* This chapter describes entering actual values directly in Project. Project Professional, when used with Project Server, offers much more sophisticated ways of collecting information (such as actual work) from resources and other stakeholders. To learn more about the enterprise collaboration tools available with Project Server, see Part 4, "Introducing Project Server."

Important   Before you can use the practice files in this chapter, be sure you install them from the book's companion CD to their default location. See "Using the Book's CD-ROM," on page xiii, for more information.

Updating a Baseline

If you completed Chapter 6, "Tracking Progress on Tasks," you saved a baseline plan for a project plan. Recall that a *baseline* is a collection of important values in a project plan, such as the planned start dates, finish dates, and costs of tasks, resources, and assignments. When you save a baseline, Project takes a "snapshot" of the existing values and saves it in the Project plan for future comparison.

Keep in mind that the purpose of the baseline is to record what you expected the project plan to look like at one point in time. As time passes, however, you might need to change your expectations. After saving an initial baseline plan, you might need to fine-tune the project plan by adding or removing tasks or assignments, and so on. To keep an accurate baseline for later comparison, you have several options:

- Update the baseline for the entire project. This simply replaces the original baseline values with the currently scheduled values.

- Update the baseline for selected tasks. This does not affect the baseline values for other tasks or resource baseline values in the project plan.

- Save a second or subsequent baseline. You can save up to 11 baselines in a single plan. The first one is called Baseline, and the rest are Baseline 1 through Baseline 10.

Tip   To learn more about baselines in Project's online Help, type **About baselines** into the **Search** box in the upper right corner of the Project window. The **Search** box initially contains the text *Type a question for help*.

Since you completed the initial planning for the short film project and saved an initial baseline, the project plan has undergone some additional fine-tuning. This included some adjustments to assignments and task durations and a new task in the pre-production phase of the project. Because of these changes, the initial baseline does not quite match the project plan as it is currently scheduled. In this exercise, you compare the project plan as it is currently scheduled with the baseline plan and update the baseline for the project plan.

Important   If you are running Project Professional, you may need to make a one-time adjustment to use the My Computer account and to work offline. This helps ensure that the practice files you work with in this chapter don't affect your Project Server data. For more information, see "Starting Project Professional," on page 10.

OPEN: Short Film Project 14a from the *My Documents\Microsoft Press\Project 2003 Step by Step* *Chapter 14 Advanced Tracking* folder. You can also access the practice files for this book by clicking **Start**, **All Programs**, **Microsoft Press**, **Project 2003 Step by Step**, and then selecting the chapter folder of the file you want to open.

1   On the **File** menu, click **Save As**.

The **Save As** dialog box appears.

2   In the **File name** box, type Short Film Project 14 Baseline, and then click the **Save** button.

Next you will switch to a different view to see baseline and scheduled values arranged for easy comparison.

3   On the **View** menu, click **Tracking Gantt**.

The Tracking Gantt view appears. Your screen should look similar to the following illustration:

In the Tracking Gantt view, the Gantt bars for the tasks as they are currently scheduled appear in blue (or if critical, red) and their baseline schedule values appear in gray.

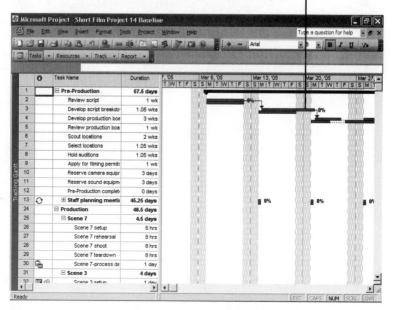

In the chart portion of this view, the tasks as they are currently scheduled appear as blue bars (if they are not critical tasks) or red bars (if they are critical). Below them, the baseline values of each task appear as gray bars.

Tip   In Gantt Chart views, the colors, patterns, and shapes of the bars represent specific things. To see what any item on the Gantt chart represents, just point your mouse pointer at it and a description will appear in a ScreenTip. To see a complete legend of Gantt chart items and their formatting, on the **Format** menu, click **Bar Styles**.

4   On the **Edit** menu, click **Go To**, enter 5 in the **ID** box, and then click **OK**.

Tip   Remember that `Ctrl`+`G` is a shortcut for displaying the **Go To** dialog box.

The Tracking Gantt view scrolls to display the Gantt bars for task 5, *Review production boards*. This task was added to the plan after the initial baseline was saved. Your screen should look similar to the following illustration:

This task was added to the project plan after its initial —
baseline was saved, so this task has no baseline.

As you can see in the Tracking Gantt view, this task has no baseline values.

To conclude this exercise, you will resave the baseline for the project plan.

5   On the **Tools** menu, point to **Tracking**, and then click **Save Baseline**.

The **Save Baseline** dialog box appears.

6   Make sure that the **Save baseline** option is selected. In the **For** area, make sure
that the **Entire project** option is selected.

Tip   To update a baseline just for selected tasks, click **Selected tasks** in the **For**
area. When you do this, the options under **Roll up baselines** become available. You
can control how baseline updates should affect the baseline values for summary
tasks. For example, you could resave a baseline for a subtask and update its
related summary task baseline values if you wanted.

7   Click **OK** to update the baseline.

Project alerts you that you are about to overwrite the previously saved baseline
values.

8   Click the **Yes** button.

Project updates the baseline values for the project plan.

Your screen should look similar to the following illustration:

After resaving the baseline for the entire project, —
the baseline start, finish, and duration values
(among others) match the scheduled values.

Task 5 now has a baseline, and all of the other tasks' baseline values now match
their scheduled values.

Save

9   On the Standard toolbar, click the **Save** button.

10 On the **File** menu, click **Close** to close the project plan.

Saving Interim Plans

After you've started tracking actual values, or any time you've adjusted your schedule, you might want to take another snapshot of the current start and finish dates. You can do this with an *interim plan*. Like a baseline, an interim plan is a set of current values from the project plan that Project saves with the file. Unlike the baseline, however, an interim plan saves only the start and finish dates of tasks, not resource or assignment values. You can save up to 10 different interim plans during a project. (If you find that you need multiple snapshots of scheduled values in addition to start and finish dates, you should instead save additional baselines.)

Depending on the scope and duration of your projects, you might want to save an interim plan at any of the following junctures:

■   At the conclusion of a major phase of work

■   At preset time intervals, such as weekly or monthly

■   Just before or after entering a large number of actual values

To save an interim plan, on the **Tools** menu, point to **Tracking**, and then click **Save Baseline**. In the **Save Baseline** dialog box, select the **Save interim plan** option. To learn more about interim plans, type Save an interim plan into the **Search** box in the upper right corner of the Project window.

Tracking Actual and Remaining Values for Tasks and Assignments

If you completed Chapter 6, "Tracking Progress on Tasks," you entered actual start, finish, and duration values for individual tasks. For tasks that have resources assigned to them, you can enter actual and remaining work values for the task as a whole or for specific assignments to that task. To help you understand how Project handles the actual values you enter, consider the following:

■   If a task has a single resource assigned to it, the actual work values you enter for the task or the assignment apply equally to both the task and the resource. For example, if you record that the assignment started on March 21 and has five hours of actual work, those values apply to the task as well.

■ If a task has multiple resources assigned to it, the actual work values you enter for the task are distributed among or *rolled down* to the assignments according to their assignment units. This level of detail is appropriate if you aren't concerned about the details at the individual assignment level.

■ If a task has multiple resources assigned to it, the actual work values you enter for one assignment are *rolled up* to the task, but don't affect the other assignments to the task. This level of detail is appropriate if details at the individual assignment level are important to you.

In this exercise, you record task-level and assignment-level actuals and see how the information is rolled up or down between tasks and assignments.

OPEN: Short Film Project 14b from the *My Documents**Microsoft Press**Project 2003 Step by Step*\\ *Chapter 14 Advanced Tracking* folder. You can also access the practice files for this book by clicking **Start**, **All Programs**, **Microsoft Press**, **Project 2003 Step by Step**, and then selecting the chapter folder of the file you want to open.

1   On the **File** menu, click **Save As**.

The **Save As** dialog box appears.

2   In the **File name** box, type Short Film Project 14 Actuals, and then click the **Save** button.

This version of the project plan includes the updated baseline values you previously saved, as well as the first actuals reported against the first pre-production task.

3   On the **View** menu, click **Task Usage**.

The Task Usage view appears. This usage view lists resources under the tasks to which they're assigned in a table on the left side of the view. On the right side of the view, you see rows organized under a timescale. The rows next to each task name show you the scheduled work values for the task. The rows next to the resource names show you the scheduled work values for each resource—in other words, the scheduled work per assignment. These are the timephased values of the assignments. The two sides of the view are split by a vertical divider bar.

4   In the **Task Name** column, click the name of task 3, **Develop script breakdown and schedule**.

Go To Selected
Task

5   On the Standard toolbar, click the **Go To Selected Task** button.

The timephased grid on the right side of the view scrolls to display the first scheduled work for the task.

Next you'll switch the table and details shown in the view.

6   On the **View** menu, point to **Table: Usage**, and then click **Work**.

The Work table appears. Your screen should look similar to the following illustration:

In a usage view, a table appears in the left pane, and a timephased grid appears in the right pane.

	Task Name	Work	Baseline	Details	S	S	M	T	W	T	F	S
							Mar 13, '05					
1	Pre-Production	1,204 hrs	1,204 hrs	Work			24h	24h	24h	24h	24h	
2	Review script	48 hrs	48 hrs	Work								
	Clair Hector	28 hrs	28 hrs	Work								
	Scott Cooper	20 hrs	20 hrs	Work								
3	Develop script breakdo	120 hrs	120 hrs	Work			18h	24h	24h	24h	24h	
	Clair Hector	40 hrs	40 hrs	Work			6h	8h	8h	8h	8h	
	Johnathan Perrera	40 hrs	40 hrs	Work			6h	8h	8h	8h	8h	
	Scott Cooper	40 hrs	40 hrs	Work			6h	8h	8h	8h	8h	
4	Develop production boa	348 hrs	348 hrs	Work								
	Johnathan Perrera	114 hrs	114 hrs	Work								
	Kim Yoshida	120 hrs	120 hrs	Work								
	Scott Cooper	114 hrs	114 hrs	Work								
5	Review production boa	80 hrs	80 hrs	Work								
	Clair Hector	40 hrs	40 hrs	Work								
	Scott Cooper	40 hrs	40 hrs	Work								
6	Scout locations	240 hrs	240 hrs	Work								
	Jan Miksovsky	80 hrs	80 hrs	Work								
	Jo Brown	80 hrs	80 hrs	Work								
	Max Benson	80 hrs	80 hrs	Work								
7	Select locations	120 hrs	120 hrs	Work								
	Clair Hector	40 hrs	40 hrs	Work								
	Max Benson	40 hrs	40 hrs	Work								

This timephased grid displays scheduled work per day for each assignment and task. Changing the timescale of the grid changes the level of detail it reports, though the underlying timephased data does not change.

This table includes the Actual Work and Remaining Work columns you will work with shortly, though they might not yet be visible. The values in the Work column are the task and assignment totals for scheduled work. Note that each task's work value is the sum of its assignment work values. For example, the work total for task 2, 48 hours, is the sum of Clair Hector's 28 hours of work on the task and Scott Cooper's 20 hours.

Next you'll change the details shown on the timephased grid on the right side of the view.

7   On the **Format** menu, point to **Details**, and then click **Actual Work**.

For each task and assignment, Project displays the Work and Actual Work rows on the timephased grid on the right side of the view. Your screen should look similar to the following illustration:

When you display the actual work details, the Act. Work row appears in the timephased grid for every assignment, task, and summary task.

	Task Name	Work	Baseline	Details	Mar 13, '05							
					S	S	M	T	W	T	F	S
1	⊟ Pre-Production	**1,204 hrs**	**1,204 hrs**	Work	■■■		24h	24h	24h	24h	24h	
				Act. W								
2	⊟ Review script	48 hrs	48 hrs	Work								
				Act. W								
	Clair Hector	28 hrs	28 hrs	Work								
				Act. W								
	Scott Cooper	20 hrs	20 hrs	Work								
				Act. W								
3	⊟ Develop script breakdo	120 hrs	120 hrs	Work			18h	24h	24h	24h	24h	
				Act. W								
	Clair Hector	40 hrs	40 hrs	Work			6h	8h	8h	8h	8h	
				Act. W								
	Johnathan Perrera	40 hrs	40 hrs	Work			6h	8h	8h	8h	8h	
				Act. W								
	Scott Cooper	40 hrs	40 hrs	Work			6h	8h	8h	8h	8h	
				Act. W								
4	⊟ Develop production bos	348 hrs	348 hrs	Work								
				Act. W								
	Johnathan Perrera	114 hrs	114 hrs	Work								
				Act. W								
	Kim Yoshida	120 hrs	120 hrs	Work								
				Act. W								
	Scott Cooper	114 hrs	114 hrs	Work								
				Act. W								
5	⊟ Review production bos	80 hrs	80 hrs	Work								

In the timephased grid, you see the scheduled work values per day. If you were to add up the daily work values for a specific task or assignment, the total would equal the value in the Work column for that task or assignment. In a usage view, you see work values at two different levels of detail: the total value for a task or assignment and the more detailed timephased level. These two sets of values are directly related.

Next you'll enter task-level and assignment-level actual work values and see how they are reflected in the timephased details.

8   Using the mouse, drag the vertical divider bar to the right until you can see all the columns in the Work table.

⊣⊢
Vertical Divider
Pointer

Tip   When the mouse pointer is in the right position to drag the vertical divider bar, it changes to a two-headed arrow that points left and right.

Your screen should look similar to this illustration:

To see more or less of the table on the left and the timephased grid on the right, drag this divider bar left or right.

	Task Name	Work	Baseline	Variance	Actual	Remaining	% W. Comp.	Details	Mar 13, '05 S	M	T
1	⊟ Pre-Production	1,204 hrs	1,204 hrs	0 hrs	48 hrs	1,156 hrs	4%	Work		24h	
								Act. W			
2	⊟ Review script	48 hrs	48 hrs	0 hrs	48 hrs	0 hrs	100%	Work			
								Act. W			
	Clair Hector	28 hrs	28 hrs	0 hrs	28 hrs	0 hrs	100%	Work			
								Act. W			
	Scott Cooper	20 hrs	20 hrs	0 hrs	20 hrs	0 hrs	100%	Work			
								Act. W			
3	⊟ Develop script breakdo	120 hrs	120 hrs	0 hrs	0 hrs	120 hrs	0%	Work		18h	
								Act. W			
	Clair Hector	40 hrs	40 hrs	0 hrs	0 hrs	40 hrs	0%	Work		6h	
								Act. W			
	Johnathan Perrera	40 hrs	40 hrs	0 hrs	0 hrs	40 hrs	0%	Work		6h	
								Act. W			
	Scott Cooper	40 hrs	40 hrs	0 hrs	0 hrs	40 hrs	0%	Work		6h	
								Act. W			
4	⊟ Develop production bos	348 hrs	348 hrs	0 hrs	0 hrs	348 hrs	0%	Work			
								Act. W			
	Johnathan Perrera	114 hrs	114 hrs	0 hrs	0 hrs	114 hrs	0%	Work			
								Act. W			
	Kim Yoshida	120 hrs	120 hrs	0 hrs	0 hrs	120 hrs	0%	Work			
								Act. W			
	Scott Cooper	114 hrs	114 hrs	0 hrs	0 hrs	114 hrs	0%	Work			
								Act. W			
5	⊟ Review production bos	80 hrs	80 hrs	0 hrs	0 hrs	80 hrs	0%	Work			

9 In the **Actual** column for task 3, *Develop script breakdown and schedule*, type or click 42h, and then press Enter.

Your screen should look similar to the following illustration:

Entering an actual value for the task causes Project to distribute the actual values among the assigned resources and adjust remaining work and other values.

	Task Name	Work	Baseline	Variance	Actual	Remaining	% W. Comp.	Details	Mar 13, '05 S	M	T
1	⊟ Pre-Production	1,204 hrs	1,204 hrs	0 hrs	90 hrs	1,114 hrs	7%	Work		24h	
								Act. W		18h	
2	⊟ Review script	48 hrs	48 hrs	0 hrs	48 hrs	0 hrs	100%	Work			
								Act. W			
	Clair Hector	28 hrs	28 hrs	0 hrs	28 hrs	0 hrs	100%	Work			
								Act. W			
	Scott Cooper	20 hrs	20 hrs	0 hrs	20 hrs	0 hrs	100%	Work			
								Act. W			
3	⊟ Develop script breakdo	120 hrs	120 hrs	0 hrs	42 hrs	78 hrs	35%	Work		18h	
								Act. W		18h	
	Clair Hector	40 hrs	40 hrs	0 hrs	14 hrs	26 hrs	35%	Work		6h	
								Act. W		6h	
	Johnathan Perrera	40 hrs	40 hrs	0 hrs	14 hrs	26 hrs	35%	Work		6h	
								Act. W		6h	
	Scott Cooper	40 hrs	40 hrs	0 hrs	14 hrs	26 hrs	35%	Work		6h	
								Act. W		6h	
4	⊟ Develop production bos	348 hrs	348 hrs	0 hrs	0 hrs	348 hrs	0%	Work			
								Act. W			
	Johnathan Perrera	114 hrs	114 hrs	0 hrs	0 hrs	114 hrs	0%	Work			
								Act. W			
	Kim Yoshida	120 hrs	120 hrs	0 hrs	0 hrs	120 hrs	0%	Work			
								Act. W			
	Scott Cooper	114 hrs	114 hrs	0 hrs	0 hrs	114 hrs	0%	Work			
								Act. W			
5	⊟ Review production bos	80 hrs	80 hrs	0 hrs	0 hrs	80 hrs	0%	Work			

Several important things happened when you pressed [Enter]:

- The amount of actual work you entered was subtracted from the Remaining column.

- The actual work was distributed to the three assignments on the task, resulting in 14 hours of actual work being recorded for each resource. Likewise, the updated remaining work value was recalculated for each assignment.

- The updated actual and remaining work values were rolled up to the pre-production summary task.

- The actual work values were also redistributed to the task and assignment timephased values.

Next you'll take a closer look at the actual work values.

10 Drag the vertical divider bar to the left until you see just the Task Name column in the Work table.

Your screen should look similar to the following illustration:

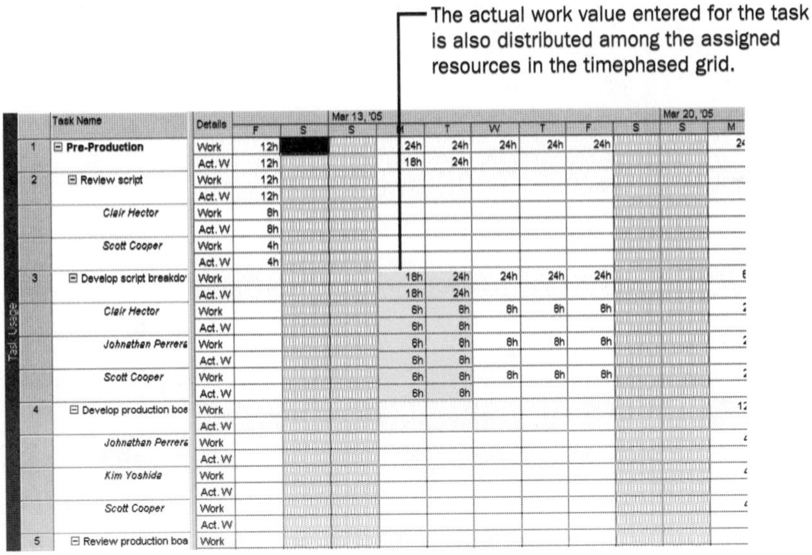

The actual work value entered for the task is also distributed among the assigned resources in the timephased grid.

In the timephased grid side of the view, you can see the daily scheduled work and actual work values for the three resources on Monday and Tuesday, March 14 and 15. Because you entered an actual work value for the entire task, Project assumes that the work was done as scheduled (six hours of scheduled work per resource on Monday and eight hours on Tuesday) and records these timephased values for the resources.

To conclude this exercise, you will enter assignment work values and see the effect on the task.

11 Drag the vertical divider bar back to the right until you see all the columns in the Work table.

12 In the **Actual** column for Clair Hector's assignment to task 3, type or click 30h, and then press [Enter].

Your screen should look similar to this illustration:

Entering an actual value for the assignment causes Project to roll up the actual to the task, but does not affect the other assignments.

	Task Name	Work	Baseline	Variance	Actual	Remaining	% W. Comp.	Details	Mar 13, '05 S	M	T
1	⊟ Pre-Production	1,204 hrs	1,204 hrs	0 hrs	106 hrs	1,098 hrs	9%	Work		24h	
								Act. W		18h	
2	⊟ Review script	48 hrs	48 hrs	0 hrs	48 hrs	0 hrs	100%	Work			
								Act. W			
	Clair Hector	28 hrs	28 hrs	0 hrs	28 hrs	0 hrs	100%	Work			
								Act. W			
	Scott Cooper	20 hrs	20 hrs	0 hrs	20 hrs	0 hrs	100%	Work			
								Act. W			
3	⊟ Develop script breakdo	120 hrs	120 hrs	0 hrs	58 hrs	62 hrs	48%	Work		18h	
								Act. W		18h	
	Clair Hector	40 hrs	40 hrs	0 hrs	30 hrs	10 hrs	75%	Work		6h	
								Act. W		6h	
	Johnathan Perrera	40 hrs	40 hrs	0 hrs	14 hrs	26 hrs	35%	Work		6h	
								Act. W		6h	
	Scott Cooper	40 hrs	40 hrs	0 hrs	14 hrs	26 hrs	35%	Work		6h	
								Act. W		6h	
4	⊟ Develop production boa	348 hrs	348 hrs	0 hrs	0 hrs	348 hrs	0%	Work			
								Act. W			
	Johnathan Perrera	114 hrs	114 hrs	0 hrs	0 hrs	114 hrs	0%	Work			
								Act. W			
	Kim Yoshida	120 hrs	120 hrs	0 hrs	0 hrs	120 hrs	0%	Work			
								Act. W			
	Scott Cooper	114 hrs	114 hrs	0 hrs	0 hrs	114 hrs	0%	Work			
								Act. W			
5	⊟ Review production boa	80 hrs	80 hrs	0 hrs	0 hrs	80 hrs	0%	Work			

Clair Hector's actual and remaining work values are updated, and those updates also roll up to the task and its summary task. However, the actual and remaining work values for the other two resources assigned to the task are not affected.

13 Drag the vertical divider bar back to the left to see the updated timephased values for the task.

Your screen should look similar to the following illustration:

The actual work value entered for the assignment is rolled up to the task and distributed across the assignment in the timephased grid.

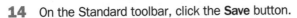

| Task Name | Details | Mar 13, '05 | | | | | | | | | Mar 20, '05 | |
		F	S	S	M	T	W	T	F	S	S	M
1 ⊟ Pre-Production	Work	12h	■			24h	24h	24h	24h	24h			24
	Act. W	12h				18h	24h	8h	8h				
2 ⊟ Review script	Work	12h											
	Act. W	12h											
Clair Hector	Work	8h											
	Act. W	8h											
Scott Cooper	Work	4h											
	Act. W	4h											
3 ⊟ Develop script breakdo	Work					18h	24h	24h	24h	24h			8
	Act. W					18h	24h	8h	8h				
Clair Hector	Work					6h	8h	8h	8h	8h			2
	Act. W					6h	8h	8h	8h				
Johnathan Perrera	Work					6h	8h	8h	8h	8h			2
	Act. W					6h	8h						
Scott Cooper	Work					6h	8h	8h	8h	8h			2
	Act. W					6h	8h						
4 ⊟ Develop production boa	Work												1:
	Act. W												
Johnathan Perrera	Work												4
	Act. W												
Kim Yoshida	Work												4
	Act. W												
Scott Cooper	Work												4
	Act. W												
5 ⊟ Review production boa	Work												

Again Project assumes that the actual work value you entered for Clair was completed as scheduled, so her work and actual work timephased values match through Thursday, March 17.

14 On the Standard toolbar, click the **Save** button.

Save

15 On the **File** menu, click **Close** to close the project plan.

Note In this exercise, you're entering actual work values but you can also enter remaining work values or percentage of work complete. All these values are related to each other—a change to one affects the others. You can update these values in the Work table or on the **Tracking** tab of the **Assignment Information** dialog box (when an assignment is selected).

Tracking a task's actual work complete value is more detailed than entering a simple percentage complete on a task. However, neither method is as detailed as entering timephased actual work for tasks or assignments (as you will see in the next section). There's nothing wrong with tracking actual work at the task or assignment level (or just entering a percentage complete, for that matter) if that level of detail meets your needs. In fact, whether you see the timephased details or not, Project always distributes any percentage complete or task-level or assignment-level actual work value you enter into corresponding timephased values, as you saw earlier. This is one reason why new Project users sometimes are surprised to encounter extremely detailed timephased values, such as 1.67 hours of work, scheduled for a day. If you generally understand the math Project is following, however, you can figure out where such numbers come from. On the other hand, you might not care about this level of scheduling detail—and that's OK too.

Manually Entering Actual Costs

Whenever you've entered actual work values in this chapter, Project has calculated actual cost values for the affected task, its summary task, the resources assigned to the task, and the entire project. By default, Project calculates actual costs and doesn't allow you to enter them directly. In most cases this is what we recommend, and what the practice files used in this book do. However if you want to enter actual cost values yourself in your own project plans, follow these steps:

1   On the **Tools** menu, click the **Options** command.

        The **Options** dialog box appears.

2   Click the **Calculation** tab.

3   Under the **Calculation options for 'Short Film Project 14 Actuals'** label, clear the **Actual costs are always calculated by Microsoft Office Project** check box.

4   Click **OK**.

After automatic cost calculation is turned off, you can enter or import task-level or assignment-level actual costs in the **Actual** field. This field is available in several locations, such as the Cost table. You can also enter actual cost values daily or at another interval in any timescale view, such as the Task Usage or the Resource Usage view. On the **Format** menu, point to the **Details** command, and then click **Actual Cost**.

Tracking Timephased Actual Work for Tasks and Assignments

Entering timephased actuals requires more work on the project manager's part and might require more work from resources to inform the project manager of their daily actuals. However, doing so gives you far more detail about the project's task and resource status than the other methods of entering actuals. Entering timephased values might be the best approach to take if you have a group of tasks or an entire project that include the following:

- High-risk tasks

- Relatively short-duration tasks in which a variance of even a fraction of a day could put the overall project at risk

- Tasks in which sponsors or other stakeholders have an especially strong interest

- Tasks that require hourly billing for labor

At this point in the short film project, the pre-production work has been completed, and the production phase has just begun. Because of the large number of resources involved, the high setup and teardown costs, and the limited availability of sites at which some scenes must be filmed, these tasks are the riskiest ones of the project. In this exercise, you enter daily actuals for production tasks in the Task Usage view.

OPEN: Short Film Project 14c from the *My Documents**Microsoft Press**Project 2003 Step by Step*\\ *Chapter 14 Advanced Tracking* folder. You can also access the practice files for this book by clicking **Start**, **All Programs**, **Microsoft Press**, **Project 2003 Step by Step**, and then selecting the chapter folder of the file you want to open.

1   On the **File** menu, click **Save As**.

The **Save As** dialog box appears.

2   In the **File name** box, type **Short Film Project 14 Timephased Actuals**, and then click the **Save** button.

3   Click the minus sign next to task 1, *Pre-Production,* to collapse this phase of the project plan.

Go To Selected
Task

4   Click the name of task 26, **Scene 7 setup**, and then on the Standard toolbar, click the **Go To Selected Task** button.

Project scrolls the timephased grid to display the first scheduled work values of the Production phase. Your screen should look similar to the following illustration:

	Task Name	Work	Details	M	T	W	T	F	S	S	M	T
1	⊞ **Pre-Production**	1,204 hrs	Work	24h	24h	8h						
			Act. W	24h	24h	8h						
24	⊟ **Production**	2,188 hrs	Work			10h	38h	113h			49h	5h
			Act. W									
25	⊟ Scene 7	215 hrs	Work			10h	38h	113h			49h	5h
			Act. W									
26	⊟ Scene 7 setup	15 hrs	Work			10h	5h					
			Act. W									
	Electrician	3 hrs	Work			2h	1h					
			Act. W									
	Jo Brown	6 hrs	Work			4h	2h					
			Act. W									
	Max Benson	6 hrs	Work			4h	2h					
			Act. W									
27	⊟ Scene 7 rehearsal	44 hrs	Work				33h	11h				
			Act. W									
	Jan Miksovsky	8 hrs	Work				6h	2h				
			Act. W									
	Jo Brown	8 hrs	Work				6h	2h				
			Act. W									
	Joseph Matthe|	8 hrs	Work				6h	2h				
			Act. W									
	Paul Borm	4 hrs	Work				3h	1h				
			Act. W									

The first timephased actual work values you will enter are at the task level, and not for specific assignments.

5   In the timephased grid, click the cell at the intersection of the Wednesday, May 25 column and the task 26 actual work row.

Tip If you point to the name of a day on the timescale, Project will display the full date of that day in a ScreenTip.

You can change the formatting of the timescale to control the time period in which you enter actual values in the timephased grid. For example, you can format it to show weeks rather than days, and when you enter an actual value at the weekly level, that value is distributed over the week. For more information about adjusting the timescale, type **Change the timescale to see a different level of detail** into the **Search** box in the upper right corner of the Project window.

6   Type **10h**, and then press the → key.

Your screen should look similar to the following illustration:

Here is the first timephased actual work value you entered.

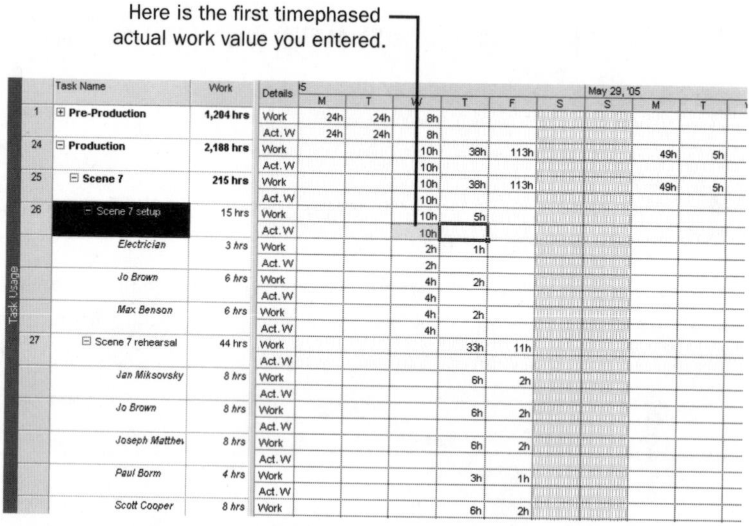

As soon as you entered the first actual value for the task, the scheduled work value changed to match it. Both work and actual work values rolled up to the task and summary task levels and were distributed among the specific assignments to the task. You can see this happen in the timephased grid.

7   In the Thursday, May 26 actual work cell, type **5h**, and then press Enter.

Your screen should look similar to the following illustration:

Here is the second timephased actual work value you entered. The timephased values for the task are distributed to the timephased assignment values and affect the task and assignment totals in the table on the left.

	Task Name	Work	Details	M	T	W		F	S	S	M	T	
1	⊞ Pre-Production	1,204 hrs	Work	24h	24h	8h							
			Act. W	24h	24h	8h							
24	⊟ Production	2,188 hrs	Work			10h	38h	113h			49h	5h	
			Act. W			10h	5h						
25	⊟ Scene 7	215 hrs	Work			10h	38h	113h			49h	5h	
			Act. W			10h	5h						
26	⊟ Scene 7 setup	15 hrs	Work			10h	5h						
			Act. W			10h	5h						
	Electrician	3 hrs	Work			2h	1h						
			Act. W			2h	1h						
	Jo Brown	6 hrs	Work			4h	2h						
			Act. W			4h	2h						
	Max Benson	6 hrs	Work			4h	2h						
			Act. W			4h	2h						
27	⊟ Scene 7 rehearsal	44 hrs	Work				33h	11h					
			Act. W										
	Jan Miksovsky	8 hrs	Work				6h	2h					
			Act. W										
	Jo Brown	8 hrs	Work				6h	2h					
			Act. W										
	Joseph Matthes	8 hrs	Work				6h	2h					
			Act. W										
	Paul Borm	4 hrs	Work				3h	1h					
			Act. W										
	Scott Cooper	8 hrs	Work				6h	2h					

That concludes the actual work for this task. Next you'll enter actual work values for the assignments on the next task.

For task 27, *Scene 7 rehearsal,* you have the actual work values for several resources for Thursday and Friday, May 26 and 27, 2005

8 If necessary, scroll the Task Usage view up so that all of the assignments to task 27 are visible.

9 In the timephased grid, click the cell at the intersection of the Thursday, May 26 column and Jan Miksovsky's actual work row for her assignment to task 27.

10 Enter the following actual work values into the timescale grid:

Resource name	Thursday's actual work	Friday's actual work
Jan Miksovsky	3h	5h
Jo Brown	3h	5h
Joseph Matthews	2h	7h
Paul Borm	3h	1h
Scott Cooper	2.5h	5.5h
Sue Jackson	6h	2h

11 When you are finished, your screen should look similar to the following illustration:

	Task Name	Work	Details		M	T	W	T	F	S	May 29, '05 S	M	T
27	⊟ Scene 7 rehearsal	45 hrs	Work					19.5h	25.5h				
			Act. W					19.5h	25.5h				
	Jan Miksovsky	8 hrs	Work					3h	5h				
			Act. W					3h	5h				
	Jo Brown	8 hrs	Work					3h	5h				
			Act. W					3h	5h				
	Joseph Matthew	9 hrs	Work					2h	7h				
			Act. W					2h	7h				
	Paul Borm	4 hrs	Work					3h	1h				
			Act. W					3h	1h				
	Scott Cooper	8 hrs	Work					2.5h	5.5h				
			Act. W					2.5h	5.5h				
	Sue Jackson	8 hrs	Work					6h	2h				
			Act. W					6h	2h				
28	⊟ Scene 7 shoot	136 hrs	Work						34h			102h	
			Act. W										
	16-mm Camera	24 hrs	Work						6h			18h	
			Act. W										
	16-mm Film	40 100 Feet	Work (						10			30	
			Act. W										
	500-Watt Light	16 hrs	Work						4h			12h	
			Act. W										
	Camera Boom	8 hrs	Work						2h			6h	
			Act. W										

12 Again, the individual resources' actual work values were rolled up to the tasks' actual work values. The original work values are also saved in the baseline, should you ever need to refer to them later.

13 On the Standard toolbar, click the **Save** button.

Save

14 On the **File** menu, click **Close** to close the project plan.

Tip   In this exercise, you have seen how task and assignment values are directly related; an update to one directly affects the other. However, if you want, you can break this relationship. Doing so enables you to record progress for resource assignments, for example, and manually enter actual values for the tasks to which those resources are assigned. You normally should not break this relationship unless you have special reporting needs within your organization—for example, you must follow a status reporting methodology based on something other than the actual values recorded for assignments in project plans. To break this relationship, on the **Tools** menu, click **Options**. On the **Calculation** tab of the **Options** dialog box, clear the **Updating task status updates resource status** check box. This setting applies to the entire project plan you have open at the time; you cannot apply it to only some tasks within a project plan.

When you need to track actual work at the most detailed level possible, use the timephased grid in the Task Usage or the Resource Usage view. In either view, you can enter actual work values for individual assignments daily, weekly, or at whatever time period you want. For example, if a task has three resources assigned to it, and you know that two resources worked on the task for eight hours one day and the third worked for six hours, you can enter these as three separate values on a timephased grid.

If your organization uses a timesheet reporting system for tracking actual work, you might be able to use this timesheet data in Project as timephased actuals. You might not need to track at this level, but if resources complete timesheets for other purposes (billing other departments within the organization, for example), you can use their data and save yourself some work.

Project Management Focus:
Collecting Actuals from Resources

The table you used in the previous exercise is similar to a time card. In fact, to enter assignment-level actual work values, you need some form of paper time card or its electronic equivalent. Several methods are used to collect such data from resources, assuming that you need to track actuals at this level of detail. Some collection methods include the following:

- Use Project Professional in conjunction with Project Server for intranet-based team collaboration, tracking, and status reporting. To learn more about Project 2002 Server, see Part 4, "Introducing Project Server."

- Collect actual values yourself. This method is feasible if you communicate with only a small group of resources on a frequent basis. It's also a good opportunity to talk directly to the resources about any surprises they might have encountered (either positive or negative) while performing the work.

- Collect actuals through a formal status reporting system. This technique might work through the already existing hierarchy of your organization and serve additional purposes besides project status reporting.

Rescheduling Incomplete Work

During the course of a project, from time to time work might be interrupted for a specific task or for the entire project. Should this happen, you can have Project reschedule the remaining work to restart after the date you specify.

When you reschedule incomplete work, you specify the date after which work can resume—the rescheduled date. Here is how Project handles tasks in relation to the rescheduled date:

- If the task does not have any actual work recorded for it prior to the rescheduled date and does not have a constraint applied, the entire task is rescheduled to begin after that date.

- If the task has some actual work recorded prior to but none after the rescheduled date, the task is split so that all remaining work starts after the rescheduled date. The actual work is not affected.

- If the task has some actual work recorded for it prior to as well as after the rescheduled date, the task is not affected.

At this point in the short film project, work on the first two scenes has been completed and the team is about to start work on the next scheduled scene, Scene 1. In this exercise, you troubleshoot a delay in work caused by a problem at the studio.

OPEN: Short Film Project 14d from the *My Documents**Microsoft Press**Project 2003 Step by Step*\ *Chapter 14 Advanced Tracking* folder. You can also access the practice files for this book by clicking **Start**, **All Programs, Microsoft Press, Project 2003 Step by Step**, and then selecting the chapter folder of the file you want to open.

1 On the **File** menu, click **Save As**.

The **Save As** dialog box appears.

2 In the **File name** box, type **Short Film Project 14 Reschedule**, and then click the **Save** button.

3 On the **Edit** menu, click **Go To**, enter **38** in the **ID** box, and then click **OK**.

The Gantt Chart view scrolls to display the Gantt bar for task 38, *Scene 1 setup*. Currently this task has one day of actual work completed and two days of scheduled work remaining.

4 Scroll the Gantt Chart view up so that the Scene 1 summary task appears near the top of the view.

Your screen should look similar to the following illustration:

Progress bars indicate the portion of —
the task that has been completed—in
this case, one day of a three-day task.

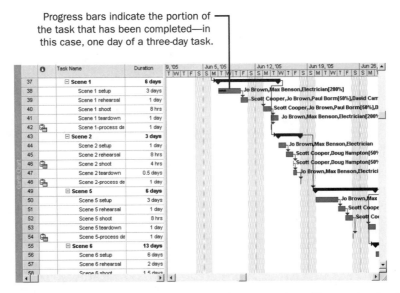

You have learned that on the evening of Tuesday, June 7, a water pipe burst in the studio where Scene 1 was to be shot. None of the project's equipment was damaged, but the cleanup will delay work until the following Monday, June 13. This effectively stops work on the production tasks for the rest of the week. Next you will reschedule incomplete work so the project can start again on Monday.

5   On the **Tools** menu, point to **Tracking**, and then click **Update Project**.

The **Update Project** dialog box appears.

6   Select the **Reschedule uncompleted work to start after** option, and in the date box, type or click 6/12/05.

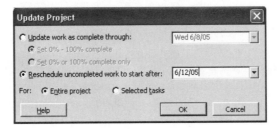

7   Click **OK** to close the **Update Project** dialog box.

Project splits task 38 so that the incomplete portion of the task is delayed until Monday. Your screen should look similar to the following illustration:

Rescheduling work for the project causes Project to split —
this task, and then reschedule the remainder of it (and
all subsequent tasks) after the date you specified.

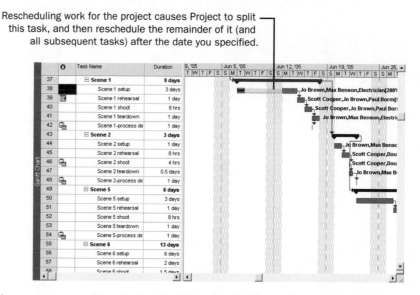

As you can see, although the duration of task 38 remains at three days, its finish date and subsequent start dates for successor tasks have been pushed out. So although we have addressed a specific problem, in doing so we have created other problems in the remainder of the project. You will address this and other problems in the project plan in later chapters.

Tip   You can turn off Project's ability to reschedule incomplete work on tasks that have any actual work. On the **Tools** menu, click the **Options** command. In the **Options** dialog box, click the **Schedule** tab, and then clear the **Split in-progress tasks** check box.

If you use status dates for reporting actuals, Project supports several options for controlling the way completed and incomplete segments of a task are scheduled around the status date. On the **Tools** menu, click the **Options** command. In the **Options** dialog box, click the **Calculation** tab. The options that control scheduling around the status date are **Move end of completed parts after status date back to status date** and the three other check boxes below it.

For more information about these and other options on the tabs of the **Options** dialog box, click the **Help** button that appears in the dialog box. To learn more about working with status dates in Project, type **About the status date** into the **Search** box in the upper right corner of the Project window.

CLOSE: the Short Film Project 14 Reschedule file.

Key Points

- Saving a baseline saves a large set of task, resource, and assignment values in a project plan. Saving an interim plan, however, saves only the start and finish dates of tasks.

- If you track work at the task level, work rolls down to the assignments. Conversely, if you track work at the assignment level, work rolls up to the task level.

- In usage views, you can change the time increments on the lower tier of the timescale to match the time period against which you wish to track. For example, if you wish to record actual work as full weeks, you can set the timescale to display weeks on the lower tier.

- Should work on a project be interrupted for some reason, you can reschedule the work to begin again on the date you specify.

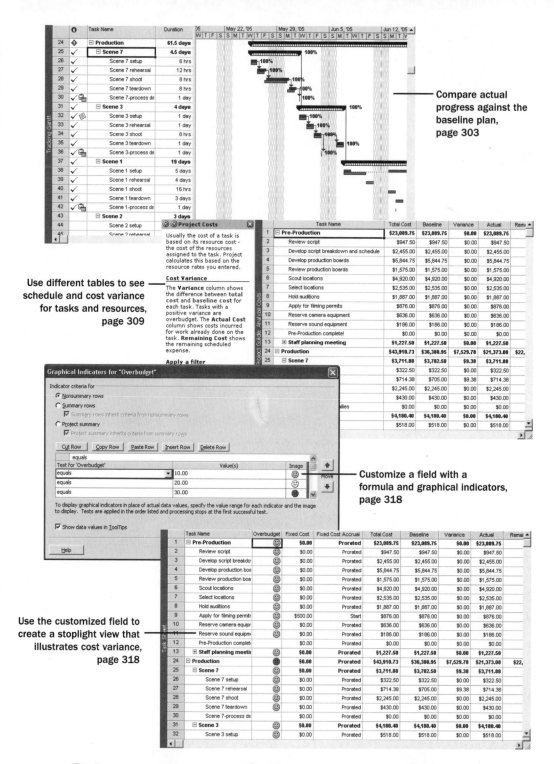

Compare actual progress against the baseline plan, page 303

Use different tables to see schedule and cost variance for tasks and resources, page 309

Customize a field with a formula and graphical indicators, page 318

Use the customized field to create a stoplight view that illustrates cost variance, page 318

15 Viewing and Reporting Project Status

In this chapter you will learn to:

✔ Determine which tasks were started or completed late.

✔ View task costs at summary and detail levels.

✔ Examine resource costs and variance.

✔ Use custom fields to create a stoplight view that illustrates each task's cost variance.

See Also Do you need a quick refresher on the topics in this chapter? See the quick reference entries on pages xxxv–xxxvi.

After a project's *baseline* has been set and work has begun, the primary focus of the project manager shifts from planning to collecting, entering, and analyzing project performance details in Microsoft Office Project 2003. For most projects, these performance details boil down to three primary questions or vital signs:

■ How much work was required to complete a task?

■ Did the task start and finish on time?

■ What was the cost of completing the task?

Comparing the answers to these questions against the baseline gives the project manager and other *stakeholders* a good way to measure the project's progress and to know when corrective action might be necessary.

Communicating project status to key stakeholders such as customers and sponsors is arguably the most important function of a project manager, and one that might occupy much of your working time. Although perfect flow of communication can't guarantee a project's success, a project with poor communications flow is almost guaranteed to fail.

A key to properly communicating project status is knowing the following:

■ Who needs to know the project's status and for what purpose?

■ What format or level of detail do these people need?

The time to answer these questions is in the initial planning phase of the project. After work on the project is under way, your main communications task will be reporting project status. This can take several forms:

■ Status reports that describe where the project is in terms of cost, scope, and schedule (these are the three sides of the *project triangle*)

■ Progress reports that document the specific accomplishments of the project team

■ Forecasts that predict future project performance

Where the scheduled or actual project performance differs from the baseline plan, you have *variance*. Variance is usually measured as time, such as days behind schedule, or as cost, such as dollars over budget. After initial project planning is complete, many project managers spend most of their time identifying, justifying, and, in many cases, responding to variance. However, before you can respond to variance, you must first identify, document, and report it. That is the subject of this chapter.

Tip *This tip describes enterprise project management (EPM) functionality.* This chapter describes reporting project status to stakeholders. Project Professional, when used with Project Server, provides much more sophisticated ways of not only publishing project status online, but collecting information (such as actual work) from resources and other stakeholders as well. To learn more about the enterprise collaboration tools available with Project Server, see Part 4, "Introducing Project Server."

Important Before you can use the practice files in this chapter, be sure you install them from the book's companion CD to their default location. See "Using the Book's CD-ROM," on page xiii, for more information.

Identifying Tasks That Have Slipped

One cause of variance is delays in starting or finishing tasks. You'd certainly want to know about tasks that started late or future tasks that might not start as scheduled. It's also helpful to identify completed tasks that did not start on time and to try to determine why.

There are different ways to see delayed tasks, depending on the type of information you want:

■ Apply the Tracking Gantt view to graphically compare tasks' baseline dates with their actual or scheduled dates.

■ Apply the Variance table to a task view to see the number of days of variance for each task's start and finish dates.

■ Filter for delayed or slipping tasks with the Slipped/Late Progress or Slipping Tasks filters.

- Follow the instructions in the Check Progress pane (select **Check the progress of the project** under **Track** in the Project Guide) or in the Compare Progress pane (select **Compare progress against baseline work** under **Reports** in the Project Guide).

In this exercise, you apply some of these and other methods to identify variance.

Important   If you are running Project Professional, you may need to make a one-time adjustment to use the My Computer account and to work offline. This helps ensure that the practice files you work with in this chapter don't affect your Project Server data. For more information, see "Starting Project Professional," on page 10.

OPEN: Short Film Project 15a from the *My Documents\Microsoft Press\Project 2003 Step by Step* *Chapter 15 Reporting Status* folder. You can also access the practice files for this book by clicking **Start**, **All Programs**, **Microsoft Press**, **Project 2003 Step by Step**, and then selecting the chapter folder of the file you want to open.

1   On the **File** menu, click **Save As**.

The **Save As** dialog box appears.

2   In the **File name** box, type Short Film Project 15, and then click the **Save** button.

To begin your analysis of tasks that have slipped, you'll start at the highest level—the project summary information.

3   On the **Project** menu, click **Project Information**.

The **Project Information** dialog box appears.

4   Click the **Statistics** button.

The **Project Statistics** dialog box appears.

Here you can see the start and finish values for
the project, including the finish date's variance.

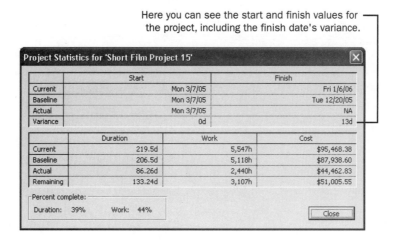

Project Statistics for 'Short Film Project 15'				☒
		Start		Finish
Current		Mon 3/7/05		Fri 1/6/06
Baseline		Mon 3/7/05		Tue 12/20/05
Actual		Mon 3/7/05		NA
Variance		0d		13d

	Duration	Work	Cost
Current	219.5d	5,547h	$95,468.38
Baseline	206.5d	5,118h	$87,938.60
Actual	86.26d	2,440h	$44,462.83
Remaining	133.24d	3,107h	$51,005.55

Percent complete:
Duration: 39%   Work: 44%   [Close]

In this dialog box you can see, among other things, that the project currently has 13 days of schedule variance on the finish date. In effect, the overall project finish date has slipped out this number of days.

5 Click the **Close** button to close the **Project Statistics** dialog box.

For the remainder of this exercise, you will use various techniques to examine the specific task variance.

6 On the **View** menu, click **Tracking Gantt**.

Project displays the Tracking Gantt view.

7 In the **Task Name** column, click the name of task 25, the Scene 7 summary task, and scroll the Tracking Gantt view up so that task 25 appears near the top of the view.

Go To Selected
Task

8 On the Standard toolbar, click the **Go To Selected Task** button.

In the chart portion of this view, the tasks as they are currently scheduled appear as blue bars (if they are not critical tasks) or red bars (if they are critical). In the lower half of each task's row, the baseline values of each task appear as gray bars.

Your screen should look similar to the following illustration:

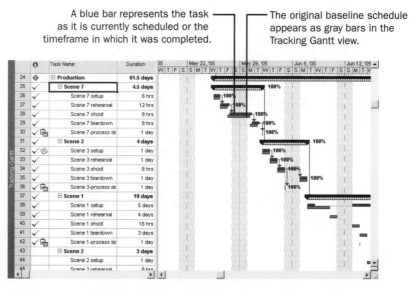

A blue bar represents the task as it is currently scheduled or the timeframe in which it was completed.

The original baseline schedule appears as gray bars in the Tracking Gantt view.

Here you can see where tasks began to vary from their baselines. Tasks 26 and 27 started as planned, but task 27 finished later than planned.

9 On the **Edit** menu, click **Go To**.

The **Go To** dialog box appears.

Tip Remember that Ctrl+G is a keyboard shortcut for displaying the **Go To** dialog box.

10 In the **ID** box, type 41, and click **OK**.

Project scrolls the Tracking Gantt view to display task 41 and its adjacent tasks.

11 Scroll the Tracking Gantt view up so that task 41 appears near the top of the view.

Your screen should look similar to the following illustration:

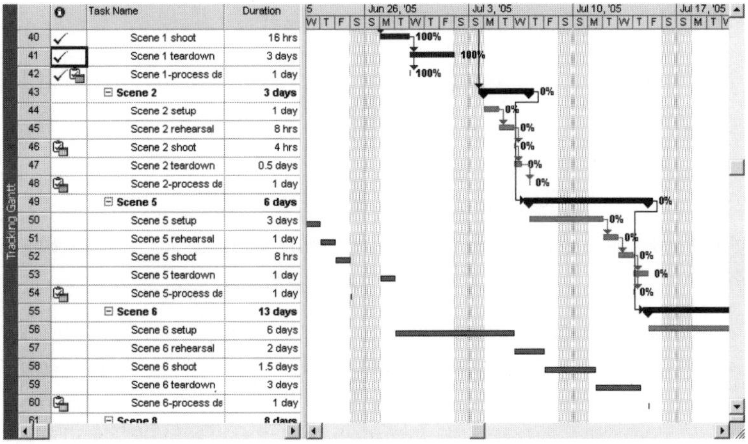

Here, you can see baseline task bars (the patterned gray bars), completed task bars (the solid blue bars), and bars for tasks scheduled but not yet not started (the red bars).

Tip To see details about any bar or other item in a Gantt Chart view, position the mouse pointer over it. After a moment, a ScreenTip appears with details.

To focus in on just the slipping tasks, you will apply a filter.

12 On the **Project** menu, point to **Filtered For: All Tasks,** and then click **More Filters**.

The **More Filters** dialog box appears. In it, you can see all the predefined filters for tasks (when in a task view) and resources (when in a resource view) available to you.

13 In the **More Filters** box, click **Slipping Tasks**, and then click the **Apply** button.

Project filters the task list to show only those tasks that, as they are now scheduled, have slipped from their baseline plan. Your screen should look similar to the following illustration:

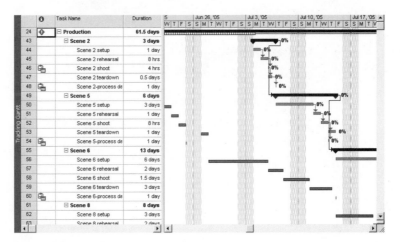

Note the gaps in the task ID numbers. Tasks 1 through 23, for example, do not appear with the filter applied, because they are already complete.

At this point in the schedule, the scheduled start date of tasks has slipped quite a bit. (To visually verify how much these tasks have slipped, you can scroll the chart portion of the Tracking Gantt view to the left to see the baseline Gantt bars for each task.) These tasks' scheduled Gantt bars are formatted red to indicate that they are critical, meaning that any delay in completing these tasks will delay the project's finish date.

14 On the **Project** menu, point to **Filtered For: Slipping Tasks**, and then click **All Tasks**.

Project removes the filter. As always, displaying or removing a filter has no effect on the original data.

The Tracking Gantt view graphically illustrates the difference between scheduled, actual, and baseline project performance. To see this information in a table format, you will display the Variance table in the Task Sheet view.

15 On the **View** menu, click **More Views**.

The **More Views** dialog box appears.

16 In the **Views** list, click **Task Sheet**, and then click the **Apply** button.

Project displays the Task Sheet view. Next you'll switch to the Variance table.

17 On the **View** menu, point to **Table: Entry**, and then click **Variance**.

> **Tip**   You also can right-click the **Select All** button in the upper left corner of the active table to switch to a different table.

The Variance table appears in the Task Sheet view. Your screen should look similar to the following illustration:

To quickly switch to a different table, right-click here, and then click the table you want.

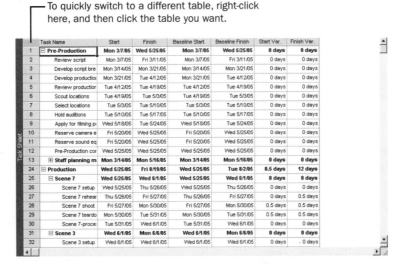

	Task Name	Start	Finish	Baseline Start	Baseline Finish	Start Var.	Finish Var.
1	⊟ Pre-Production	**Mon 3/7/05**	**Wed 5/25/05**	**Mon 3/7/05**	**Wed 5/25/05**	**0 days**	**0 days**
2	Review script	Mon 3/7/05	Fri 3/11/05	Mon 3/7/05	Fri 3/11/05	0 days	0 days
3	Develop script bre	Mon 3/14/05	Mon 3/21/05	Mon 3/14/05	Mon 3/21/05	0 days	0 days
4	Develop production	Mon 3/21/05	Tue 4/12/05	Mon 3/21/05	Tue 4/12/05	0 days	0 days
5	Review production	Tue 4/12/05	Tue 4/19/05	Tue 4/12/05	Tue 4/19/05	0 days	0 days
6	Scout locations	Tue 4/19/05	Tue 5/3/05	Tue 4/19/05	Tue 5/3/05	0 days	0 days
7	Select locations	Tue 5/3/05	Tue 5/10/05	Tue 5/3/05	Tue 5/10/05	0 days	0 days
8	Hold auditions	Tue 5/10/05	Tue 5/17/05	Tue 5/10/05	Tue 5/17/05	0 days	0 days
9	Apply for filming p	Wed 5/18/05	Tue 5/24/05	Wed 5/18/05	Tue 5/24/05	0 days	0 days
10	Reserve camera e	Fri 5/20/05	Wed 5/25/05	Fri 5/20/05	Wed 5/25/05	0 days	0 days
11	Reserve sound eq	Fri 5/20/05	Wed 5/25/05	Fri 5/20/05	Wed 5/25/05	0 days	0 days
12	Pre-Production cor	Wed 5/25/05	Wed 5/25/05	Wed 5/25/05	Wed 5/25/05	0 days	0 days
13	⊞ Staff planning m	**Mon 3/14/05**	**Mon 5/16/05**	**Mon 3/14/05**	**Mon 5/16/05**	**0 days**	**0 days**
24	⊟ Production	**Wed 5/25/05**	**Fri 8/19/05**	**Wed 5/25/05**	**Tue 8/2/05**	**0.5 days**	**12 days**
25	⊟ Scene 7	**Wed 5/25/05**	**Wed 6/1/05**	**Wed 5/25/05**	**Wed 6/1/05**	**0 days**	**0 days**
26	Scene 7 setup	Wed 5/25/05	Thu 5/26/05	Wed 5/25/05	Thu 5/26/05	0 days	0 days
27	Scene 7 rehear	Thu 5/26/05	Fri 5/27/05	Thu 5/26/05	Fri 5/27/05	0 days	0.5 days
28	Scene 7 shoot	Fri 5/27/05	Mon 5/30/05	Fri 5/27/05	Mon 5/30/05	0.5 days	0.5 days
29	Scene 7 teardo	Mon 5/30/05	Tue 5/31/05	Mon 5/30/05	Tue 5/31/05	0.5 days	0.5 days
30	Scene 7-proce:	Tue 5/31/05	Wed 6/1/05	Tue 5/31/05	Wed 6/1/05	0 days	0 days
31	⊟ Scene 3	**Wed 6/1/05**	**Mon 6/6/05**	**Wed 6/1/05**	**Mon 6/6/05**	**0 days**	**0 days**
32	Scene 3 setup	Wed 6/1/05	Wed 6/1/05	Wed 6/1/05	Wed 6/1/05	0 days	. 0 days

In this table you can see the scheduled, baseline, and variance values per task.

Here are a few more tips and suggestions for viewing slipped tasks:

- To see a legend of all Gantt bar color coding and symbols, switch to a Gantt Chart view and on the **Format** menu, click **Bar Styles**, and in the **Bar Styles** dialog box, look at the **Name** and **Appearance** columns.

All Tasks

Filter

- All filters are available to you via the **Filter** button on the Formatting toolbar. The name of the active filter appears in this button; click the arrow next to the filter name to see other filters. If no filter is applied to the current view, **All Tasks** or **All Resources** appears on the button, depending on the type of view currently displayed.

- You can see the criteria that most filters use to determine which tasks or resources they will display or hide. On the **Project** menu, point to **Filter For: All Tasks**, and then click **More Filters**. In the **More Filters** dialog box, click a filter and click the **Edit** button. In the **Filter Definition** dialog box, you can see the tests applied to various fields for the filter.

- The Slipping Tasks report describes tasks that are off-schedule. On the **View** menu, click **Reports**. In the **Reports** dialog box, double-click **Current Activities**, and then double-click **Slipping Tasks**.

- In this exercise you have viewed variance for a task. To see variance for assignments to a task, switch to the Task Usage view, and then apply the Variance table (to see scheduled variance) or the Work table (to see work variance).

Project Management Focus: Getting the Word Out

If you work in an organization that is highly focused on projects and project management, chances are that standard methods and formats already exist within your organization for reporting project status. If not, you might be able to introduce project status formats that are based on clear communication and project management principles.

Techniques you can use in Project to help you report project status include the following:

- Printing the Project Summary report.

- Copying Project data to other applications—for example, use the Copy Picture To Office Wizard (Analysis toolbar) to copy the Gantt Chart view to Word or to PowerPoint.

- Saving Project data in other formats, such as HTML, using the Compare To Baseline export map.

- For Project Professional users, sharing project status through Project Server, which enables the stakeholders you choose to view project details through their Web browsers.

All these status-reporting tools are described elsewhere in this book.

Examining Task Costs

The schedule's status (Did tasks start and finish on time?), although critical to nearly all projects, is only one indicator of overall project health. For projects that include cost information, another critical indicator is cost variance: Are tasks running over or under budget? Task costs in Project consist of fixed costs applied directly to tasks, resource costs derived from assignments, or both. When tasks cost more or less than planned to complete, cost variance is the result. Evaluating cost variance enables you to make incremental budget adjustments for individual tasks to avoid exceeding your project's overall budget.

Tip Another way of using project costs to measure past performance and predict future performance is earned value analysis. For more information about earned value analysis, type **About earned value analysis** into the **Search** box in the upper right corner of the Project window. The **Search** box initially contains the text *Type a question for help*. You can also see Chapter 19, "Measuring Performance with Earned Value Analysis."

Although tasks and resources (and their costs) are directly related, it's informative to evaluate each individually. In this exercise, you view task cost variance. Again you'll start at the highest level—the project summary information.

1   On the **Project** menu, click **Project Information**.

The **Project Information** dialog box appears.

2   Click the **Statistics** button.

The **Project Statistics** dialog box appears.

Here you can see the project's cost values. ⌐

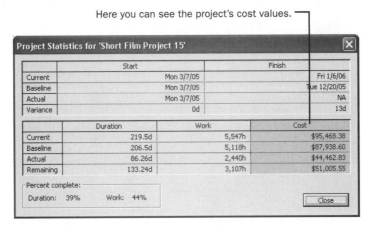

In the Cost column, you can see the current, baseline, actual, and remaining cost values for the entire project:

- ▪   The current cost value is the sum of the actual and remaining cost values.

- ▪   The baseline cost value is the project's total planned cost when its baseline was saved.

- ▪   The actual cost is the cost that's been incurred so far, that is, after 39 percent of the project's duration and 44 percent of the total work have been completed.

- ▪   The remaining cost is the difference between the current cost and actual cost.

Clearly, some cost variance has occurred, but you can't tell from this information when or where it occurred.

3   Click the **Close** button to close the **Project Statistics** dialog box.

Next you will switch to views where you can examine cost variance more closely, starting with the Cost table.

4   On the **View** menu, point to **Table: Variance**, and click **Cost**.

Tip You also can right-click the upper left corner of the active table, and in the shortcut menu that appears, click **Cost**.

The Cost table appears in the Task Sheet view. Your screen should look similar to the following illustration:

	Task Name	Fixed Cost	Fixed Cost Accrual	Total Cost	Baseline	Variance	Actual	Remaining
1	⊟ Pre-Production	$0.00	Prorated	$23,089.75	$23,089.75	$0.00	$23,089.75	$0.00
2	Review script	$0.00	Prorated	$947.50	$947.50	$0.00	$947.50	$0.00
3	Develop script breakdo	$0.00	Prorated	$2,455.00	$2,455.00	$0.00	$2,455.00	$0.00
4	Develop production boa	$0.00	Prorated	$5,844.75	$5,844.75	$0.00	$5,844.75	$0.00
5	Review production boa	$0.00	Prorated	$1,575.00	$1,575.00	$0.00	$1,575.00	$0.00
6	Scout locations	$0.00	Prorated	$4,920.00	$4,920.00	$0.00	$4,920.00	$0.00
7	Select locations	$0.00	Prorated	$2,535.00	$2,535.00	$0.00	$2,535.00	$0.00
8	Hold auditions	$0.00	Prorated	$1,887.00	$1,887.00	$0.00	$1,887.00	$0.00
9	Apply for filming permit:	$500.00	Start	$876.00	$876.00	$0.00	$876.00	$0.00
10	Reserve camera equipr	$0.00	Prorated	$636.00	$636.00	$0.00	$636.00	$0.00
11	Reserve sound equipm	$0.00	Prorated	$186.00	$186.00	$0.00	$186.00	$0.00
12	Pre-Production complet	$0.00	Prorated	$0.00	$0.00	$0.00	$0.00	$0.00
13	⊞ Staff planning meetii	$0.00	Prorated	$1,227.50	$1,227.50	$0.00	$1,227.50	$0.00
24	⊟ Production	$0.00	Prorated	$43,910.73	$36,380.95	$7,529.78	$21,373.08	$22,537.65
25	⊟ Scene 7	$0.00	Prorated	$3,711.88	$3,702.50	$9.38	$3,711.88	$0.00
26	Scene 7 setup	$0.00	Prorated	$322.50	$322.50	$0.00	$322.50	$0.00
27	Scene 7 rehearsal	$0.00	Prorated	$714.38	$705.00	$9.38	$714.38	$0.00
28	Scene 7 shoot	$0.00	Prorated	$2,245.00	$2,245.00	$0.00	$2,245.00	$0.00
29	Scene 7 teardown	$0.00	Prorated	$430.00	$430.00	$0.00	$430.00	$0.00
30	Scene 7-process de	$0.00	Prorated	$0.00	$0.00	$0.00	$0.00	$0.00
31	⊟ Scene 3	$0.00	Prorated	$4,180.40	$4,180.40	$0.00	$4,180.40	$0.00
32	Scene 3 setup	$0.00	Prorated	$518.00	$518.00	$0.00	$518.00	$0.00

In this table, you can see each task's baseline cost, scheduled cost (in the **Total Cost** column), actual cost, and variance. The variance is the difference between the baseline cost and the scheduled cost. Of course, costs aren't scheduled in the same sense that work is scheduled; however, costs (other than fixed costs) are derived directly from the scheduled work.

Next you'll focus on the top-level costs.

5 Click the **Task Name** column heading.

6 On the Formatting toolbar, click the **Hide Subtasks** button.

Hide Subtasks

Project displays only the top three summary tasks, which in this project correspond to the major phases of the short film project. Because we're currently working on tasks in the Production phase, we'll direct our attention there.

7 Click the plus sign next to task 24, *Production*.

Project expands the Production summary task to show the summary tasks for the individual scenes. Your screen should look similar to the following illustration:

Here is the most significant variance ⎯
in the Production phase at this point.

	Task Name	Fixed Cost	Fixed Cost Accrual	Total Cost	Baseline	Variance	Actual	Remaining
1	⊞ Pre-Production	$0.00	Prorated	$23,089.75	$23,089.75	$0.00	$23,089.75	$0.00
24	⊟ Production	$0.00	Prorated	$43,910.73	$36,380.95	$7,529.78	$21,373.08	$22,537.65
25	⊞ Scene 7	$0.00	Prorated	$3,711.88	$3,702.50	$9.38	$3,711.88	$0.00
31	⊞ Scene 3	$0.00	Prorated	$4,180.40	$4,180.40	$0.00	$4,180.40	$0.00
37	⊞ Scene 1	$0.00	Prorated	$13,480.80	$5,960.40	$7,520.40	$13,480.80	$0.00
43	⊞ Scene 2	$0.00	Prorated	$2,257.10	$2,257.10	$0.00	$0.00	$2,257.10
49	⊞ Scene 5	$0.00	Prorated	$4,547.40	$4,547.40	$0.00	$0.00	$4,547.40
55	⊞ Scene 6	$0.00	Prorated	$8,723.40	$8,723.40	$0.00	$0.00	$8,723.40
61	⊞ Scene 8	$0.00	Prorated	$5,278.20	$5,278.20	$0.00	$0.00	$5,278.20
67	⊞ Scene 4	$0.00	Prorated	$1,731.55	$1,731.55	$0.00	$0.00	$1,731.55
73	⊞ Post-Production	$0.00	Prorated	$28,467.90	$28,467.90	$0.00	$0.00	$28,467.90

Looking at the **Variance** column, you can see that Scene 7 had some modest variance, but Scene 1 had significantly more. Next you'll focus on the details for Scene 1.

8 Click the plus sign next to summary task 37, *Scene 1*.

Project expands the Scene 1 summary task to show the subtasks. Your screen should look similar to the following illustration:

	Task Name	Fixed Cost	Fixed Cost Accrual	Total Cost	Baseline	Variance	Actual	Remaining
1	⊞ Pre-Production	$0.00	Prorated	$23,089.75	$23,089.75	$0.00	$23,089.75	$0.00
24	⊟ Production	$0.00	Prorated	$43,910.73	$36,380.95	$7,529.78	$21,373.08	$22,537.65
25	⊞ Scene 7	$0.00	Prorated	$3,711.88	$3,702.50	$9.38	$3,711.88	$0.00
31	⊞ Scene 3	$0.00	Prorated	$4,180.40	$4,180.40	$0.00	$4,180.40	$0.00
37	⊟ Scene 1	$0.00	Prorated	$13,480.80	$5,960.40	$7,520.40	$13,480.80	$0.00
38	Scene 1 setup	$0.00	Prorated	$3,470.00	$2,082.00	$1,388.00	$3,470.00	$0.00
39	Scene 1 rehearsal	$0.00	Prorated	$3,120.00	$780.00	$2,340.00	$3,120.00	$0.00
40	Scene 1 shoot	$0.00	Prorated	$4,808.80	$2,404.40	$2,404.40	$4,808.80	$0.00
41	Scene 1 teardown	$0.00	Prorated	$2,082.00	$694.00	$1,388.00	$2,082.00	$0.00
42	Scene 1-process de	$0.00	Prorated	$0.00	$0.00	$0.00	$0.00	$0.00
43	⊞ Scene 2	$0.00	Prorated	$2,257.10	$2,257.10	$0.00	$0.00	$2,257.10
49	⊞ Scene 5	$0.00	Prorated	$4,547.40	$4,547.40	$0.00	$0.00	$4,547.40
55	⊞ Scene 6	$0.00	Prorated	$8,723.40	$8,723.40	$0.00	$0.00	$8,723.40
61	⊞ Scene 8	$0.00	Prorated	$5,278.20	$5,278.20	$0.00	$0.00	$5,278.20
67	⊞ Scene 4	$0.00	Prorated	$1,731.55	$1,731.55	$0.00	$0.00	$1,731.55
73	⊞ Post-Production	$0.00	Prorated	$28,467.90	$28,467.90	$0.00	$0.00	$28,467.90

Looking at the **Variance** column, you can see that the Scene 1 rehearsal accounts for much of the variance for the Scene 1 summary task.

9 Click the **Task Name** column heading.

10 On the Formatting toolbar, click the **Show Subtasks** button.

Show Subtasks

Project expands the task list to show all subtasks.

To conclude this exercise, you will use the Project Guide to examine task costs. The information is similar to what you've seen before, but the Project Guide includes a handy explanation of variance and a short list of the most relevant filters.

11 On the **Project Guide** toolbar, click the **Report** button.

12 In the Report pane, click the **See project costs** link.

The Project Guide: Analyze Costs view appears. Your screen should look similar to the following illustration:

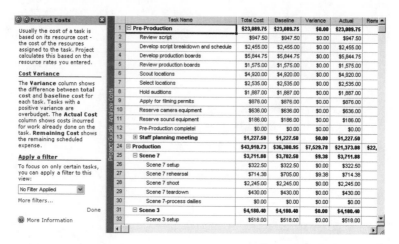

This view is similar to the Task Sheet view with the Cost table applied, which you displayed in step 4 of this exercise. In the Project Costs pane, you also have quick access to the filters most relevant to project costs.

13 In the Project Costs pane, under **Apply a filter**, click **Cost Overbudget** in the drop-down list.

Project filters the task list to show only those tasks that had actual and scheduled costs greater than their baseline costs. Your screen should look similar to this illustration:

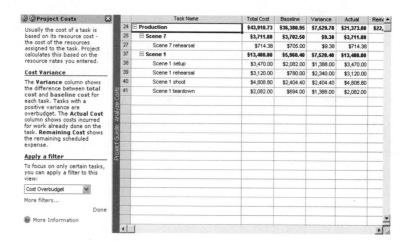

Note the gaps in the task ID numbers, indicating which tasks are not shown with this filter applied.

14 In the **Apply a filter** box, click **No Filter Applied**.

Project removes the filter.

Show/Hide
Project Guide

15 Click the **Show/Hide Project Guide** button on the **Project Guide** toolbar.

The Project Guide closes.

What caused the task cost variance in the short film project? Because this project's costs are almost entirely derived from work performed by resources, we can conclude that more work than scheduled has been required to complete the tasks up to now.

As we noted earlier, task and resource costs are closely related; in most cases the task costs are mostly or fully derived from the costs of resources assigned to tasks. Examining resource costs is the subject of the next exercise.

Here are a few more tips and suggestions for working with cost data:

■ To see tasks that are over budget, you can use the Overbudget Tasks report. On the **View** menu, click **Reports**. In the **Reports** dialog box, double-click **Costs**, and then double-click **Overbudget Tasks**.

■ The Cost Overbudget filter and all the other filters in the Project Costs pane of the Project Guide are also available in the **More Filters** dialog box (on the **Project** menu, point to **Filtered For: All Tasks**, and then click **More Filters**) and via the **Filter** button on the Formatting toolbar.

■ To see work variance in the Work table, in a task view on the **View** menu point to **Table**, and then click **Work**. You can also compare timephased baseline and scheduled work in a usage view. For example, in the Task Usage view, on the **Format** menu, point to **Details**, and click **Baseline Work**.

■ In this exercise, you have viewed cost variance for a task. To see cost variance for assignments to a task, switch to the Task Usage view, and then apply the Cost table.

Examining Resource Costs

Project managers sometimes focus on resource costs as a means of measuring progress and variance within a project. However, resource cost information also serves other people and other needs. For many organizations, resource costs are the primary or even the only costs of doing projects, so keeping an eye on resource costs might directly relate to the financial health of an organization. It might not be a project manager, but an executive, cost accountant, or *resource manager* who is most interested in resource costs on projects as they relate to organizational costs.

Another common reason to track resource costs is for billing either within an organization (for example, billing another department for services your department has provided) or externally. In either case, the resource cost information stored in project plans can serve as the basis for billing out your department's or organization's services to others.

Because cost values in the short film project are almost entirely derived from the costs of resource assignments, you'll look at resource cost variance next.

1   On the **View** menu, click **Resource Sheet**.

The Resource Sheet view appears.

2   On the **View** menu, point to **Table: Entry** and click **Cost**.

The Cost table appears. Your screen should look similar to the following illustration:

	Resource Name	Cost	Baseline Cost	Variance	Actual Cost	Remaining
1	16-mm Camera	$1,050.00	$900.00	$150.00	$550.00	$500.00
2	16-mm Film	$6,600.00	$5,800.00	$800.00	$3,200.00	$3,400.00
3	500-Watt Light	$350.00	$330.00	$20.00	$160.00	$190.00
4	Anne L. Paper	$731.25	$731.25	$0.00	$150.00	$581.25
5	Camera Boom	$0.00	$0.00	$0.00	$0.00	$0.00
6	Clair Hector	$8,320.00	$8,320.00	$0.00	$4,160.00	$4,160.00
7	Crane	$0.00	$0.00	$0.00	$0.00	$0.00
8	Daniel Penn	$412.50	$412.50	$0.00	$0.00	$412.50
9	David Campbell	$2,775.00	$2,475.00	$300.00	$450.00	$2,325.00
10	Dolly	$0.00	$0.00	$0.00	$0.00	$0.00
11	Doug Hampton	$1,950.00	$1,887.60	$62.40	$499.20	$1,450.80
12	Editing Lab	$5,100.00	$5,100.00	$0.00	$0.00	$5,100.00
13	Electrician	$3,586.00	$2,178.00	$1,408.00	$3,322.00	$264.00
14	Eric Lang	$372.00	$372.00	$0.00	$372.00	$0.00
15	Eric Miller	$975.00	$675.00	$300.00	$600.00	$375.00
16	Florian Voss	$2,024.00	$2,024.00	$0.00	$0.00	$2,024.00
17	Frank Lee	$924.00	$812.00	$112.00	$448.00	$476.00
18	Jan Miksovsky	$4,237.00	$3,637.00	$600.00	$3,412.00	$825.00
19	Jim Hance	$412.50	$412.50	$0.00	$150.00	$262.50
20	Jo Brown	$10,237.50	$9,037.50	$1,200.00	$4,762.50	$5,475.00
21	Johnathan Perrera	$3,828.00	$3,828.00	$0.00	$3,828.00	$0.00
22	Joseph Matthews	$365.63	$356.25	$9.37	$309.38	$56.25

In the Cost table you can see each resource's cost, baseline cost, and related cost values. In most cases, the resource cost values are derived from each resource's cost rate multiplied by the work on their assignments to tasks in the project plan.

Currently, the resource sheet is sorted by resource ID. Next you will sort it by resource cost.

3   On the **Project** menu, point to **Sort** and click **Sort By**.

The **Sort** dialog box appears.

4   In the **Sort By** box, click **Cost** in the drop-down list, and click **Descending**.

5   Make sure the **Permanently renumber resources** check box is cleared, and then click the **Sort** button.

Project sorts the resources by cost, from highest to lowest. Your screen should look similar to the following illustration:

With resources sorted by cost in descending order, you can quickly identify the most expensive resources working on the project.

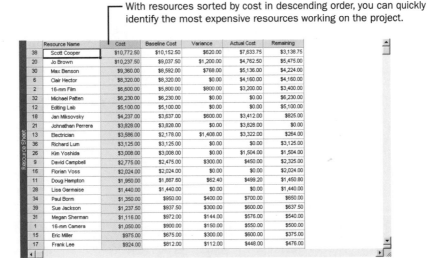

	Resource Name	Cost	Baseline Cost	Variance	Actual Cost	Remaining
38	Scott Cooper	$10,772.50	$10,152.50	$620.00	$7,633.75	$3,138.75
20	Jo Brown	$10,237.50	$9,037.50	$1,200.00	$4,762.50	$5,475.00
30	Max Benson	$9,360.00	$8,592.00	$768.00	$5,136.00	$4,224.00
6	Clair Hector	$8,320.00	$8,320.00	$0.00	$4,160.00	$4,160.00
2	16-mm Film	$6,600.00	$5,800.00	$800.00	$3,200.00	$3,400.00
32	Michael Patten	$6,230.00	$6,230.00	$0.00	$0.00	$6,230.00
12	Editing Lab	$5,100.00	$5,100.00	$0.00	$0.00	$5,100.00
18	Jan Miksovsky	$4,237.00	$3,637.00	$600.00	$3,412.00	$825.00
21	Johnathan Perrera	$3,828.00	$3,828.00	$0.00	$3,828.00	$0.00
13	Electrician	$3,586.00	$2,178.00	$1,408.00	$3,322.00	$264.00
36	Richard Lum	$3,125.00	$3,125.00	$0.00	$0.00	$3,125.00
26	Kim Yoshida	$3,008.00	$3,008.00	$0.00	$1,504.00	$1,504.00
9	David Campbell	$2,775.00	$2,475.00	$300.00	$450.00	$2,325.00
16	Florian Voss	$2,024.00	$2,024.00	$0.00	$0.00	$2,024.00
11	Doug Hampton	$1,950.00	$1,887.60	$62.40	$499.20	$1,450.80
28	Lisa Garmaise	$1,440.00	$1,440.00	$0.00	$0.00	$1,440.00
34	Paul Borm	$1,350.00	$950.00	$400.00	$700.00	$650.00
39	Sue Jackson	$1,237.50	$937.50	$300.00	$600.00	$637.50
31	Megan Sherman	$1,116.00	$972.00	$144.00	$576.00	$540.00
1	16-mm Camera	$1,050.00	$900.00	$150.00	$550.00	$500.00
15	Eric Miller	$975.00	$675.00	$300.00	$600.00	$375.00
17	Frank Lee	$924.00	$812.00	$112.00	$448.00	$476.00

This sort quickly tells you who the most and least expensive resources are (as indicated in the **Cost** column), but it doesn't help you see variance patterns. You will do that next.

6   On the **Project** menu, point to **Sort** and click **Sort By**.

The **Sort** dialog box appears.

7   In the **Sort By** box, click **Cost Variance**, and make sure **Descending** is still selected.

8   Make sure the **Permanently renumber resources** check box is cleared, and then click the **Sort** button.

Project re-sorts the resources by cost variance, from highest to lowest. Your screen should look similar to the following illustration:

With resources sorted by variance in descending order, you can quickly identify those whose cost varied the most from planned costs.

	Resource Name	Cost	Baseline Cost	Variance	Actual Cost	Remaining
13	Electrician	$3,586.00	$2,178.00	$1,408.00	$3,322.00	$264.00
20	Jo Brown	$10,237.50	$9,037.50	$1,200.00	$4,762.50	$5,475.00
2	16-mm Film	$6,600.00	$5,800.00	$800.00	$3,200.00	$3,400.00
30	Max Benson	$9,360.00	$8,592.00	$768.00	$5,136.00	$4,224.00
38	Scott Cooper	$10,772.50	$10,152.50	$620.00	$7,633.75	$3,138.75
18	Jan Miksovsky	$4,237.00	$3,637.00	$600.00	$3,412.00	$825.00
34	Paul Borm	$1,350.00	$950.00	$400.00	$700.00	$650.00
39	Sue Jackson	$1,237.50	$937.50	$300.00	$600.00	$637.50
9	David Campbell	$2,775.00	$2,475.00	$300.00	$450.00	$2,325.00
15	Eric Miller	$975.00	$675.00	$300.00	$600.00	$375.00
1	16-mm Camera	$1,050.00	$900.00	$150.00	$550.00	$500.00
31	Megan Sherman	$1,116.00	$972.00	$144.00	$576.00	$540.00
17	Frank Lee	$924.00	$812.00	$112.00	$448.00	$476.00
25	Keith Harris	$924.00	$812.00	$112.00	$448.00	$476.00
40	Ted Bremer	$924.00	$812.00	$112.00	$448.00	$476.00
41	Tim O'Brien	$896.00	$784.00	$112.00	$448.00	$448.00
11	Doug Hampton	$1,950.00	$1,887.60	$62.40	$499.20	$1,450.80
3	500-Watt Light	$350.00	$330.00	$20.00	$160.00	$190.00
22	Joseph Matthews	$365.63	$356.25	$9.37	$309.38	$56.25
4	Anne L. Paper	$731.25	$731.25	$0.00	$150.00	$581.25
5	Camera Boom	$0.00	$0.00	$0.00	$0.00	$0.00
6	Clair Hector	$8,320.00	$8,320.00	$0.00	$4,160.00	$4,160.00

With the resource list sorted by cost variance, you can quickly zero in on those resources with the greatest variance, and, if you want, begin to investigate why.

9   On the **Project** menu, point to **Sort**, and then click **By ID**.

Project re-sorts the resources by ID.

Here are a few more tips and suggestions for working with resource costs:

- You can use the Overbudget Resources report to list resources who are over budget. On the **View** menu, click **Reports**. In the **Reports** dialog box, double-click **Costs**, and then double-click **Overbudget Resources**.

- You can also see timephased cost values in a usage view. For example, in the Resource Usage view, on the **Format** menu, click **Detail Styles**. In the **Usage Details** tab, show the **Baseline Cost** and **Cost** fields. This also works in the Task Usage view.

Project Management Focus: What About All Those Other Costs?

In many projects, cost budgets don't fully reflect all the costs of completing the project. For example, in the short film project, we're not accounting for such overhead costs as renting or acquiring studio space, electricity, or replacement parts for equipment. Depending on your organization's needs and practices, you might need to track such overhead costs in your project plan. If you do need to track overhead costs, you might be able to use a *burdened labor rate*—resource rates that factor in such overhead costs. Using burdened labor rates has the additional benefit of hiding each resource's exact pay rate—often considered highly confidential information—in the project plan. Here's one caveat, though: if you plan to use cost information from your project plan for accounting purposes, especially for capitalizing specific task types, check with an accounting expert about how salary, benefit, and overhead cost rates should be handled.

Reporting Project Cost Variance with a Stoplight View

There are many different ways to report a project's status in terms of task or budget variance, or other measures. There is no shortage of features in Project that support reporting project status, but the main thing to keep in mind is that how you report project status is less a technical question than a communications question. For example, what format and level of detail do your stakeholders need to see? Should project sponsors see different aspects of a project's performance than its resources see? These questions are central to the job of the project manager. Fortunately, as noted earlier, Project is a rich communications tool that you can use to put together the type of project status information that best meets the needs of your stakeholders.

Tip   Creating a stoplight view involves using formulas in custom fields. Custom fields are a very powerful and flexible feature, and the stoplight view is just one example of what you can do with them. To learn more about custom fields, type **About custom fields** into the **Search** box in the upper right corner of the Project window.

In this exercise, you focus on creating what is often called a *stoplight* report. This status report represents key indicators for tasks, such as schedule or budget status, as a simple red, yellow, or green light, much as you'd find on a traffic signal. Such status reports are easy for anybody to understand, and they quickly provide a general sense of the health of a project. Strictly speaking, what you'll create here is not a *report* in Project, so we'll call it a *stoplight view* instead.

1   On the **View** menu, click **More Views**.

The **More Views** dialog box appears.

2   Click **Task Sheet**, and click the **Apply** button.

Project displays the Task Sheet view. It currently contains the Cost table.

To save you time, we have added a customized field in this Project file containing a formula that evaluates each task's cost variance. Next you will view the formula to understand what it does, and then view the graphical indicators assigned to the field.

3   On the **Tools** menu, point to **Customize**, and then click **Fields**.

The **Customize Fields** dialog box appears.

4   Click the **Custom Fields** tab.

5   In the **Type** box, click **Number** in the drop-down list.

6   In the list box, click **Overbudget (Number3)**.

Your screen should look similar to the following illustration:

The Number3 field has been renamed "Overbudget" and customized with a formula and graphical indicators.

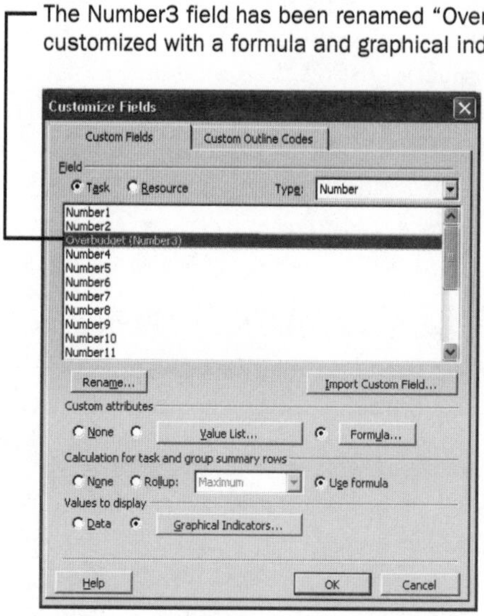

7   Under **Custom attributes**, click the **Formula** button.

The **Formula** dialog box appears. Your screen should look similar to the following illustration:

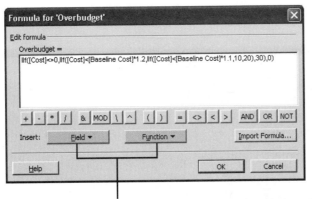

When writing a formula, use these buttons to
insert Project fields or functions into your formula.

This formula evaluates each task's cost variance. If the task's cost is 10 percent or
less above baseline, the formula assigns the number 10 to the task. If the cost is
between 10 and 20 percent above baseline, it is assigned a 20. If the cost is more
than 20 percent above baseline, it receives a 30.

8   Click **Cancel** to close the **Formula** dialog box.

9   In the **Customize Fields** dialog box, under **Values to display**, click the **Graphical Indicators** button.

The **Graphical Indicators** dialog box appears. Here you specify a unique graphical
indicator to display, depending on the value of the field for each task. Again, to
save you time, the indicators are already selected.

Depending on the value returned by the formula, Project will display
one of these three graphical indicators in the Overbudget column.

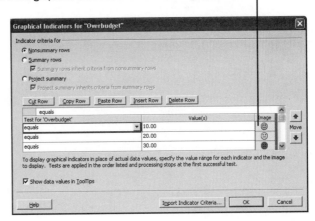

10   In the first cell under the **Image** column heading, click the drop-down arrow.

Here you can see the many graphical indicators you can associate with the values of fields.

11 Click **Cancel** to close the **Graphical Indicators** dialog box, and then click **Cancel** again to close the **Customize Fields** dialog box.

To conclude this exercise, you will display the Overbudget (Number3) column in the Cost table.

12 Click the **Fixed Cost** column heading.

13 On the **Insert** menu, click **Column**.

The **Column Definition** dialog box appears.

14 In the **Field Name** box, click **Overbudget (Number3)** in the drop-down list, and then click **OK**.

Project displays the Overbudget column in the Cost table. Your screen should look similar to the following illustration:

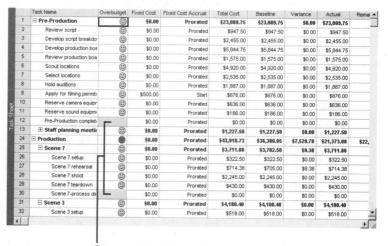

	Task Name	Overbudget	Fixed Cost	Fixed Cost Accrual	Total Cost	Baseline	Variance	Actual	Remai
1	⊟ Pre-Production	☺	$0.00	Prorated	$23,089.75	$23,089.75	$0.00	$23,089.75	
2	Review script	☺	$0.00	Prorated	$947.50	$947.50	$0.00	$947.50	
3	Develop script breakdov	☺	$0.00	Prorated	$2,455.00	$2,455.00	$0.00	$2,455.00	
4	Develop production bos	☺	$0.00	Prorated	$5,844.75	$5,844.75	$0.00	$5,844.75	
5	Review production boa	☺	$0.00	Prorated	$1,575.00	$1,575.00	$0.00	$1,575.00	
6	Scout locations	☺	$0.00	Prorated	$4,920.00	$4,920.00	$0.00	$4,920.00	
7	Select locations	☺	$0.00	Prorated	$2,535.00	$2,535.00	$0.00	$2,535.00	
8	Hold auditions	☺	$0.00	Prorated	$1,887.00	$1,887.00	$0.00	$1,887.00	
9	Apply for filming permit:	☺	$500.00	Start	$876.00	$876.00	$0.00	$876.00	
10	Reserve camera equipr	☺	$0.00	Prorated	$636.00	$636.00	$0.00	$636.00	
11	Reserve sound equipm	☺	$0.00	Prorated	$186.00	$186.00	$0.00	$186.00	
12	Pre-Production complet		$0.00	Prorated	$0.00	$0.00	$0.00	$0.00	
13	⊞ Staff planning meetii	☺	$0.00	Prorated	$1,227.50	$1,227.50	$0.00	$1,227.50	
24	⊟ Production	●	$0.00	Prorated	$43,910.73	$36,380.95	$7,529.78	$21,373.08	$22,
25	⊟ Scene 7	☺	$0.00	Prorated	$3,711.88	$3,702.50	$9.38	$3,711.88	
26	Scene 7 setup	☺	$0.00	Prorated	$322.50	$322.50	$0.00	$322.50	
27	Scene 7 rehearsal	☺	$0.00	Prorated	$714.38	$705.00	$9.38	$714.38	
28	Scene 7 shoot	☺	$0.00	Prorated	$2,245.00	$2,245.00	$0.00	$2,245.00	
29	Scene 7 teardown	☺	$0.00	Prorated	$430.00	$430.00	$0.00	$430.00	
30	Scene 7-process de		$0.00	Prorated	$0.00	$0.00	$0.00	$0.00	
31	⊟ Scene 3	☺	$0.00	Prorated	$4,180.40	$4,180.40	$0.00	$4,180.40	
32	Scene 3 setup	☺	$0.00	Prorated	$518.00	$518.00	$0.00	$518.00	

Because these tasks have no cost, no indicators are displayed.

As each task's cost variance changes, so do the graphical indicators according to the ranges specified in the formula. This is a handy format for identifying tasks whose cost variance is higher than you'd like, as indicated by the yellow or red lights.

Tip To see a graphical indicator's numeric value in a ScreenTip, just point to the indicator.

Up to now, you've identified schedule and budget variance in a task view and budget variance in a resource view—each an important measure of project status. This is a good time to remind yourself that the final qualifier of project status is not the exact formatting of the data in Project, but the needs of your project's stakeholders. Determining what these needs are requires your good judgment and communication skills.

CLOSE: the Short Film Project 15 file.

Key Points

- Schedule variance is caused by tasks that have slipped from their planned start or finish dates (as recorded in a baseline). You can use a combination of views, tables, filters, and reports to identify which tasks have slipped and caused variance.

- Schedule and cost variance are closely related—if a project plan has one, it likely has the other. As with schedule variance, you can apply a combination of views, tables, filters, and reports to locate cost variance.

- You can use formulas and graphical indicators in custom fields to create a highly customized view, such as a stoplight view, to communicate key project health indicators to your stakeholders.

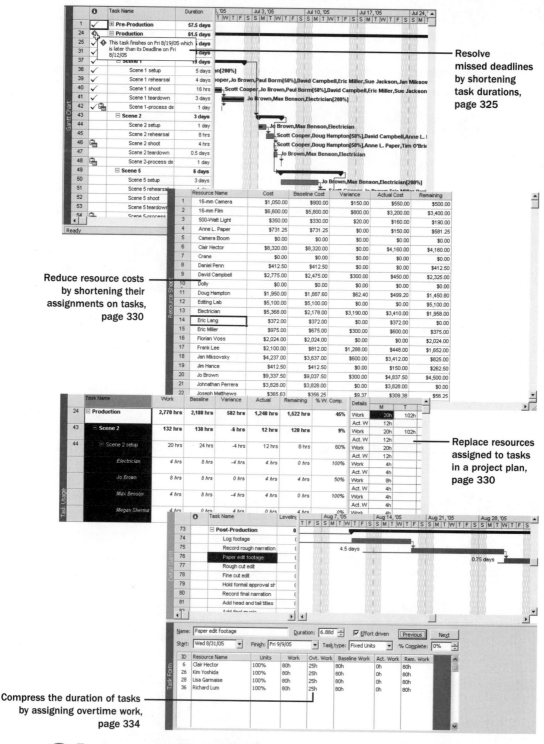

Resolve missed deadlines by shortening task durations, page 325

Reduce resource costs by shortening their assignments on tasks, page 330

Replace resources assigned to tasks in a project plan, page 330

Compress the duration of tasks by assigning overtime work, page 334

Chapter 16 at a Glance

16 Getting Your Project Back on Track

In this chapter you will learn to:

✔ Assign additional resources to tasks to reduce task durations.

✔ Edit work values for resource assignments and replace resources assigned to tasks.

✔ Assign overtime work to assignments and change task relationships to compress the overall project duration.

See Also Do you need a quick refresher on the topics in this chapter? See the quick reference entries on page xxxvii.

After work has started on a project, addressing *variance* is not a one-time event. Instead it is an ongoing effort by the project manager. The specific way you should respond to variance depends on the type of variance and the nature of the project. In this chapter, we'll focus on some of the many variance problems that can arise during a project as work progresses. We'll frame these problems around the *project triangle* described in detail in Appendix A, "A Short Course in Project Management."

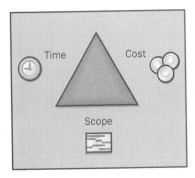

In short, the project triangle model frames a project in terms of the *time* (or duration), *cost* (or budget), and *scope* (the project work required to produce a satisfactory *deliverable*). In virtually any project of any complexity, one of these factors will be more important than the other two. The most important factor is sometimes called the driving constraint because meeting it drives your actions as a project manager. For example, for a project that must be concluded by a specific date, you might have to make cost and scope compromises to meet the deadline. Working with the project triangle gives you a good way to think about the trade-offs that nearly always must be made in projects. Just as importantly, it gives you a clear way of explaining the pros and cons of trade-offs to the project's *resources*, *sponsors*, and other *stakeholders*.

In the project triangle model, time, cost, and scope are interconnected; changing one element can affect the other two. However, for purposes of identifying, analyzing, and addressing problems in project management, it's useful to fit problems into one of these three categories.

The specific issues we'll focus on in this chapter aren't necessarily the most common problems you'll face in your own projects. Because every project is unique, there's no way to anticipate what you'll run into. However, we've attempted to highlight the most pressing issues at the midpoint of the short film project's duration and to apply solutions to many common problems. Note that some of the features you'll use in this chapter you might also use when planning a project. Here, however, your intent is different—getting the project plan back on track.

Important   Before you can use the practice files in this chapter, be sure you install them from the book's companion CD to their default location. See "Using the Book's CD-ROM," on page xiii, for more information.

Troubleshooting Time and Schedule Problems

Schedule variance will almost certainly appear in any lengthy project. Maintaining control over the schedule requires that the project manager know when variance has occurred and to what extent, and then take timely corrective action to stay on track. To help you identify when variance has occurred, the short film project plan includes the following:

- Deadline dates applied to key milestones.
- A project baseline against which you can compare actual performance.

The deadline dates and project baseline will help you troubleshoot time and schedule problems in Microsoft Office Project 2003. In this exercise, you address the missed deadline for the production phase of the short film project and shorten the durations of some tasks on the critical path.

Important   If you are running Project Professional, you may need to make a one-time adjustment to use the My Computer account and to work offline. This helps ensure that the practice files you work with in this chapter don't affect your Project Server data. For more information, see "Starting Project Professional," on page 10.

OPEN: Short Film Project 16a from the *My Documents**Microsoft Press**Project 2003 Step by Step*\ *Chapter 16 Getting Back on Track* folder. You can also access the practice files for this book by clicking **Start**, **All Programs**, **Microsoft Press**, **Project 2003 Step by Step**, and then selecting the chapter folder of the file you want to open.

1   On the **File** menu, click **Save As**.

The **Save As** dialog box appears.

2   In the **File name** box, type Short Film Project 16, and then click the **Save** button.

To begin troubleshooting the time and schedule issues, you'll get a top-level view of the degree of schedule variance in the project plan now.

3   On the **Project** menu, click **Project Information**.

The **Project Information** dialog box appears.

The current date you see will probably differ.

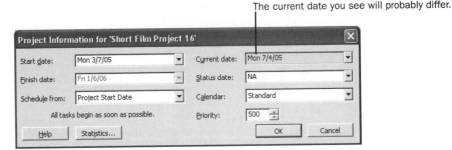

In it you can see the scheduled finish date for the project: January 6, 2006. However, you know this date must be pulled in so the project concludes before the end of 2005.

Next you will look at the duration values for this project.

4   In the **Project Information** dialog box, click the **Statistics** button.

The **Project Statistics** dialog box appears:

Based on current project performance and the remaining
work as scheduled, the project will finish 13 days later than
planned in the baseline.

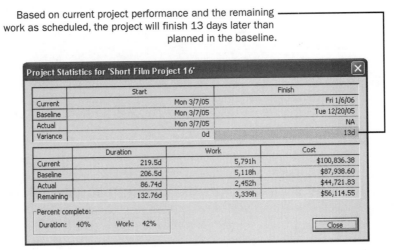

Here you can see, among other things, that overall the project plan now has 13 days of finish variance.

The **Project Statistics** dialog box also indicates some cost variance—the difference between the current and baseline cost values. You will examine this more closely in a later exercise.

5 Click the **Close** button to close the **Project Statistics** dialog box.

Before you address the overall project duration, you'll examine the missed deadline for the production phase.

6 Point to the missed deadline indicator in the Indicators column for task 24, the *Production* summary task.

Your screen should look similar to the following illustration:

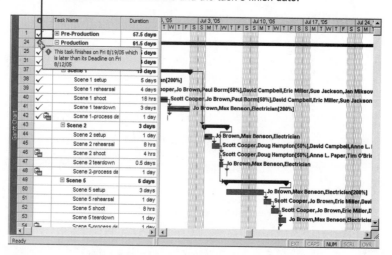

Positioning the mouse pointer over the missed deadline indicator displays a ScreenTip in which you can see the details of the deadline and the task's finish date.

Enough schedule variance has occurred in the pre-production phase and the completed portion of the production phase to cause the scheduled completion of the production phase to move out beyond its deadline date of August 12.

Take a moment to look over the remaining tasks in the production phase. These consist of several more scenes to be shot. Because of the nature of this work, you can't change task relationships (for example, from finish-to-start to start-to-start) to decrease the duration of each scene's summary task; the tasks follow a logical finish-to-start relationship. Nor can you schedule two or more scenes to be shot in parallel, because many of the same resources are required for all of them. To get the production phase back down to an acceptable duration, you'll have to shorten the duration of some of its subtasks. To do this, you'll assign additional resources to some tasks.

Looking over the remaining production tasks, you see that some of the setup and teardown tasks seem to be the longest, so you'll focus on these.

7 Click the name of task 50, **Scene 5 setup**, and then scroll the Gantt Chart view up so the task appears at the top of the view.

This three-day task currently has three resources assigned. After conferring with these resources, you all agree that they could complete the task more quickly with additional resources.

Assign
Resources

8 On the Standard toolbar, click the **Assign Resources** button.

9 In the **Assign Resources** dialog box, under the **Resource Name** column, click **Frank Lee**, and then click the **Assign** button.

Project assigns Frank Lee to the task, and because *effort-driven scheduling* is enabled for this task, Project reduces the duration of the task to 2.4 days. Your screen should look similar to the following illustration:

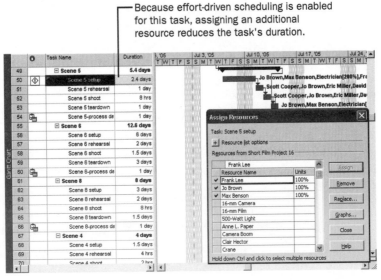

To further reduce the task's duration, you'll assign another resource.

10 In the **Resource Name** column, click **Keith Harris**, and then click the **Assign** button.

Project further reduces the duration of the task to 2 days.

Next you will reduce the durations of the setup and teardown tasks of Scene 6. This time, however, you'll make multiple assignments to multiple tasks simultaneously, because it's quicker.

11 In the **Task Name** column, click the name of task 56, **Scene 6 setup**. While holding down the Ctrl key, click the name of task 59, **Scene 6 teardown**.

12 In the **Resource Name** column of the **Assign Resources** dialog box, while holding down the Ctrl key, click **Keith Harris** and then **Frank Lee**.

13 Click the **Assign** button.

Project assigns these two resources to tasks 56 and 59 and correspondingly reduces the durations of the two tasks. Your screen should look similar to the following illustration:

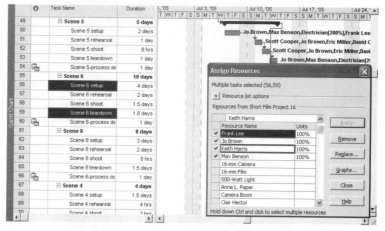

14 Scroll up to see task 24, the *Production* summary task.

Note that the missed deadline indicator is still visible. If you point at it with your mouse pointer you'll see that the additional assignments you just made did indeed move up the completion date of the production phase, but not enough to meet its deadline date. To remedy this, you'll make some additional assignments to other tasks.

15 In the **Task Name** column, click the name of task 62, **Scene 8 setup**. While holding down the Ctrl key, click the name of task 65, **Scene 8 teardown**.

16 In the **Resource Name** column of the **Assign Resources** dialog box, while holding down the Ctrl key, click **Keith Harris** and then **Frank Lee**.

17 Click the **Assign** button.

18 Click the **Close** button to close the **Assign Resources** dialog box.

19 Scroll up to see task 24, the *Production* summary task.

Your screen should look similar to the following illustration:

Reducing the durations of subtasks also reduced the duration of this summary task enough so that, as scheduled, it no longer misses its deadline.

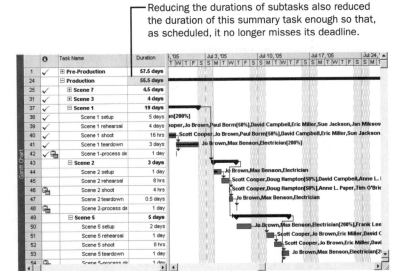

The missed deadline indicator is gone. Next you'll see how the production phase is now scheduled. Recall that the deadline date of the Production summary task was August 12.

20 On the **Edit** menu, click **Go To**.

21 In the **Date** box (not the *ID* box), type or click **8/12/05**, and then click **OK**.

Project scrolls the Gantt Chart to show the end of the Production summary task. Your screen should look similar to the following illustration:

You can visually verify that the summary task concludes prior to its deadline in the chart portion of the Gantt Chart view.

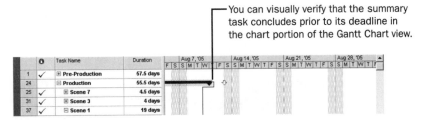

Task
Information

Tip You can also see the summary task's scheduled finish date and deadline date by clicking the **Task Information** button on the Standard toolbar.

With the updated setup and teardown durations, the overall duration of the production phase now ends on August 11, just one day before its deadline. Given the amount of variance that occurred in the production phase already, however, you should keep a close watch on this phase as work progresses.

Troubleshooting Cost and Resource Problems

In projects where you've entered cost information for resources, you might find that to address many cost problems you must fine-tune resource and assignment details. Whether or not it's your intention, changing resource assignment details not only affects costs but can affect task durations as well.

As you saw in the previous exercise, the short film project plan has some cost variance. As it is currently scheduled, the project plan will end up costing about $11,000 more than planned, or about 9 percent over budget. This cost variance has resulted from longer-than-expected assignment durations and the resulting higher costs of the assigned resources.

After doing some research into the high cost of the electricians on the setup and tear-down assignments, you learn that in most cases, they're really needed for only a portion of the tasks' durations. After discussing the issue with the production manager, you agree that the electricians' assignments on the remaining setup and teardown tasks should be halved. While you're updating the project, you'll also handle the upcoming departure of another resource.

In this exercise, you adjust work values for resource assignments and replace one resource with another on upcoming assignments. You begin, however, by checking the total cost of the electricians' assignments.

1   On the **View** menu, click **Resource Sheet**.

The Resource Sheet view appears. Note the current total cost of resource 13, Electrician: $7,370. This is a combination of the electricians' actual cost to date and their anticipated cost for scheduled assignments yet to be completed. You would like to reduce this cost by reducing the electricians' work on tasks.

2   On the **View** menu, click **Resource Usage**.

The Resource Usage view appears.

3   In the **Resource Name** column, click the plus sign next to the name of resource 13, *Electrician*. Then scroll the Resource Usage view so that all of the electricians' assignments are visible.

Because scenes 7, 3, and 1 have already been completed, you'll focus on the electricians' assignments to the remaining scenes.

4   In the **Work** column for **Scene 2 setup**, type **4h**, and then press the ⌷Enter⌷ key.

Project adjusts the work of the electricians on this task to four hours.

5   Enter the new work values in the following list for the electricians' remaining assignments:

For this assignment	Enter this work value
Scene 2 teardown	2h
Scene 5 setup	16h
Scene 5 teardown	8h
Scene 6 setup	32h
Scene 6 teardown	7h
Scene 8 setup	8h
Scene 8 teardown	4h
Scene 4 setup	6h
Scene 4 teardown	6h

When you're done, your screen should look similar to the following illustration:

After reducing the work on the electricians' assignments, their total work (and resulting costs) is correspondingly reduced.

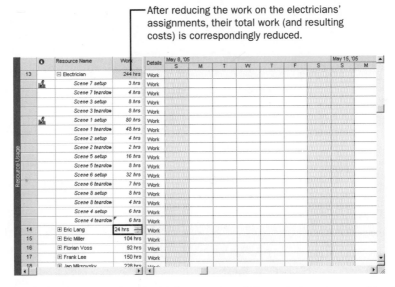

Note that because the electricians were not the only resource assigned to these tasks, reducing the electricians' scheduled work in this way will reduce the cost of their assignments, but not necessarily the durations of these tasks. The other resources assigned to these tasks may have assignments of longer durations.

To verify the reduction in the electricians' costs, you'll switch back to the Resource Sheet view.

6   On the **View** menu, click **Resource Sheet**.

The Resource Sheet view appears. Your screen should look similar to the following illustration:

The electricians' updated cost includes their actual cost plus remaining cost. Only remaining cost is affected by changing the upcoming assignments for the electricians.

	Resource Name	Cost	Baseline Cost	Variance	Actual Cost	Remaining
1	16-mm Camera	$1,050.00	$900.00	$150.00	$550.00	$500.00
2	16-mm Film	$6,600.00	$5,800.00	$800.00	$3,200.00	$3,400.00
3	500-Watt Light	$350.00	$330.00	$20.00	$160.00	$190.00
4	Anne L. Paper	$731.25	$731.25	$0.00	$150.00	$581.25
5	Camera Boom	$0.00	$0.00	$0.00	$0.00	$0.00
6	Clair Hector	$8,320.00	$8,320.00	$0.00	$4,160.00	$4,160.00
7	Crane	$0.00	$0.00	$0.00	$0.00	$0.00
8	Daniel Penn	$412.50	$412.50	$0.00	$0.00	$412.50
9	David Campbell	$2,775.00	$2,475.00	$300.00	$450.00	$2,325.00
10	Dolly	$0.00	$0.00	$0.00	$0.00	$0.00
11	Doug Hampton	$1,950.00	$1,887.60	$62.40	$499.20	$1,450.80
12	Editing Lab	$5,100.00	$5,100.00	$0.00	$0.00	$5,100.00
13	Electrician	$5,368.00	$2,178.00	$3,190.00	$3,410.00	$1,958.00
14	Eric Lang	$372.00	$372.00	$0.00	$372.00	$0.00
15	Eric Miller	$975.00	$675.00	$300.00	$600.00	$375.00
16	Florian Voss	$2,024.00	$2,024.00	$0.00	$0.00	$2,024.00
17	Frank Lee	$2,100.00	$812.00	$1,288.00	$448.00	$1,652.00
18	Jan Miksovsky	$4,237.00	$3,637.00	$600.00	$3,412.00	$825.00
19	Jim Hance	$412.50	$412.50	$0.00	$150.00	$262.50
20	Jo Brown	$9,337.50	$9,037.50	$300.00	$4,837.50	$4,500.00
21	Johnathan Perrera	$3,828.00	$3,828.00	$0.00	$3,828.00	$0.00
22	Joseph Matthews	$365.63	$356.25	$9.37	$309.38	$56.25

Note the updated total cost of resource 13, Electrician: $5,368. Only the Cost and Remaining Cost values changed; the costs relating to work already performed (that is, actual work) are not affected, nor is the baseline cost.

To conclude this exercise, you will update the project plan to reflect that a resource will be leaving the project early and his assignments will be taken over by another resource. Max Benson will be leaving the project just after the start of work on scene 2. You will reassign Max Benson's work on subsequent tasks to Megan Sherman. Megan also happens to be a slightly less expensive resource, so the replacement will help a little with the cost variance too.

7   On the **View** menu, click **Task Usage**.

The Task Usage view appears. It currently displays the Work table.

8   Drag the vertical divider bar to the right to show all columns in the Work table.

9   On the **Edit** menu, click **Go To**.

10   In the **ID** box, type 44, and then click **OK**.

Project displays the assignments for the most recent task for which Max Benson has any actual work reported.

Your screen should look similar to the following illustration:

Task Name	Work	Baseline	Variance	Actual	Remaining	% W. Comp.	Details	M	T
44	⊟ Scene 2 setup	20 hrs	24 hrs	-4 hrs	12 hrs	8 hrs	60%	Work	20h	
								Act. W	12h	
	Electrician	4 hrs	8 hrs	-4 hrs	4 hrs	0 hrs	100%	Work	4h	
								Act. W	4h	
	Jo Brown	8 hrs	8 hrs	0 hrs	4 hrs	4 hrs	50%	Work	8h	
								Act. W	4h	
	Max Benson	8 hrs	8 hrs	0 hrs	4 hrs	4 hrs	50%	Work	8h	
								Act. W	4h	
45	⊟ Scene 2 rehearsal	36 hrs	36 hrs	0 hrs	0 hrs	36 hrs	0%	Work		36h
								Act. W		
	Anne L. Paper	8 hrs	8 hrs	0 hrs	0 hrs	8 hrs	0%	Work		8h
								Act. W		
	David Campbe.	8 hrs	8 hrs	0 hrs	0 hrs	8 hrs	0%	Work		8h
								Act. W		
	Doug Hampton	4 hrs	4 hrs	0 hrs	0 hrs	4 hrs	0%	Work		4h
								Act. W		
	Jan Miksovsky	8 hrs	8 hrs	0 hrs	0 hrs	8 hrs	0%	Work		8h
								Act. W		
	Scott Cooper	8 hrs	8 hrs	0 hrs	0 hrs	8 hrs	0%	Work		8h
								Act. W		
46	⊟ Scene 2 shoot	66 hrs	66 hrs	0 hrs	0 hrs	66 hrs	0%	Work		66h
								Act. W		
	16-mm Camera	8 hrs	8 hrs	0 hrs	0 hrs	8 hrs	0%	Work		8h
								Act. W		

You can see that Max Benson's assignment to task 44, *Scene 2 setup,* is 50 percent complete. This value appears in the Percent Work Complete column, labeled *% W. Comp.*

Next you'll filter the Task Usage view to show only incomplete tasks. That way, when you replace Max Benson with Megan Sherman, the replacement will affect only the incomplete tasks to which Max Benson is assigned.

11 On the **Project** menu, point to **Filtered For: All Tasks**, and then click **Incomplete Tasks**.

Project filters the Task Usage view to show only those tasks that are not yet complete. Next you will make the resource replacement. Keep an eye on Max Benson's partial work on task 44.

12 Click the **Task Name** column heading.

Assign
Resources

13 On the Standard toolbar, click the **Assign Resources** button.

The **Assign Resources** dialog box appears.

14 In the **Resource Name** column, click **Max Benson**, and then click the **Replace** button.

The **Replace Resource** dialog box appears.

15 In the **Resource Name** column, click **Megan Sherman**, and then click **OK**.

Project replaces Max Benson's future assignments with Megan Sherman.

16 Click **Close** to close the **Assign Resources** dialog box.

Your screen should look similar to the following illustration:

After replacing Max Benson with Megan
Sherman, Max's actual work on the
partially completed task is preserved...

...and his remaining work on the task is assigned to Megan.

Note that for task 44, Project preserved Max Benson's four hours of work on the task and assigned the remainder of his work on the task (four hours) to Megan. For the subsequent tasks to which Max was assigned, he has been replaced by Megan.

17 On the **Project** menu, point to **Filtered For: Incomplete Tasks**, and then click **All Tasks**.

Project unfilters the Task Usage view. Note that Max's historical actual work is still recorded in the project plan.

Troubleshooting Scope-of-Work Problems

The project's scope includes all the work required—and only the work required—to successfully deliver the product of the project to its intended customer. After project work has started, managing its scope usually requires making trade-offs: trading time for money, quality for time, and so on. You might have the goal of never making such trade-offs, but a more realistic goal might be to make the best-informed trade-offs possible.

Recall from the previous exercises that the project finish date extended into 2006. With the actions taken in the previous exercise, the finish date has been pulled into 2005, but you want it to end around mid-December 2005 at the latest. In this exercise, you focus on the project's finish date and make several trade-offs to ensure that the project will deliver its product within the time frame that you want.

1 On the **Project** menu, click **Project Information**.

The **Project Information** dialog box appears. As the schedule is now, if all the remaining work is completed as scheduled, the project will be completed on

December 29, 2005. However, realistically, you expect the holiday season to interfere with concluding the project, so you'll need to take steps to pull in the finish date.

2   Click **Cancel** to close the **Project Information** dialog box.

Because the project finish date is controlled by tasks on the critical path, you'll begin by viewing only those tasks.

3   On the **View** menu, click **More Views**.

4   In the **More Views** dialog box, click **Detail Gantt**, and then click the **Apply** button.

The Detail Gantt view appears.

5   On the **Project** menu, point to **Filtered For: All Tasks**, and then click **Critical**.

Project displays only the critical tasks. The remaining production tasks are already as compressed as they can be, so you'll focus on compressing the post-production tasks. To begin, you'll allow overtime work for several tasks, to shorten their durations.

6   On the **Edit** menu, click **Go To**.

7   In the **ID** box, type 74, and then click **OK**.

Project displays task 74, *Log footage*.

Your screen should look similar to the following illustration:

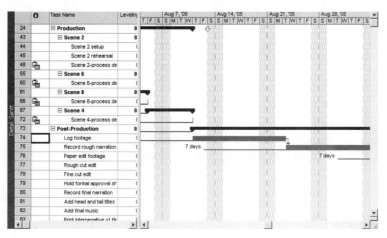

8   On the **Window** menu, click **Split**.

The Task Form appears below the Detail Gantt view.

9   Click anywhere in the Task Form. Then on the **Format** menu, point to **Details**, and click **Resource Work**.

The Resource Work details appear in the Task Form.

10 To see the effect of the following steps on the duration of task 74 and successor tasks, scroll the Detail Gantt view in the upper pane until task 74 is visible.

11 In the Task Form, in the **Ovt. Work** column for the resource named *Editing Lab,* type or click 20h, and press Enter .

12 In the **Ovt. Work** column for *Florian Voss*, type or click 20h, and click **OK** in the upper right corner of the Task Form.

The overtime work values cause Project to adjust the daily work assignments for these resources and to shorten the overall duration of the task. Your screen should look similar to the following illustration:

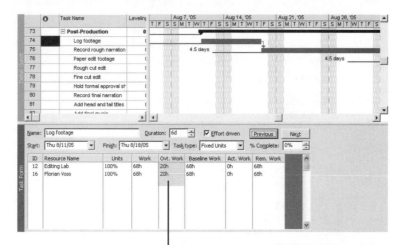

Assigning overtime work reduces the duration of the task but not the total amount of work required to complete the task.

Note that each resource's total work on this task remains at 68 hours. Now, however, 20 of those 68 hours per resource will be scheduled as overtime. The same amount of work will be performed, but in a shorter time span. Project will apply overtime cost rates, if they have been set up, to the overtime portion of the assignment.

13 In the Gantt Chart view, click the name of task 75, **Record rough narration**.

14 In the Task Form, enter 30 hours (30h) of overtime work for both of the assigned resources, and then click **OK**.

Project schedules the overtime work and recalculates the task's duration.

15 In the Gantt Chart view, click the name of task 76, **Paper edit footage**.

16 In the Task Form, enter 25 hours (**25h**) of overtime work for each of the four assigned resources, and then click **OK**.

Project schedules the overtime work and recalculates the task's duration.

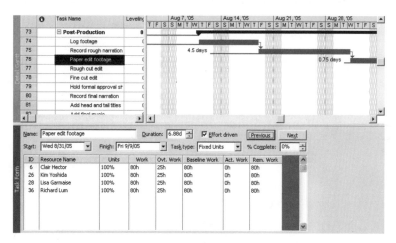

17 On the **Window** menu, click **Remove Split**.

18 On the **Project** menu, click **Project Information**.

The **Project Information** dialog box appears. The adjustments you've made to the schedule have pulled in the project's finish date to 12/16/05. Although that meets the target you had in mind, given the overall performance to date, you can expect some additional variance. In anticipation of this, you'll make further adjustments to the post-production tasks.

19 Click **Cancel** to close the **Project Information** dialog box.

Task 81, *Add head and tail titles,* is a fairly long task. After talking with the resources assigned to it and its predecessor task, you all agree that given the schedule crunch, work on task 81 can begin at the same time as its predecessor, task 80.

20 In the **Task Name** column, click the name of task 81, **Add head and tail titles**.

Task
Information

21 On the Standard toolbar, click the **Task Information** button.

The **Task Information** dialog box appears.

22 Click the **Predecessors** tab.

23 In the **Type** field for the task's predecessor, click **Start-to-Start (SS)** in the drop-down list.

24 Click **OK** to close the **Task Information** dialog box.

Go To Selected
Task

25 On the Standard toolbar, click the **Go To Selected Task** button.

Your screen should look similar to the following illustration:

Changing the predecessor relationship between
these tasks to start-to-start decreases the
overall duration of the project because these
tasks are on the critical path.

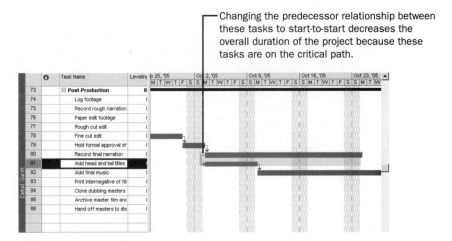

Project reschedules task 81 to start when 80 starts and reschedules all subsequent linked tasks as well. Note that now task 82 as well as task 81 will now start before task 80 is completed.

26 On the **Project** menu, click **Project Information**.

The **Project Information** dialog box appears. The project's finish date is now pulled back to late November—a workable date at this time.

To conclude this exercise, you'll see what effects these final adjustments have had on the project's final cost values as well.

27 Click the **Statistics** button.

The **Project Statistics** dialog box appears.

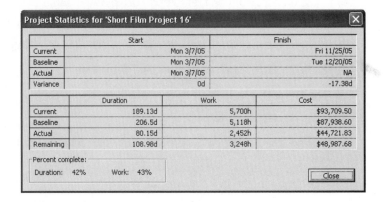

Project Statistics for 'Short Film Project 16'			
	Start		Finish
Current	Mon 3/7/05		Fri 11/25/05
Baseline	Mon 3/7/05		Tue 12/20/05
Actual	Mon 3/7/05		NA
Variance	0d		-17.38d

	Duration	Work	Cost
Current	189.13d	5,700h	$93,709.50
Baseline	206.5d	5,118h	$87,938.60
Actual	80.15d	2,452h	$44,721.83
Remaining	108.98d	3,248h	$48,987.68

Percent complete:
Duration: 42%   Work: 43%

Close

The current cost calculation is now closer to its baseline cost, although you know it's likely to go up.

28 Click the **Close** button to close the **Project Statistics** dialog box.

You confer with the project sponsors, who are pleased that you can wrap up the short film project before the holiday season. Although producing the project deliverable within these constraints will be a challenge, you're both realistic and optimistic about the project's future performance and comfortable with your project management skills and your knowledge of Project. Good luck!

CLOSE: the Short Film Project 16 file.

Key Points

- When addressing variance in a project plan, it is useful to evaluate your plan (and variance) in terms of time, cost, and scope: the three sides of the project triangle.

- When addressing schedule problems, focus your remedies on tasks on the critical path; these drive the finish date of the project.

- When addressing cost or scope problems, focus on expensive resources and especially on their longer assignments.

III
Special Subjects

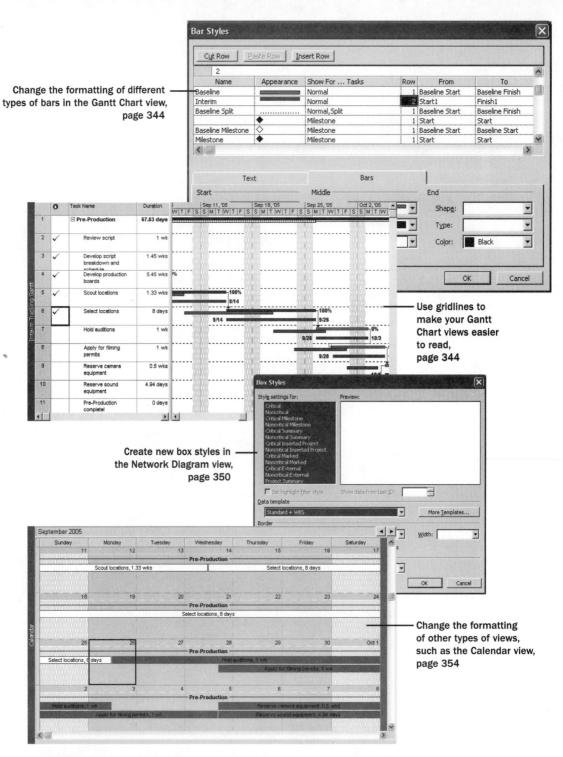

Change the formatting of different types of bars in the Gantt Chart view, page 344

Use gridlines to make your Gantt Chart views easier to read, page 344

Create new box styles in the Network Diagram view, page 350

Change the formatting of other types of views, such as the Calendar view, page 354

17 Applying Advanced Formatting

In this chapter you will learn to:

✔ Format the Gantt Chart view.

✔ Format the Network Diagram view.

✔ Format the Calendar view.

See Also Do you need a quick refresher on the topics in this chapter? See the quick reference entries on pages xxxvii–xxxviii.

This chapter introduces you to some of the more advanced formatting features in Microsoft Office Project 2003. A well-formatted project plan is essential for communicating details to resources, customers, and other stakeholders. Some of the formatting capabilities in Project are similar to those of a style-based word processor such as Word, in which defining a style once affects all content in the document to which that style has been applied. In Project you can use styles to change the appearance of a specific type of Gantt bar, such as a summary bar, throughout a project plan. Other formatting options you're introduced to in this chapter focus on the different ways of identifying tasks and formatting some of the more commonly used views.

 Important Before you can use the practice files in this chapter, be sure you install them from the book's companion CD to their default location. See "Using the Book's CD-ROM," on page xiii, for more information.

Formatting Bar Styles in a Gantt Chart View

You can directly format specific items (a milestone, for example) in a Gantt chart view or use the Gantt Chart Wizard (on the **Format** menu) to change the look of a Gantt chart view in limited ways. To change the overall appearance of a Gantt chart view, however, you use the **Bar Styles** command on the **Format** menu.

Note Remember that several views are Gantt chart views, even though only one view is specifically called the Gantt Chart view. Other Gantt chart views include the Detail Gantt, Leveling Gantt, Multiple Baselines Gantt, and Tracking Gantt. *Gantt chart view* generally refers to a type of presentation that shows Gantt bars organized along a timescale.

In addition to changing the formatting of objects that appear by default in a Gantt chart view (such as a task's Gantt bar), you can add or remove objects. For example, it may be useful to compare *baseline, interim,* and *actual* plans in a single view. Doing so helps you evaluate the schedule adjustments you have made.

In this exercise, you display the current schedule along with the baseline and the interim plan. (The baseline and the interim plan were previously saved in the project plan.) You begin by customizing a copy of the Tracking Gantt chart view.

OPEN: Parnell Film 17a from the *\My Documents\Microsoft Press\Project 2003 Step by Step\Chapter 17 Advanced Formatting* folder. You can also access the practice files for this book by clicking **Start**, **All Programs**, **Microsoft Press**, **Project 2003 Step by Step**, and then selecting the chapter folder of the file you want to open.

1 On the **File** menu, click **Save As**.

The **Save As** dialog box appears.

2 In the **File name** box, type Parnell Film 17, and then click the **Save** button.

3 On the **View** menu, click **More Views**.

The **More Views** dialog box appears.

4 In the **Views** list, click **Tracking Gantt**, and click the **Copy** button.

The **View Definition** dialog box appears:

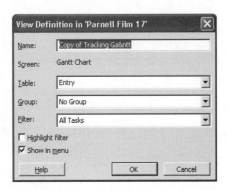

5 In the **Name** box, type Interim Tracking Gantt, and click **OK**.

The new view is listed in the **More Views** dialog box.

6 Click the **Apply** button.

Project displays the new view, which at this point is identical to the Tracking Gantt view.

Next you will add the interim plan bars to the view.

7 On the **Format** menu, click **Bar Styles**.

The **Bar Styles** dialog box appears.

Tip You can also display this dialog box by double-clicking the background of the chart portion of a Gantt chart view.

8 Scroll down the list of the bar styles, and in the **Name** column, click **Baseline Split**.

9 Click the **Insert Row** button.

Project inserts a row for a new bar style in the table.

10 In the new cell, type Interim.

Interim is the name you'll give to the new task bar that will appear on the chart portion of the view.

Tip The names of most task bars will appear in the legend of printed Gantt chart views. If you do not want your custom task bar name to appear in the legend, type an asterisk (*) at the beginning of the task bar name. For example, if you wanted to prevent Interim from appearing in the legend, you would enter it's name here as *Interim. For example, in the **Bar Styles** dialog box you can see that the Rolled Up Task bar name (among others) is prefaced with an asterisk, so it does not appear in the legend of a printed Gantt chart view.

11 In the same row, click the cell under the **Show For...Tasks** column heading, and then click **Normal** in the drop-down list.

The **Show For ... Tasks** value indicates the type of task the bar will represent, (such as a normal task, a summary task, or a milestone) or the status of the task (such as critical or in progress).

Tip This is a fairly complex dialog box in Project, but it is extensively documented in online Help. To see Help for this dialog box, click the **Help** button.

12 Click the cell under the **From** column heading, and click **Start1** in the drop-down list.

13 Click the cell under the **To** column heading, and then click **Finish1** in the drop-down list.

The From and To values represent the start and end points for the bar. Your screen should look similar to the following illustration:

Here is the new bar style you are creating.

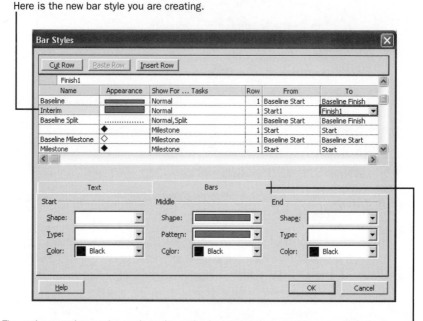

The options on these tabs apply to the active bar style above; in this case, "Interim."

The Start1 and Finish1 items are the fields in which the first interim plan values were previously saved for you in the project plan. The current start date and finish date of each task in the project were saved to these fields when the interim plan was saved.

You have now instructed Project to display the first interim plan start and finish dates as bars; next you will specify what these bars should look like.

14 Click the cell under the **Row** column heading, and click **2** in the drop-down list.

This causes Project to display multiple rows of Gantt bars for each task in the view. Next focus your attention on the lower half of the **Bar Styles** dialog box.

15   In the **Shape** box under the **Middle** label, click the half-height bar, the third option from the top of the list.

Troubleshooting   The **Bar Styles** dialog box is one of several dialog boxes in Project that contains tabs (and is referred to as a *tabbed dialog box*). If you don't see the Shape box mentioned in the previous step, verify that the **Bars** tab is active and not the **Text** tab.

16   In the **Pattern** box under the **Middle** label, click the solid bar, the second option from the top of the list.

17   In the **Color** box, click **Green**.

Your screen should look similar to the following illustration:

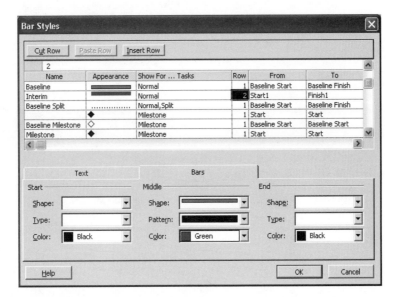

Because this custom view focuses on the interim plan, next you'll format the interim bars to include their start and finish dates.

18   In the **Bar Styles** dialog box, click the **Text** tab.

19   In the **Left** box, click **Start1** in the drop-down list.

Tip   You can type a letter in a field name list to go directly to fields that begin with that letter. For example, you can type **S** to go to the items that begin with S.

20 In the **Right** box, click **Finish1** in the drop-down list.

Selecting these values will cause the Start1 and Finish1 dates to appear on either side of the bar. Your screen should look similar to the following illustration:

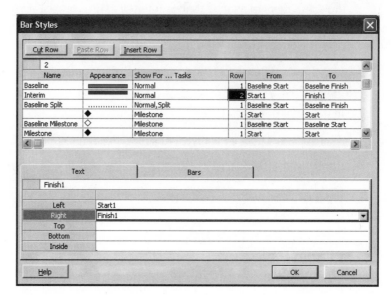

21 Click **OK** to close the **Bar Styles** dialog box.

Project displays the interim bars on the Interim Tracking Gantt view, although it's possible that no Gantt bars will be visible on your screen yet. Next you will get a better look at the Gantt bars.

22 On the **Edit** menu, click **Go To**.

The **Go To** dialog box appears.

23 In the **ID** box, type 6, and click **OK**.

Project scrolls the view to display the Gantt bars for task 6 and its adjacent tasks. Your screen should look similar to the following illustration.

In this custom view, the interim plan appears as green bars and the interim start and finish dates appear at either end of the interim bars.

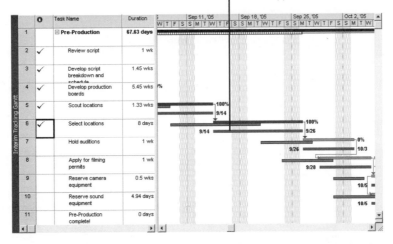

Here you can see that the completed task 6 (shown as a solid blue bar at the top of the task row) corresponds exactly to its interim plan bar (the green bar at the bottom of the task row) and that both were scheduled later than the baseline (the patterned gray bar in the middle of the task row). That is because after the baseline was saved, changes to the schedule were made that pushed out the scheduled start date of the task.

To conclude this exercise, you'll display horizontal gridlines on the chart portion of the Interim Tracking Gantt view to better distinguish the rows of Gantt bars per task.

24 On the **Format** menu, click **Gridlines**.

The **Gridlines** dialog box appears.

25 In the **Line to change** box, make sure that **Gantt Rows** is selected, and then in the **Type** box, click the long dashed line, the last option in the list.

Your screen should look similar to the following illustration:

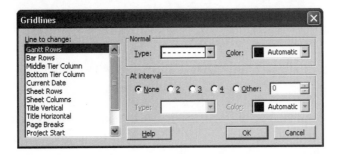

26 Click **OK** to close the **Gridlines** dialog box.

Project draws gridlines between task rows in the chart. Your screen should look similar to the following illustration:

Horizontal gridlines help separate the sets of Gantt bars for each task from those of the other tasks.

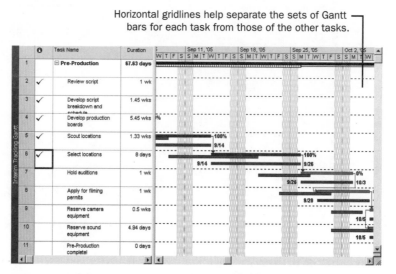

Displaying gridlines like this is a great idea when you print multiple Gantt bars for each task.

Formatting the Network Diagram View

In traditional project management, the Network Diagram is a standard way of representing project activities and their relationships. Tasks are represented as boxes, or nodes, and the relationships between tasks are drawn as lines connecting nodes. Unlike a Gantt chart, which is a timescaled view, a network diagram enables you to see project activities in more of a flowchart format. This is useful if you'd like to focus more on the relationships between activities rather than on their durations.

Project provides substantial formatting options for the Network Diagram. In this section, you will use just a few of these formatting options. If you're a heavy-duty Network Diagram user, you'll want to explore the formatting options in greater detail on your own.

In this exercise, you format items in the Network Diagram view.

1 On the **View** menu, click **Network Diagram**.

The Network Diagram view appears. In this view, each task is represented by a box or node, and each node contains several pieces of information about the task. Your screen should look similar to the following illustration:

The Network Diagram view focuses more on
task relationships than on durations or sequence.
Each task is represented as a box or node, and the
relationships between tasks are represented as arrows.

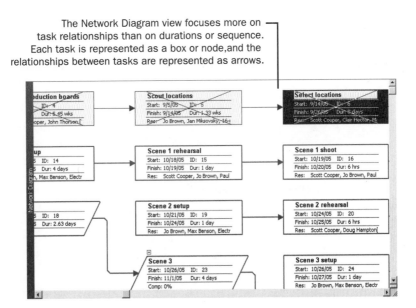

Note   Nodes with an *X* drawn through them represent completed tasks.

Next you'll replace the task ID values with the Work Breakdown Structure (WBS)
codes.

2   On the **Format** menu, click **Box Styles.**

The **Box Styles** dialog box appears. Your screen should look similar to the following
illustration:

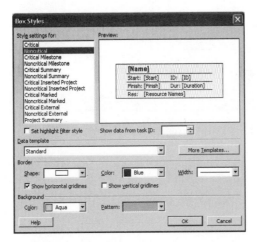

In the **Style settings for** list, you can see all of the node box styles available in
Project. The **Preview** box shows you the specific labels and fields displayed in each
box style.

3   Click the **More Templates** button.

The **Data Templates** dialog box appears. Templates determines what fields appear in boxes (nodes) and their layout.

4   In the **Templates in Network Diagram** list, make sure that **Standard** is selected, and then click the **Copy** button.

The **Data Template Definition** dialog box appears. You want to add the WBS code value to the upper right corner of the node.

5   In the **Template name** box, type Standard + WBS.

6   Below **Choose cell(s)**, click the cell in the upper right corner; it currently contains *ID*.

7   In the drop-down list of fields, click **WBS**, and then press the [Enter] key.

Pressing the [Enter] key causes Project to update the preview in the dialog box. Your screen should look similar to the following illustration:

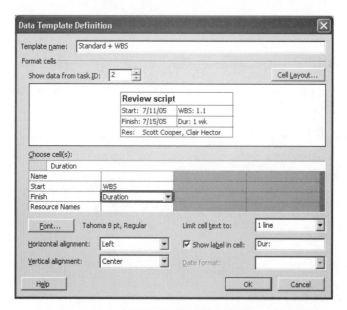

8   Click **OK** to close the **Data Template Definition** dialog box.

9   Click the **Close** button to close the **Data Templates** dialog box.

10   In the **Box Styles** dialog box, under **Style settings for**, drag to select all the items in the box: **Critical** through **Project Summary**.

11   In the **Data template** box, select **Standard + WBS** from the drop-down list.

Your screen should look similar to the following illustration:

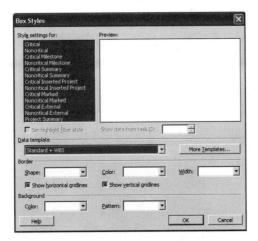

12 Click **OK** to close the **Box Styles** dialog box.

Project applies the revised box style to nodes in the Network Diagram. Your screen should look similar to the following illustration:

After you reformat the box style in the Network Diagram view, the WBS code replaces the task ID in each node.

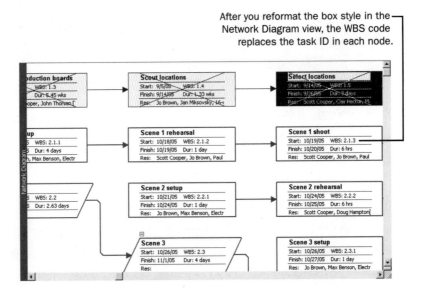

Formatting the Calendar View

The Calendar view is probably the simplest view available in Project; however, even the Calendar view offers several formatting options. This view is especially useful for sharing schedule information with resources or other stakeholders who prefer a traditional "month-at-a-glance" format rather than a more detailed view, such as the Gantt Chart view.

In this exercise, you reformat summary and critical tasks in the Calendar view.

1   On the **View** menu, click **Calendar**.

The Calendar view appears. It displays four weeks at a time, and it draws task bars on the days on which tasks are scheduled. Depending on your screen resolution, you might see additional task bars in the Calendar view.

The Calendar view resembles a traditional "month-at-a-glance" calendar and displays tasks as bars spanning the days on which they are scheduled to occur.

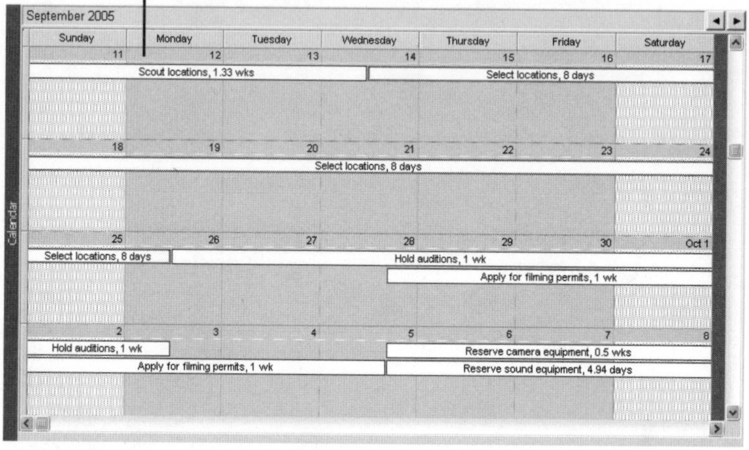

2   On the **Format** menu, click **Bar Styles**.

The **Bar Styles** dialog box appears. The additional item type you would like to show on the Calendar view is a summary bar.

3   In the **Task type** box, click **Summary**.

4   In the **Bar type** box, click **Line** in the drop-down list.

The next item type to reformat is critical tasks.

5   In the **Task type** box, click **Critical**.

6   In the **Pattern** box, select the second option in the drop-down list: the solid black bar.

7   In the **Color** box, select **Red** from the drop-down list.

Your screen should look similar to the following illustration:

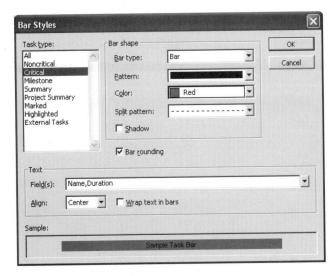

8 Click **OK** to close the **Bar Styles** dialog box.

9 On the **Format** menu, click **Layout Now**.

Project applies the format options to the Calendar view. Rather than scrolling through the Calendar view, you can jump right to a specific date.

10 On the **Edit** menu, click **Go To**.

11 In the **Date** box (*not* the **ID** box), type or select 9/26/05, and then click **OK**.

The Calendar view displays the first critical tasks. Your screen should look similar to the following illustration:

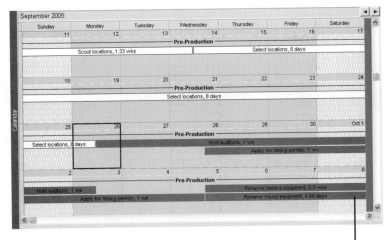

After you reformat the Calendar view, critical tasks appear in red and summary tasks appear as lines.

CLOSE: the Parnell Film 17 file.

Key Points

- Many different types of bars can appear in the chart portion of a Gantt chart view. Each type of bar can represent a kind of task (such as a summary task) or a condition of a task (such as completed).

- The Gantt Chart Wizard offers limited Gantt bar formatting, but the **Format Bar Styles** command (**Format** menu) gives you complete control over Gantt bar formatting.

- Although the Gantt Chart view is often synonymous with project plans, the Network Diagram view (sometimes incorrectly referred to as a *PERT chart*) is useful for focusing on the relationships between activities.

- The Calendar view is especially helpful for those who prefer a traditional "month-at-a-glance" format.

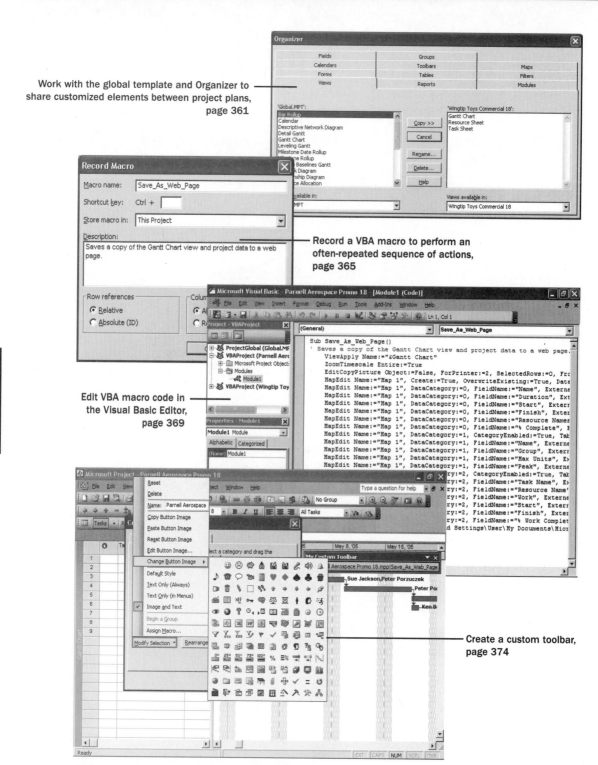

Work with the global template and Organizer to share customized elements between project plans, page 361

Record a VBA macro to perform an often-repeated sequence of actions, page 365

Edit VBA macro code in the Visual Basic Editor, page 369

Create a custom toolbar, page 374

18 Customizing Project

In this chapter you will learn to:

- ✔ Copy a customized element, such as a table, from one project plan to another by using the Organizer.
- ✔ Record and play back a simple macro.
- ✔ Edit a macro in the Visual Basic Editor.
- ✔ Create a custom toolbar.

This chapter describes some of the ways you can customize Microsoft Office Project 2003 to fit your own preferences. Some of the customization options in Project are similar to those you see in other programs in the Microsoft Office System such as Word or Excel. Some customization options even apply to all programs in the Microsoft Office System regardless of the specific program in which you set them. Other options are unique to Project.

Important Some of the actions you perform in this chapter can affect your overall settings in Project regardless of the specific project plan you are using. To keep your Project environment unaffected or at the "factory settings," after you complete this chapter, we include steps to undo some actions.

Important Before you can use the practice files in this chapter, be sure you install them from the book's companion CD to their default location. See "Using the Book's CD-ROM," on page xiii, for more information.

Working with the Organizer

The *Organizer* is the feature you use to share customized elements among project plans. The complete list of elements you can copy between files with the Organizer is indicated by the names of the tabs in the **Organizer** dialog box, which you will see shortly.

One feature of Project that you can work with through the Organizer is the *global template*. This is a Project template named Global.mpt, and it is installed as part of

Project. The global template provides the default *views*, *tables*, and other elements in Project. The list of elements provided by the global template includes the following:

■ Calendars	■ Reports
■ Filters	■ Tables
■ Forms	■ Menus and toolbars
■ Groups	■ Modules (VBA macros)
■ Maps (import/export)	■ Views

Tip   *This tip describes enterprise project management (EPM) functionality.* Project Standard always uses the global template, and Project Professional uses the global template when not connected to Project Server. However, when Project Professional is connected to Project Server, it uses the enterprise global template rather than the global template. The enterprise global template is stored within Project Server and generally provides the same services as does the global template, but on an enterprise project management scale. For more information, see Part 4, "Introducing Project Server."

Initially, the specific definitions of all views, tables, and similar elements are contained in the global template. For example, the fact that the default usage table contains one set of fields and not others is determined by the global template. The very first time you display a view, table, or similar element in a project plan, it is automatically copied from the global template to that project plan. Thereafter, the element resides in the project plan. Any subsequent customization of that element in the project plan (for example, changing the fields displayed in a table) applies to only that one project plan and does not affect the global template. The exception to this is macros, toolbars, and import/export maps. Project always stores these elements in the global template rather than in the active project plan.

You could use Project extensively and never need to touch the global template. When you do work with the global template, you do so through the Organizer. There are two primary actions you can accomplish relating to the global template:

■ Create a customized element, such as a custom view, and make it available in all project plans you work with by copying the custom view into the global template.

■ Replace a customized element such as a view or table in a project plan by copying the original, unmodified element from the global template to the project plan in which you've customized the same element.

The settings in the global template apply to all project plans you work with in Project. Because we don't want to alter the global template you use, in this exercise we'll focus on copying customized elements between two project plans. Keep in mind, though, that the general process of using the Organizer shown here is the same whether you are working with the global template and a project plan or two project plans. In fact, any custom element you copy into the global template becomes available in all the project plans you use.

Important   In the Organizer, when you attempt to copy a view, table, or other element from a project plan to the global template, Project alerts you if you will overwrite that same element in the global template. If you choose to overwrite it, that customized element (such as a customized view) will be available in all new project plans and any other project plans that do not already contain that element. If you choose to rename the customized element, it becomes available in all project plans but does not affect the existing elements already stored in the global template. It's generally a good idea to give your customized elements unique names, like *Custom Gantt Chart,* so that you can keep the original element intact.

In this exercise, you will copy a custom table from one project plan to another.

Important   If you are running Project Professional, you may need to make a one-time adjustment to use the My Computer account and to work offline. This helps ensure that the practice files you work with in this chapter don't affect your Project Server data. For more information, see "Starting Project Professional," on page 10.

OPEN: Parnell Aerospace Promo 18a and Wingtip Toys Commercial 18b from the *My Documents*\\ *Microsoft Press**Project 2003 Step by Step**Chapter 18 Customizing* folder. You can also access the practice files for this book by clicking **Start**, **All Programs**, **Microsoft Press**, **Project 2003 Step by Step**, and then selecting the chapter folder of the file you want to open.

1   On the **File** menu, click **Save As**.

   The **Save As** dialog box appears.

2   In the **File name** box, type Wingtip Toys Commercial 18, and then click the **Save** button.

3   Repeat steps 1 and 2 to save **Parnell Aerospace Promo 18a** as Parnell Aerospace Promo 18.

The Wingtip Toys Commercial 18 project plan contains a custom table named *Custom Entry Table,* which is currently displayed in the Task Sheet view. Your screen should look similar to the following illustration:

The table in this view has been customized by inserting and removing columns.

You'd like to copy this custom table to the Parnell Aerospace Promo 18 project plan.

4 On the **Tools** menu, click **Organizer**.

The **Organizer** dialog box appears. Your screen should look similar to the following illustration:

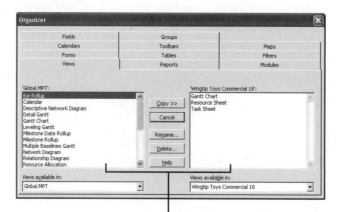

Every tab in the Organizer dialog box has a similar structure—the elements in the global template are on the left, and those in the active project plan are on the right.

5   Click several of the tabs in the dialog box to get an overview of the available
options, and then click the **Tables** tab.

As you can see, every tab of the **Organizer** dialog box has a similar structure: elements from the global template appear on the left side of the dialog box, and the
same types of elements from the active project plan appear on the right.

You might notice that the list of tables in the Wingtip plan is not the complete list
of tables you can display. The list you see for the Wingtip plan in the Organizer
includes only the tables that have actually been displayed already in the Wingtip
plan. If you were to display another table, the Schedule table, for example, Project
would copy that table definition from the global template into the Wingtip plan.

Selecting an element on the left side of the dialog box and then clicking the **Copy**
button will copy that element to the project plan listed on the right. Conversely,
selecting an element on the right side of the dialog box and then clicking the **Copy**
button will copy that element to the file listed on the left.

6   In the **Tables available in** drop-down list on the left side of the **Organizer** dialog box,
select **Parnell Aerospace Promo 18**.

This project plan appears in the list because it is open in Project. Your screen
should look similar to the following illustration:

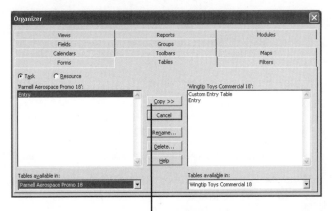

        The side of the dialog box in which you've
        selected an element determines the
        direction in which you copy the element.

As you can see, the Parnell plan (on the left) does not have the Custom Entry Table,
and the Wingtip plan (on the right) does.

7   In the list of tables on the right side of the dialog box, click **Custom Entry Table**.

Tip   Notice that the two arrow symbols (>>) in the **Copy** button switch direction
(<<) when you select an element on the right side of the dialog box.

8 Click **Copy**.

Project copies the Custom Entry Table from the Wingtip plan to the Parnell plan. Your screen should look similar to the following illustration:

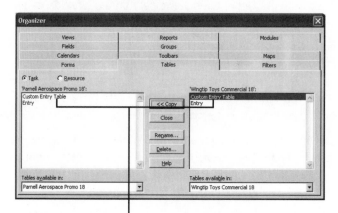

After clicking the Copy button, the Custom Entry Table is copied from the Wingtip plan to the Parnell plan.

9 Click **Close** to close the **Organizer** dialog box.

To conclude this exercise, you will display the newly copied custom table.

10 On the **Window** menu, click **Parnell Aerospace Promo 18**.

Project switches to the Parnell plan, the plan to which you just copied the custom table.

11 On the **View** menu, click **More Views**.

The **More Views** dialog box appears.

12 In the **Views** list, click **Task Sheet**, and then click **Apply**.

13 On the **View** menu, point to **Table: Entry**, and then click **Custom Entry Table**.

Project displays the custom table in the Parnell plan. Your screen should look similar to the following illustration:

14 On the **View** menu, click **Gantt Chart**.

Important   In this exercise, you copied a table between project plans. When copying an entire view, however, keep in mind that it is comprised of tables, filters, and groups. When copying custom views between plans, you might also need to copy a custom table, filter, or group that is part of the custom view.

Recording Macros

Many activities you perform in Project can be repetitive. To save time, you can record a *macro* that captures keystrokes and mouse actions. The macro is recorded in Microsoft Visual Basic for Applications (VBA), the built-in macro programming language of the Microsoft Office System. You can do sophisticated things with VBA, but you can record and play back simple macros without ever directly seeing or working with VBA code.

The macros you create are stored in the global template by default, so they are available to you whenever Project is running. (In fact, macros, toolbars, and import/export maps are unique in that when you create or customize them, Project will store them in the global template rather than the active project plan by default.) The project plan for which you originally created the macro need not be open to run the macro in other project plans. If you want, you can use the Organizer to copy the macro from the global template to another project plan to give it to a friend, for example.

Publishing a project plan in HTML format is a great way to share project details on an intranet or the World Wide Web. However, it's likely the details you initially publish will become obsolete quickly as the project plan is updated. Republishing is a repetitive task that is ideal for automation through a macro. In this exercise, you record and run a macro in the Parnell Aerospace Promo 18 project plan that publishes the project plan to HTML format.

1   On the **Tools** menu, point to **Macro**, and then click **Record New Macro**.

The **Record Macro** dialog box appears.

2   In the **Macro name** box, type Save_As_Web_Page

Tip   Macro names must begin with a letter and cannot contain spaces. To improve the readability of your macro names, you can use an underscore (_) in place of a space. For example, rather than naming a macro *SaveAsWebPage*, you can name it *Save_As_Web_Page*.

For this macro, we will not use a shortcut key. When recording other macros, note that you cannot use a ⎈+ key combination already reserved by Project, so combinations like ⎈+F (the keyboard shortcut for Find) and ⎈+G (Go To) are unavailable. When you click **OK** to close the dialog box, Project alerts you if you need to choose a different key combination.

3   In the **Store macro in** box, click **This Project** to store the macro in the active project plan.

When a macro is stored in a project plan, the macro can be used by any project plan when the project plan that contains the macro is open. The other option, **Global File**, refers to the global template. In this exercise, you will not customize your global template.

4   In the **Description** box, select the boilerplate text, and replace it by typing Saves a copy of the Gantt Chart view and project data to a web page.

Your screen should look similar to the following illustration:

The description is useful to help identify the actions the macro will perform.

5   Click **OK.**

Project begins recording the new macro. Project does not literally record and play back every mouse movement and passing second, but records only the results of the keystrokes and mouse actions you make. Do not feel rushed to complete the recording of the macro.

6   On the **View** menu, click **Gantt Chart.**

Even though the project plan is already showing the Gantt Chart view, including this step in the macro records the action so that if the project plan were initially in a different view, the macro would switch to the Gantt Chart view.

7   On the **View** menu, click **Zoom.**

8   In the **Zoom** dialog box, select **Entire Project**, and then click **OK.**

Project adjusts the timescale to display the entire project. Your screen should look similar to the following illustration:

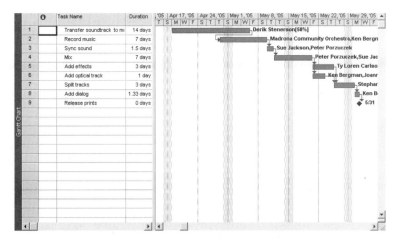

Copy Picture

9 On the Standard toolbar click the **Copy Picture** button.

The **Copy Picture** dialog box appears.

10 Under **Render image**, click **To GIF image file**, and then click **OK**.

The folder location and file name proposed for the GIF image are the same as those of the project plan, which is fine.

11 On the **File** menu, click **Save As Web Page**, and then click **Save**.

Again, the folder location and file name proposed for the HTML file are the same as those of the project plan, which is fine.

When you click **Save**, the Export Wizard appears.

12 In the Export Wizard, click the **Next** button.

The Map page of the Export Wizard appears.

13 Click **Use existing map**, and then click the **Next** button.

The Map Selection page of the Export Wizard appears.

14 Under **Choose a map for your data**, click **Export to HTML using standard template**, and then click the **Next** button.

The Map Options page of the Export Wizard appears.

15 Under **HTML Options**, click **Include image file in HTML page**, and then click **Finish**.

The Export Wizard saves the Web page as you've specified. To wrap up the actions recorded in the macro, you will reset the timescale.

16   On the **View** menu, click **Zoom**, click **Reset**, and then click **OK**.

Now you are ready to stop recording.

17   On the **Tools** menu, point to **Macro**, and then click **Stop Recorder**.

Next you will run the macro to see it play back.

18   On the **Tools** menu, point to **Macro**, and then click **Macros**.

The **Macros** dialog box appears.

19   In the **Macro name** box, click **Parnell Aerospace Promo 18.mpp! Save_As_Web_Page**, and then click the **Run** button.

The macro begins running but pauses as soon as Project generates a confirmation message to replace the existing GIF image file.

Important   Your security level setting in Project affects Project's ability to run macros that you record, or that you get from others. You may not have set the security level directly, but it may have been set when you installed Project, or by a system policy within your organization.

20   Click **Overwrite**, and then click **OK** to overwrite the previously created Web page.

The macro republishes the project plan to HTML format. Next you'll see the results of the macro's actions.

21   In Windows Explorer, navigate to the **Chapter 18 Customizing** folder, and double-click the **Parnell Aerospace Promo 18.html** file to open it in your browser.

The Web page (consisting of the HTML file and related GIF image) appears in your browser. Your screen should look similar to the following illustration:

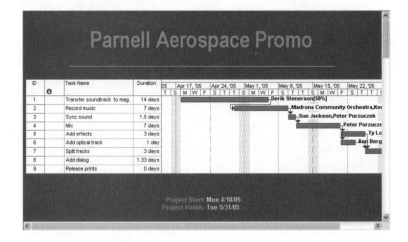

Leave the Web page open in your browser; you'll return to it in the next exercise.

22 Switch back to the Parnell Aerospace Promo 18 project plan in Project.

This macro would be very useful if the Parnell project manager needed to republish the details of the project plan frequently. For example, the project manager could republish it at regular intervals during the planning stage, when the details are being developed, and then again during the execution stage, when the effects of actual progress change the remaining scheduled work.

Editing Macros

As handy as the Save_As_Web_Page macro is, it can be improved. Remember that when you ran it in the previous exercise, you had to confirm that Project should over-write the existing GIF image and HTML files. Because the intent of the macro is to publish the most current information, you would always want to overwrite the older information. You can change the macro code directly to accomplish this. The macro code resides in a VBA module, and you work with the code in the Visual Basic Environment.

Tip The VBA language and Visual Basic Environment are standard in many of the programs in the Microsoft Office System (including Project). Although the specific details of each program differ, the general way you use VBA in each is the same. VBA automation is a powerful tool you can master, and that knowledge can be used in many Microsoft programs.

In this exercise, you work in the Visual Basic Editor to fine-tune the macro you recorded in the previous exercise and then run it.

1 On the **Tools** menu, point to **Macro**, and then click **Macros.**

2 Under **Macro name**, click **Parnell Aerospace Promo 18.mpp!Save_As_Web_Page,** and then click the **Edit** button.

Project loads the module that contains the macro in the Visual Basic Editor. Your screen should look similar to the following illustration:

This VBA code was generated when Project recorded your macro.

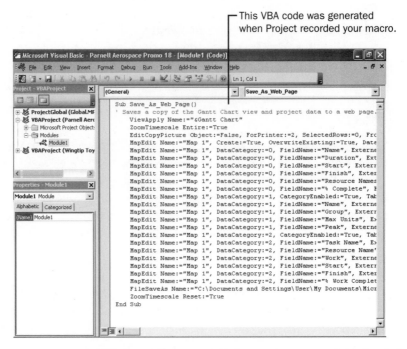

A full explanation of the VBA language is beyond the scope of this book, but we can walk you through some steps to change the behavior of the previously recorded macro. You might also recognize some of the actions that you recorded earlier by the names used in the VBA code.

3 Click at the beginning of the line **ViewApply Name:="&Gantt Chart"**, and press Enter.

4 Click in the new line you just created, press Tab, and type **Application.Alerts False**

Your screen should look similar to the following illustration:

Here is the text you typed.

```
Sub Save_As_Web_Page()
' Saves a copy of the Gantt Chart view and project data to a web page.
    Application.Alerts False
    ViewApply Name:="&Gantt Chart"
    ZoomTimescale Entire:=True
    EditCopyPicture Object:=False, ForPrinter:=2, SelectedRows:=0, Frc
    MapEdit Name:="Map 1", Create:=True, OverwriteExisting:=True, Date
```

This will prevent the two prompts you received when running the macro and accept the default option of replacing the existing files with the same name.

Tip   Note that as you were typing, selection boxes and ScreenTips might have appeared. The Visual Basic Editor uses such tools and feedback to help you enter text in a module correctly.

5   In the line that begins with **EditCopyPicture**, select the text that follows **FromDate:=** text **"4/14/05 12:00 AM"** (including the quotation marks), and type **ActiveProject.ProjectStart**.

Note that the specific date you see might not be 4/14/05.

This VBA code describes the project start date of the active project. Your screen should look similar to the following illustration:

Here is the text string you typed ‾|
to return the project start date.

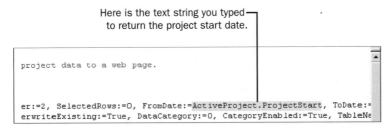

This causes the macro to get the current start date of the active project for the GIF image the macro creates.

6   In the same row, select the text that follows **ToDate:=** text **"6/5/05 12:00 PM"** (including the quotation marks), and type **ActiveProject.ProjectFinish**

Again, note that the specific date you see might not be 6/5/05. Your screen should look similar to the following illustration:

Here is the text string you typed ‾|
to return the project finish date.

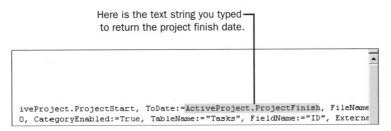

This causes the macro to get the current finish date of the active project for the GIF image that the macro creates. Now if the project plan's start or finish date changes, the date range for the GIF image will change as well.

7   On the **File** menu in the Visual Basic Editor, click **Close and Return to Microsoft Project**.

The Visual Basic Editor closes, and you return to the Parnell plan.

You could run the updated macro now, but to test whether it really uses the most current project start and finish dates, you'll change the start date of the project plan.

8 On the **Project** menu, click **Project Information**.

The **Project Information** dialog box appears. Your screen should look similar to the following illustration:

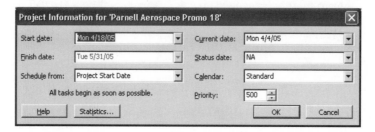

Note the current start and finish dates: 4/18/05 and 5/31/05.

9 In the **Start date** box, type or select **4/25/05**, and then click **OK** to close the **Project Information** dialog box.

Project reschedules the start (and all subsequent dates) of the project plan. Before you rerun the macro, however, you'll make one more major change to the plan. You'll change the duration of task 1 from 14 days to 7.

10 In the **Duration** field for task 1, **Transfer soundtrack to mag. stock**, type or select **7d**, and then press Enter.

Project adjusts the duration for task 1 and reschedules all successor tasks. Your screen should look similar to the following illustration:

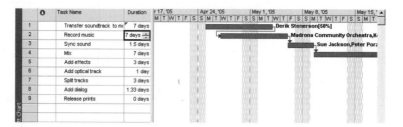

Now you are ready to rerun the macro.

11 On the **Tools** menu, point to **Macro**, and then select **Macros**.

The **Macros** dialog box appears.

12 In the **Macro name** box, click **Parnell Aerospace Promo 18.mpp!Save_As_Web_Page**, and then click **Run**.

The macro runs, and this time you are not prompted to overwrite the previously saved files.

To verify that the macro ran correctly, you'll view the updated Web page in your browser.

13 Switch back to your browser. The previously viewed project plan should still be visible.

14 Click the **Refresh** button to reload the most recently saved HTML file and related GIF image.

The updated HTML file and related GIF image appear in your browser. Your screen should look similar to the following illustration:

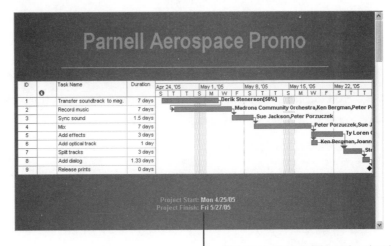

The macro detected the updated project start and finish dates and adjusted the GIF image and other details on the Web page.

Now you can run the macro as frequently as needed to keep the most up-to-date information published.

Tip VBA is a rich and well-documented programming language. If you would like to take a closer look at VBA in Project, on the **Tools** menu, click **Macro**, and then click **Visual Basic Editor**. In the Microsoft Visual Basic window, on the **Help** menu, click **Microsoft Visual Basic Help**. To get help on specific items in a module such as objects, properties, and methods, click a word, and then press the [F1] key. To return to Project, on the **File** menu, click **Close and Return to Microsoft Project**.

Customizing a Toolbar

As with other Office applications, you have several choices about how to work with Project. In fact, some of the preferences you set in Project automatically apply in the other Office applications and vice versa. Some of the customization settings include the following:

■ Displaying or hiding the Office Assistant. (It's hidden by default in Project 2003.) To display the Office Assistant, click **Show the Office Assistant** on the **Help** menu. To hide the Office Assistant, click **Hide the Office Assistant** on the **Help** Menu.

■ Setting up Project to save the active file or all open files automatically at the time interval you specify. (On the **Tools** menu click **Options**, and on the **Save** tab of the **Options** dialog box, select **Save Every** and enter the time interval you want.)

■ Creating customized toolbars that include buttons for any commands you want. (You will do this in the following exercise.)

In this exercise, you create a custom toolbar and assign the macro you recorded earlier to a button on the custom toolbar.

1 Switch back to the Project window that displays the Parnell project plan.

2 On the **Tools** menu, point to **Customize**, and then click **Toolbars**.

The **Customize** dialog box appears.

3 Click the **Toolbars** tab.

Your screen should look similar to the following illustration:

A check mark indicates the toolbars that are currently displayed; what you see might differ.

Tip Toolbars are either docked or floating. When docked, a toolbar appears at one edge of the Project window. Normally this is the top edge, but you can dock a toolbar at any edge of the window. When a toolbar is floating, it has a title bar that tells you the toolbar's name. To move a docked toolbar, point to the far left edge, and drag the toolbar either into the Project window to make it float or to another edge of the window to redock it.

4 Click **New**.

The **New Toolbar** dialog box appears.

5 In the **Toolbar Name** box, type My Custom Toolbar, and then click **OK**.

The new toolbar appears in the list of toolbars and is displayed by default. (Initially it's a floating, empty toolbar.) Your screen should look similar to the following illustration:

Initially the new toolbar floats in the Project window; — it might not appear in this exact spot on your screen.

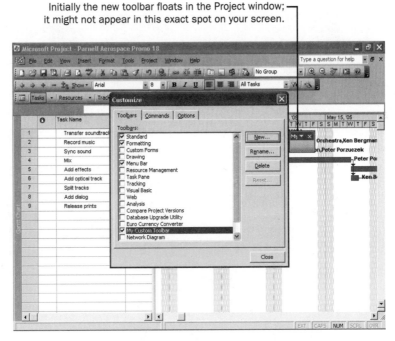

Next you'll add a command to the toolbar that runs the previously recorded macro.

6 Click the **Commands** tab.

In the **Categories** list, you can see several categories of commands. Many of these, such as File and Edit, correspond to menu names.

7 In the **Categories** list, click **All Macros**.

The commands in the All Macros category appear in the **Commands** list on the right. Your screen should look similar to the following illustration:

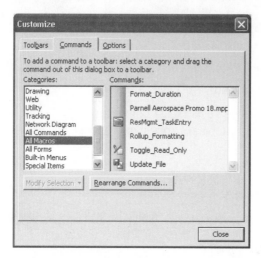

Most of the commands listed for the All Macros category relate to macros included with Project, and what you see might differ. However you should see the Parnell Aerospace Promo 18.mpp!Save_As_Web_Page macro listed because it is stored in the active project plan.

8 Drag the **Parnell Aerospace Promo 18.mpp!Save_As_Web_Page** macro from the **Customize** dialog box onto **My Custom Toolbar**.

My Custom Toolbar widens to show the full title of the macro. If necessary, drag the toolbar so you can see all of it. Your screen should look similar to the following illustration:

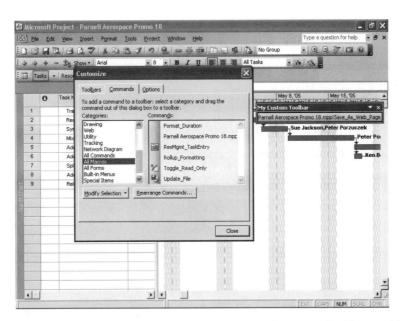

Next you'll change the text that appears on the button and add a graphic image.

9 In the **Customize** dialog box, click **Modify Selection,** and then click **Image and Text.**

This setting makes room on the button for an image as well as a text label.

10 Click **Modify Selection,** and then point to **Change Button Image.**

A submenu of button images appears. Your screen should look similar to the following illustration:

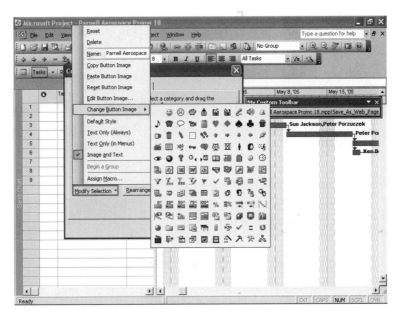

11   Click the last item on the fourth row, the running figure.

Project adds the button image to the button. Next you will change the text label of the button.

12   Click **Modify Selection**, and then position your mouse pointer in the **Name** box and select the full name of the macro.

13   With the name of the macro selected, type Publish To Web, and then press Enter.

Project changes the text label on the button. Your screen should look similar to the following illustration:

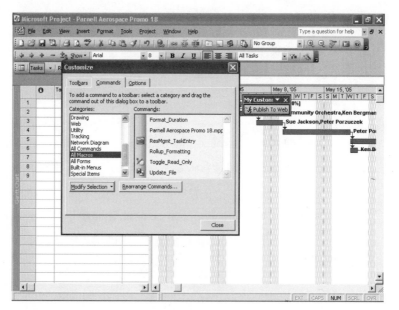

14   Click **Close** to close the **Customize** dialog box.

The custom toolbar remains floating in your Project window.

15   On **My Custom Toolbar**, click the **Publish To Web** button.

The Save_As_Web_Page macro runs. If you want, switch back to your browser and refresh it to see the results, and then switch back to Project.

Custom toolbars and any other customizations made to built-in toolbars apply to all project plans you view in Project. This is because toolbar settings must reside in the global template. To conclude this exercise, you'll delete My Custom Toolbar and the map created by the Export Wizard from your global template so it doesn't affect your overall Project environment.

16   On the **Tools** menu click **Organizer**.

The **Organizer** dialog box appears.

17 Click the **Toolbars** tab.

Your screen should look similar to the following illustration:

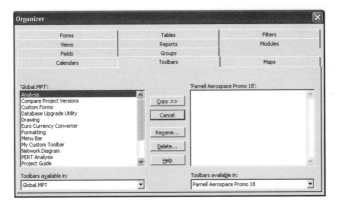

18 In the **Global.MPT** box, click **My Custom Toolbar**, and then click **Delete**.

19 Project prompts you to confirm that you want to delete the toolbar; click **Yes**.

20 Click the **Maps** tab.

21 In the **Global.MPT** box, click **Map 1**, and then click **Delete**.

22 Project prompts you to confirm that you want to delete the map; click **Yes**.

23 Click **Close** to close the **Organizer** dialog box.

Tip You can also delete a toolbar on the **Toolbars** tab of the **Customize** dialog box (**Tools** menu).

CLOSE: the Parnell Aerospace Promo 18 and Wingtip Toys Commercial 18 files.

Key Points

- In Project you share elements you customize, such as tables or filters, between project plans via the Organizer.

- Project, like many other programs in the Microsoft Office System, uses the Visual Basic for Applications (VBA) macro programming language. Among other things, macros enable you to automate repetitive tasks.

- If you want to work directly with VBA code, you do so in the Visual Basic Editor, which is included in Project as well as other Office applications.

- You can substantially customize the toolbars in Project to include the commands and features that interest you the most.

Set the status date, and see earned value schedule indicators to evaluate past schedule performance and forecast future performance, page 383

	Task Name	BCWS	BCWP	SV	SV%	SPI
0	⊟ Short Film Project	$44,763.55	$36,636.37	($8,127.19)	-18%	0.82
1	⊞ Pre-Production	$23,089.75	$23,089.75	$0.00	0%	1
24	⊟ Production	$21,673.80	$13,546.62	($8,127.19)	-37%	0.63
25	⊞ Scene 7	$3,702.50	$3,702.50	$0.00	0%	1
31	⊞ Scene 3	$4,180.40	$4,180.40	$0.00	0%	1
37	⊟ Scene 1	$5,960.40	$5,663.72	($296.69)	-4%	0.95
38	Scene 1 setup	$2,082.00	$2,082.00	$0.00	0%	1
39	Scene 1 rehears:	$780.00	$780.00	$0.00	0%	1
40	Scene 1 shoot	$2,404.40	$2,404.40	$0.00	0%	1
41	Scene 1 teardow	$694.00	$397.32	($296.69)	-42%	0.57
42	Scene 1-process	$0.00	$0.00	$0.00	0%	0
43	⊟ Scene 2	$2,257.10	$0.00	($2,257.10)	-100%	0
44	Scene 2 setup	$518.00	$0.00	($518.00)	-100%	0
45	Scene 2 rehears:	$517.40	$0.00	($517.40)	-100%	0
46	Scene 2 shoot	$962.70	$0.00	($962.70)	-100%	0
47	Scene 2 teardow	$259.00	$0.00	($259.00)	-100%	0
48	Scene 2-process	$0.00	$0.00	$0.00	0%	0
49	⊟ Scene 5	$4,547.40	$0.00	($4,547.40)	-100%	0
50	Scene 5 setup	$1,026.00	$0.00	($1,026.00)	-100%	0
51	Scene 5 rehears:	$755.00	$0.00	($755.00)	-100%	0
52	Scene 5 shoot	$2,424.40	$0.00	($2,424.40)	-100%	0
53	Scene 5 teardow	$342.00	$0.00	($342.00)	-100%	0

	Task Name	BCWS	BCWP	CV	CV%	CPI	BAC	EAC	VAC
0	⊟ Short Film Project	$44,763.55	$36,636.37	$30.71	0%	1	CPI	$87,864.88	$73.72
1	⊞ Pre-Production	$23,089.75	$23,089.75	$0.00	0%	1	Help on CPI	$23,089.75	$0.00
24	⊟ Production	$21,673.80	$13,546.62	$30.71	0%	1	$36,380.95	$36,298.47	$82.48
25	⊞ Scene 7	$3,702.50	$3,702.50	($9.38)	0%	1	$3,702.50	$3,711.88	($9.38)
31	⊞ Scene 3	$4,180.40	$4,180.40	$0.00	0%	1	$4,180.40	$4,180.40	$0.00
37	⊟ Scene 1	$5,960.40	$5,663.72	$40.09	0%	1.01	$5,960.40	$5,918.21	$42.19
38	Scene 1 setup	$2,082.00	$2,082.00	$0.00	0%	1	$2,082.00	$2,082.00	$0.00
39	Scene 1 rehears:	$780.00	$780.00	$195.00	25%	1.33	$780.00	$585.00	$195.00
40	Scene 1 shoot	$2,404.40	$2,404.40	($154.80)	-6%	0.94	$2,404.40	$2,559.20	($154.80)
41	Scene 1 teardow	$694.00	$397.32	($0.11)	0%	1	$694.00	$694.19	($0.19)
42	Scene 1-process	$0.00	$0.00	$0.00	0%	0	$0.00	$0.00	$0.00
43	⊟ Scene 2	$2,257.10	$0.00	$0.00	0%	0	$2,257.10	$2,077.10	$180.00
44	Scene 2 setup	$518.00	$0.00	$0.00	0%	0	$518.00	$406.00	$112.00
45	Scene 2 rehears:	$517.40	$0.00	$0.00	0%	0	$517.40	$517.40	$0.00
46	Scene 2 shoot	$962.70	$0.00	$0.00	0%	0	$962.70	$962.70	$0.00
47	Scene 2 teardow	$259.00	$0.00	$0.00	0%	0	$259.00	$191.00	$68.00
48	Scene 2-process	$0.00	$0.00	$0.00	0%	0	$0.00	$0.00	$0.00
49	⊟ Scene 5	$4,547.40	$0.00	$0.00	0%	0	$4,547.40	$5,213.40	($666.00)
50	Scene 5 setup	$1,026.00	$0.00	$0.00	0%	0	$1,026.00	$1,388.00	($362.00)
51	Scene 5 rehears:	$755.00	$0.00	$0.00	0%	0	$755.00	$755.00	$0.00
52	Scene 5 shoot	$2,424.40	$0.00	$0.00	0%	0	$2,424.40	$2,424.40	$0.00
53	Scene 5 teardow	$342.00	$0.00	$0.00	0%	0	$342.00	$646.00	($304.00)

See earned value cost indicators to compare the project's performance to the baseline plan, page 385

Chapter 19 at a Glance

19 Measuring Performance with Earned Value Analysis

In this chapter you will learn to:

✔ Set a status date and see earned value indicators for schedule performance.

✔ See earned value cost performance indicators.

Looking at task and resource *variance* throughout a project's duration is an essential project management activity, but it does not give you a complete picture of the project's long-term health. For example, a task might be over budget and ahead of schedule (possibly not good) or over budget and behind schedule (definitely not good). Viewing schedule or cost variance alone does not tell you much about performance trends that might continue for the duration of the project.

To get a more complete picture of overall project performance in terms of both time and cost, you can use *earned value analysis*. The purpose of earned value analysis is to measure the project's progress and help predict its outcome. Earned value analysis involves comparing the project's progress to what you expected to achieve (as reflected in a baseline plan) by a specific point in the schedule or budget of a project plan, and forecasting future project performance.

The main differences between earned value analysis and simpler schedule and cost variance analysis can be summed up like this:

■ Simple variance analysis answers the question, "What current performance results are we getting?"

■ Earned value analysis addresses the question, "For the current performance results we are getting, are we getting our money's worth?"

The difference is subtle but important. Here is an example. Let's say a project has a baseline *duration* of 160 days and a budget of $82,000. After about half of the baseline duration has elapsed, the actual costs incurred are about $40,000. But what is the project's status? You cannot tell based on this information alone. A simple distribution of cost over time would suggest that $40,000 spent by the midpoint of an

$82,000 project is just about right. But perhaps the project is running ahead of schedule—more work has been completed by midpoint than planned. That would be good news; the project might finish ahead of schedule. On the other hand, the project might be running behind schedule—less work has been accomplished than was planned. This would be bad news; the project will likely miss its planned finish date, exceed its budget, or both.

Earned value analysis enables you to look at project performance in a more sophisticated way. It helps you to determine two important things: the true cost of project results to date and the performance trend that is likely to continue for the remainder of the project.

Earned value analysis has its origins in large projects carried out for the U.S. government, and it remains an essential project status reporting tool for major government projects. However, because of the usefulness of earned value analysis in predicting future project performance, it is gaining popularity in the private sector and on smaller projects as well.

 Important Before you can use the practice files in this chapter, be sure you install them from the book's companion CD to their default location. See "Using the Book's CD-ROM," on page xiii, for more information.

Viewing Earned Value Schedule Indicators

For Microsoft Office Project 2003 to calculate earned value amounts for a project plan, you must first do the following:

- Save a baseline plan so Project can calculate the budgeted cost of the work scheduled before you start tracking actual work. (On the **Tools** menu, point to **Tracking**, and then click **Save Baseline**.)

- Record *actual* work on tasks or assignments.

- Set the *status date* so Project can calculate actual project performance up to a certain point in time. (On the **Project** menu, click **Project Information**, and then select a status date.) If you do not specify a status date, Project uses the current date.

Earned value analysis uses the following three key values to generate all schedule indicator and cost indicator values:

- The budgeted cost of work scheduled, called *BCWS*. This is the value of the work scheduled to be completed as of the status date. Project calculates this value by adding up all the timephased baseline values for tasks up to the status date.

- The actual cost of work performed, called *ACWP*. This is the actual cost incurred to complete each task's actual work up to the status date.

■ · The budgeted cost of work performed, called *BCWP* or earned value. This is the portion of the budgeted cost that should have been spent to complete each task's actual work performed up to the status date. This value is called *earned value* because it is literally the value earned by the work performed.

The earned value analysis schedule and the cost variance are directly related, but it's simpler to examine each independently. To accommodate this, Project groups the earned value schedule indicator fields into one *table*, and the earned value cost indicator fields into another table. A third table combines the key fields of both schedule and cost indicators.

In this exercise, you set the status date and view earned value schedule indicators for the project plan.

Important   If you are running Project Professional, you may need to make a one-time adjustment to use the My Computer account and to work offline. This helps ensure that the practice files you work with in this chapter don't affect your Project Server data. For more information, see "Starting Project Professional," on page 10.

OPEN: Short Film Project 19a from the *\My Documents\Microsoft Press\Project 2003 Step by Step\ Chapter 19 Earned Value* folder. You can also access the practice files for this book by clicking **Start**, **All Programs**, **Microsoft Press**, **Project 2003 Step by Step**, and then selecting the chapter folder of the file you want to open.

1   On the **File** menu, click **Save As**.

The **Save As** dialog box appears.

2   In the **File name** box, type Short Film Project 19, and then click the **Save** button.

Next you will set the project status date. Unless you specify a status date, Project uses the current date when performing earned value calculations.

3   On the **Project** menu, click **Project Information**.

The **Project Information** dialog box appears.

4   In the **Status Date** box, type or select June 30, 2005, and click **OK**.

Now you will view the first earned value indicators table.

5   On the **View** menu, point to **Table: Entry**, and click **More Tables**.

The **More Tables** dialog box appears. In it, you see the three earned value tables.

6   In the **Tables** list, select **Earned Value Schedule Indicators**, and click the **Apply** button.

Project displays the Earned Value Schedule Indicators table in the Task Sheet view.

7   Double-click between the column headings to widen any columns that display pound signs (##).

Your screen should look similar to the following illustration:

Project-level earned value indicators — Summary task-level earned value indicators — Task-level earned value indicators

	Task Name	BCWS	BCWP	SV	SV%	SPI
0	Short Film Project	$44,763.55	$36,636.37	($8,127.19)	-18%	0.82
1	Pre-Production	$23,089.75	$23,089.75	$0.00	0%	1
24	Production	$21,673.80	$13,546.62	($8,127.19)	-37%	0.63
25	Scene 7	$3,702.50	$3,702.50	$0.00	0%	1
31	Scene 3	$4,180.40	$4,180.40	$0.00	0%	1
37	Scene 1	$5,960.40	$5,663.72	($296.69)	-4%	0.95
38	Scene 1 setup	$2,082.00	$2,082.00	$0.00	0%	1
39	Scene 1 rehears	$780.00	$780.00	$0.00	0%	1
40	Scene 1 shoot	$2,404.40	$2,404.40	$0.00	0%	1
41	Scene 1 teardow	$694.00	$397.32	($296.69)	-42%	0.57
42	Scene 1-process	$0.00	$0.00	$0.00	0%	0
43	Scene 2	$2,257.10	$0.00	($2,257.10)	-100%	0
44	Scene 2 setup	$518.00	$0.00	($518.00)	-100%	0
45	Scene 2 rehears	$517.40	$0.00	($517.40)	-100%	0
46	Scene 2 shoot	$962.70	$0.00	($962.70)	-100%	0
47	Scene 2 teardow	$259.00	$0.00	($259.00)	-100%	0
48	Scene 2-process	$0.00	$0.00	$0.00	0%	0
49	Scene 5	$4,547.40	$0.00	($4,547.40)	-100%	0
50	Scene 5 setup	$1,026.00	$0.00	($1,026.00)	-100%	0
51	Scene 5 rehears	$755.00	$0.00	($755.00)	-100%	0
52	Scene 5 shoot	$2,424.40	$0.00	($2,424.40)	-100%	0
53	Scene 5 teardow	$342.00	$0.00	($342.00)	-100%	0

Here you can see the earned value schedule indicators for the project plan, summary tasks, and subtasks. All earned value numbers are reported either as dollars or as index ratios for easy comparison; negative cost values appear in parentheses. Note the information in the following columns:

- *BCWS* is the budgeted cost of work scheduled, as described earlier. As of the status date, a total of $44,763.55 was scheduled to be spent on tasks. In the baseline plan, the short film project would have incurred this amount by the status date. Project uses this value for comparison to the BCWP and to derive other values.

- *BCWP* is the budgeted cost of work performed. The value of the work performed as of the status date in the short film project is only $36,636.37— quite a bit less than the BCWS value.

- *SV* is the schedule variance, which is simply the difference between the BCWP and the BCWS. The short film project has negative schedule variance of $8,127.19.

- *SV%* is the ratio of the schedule variance to the BCWS, expressed as a percentage. This value tells you whether the current level of completion on tasks is ahead of or behind the performance predicted in the baseline. The short film project is 18 percent behind or under baseline performance.

■   *SPI* is the schedule performance index. This is the BCWP divided by the BCWS, and it is the most common way to compare earned value schedule performance between tasks, summary tasks, or projects. For example, you can see that the pre-production phase of the short film project has an SPI of 1; the budgeted cost of work scheduled was equal to the budgeted cost of work performed. However, the second phase, Production, has a considerably worse SPI value: 0.63. The project summary task has a 0.82 SPI value. One way you can interpret this is that for every dollar's worth of work we had planned to accomplish by the status date, only 82 cents' worth was actually accomplished.

Tip   Here's a quick way to get help about an earned value field or any field in a table in Project. Point to the column heading, and in the ScreenTip that appears, click the **Help On <Field Name>** link. Information about that field appears in the Help window.

You can use these schedule indicator values to address the question, "At the rate you're making progress, is there enough time left to complete the project?" In the case of the short film project, one area to investigate is the low SPI for the production work completed thus far—and whether the cause of that problem is likely to affect the remaining production work.

The values in the Earned Value Schedule Indicators table inform us about schedule performance, but they do not directly inform us about cost performance. You examine cost performance in the next section.

Viewing Earned Value Cost Indicators

The flip side of the question, "Is there enough time left to complete the project?" relates to cost: "Is there enough money available to complete the project?" Focusing on earned value cost indicators can help you answer this question. To calculate cost indicators, Project uses the actual cost of work performed, or ACWP, as derived from the actual work values recorded in a project plan.

In this exercise, you display earned value cost indicators for the project plan.

1   On the **View** menu, point to **Table: Earned Value Schedule Indicators**, and click **More Tables.**

    The **More Tables** dialog box appears.

2   In the **Tables** list, select **Earned Value Cost Indicators**, and click the **Apply** button.

    Project displays the Earned Value Cost Indicators table in the Task Sheet view.

3 Double-click between the column headings to widen any columns that display pound signs (##).

Your screen should look similar to the following illustration:

To get help about any field in a table, point to the column heading, and in the ScreenTip that appears, click the Help link.

	Task Name	BCWS	BCWP	CV	CV%	CPI	BAC	EAC	VAC
0	⊟ Short Film Project	$44,763.55	$36,636.37	$30.71	0%	1	$87,864.88	$87,864.88	$73.72
1	⊞ Pre-Production	$23,089.75	$23,089.75	$0.00	0%	1	Help on CPI	$23,089.75	$0.00
24	⊟ Production	$21,673.80	$13,546.62	$30.71	0%	1	$36,380.95	$36,298.47	$82.48
25	⊞ Scene 7	$3,702.50	$3,702.50	($9.38)	0%	1	$3,702.50	$3,711.88	($9.38)
31	⊞ Scene 3	$4,180.40	$4,180.40	$0.00	0%	1	$4,180.40	$4,180.40	$0.00
37	⊟ Scene 1	$5,960.40	$5,663.72	$40.09	0%	1.01	$5,960.40	$5,918.21	$42.19
38	Scene 1 setup	$2,082.00	$2,082.00	$0.00	0%	1	$2,082.00	$2,082.00	$0.00
39	Scene 1 rehears:	$780.00	$780.00	$195.00	25%	1.33	$780.00	$585.00	$195.00
40	Scene 1 shoot	$2,404.40	$2,404.40	($154.80)	-6%	0.94	$2,404.40	$2,559.20	($154.80)
41	Scene 1 teardow	$694.00	$397.32	($0.11)	0%	1	$694.00	$694.19	($0.19)
42	Scene 1-process	$0.00	$0.00	$0.00	0%	0	$0.00	$0.00	$0.00
43	⊟ Scene 2	$2,257.10	$0.00	$0.00	0%	0	$2,257.10	$2,077.10	$180.00
44	Scene 2 setup	$518.00	$0.00	$0.00	0%	0	$518.00	$406.00	$112.00
45	Scene 2 rehears:	$517.40	$0.00	$0.00	0%	0	$517.40	$517.40	$0.00
46	Scene 2 shoot	$962.70	$0.00	$0.00	0%	0	$962.70	$962.70	$0.00
47	Scene 2 teardow	$259.00	$0.00	$0.00	0%	0	$259.00	$191.00	$68.00
48	Scene 2-process	$0.00	$0.00	$0.00	0%	0	$0.00	$0.00	$0.00
49	⊟ Scene 5	$4,547.40	$0.00	$0.00	0%	0	$4,547.40	$5,213.40	($666.00)
50	Scene 5 setup	$1,026.00	$0.00	$0.00	0%	0	$1,026.00	$1,388.00	($362.00)
51	Scene 5 rehears:	$755.00	$0.00	$0.00	0%	0	$755.00	$755.00	$0.00
52	Scene 5 shoot	$2,424.40	$0.00	$0.00	0%	0	$2,424.40	$2,424.40	$0.00
53	Scene 5 teardow	$342.00	$0.00	$0.00	0%	0	$342.00	$646.00	($304.00)

Here you can see the earned value cost indicators for the project plan, summary tasks, and subtasks. Because BCWS and BCWP are key values for both schedule and cost indicators, they appear in both tables and were described in the previous section. (Note that the ACWP field does not appear on either the schedule indicators or cost indicators tables; it does appear on the Earned Value table, however.) Note the information in the following columns:

- *CV* is the cost variance, the difference between BCWP and ACWP. The short film project has very low cost variance.

- *CV%* is the ratio of cost variance to BCWS, expressed as a percentage. This value tells you how close you are (under or over) to the budget plan per task. The short film project is essentially right on baseline cost performance.

- *CPI* is the cost performance index. The short film project's CPI (as of the status date) is 1. One way you can interpret this is that for every dollar's worth of work we have paid for, a full dollar's worth of work was actually accomplished.

- *BAC* is the budget at completion. This is simply the total baseline cost of a task, summary task, or the project. You evaluate this figure against the EAC to derive the VAC.

- *EAC* is the estimate at completion. This value represents the forecasted cost to complete a task, summary task, or the project based on performance so far (up to the status date).

- *VAC* is the variance at completion, or the difference between the BAC and the EAC. The VAC represents the forecasted cost variance to complete a task, summary task, or the project based on performance so far (up to the status date). The short film project has a very low variance at completion value.

- *TCPI* is the to complete performance index. This index value shows the ratio of remaining work to remaining budget, as of the status date. The short film project's TCPI value is 1, meaning remaining work and remaining budget are essentially equal. Depending on your screen resolution, you might need to scroll right to see this column.

Note   Although it might seem odd and even confusing to think of being ahead of or behind schedule in terms of dollars, remember that dollars buy work and work drives the completion of tasks.

From a pure cost variance analysis standpoint, the short film project appears to be in very good shape. Yet the schedule variance analysis suggests otherwise. The heart of the issue is that as of the status date, quite a bit of work has started later than planned but hasn't cost more than planned. The true health of the project is often not obvious and requires a comparison of both cost and schedule variance based on past performance, as well as forecasts of future performance.

Now let's all take a deep breath. Earned value analysis is one of the more complicated things you can do in Project, but the information it provides on project status is invaluable. Earned value analysis is also a great example of the benefits of entering task and resource cost information in a project plan.

Tip   A quick way to view a task's earned value numbers in any task view is to display the Earned Value form. On the **Tools** menu, point to **Customize**, and then click **Forms**. In the **Customize Forms** dialog box, click **Earned Value**, and then click the **Apply** button.

Changing How Project Calculates Earned Value Numbers

All the earned value calculations shown in the previous exercises use the default calculation options in Project. However, you can change settings to give yourself more flexibility in how earned value is calculated. Some important settings you can change include the following:

- Rather than using the percent complete of tasks that is based on actuals recorded in a project plan, you can tell Project to use a percent complete value you enter—regardless of a task's calculated percent complete. The manual or override value is called physical percent complete.

- Rather than using the initial baseline values stored in the default Baseline fields for earned value comparisons, you can tell Project to use any baseline set you want—Baseline or Baseline 1 through Baseline 10.

You can set these options for an entire project plan or change only the calculation method for a specific task:

- To change these options for an entire project plan, on the **Tools** menu click **Options**, and then in the **Options** dialog box, click the **Calculation** tab. Next click the **Earned Value** button. In the **Earned Value** dialog box, choose the calculation method and baseline options you want.

- To change the earned value calculation method for a selected task, on the **Project** menu, click **Task Information**, and then in the **Task Information** dialog box, click the **Advanced** tab. In the **Earned Value Method** box, click the method you want.

If you choose to use the physical percent complete method for either an entire project plan or for a specific task, you must enter a percent complete value manually. This field is displayed in the Tracking table, and you can insert it into any other task table.

CLOSE: the Short Film Project 19 file.

Key Points

- Earned value analysis is a complex and robust means of evaluating project performance and predicting its outcome.

- When performing earned value analysis, remember that it is essential to set the project status date.

- Project organizes key earned value indicators into schedule indicators and cost indicators tables, as well as an overall earned value table.

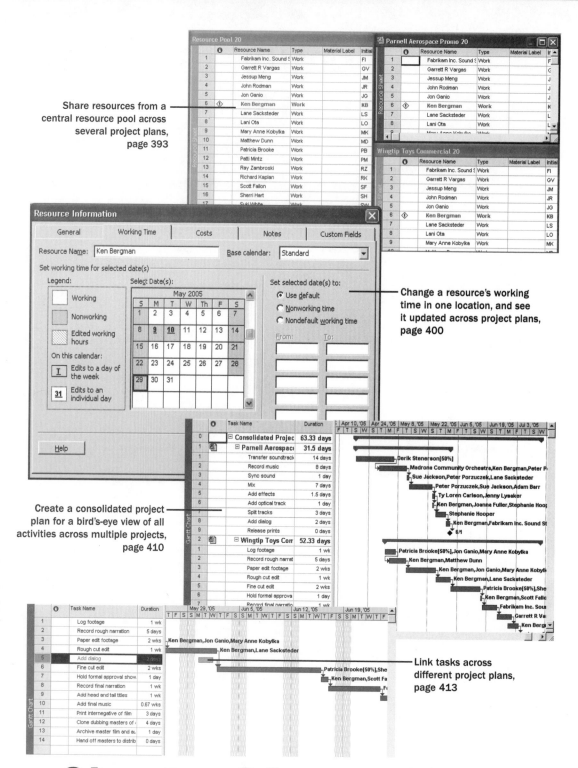

Share resources from a central resource pool across several project plans, page 393

Change a resource's working time in one location, and see it updated across project plans, page 400

Create a consolidated project plan for a bird's-eye view of all activities across multiple projects, page 410

Link tasks across different project plans, page 413

20 Consolidating Projects and Resources

In this chapter you will learn to:

- ✔ Create a resource pool to share resources across multiple projects.
- ✔ Look at resource allocation across multiple projects.
- ✔ Change resource assignments in a sharer plan, and see the effects in the resource pool.
- ✔ Change a resource's working time in the resource pool, and see the effects in the sharer plan.
- ✔ Make a specific date nonworking time in the resource pool, and see the effects in the sharer plan.
- ✔ Create a project plan, and make it a sharer plan for the resource pool.
- ✔ Manually update the resource pool from a sharer plan.
- ✔ Insert project plans to create a consolidated project.
- ✔ Link tasks between two project plans.

Important This chapter describes various ways of sharing resources and managing multiple projects. This process is more generally called portfolio management or enterprise project management. Project Professional, when used with Project Server, offers much more sophisticated ways of managing a portfolio of projects and resources across an enterprise. To learn more about the portfolio management tools available with Project Server, see Part 4, "Introducing Project Server."

Most project managers must juggle more than one project at a time. These projects often share resources and are worked on simultaneously. Microsoft Office Project 2003 has several features to make it easier to work with multiple projects. In this chapter, you share resource information between multiple project plans and join separate project plans as a single consolidated plan.

Important Before you can use the practice files in this chapter, be sure you install them from the book's companion CD to their default location. See "Using the Book's CD-ROM," on page xiii, for more information.

Creating a Resource Pool

When managing multiple projects, it is common for *work resources* (people and equipment) to be assigned to more than one project at a time. It might become difficult to coordinate the resources' time among the multiple projects, especially if those projects are managed by different people. For example, a sound engineer in a film studio might have task assignments for a TV commercial, a promotional program, and a documentary film—three projects proceeding simultaneously. In each project, the engineer might be *fully allocated* or even *underallocated*. However, if you add together all her tasks from these projects, you might discover that she has been overallocated, or assigned to work on more tasks than she can handle at one time.

A *resource pool* can help you see how resources are utilized across multiple projects. The resource pool is a project plan from which other project plans draw their resource information. It contains information about all resources' task assignments from all the project plans linked to the resource pool. You can change resource information—such as maximum units, cost rates, and nonworking time—in the resource pool, and all linked project plans will use the updated information.

The project plans that are linked to the resource pool are called sharers. Here is one way of visualizing a resource pool and *sharer plans*:

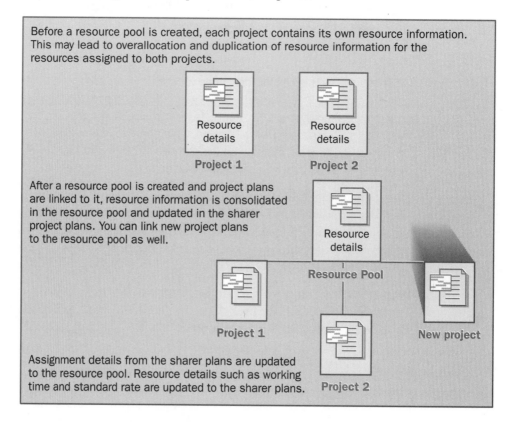

Before a resource pool is created, each project contains its own resource information. This may lead to overallocation and duplication of resource information for the resources assigned to both projects.

Resource details

Project 1

Resource details

Project 2

After a resource pool is created and project plans are linked to it, resource information is consolidated in the resource pool and updated in the sharer project plans. You can link new project plans to the resource pool as well.

Resource details

Resource Pool

Resource details

Project 1

Resource details

Project 2

New project

Assignment details from the sharer plans are updated to the resource pool. Resource details such as working time and standard rate are updated to the sharer plans.

If you manage just one project with resources that are not used in other projects, a resource pool provides you no benefit. However, if your organization plans to manage multiple projects, setting up a resource pool enables you to do the following:

- Enter resource information once but use it in multiple project plans.

- View resources' assignment details from multiple projects in a single location.

- View assignment costs per resource across multiple projects.

- Find resources who are overallocated across multiple projects, even if those resources are underallocated in individual projects.

- Enter resource information, such as nonworking time, in any of the sharer plans or in the resource pool so that it is available in the other sharer plans.

A resource pool is especially beneficial when working with other Project users across a network. In those cases, the resource pool is stored in a central location, such as a network server, and the individual owners of the sharer plans (which might be stored locally or on a network server) share the common resource pool.

In this exercise, you arrange the windows of two project plans that will become sharer plans; this helps you see the effects of creating a resource pool. You then create a project plan that will become a resource pool and you link the two sharer plans to it.

Important   If you are running Project Professional, you may need to make a one-time adjustment to use the My Computer account and to work offline. This helps ensure that the practice files you work with in this chapter don't affect your Project Server data. For more information, see "Starting Project Professional," on page 10.

OPEN: Wingtip Toys Commercial 20a from the \My Documents\Microsoft Press\Project 2003 Step by Step\Chapter 20 Consolidating folder. You can also access the practice files for this book by clicking **Start, All Programs, Microsoft Press, Project 2003 Step by Step,** and then selecting the chapter folder of the file you want to open.

1   On the **File** menu, click **Save As.**

The **Save As** dialog box appears.

2   In the **File name** box, type Wingtip Toys Commercial 20, and then click the **Save** button.

3   On the Standard toolbar, click the **Open** button.

The **Open** dialog box appears.

4   Double-click the **Parnell Aerospace Promo 20b** file.

5   On the **File** menu, click **Save As.**

The **Save As** dialog box appears.

6 In the **File name** box, type Parnell Aerospace Promo 20, and then click the **Save** button.

These two project plans were previously created, and both contain resource information. Next you will create a new project plan that will become a resource pool.

New

7 On the Standard toolbar, click the **New** button.

Show/Hide
Project Guide

8 Click the **Show/Hide Project Guide** button on the **Project Guide** toolbar.

The Project Guide closes.

9 On the **File** menu, click **Save As**.

10 In the **File name** box, type Resource Pool 20, and then click the **Save** button.

Tip You can name a resource pool anything you want, but it is a good idea to indicate that it is a resource pool in the file name.

11 On the **Window** menu, click **Arrange All**.

Project arranges the three project plan windows within the Project window. You do not need to arrange the project windows in this way to create a resource pool, but it is helpful to see the results as they occur in this chapter.

Next you will switch the resource pool to the Resource Sheet view.

12 On the **View** menu, click **Resource Sheet**. Your screen should look similar to the following illustration:

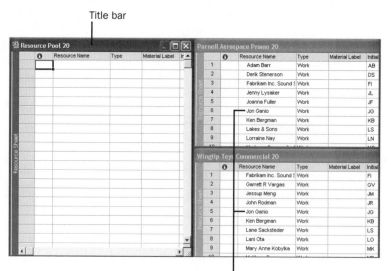

Title bar

Prior to being linked to a resource pool, some resource names and other details are duplicated in these project plans.

Looking at the resource names in the two project plans (Parnell Aerospace Promo 20 and Wingtip Toys Commercial 20), you can see that several of the same resources appear in both project plans. These include Fabrikam Inc. Sound Studio, Jon Ganio, Ken Bergman, and others. None of these resources are overallocated in either project.

13 Click the title bar of the Wingtip Toys Commercial 20 window.

14 On the **Tools** menu, point to **Resource Sharing**, and click **Share Resources**.

The **Share Resources** dialog box appears.

15 Under **Resources for 'Wingtip Toys Commercial 20'**, select the **Use resources** option.

The **Use resources From** list contains the open project plans that can be used as a resource pool.

16 In the **From** list, click **Resource Pool 20** in the drop-down list.

Your screen should look similar to the following illustration:

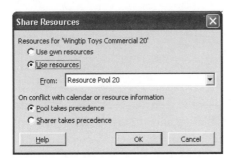

17 Click **OK** to close the **Share Resources** dialog box.

You see the resource information from the Wingtip Toys Commercial 20 project plan appear in the Resource Pool 20 plan. Next you will set up the Parnell Aerospace Promo 20 project plan as a sharer plan with the same resource pool.

18 Click the title bar of the Parnell Aerospace Promo 20 window.

19 On the **Tools** menu, point to **Resource Sharing**, and then click **Share Resources**.

20 Under **Resources for 'Parnell Aerospace Promo 20'**, click the **Use resources** option.

21 In the **From** list, make sure that **Resource Pool 20** is selected.

22 Under **On conflict with calendar or resource information**, make sure that the **Pool takes precedence** option is selected.

Selecting this option causes Project to use resource information (such as cost rates) in the resource pool rather than in the sharer plan should it find any differences between the two project plans.

23 Click **OK** to close the **Share Resources** dialog box.

You see the resource information from the Wingtip Toys Commercial 20 project plan appear in the resource pool. Your screen should look similar to the following illustration:

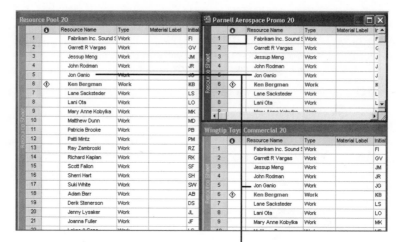

After these two sharer plans have been linked to the resource pool, the combined resource information appears in all three files.

The resource pool contains the resource information from both sharer plans. Project will consolidate resource information from the sharer plans based on the name of the resource. Jon Ganio, for example, is listed only once in the resource pool, no matter how many sharer plans list him as a resource. However, Project cannot match variations of a resource's name—for example, Jon Ganio from one sharer plan and J. Ganio from another. For this reason, it is a good idea to develop a convention for naming resources and stick with it.

Again, you do not have to arrange the project windows as you did in this exercise to link the sharer plans to the resource pool. But it is helpful in this chapter to see the results as they occur.

Tip   If you decide you do not want to use a resource pool with a project plan, you can break the link. On the **Tools** menu, point to **Resources Sharing**, and click **Share Resources**. Under **Resources for <Current Project Name>**, select the **Use own resources** option.

Creating a Dedicated Resource Pool

Any project plan, with or without tasks, can serve as a resource pool. However, it is a good idea to designate a project plan that does not contain tasks as the resource pool. This is because any project with tasks will almost certainly conclude at some point, and you might not want assignments for those tasks (with their associated costs and other details) to be included indefinitely in the resource pool.

Moreover, a dedicated resource pool without tasks can enable people such as *line managers* or resource managers to maintain some information about their resources, such as nonworking time, in the resource pool. These people might not have a role in project management, and they will not need to deal with task-specific details in the resource pool.

Viewing Assignment Details in a Resource Pool

One of the most important benefits of using a resource pool is that it allows you to see how resources are allocated across projects. For example, you can identify resources that are overallocated across the multiple projects to which they are assigned.

For example, as you might have noticed in the previous section, the resource Ken Bergman, who was not overallocated in either of the individual project plans, did appear overallocated after Project accounted for all his assignments across the two project plans. This is because when Ken's assignments from the two sharer plans were combined, they exceeded his capacity to work on at least one day. Although Ken most likely was well aware of this problem, the project manager may not have known about it without setting up a resource pool (or hearing about the problem directly from Ken).

In this exercise, you look at the information in the resource pool.

1   Double-click the title bar of the Resource Pool 20 window.

The resource pool window is maximized to fill the Project window. In the resource pool, you can see all of the resources from the two sharer plans. To get a better view of resource usage, you will change views.

2   On the **View** menu, click **Resource Usage**.

The Resource Usage view appears.

3   In the **Resource Name** column, click the name of resource 6, **Ken Bergman**, and then scroll the Resource Usage view to display all of Ken's assignments below his name.

Go To Selected
Task

4   On the Standard toolbar, click the **Go To Selected Task** button.

The timescale details on the right side of the Project window scroll horizontally to show Ken Bergman's earliest task assignments.

5   Scroll the timescale details to the right to see more of Ken's assignments during the week of May 1 if they are not already visible.

The red numbers (for example, 16 hours on Wednesday through Friday, May 4 through 6) indicate days on which Ken is overallocated. Next you will display the Resource Form to get more detail about Ken's assignments.

6   On the **Window** menu, click **Split**.

Your screen should look similar to the following illustration:

> In this combination view, you can see both the resource's assigned tasks and details about each assignment.

	0	Resource Name	Work	Details	May 1, '05								May 8, '0
					S	S	M	T	W	T	F	S	S
6	◆	⊟ Ken Bergman	261.33 hrs	Work			8h	8h	16h	16h	16h		
		Record rough na	32 hrs	Work					8h	8h	8h		
		Paper edit footag	80 hrs	Work									
		Rough cut edit	40 hrs	Work									
		Hold formal appr	8 hrs	Work									
		Add final music	26.67 hrs	Work									
		Record music	56 hrs	Work			8h	8h	8h	8h	8h		
		Add optical trac	8 hrs	Work									
		Add dialog	10.67 hrs	Work									
		⊟ Lana Seoletedea	00.07 hrs										

Name: Ken Bergman   **Initials:** KB   **Max units:** 100%   Previous   Next

Costs
Std rate: $17.00/h   **Per use:** $0.00   **Base cal:** Standard
Ovt rate: $25.50/h   **Accrue at:** Prorated   **Group:**
                                                       Code:

Project	ID	Task Name	Work	Leveling Delay	Delay	Start	Finish
Wingtip To	2	Record rough narratio	32h	0d	0d	Wed 5/4/05	Mon 5/9/05
Wingtip To	9	Add final music	26.67h	0d	0d	Mon 6/27/05	Thu 6/30/05
Wingtip To	3	Paper edit footage	80h	0d	0d	Tue 5/10/05	Mon 5/23/05
Wingtip To	6	Hold formal approval s	8h	0d	0d	Tue 6/14/05	Tue 6/14/05
Wingtip To	4	Rough cut edit	40h	0d	0d	Tue 5/24/05	Mon 5/30/05
Parnell Aer	2	Record music	56h	0d	0d	Fri 4/29/05	Mon 5/9/05

In this combination view, you can see all resources in the resource pool and their assignments (in the upper pane), as well as each resource's details (in the lower pane) from all sharer plans. You can see, for example, that the Record rough narration task to which Ken is assigned is from the Wingtip Toys Commercial 20 project, and the Record music task is from the Parnell Aerospace Promo 20 project. Ken was not overallocated in either project, but he is overallocated when you see his assignments across projects in this way.

If you want, click different resource names in the Resource Usage view to see their assignment details in the Resource Form.

7   On the **Window** menu, click **Remove Split**.

Tip   In a resource pool, the Resource Form is just one way to see the details of specific assignments from sharer files. Other ways include inserting the **Project** or **Task Summary Name** columns into the table portion of the Resource Usage view. (On the **Insert** menu, click **Column**.)

Updating Assignments in a Sharer Plan

You might recall that an assignment is the matching of a resource to a task. Because a resource's assignment details originate in sharer plans, Project updates the resource pool with assignment details as you make them in the sharer plan.

In this exercise, you change resource assignments in a sharer plan, and you see the changes posted to the resource pool.

1   In the Resource Usage view, scroll down until you see resource 20, **Jenny Lysaker**, in the **Resource Name** column, and then click her name.

You can see that Jenny Lysaker has no task assignments in either sharer plan. (The value of her **Work** field is zero.) Next you will assign Jenny to a task in one of the sharer plans, and you will see the result in the resource pool as well as in the project.

2   On the **Window** menu, click **Parnell Aerospace Promo 20**.

3   On the **View** menu, click **Gantt Chart**.

Assign
Resources

4   On the Standard toolbar, click the **Assign Resources** button.

5   In the **Task Name** column, click the name of task 5, **Add effects**.

6   In the **Resource Name** column in the **Assign Resources** dialog box, click **Jenny Lysaker**, and click the **Assign** button.

7   Click the **Close** button to close the **Assign Resources** dialog box.

8   On the **Window** menu, click **Resource Pool 20** to switch back to the resource pool.

Go To Selected
Task

9   On the Standard toolbar, click the **Go To Selected Task** button.

Your screen should look similar to the following illustration:

	❶	Resource Name	Work	Details	W	T	F	S	S	M	T	W	T
20		⊟ Jenny Lysaker	12 hrs	Work			4h			8h			
		Add effects	12 hrs	Work			4h			8h			
21		⊟ Joanna Fuller	8 hrs	Work			4h			4h			
		Add optical track	8 hrs	Work			4h			4h			

As expected, Jenny Lysaker's new task assignment appears in the resource pool.

When the resource pool is open in Project, any changes you make to resource assignments or other resource information in any sharer immediately show up in all other open sharers and the resource pool. You don't need to switch between sharers and the resource pool, as you did in this chapter, to verify the updated resource assignments.

Updating a Resource's Information in a Resource Pool

Another important benefit of using a resource pool is that it gives you a central location in which to enter resource details, such as cost rates and working time. When a resource's information is updated in the resource pool, the new information is available in all the sharer plans. This can be especially useful in organizations with a large number of resources working on multiple projects. In larger organizations, people such as line managers, resource managers, or staff in a *program office* are often responsible for keeping general resource information up to date.

Ken Bergman has told you that he will be unavailable to work on May 9 and 10. In this exercise, you update a resource's working time in the resource pool, and you see changes in the sharer plans.

Resource
Information

1   In the **Resource Name** column, click the name of resource 6, **Ken Bergman**.

2   On the Standard toolbar, click the **Resource Information** button.

     The **Resource Information** dialog box appears.

3   Click the **Working Time** tab.

4   In the calendar below the **Select Date(s)** label, drag the vertical scroll bar or click the up or down arrow button until May 2005 appears.

5   Select the dates **May 9** and **10**.

     Tip   To select this date range with the mouse, drag from **9** to **10**.

6   Under **Set selected date(s) to**, select the **Nonworking time** option, and then click **OK** to close the **Resource Information** dialog box.

     Tip   When making such changes in the resource pool, you should have it open as read-write (as you do now). Whenever you open a resource pool, Project asks whether you want to open it as read-only (the default) or read-write.

7   Scroll the timescale details to see that on May 9 and 10 Ken has no work scheduled. (Previously he did.) Your screen should look similar to the following illustration:

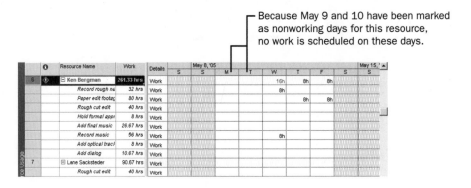

Because May 9 and 10 have been marked as nonworking days for this resource, no work is scheduled on these days.

To verify that Ken's nonworking time setting was updated in the sharer plans, you will look at his working time in one of those project plans.

8   On the **Window** menu, click **Parnell Aerospace Promo 20**.

9   On the Standard toolbar, click the **Assign Resources** button.

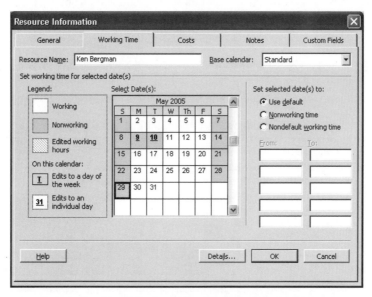

*Assign
Resources*

10   In the **Assign Resources** dialog box, double-click **Ken Bergman**.

The **Resource Information** dialog box appears.

11   Click the **Working Time** tab.

12   In the calendar below **Select Date(s)**, drag the vertical scroll bar or click one of the scroll arrows until May 2005 appears.

May 9 and 10 are flagged as nonworking days for Ken; the change to this resource's working time in the resource pool has been updated in the sharer plans.

13   Click **Cancel** to close the **Resource Information** dialog box, and then click the **Close** button to close the **Assign Resources** dialog box.

Updating All Projects' Working Times in a Resource Pool

In the previous exercise, you changed an individual resource's working time in the resource pool, and you saw the change posted to the sharer plans. Another powerful capability of a resource pool is to enable you to change working times for a base calendar and to see the changes updated to all sharer plans that use that calendar. For example, if you specify that certain days (such as holidays) are to be nonworking days in the resource pool, that change is posted to all sharer plans.

Note By default, all sharer plans share the same base calendars, and any changes you make to a base calendar in one sharer plan are reflected in all other sharer plans through the resource pool. If you have a specific sharer plan for which you want to use different base calendar working times, change the base calendar that sharer plan uses.

In this exercise, you set nonworking time in a base calendar in the resource pool, and you see this change in all sharer plans.

1   On the **Window** menu, click **Resource Pool 20**.

The entire company will be attending a local film festival on May 9, and you want this to be a nonworking day for all sharer projects.

2   On the **Tools** menu, click **Change Working Time**.

The **Change Working Time** dialog box appears.

3   In the **For** box, select **Standard (Project Calendar)** in the drop-down list.

4   In the calendar below **Select Date(s)**, drag the vertical scroll bar or click one of the scroll arrows until May 2005 appears, and then click **May 9**.

5   Under **Set selected date(s) to**, select the **Nonworking time** option.

May 9 is marked as a nonworking day in the resource pool.

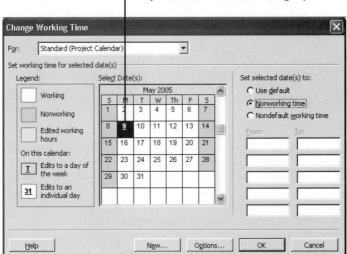

6   Click **OK** to close the **Change Working Time** dialog box.

To verify that this change to the resource pool's Standard base calendar was updated in the sharer plans, you will look at working time in one of the sharer plans.

7 On the **Window** menu, click **Wingtip Toys Commercial 20**.

8 On the **Tools** menu, click **Change Working Time**.

The **Change Working Time** dialog box appears.

9 In the **For** box, click **Standard (Project Calendar)** in the drop-down list.

10 In the calendar below **Select Date(s)**, drag the vertical scroll bar or click one of the scroll arrows until May 2005 appears.

May 9 is flagged as a nonworking day. All project plans that are sharer plans of the same resource pool will see this change in this base calendar.

In the sharer plans linked to the resource pool, May 9 appears as a nonworking day in the Standard base calendar.

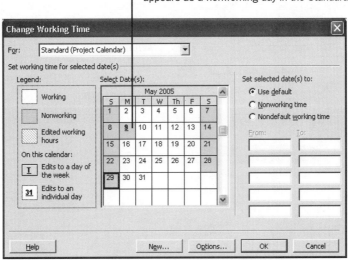

11 Click **Cancel** to close the **Change Working Time** dialog box.

If you want, you can switch to the Parnell Aerospace Promo 20 project plan and verify that May 9 is also a nonworking day for that project.

12 Close and save changes to all open project plans, including the resource pool.

Important When working with sharer plans and a resource pool, it is important to understand that when you open a sharer plan, you must also open the resource pool if you want the sharer plan to be updated with the most recent changes to the resource pool. For example, if you change the project calendar's working time in the resource pool, save and close it, and then later open a sharer plan but don't also open the resource pool, that sharer plan will not reflect the updated project calendar's working time.

Linking New Project Plans to a Resource Pool

You can make a project plan a sharer plan for a resource pool at any time: when initially entering the project plan's tasks, after you have assigned resources to tasks, or even after work has begun. After you have set up a resource pool, you might find it helpful to make sharer plans of not only projects already under way but also all new projects. That way, you get used to relying on the resource pool for resource information.

Tip   A big timesaving advantage of making new project plans sharers of a resource pool is that your resource information is instantly available. You don't have to reenter any resource data.

In this exercise, you create a project plan and make it a sharer plan for the resource pool.

Open

1   On the Standard toolbar, click the **Open** button.

The **Open** dialog box appears.

2   Navigate to the Chapter 20 Consolidating folder, and double-click **Resource Pool 20**.

Project prompts you to select how you want to open the resource pool.

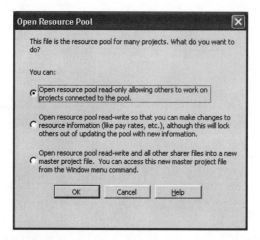

Important   The default option is to open the resource pool as read-only. You might want to choose this option if you and other Project users are sharing a resource pool across a network. If you store the resource pool locally, however, you should open it as read-write. To read more about how to open a resource pool, click the **Help** button in the **Open Resource Pool** dialog box.

3   Click the second option to open the project plan as read-write, and then click **OK**.

4   On the **View** menu, click **Resource Sheet**.

The Resource Sheet view appears.

New

5   On the Standard toolbar, click the **New** button.

Show/Hide
Project Guide

6   Click the **Show/Hide Project Guide** button on the **Project Guide** toolbar.

The Project Guide closes.

7   On the **File** menu, click **Save As**.

The **Save As** dialog box appears.

8   In the **File name** box, type Hanson Brothers Project 20, and then click the **Save** button.

Assign
Resources

9   On the Standard toolbar, click the **Assign Resources** button.

The **Assign Resources** dialog box is initially empty because you have not yet entered any resource information in this project plan.

10   On the **Tools** menu, point to **Resource Sharing**, and then click **Share Resources**.

The **Share Resources** dialog box appears.

11   Under **Resources for 'Hanson Brothers Project 20'**, select the **Use resources** option.

12   In the **From** list, make sure that **Resource Pool 20** is selected in the drop-down list, and then click **OK** to close the **Share Resources** dialog box.

In the **Assign Resources** dialog box, you see all of the resources from the resource pool appear.

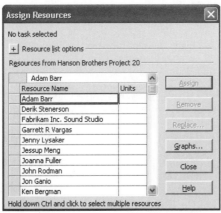

Now these resources are ready for assignments to tasks in this project.

13 Click the **Close** button to close the **Assign Resources** dialog box.

14 On the **File** menu, click **Close**. When prompted, click the **Yes** button to save your changes.

The Hanson Brothers Project 20 project plan closes, and the Resource Pool 20 plan remains open.

15 On the **File** menu, click **Close**. When prompted, click the **Yes** button to save your changes to Resource Pool 20.

You save changes to the resource pool because it records the names and locations of its sharer plans.

Opening a Sharer Plan and Updating a Resource Pool

If you are sharing a resource pool with other Project users across a network, whoever has the resource pool open as read-write prevents others from updating resource information such as standard cost rates or making other project plans sharers of that resource pool. For this reason, it is a good idea to open the resource pool as read-only and to use the **Update Resource Pool** command only when you need to update the resource pool with assignment information. You can click the **Update Resource Pool** command from the **Resource Sharing** submenu of the **Tools** menu. This command updates the resource pool with new assignment information; once that is done, any-one else who opens the resource pool will see the latest assignment information.

In this chapter, you are working with the resource pool and sharer plans locally. If you are going to use a resource pool over a network, it is a good idea to understand the updating process. This exercise introduces you to that process.

In this exercise, you change assignments in a sharer plan, and then you manually update the assignment information in the resource pool.

Open

1 On the Standard toolbar, click the **Open** button.

The **Open** dialog box appears.

2 Navigate to the Chapter 20 Consolidating folder, and double-click the **Parnell Aerospace Promo 20** file.

Because this project plan is a sharer plan linked to a resource pool, Project gives you the following options:

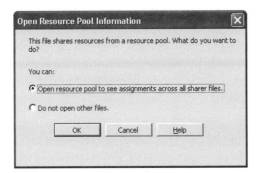

3   Click the **Open resource pool to see assignments across all sharer files** option, and then click **OK**.

Choosing the second option, **Do not open other files**, enables you to see assignments only in the one sharer.

The resource pool opens as read-only in the background. (If you want to verify this, look at the items on the **Window** menu.) Next you will change some assignments in the sharer plan.

Assign
Resources

4   On the Standard toolbar, click the **Assign Resources** button. The **Assign Resources** dialog box appears.

5   In the **Task Name** column, click the name of task 6, **Add optical track**.

6   In the **Resource Name** column in the **Assign Resources** dialog box, click **Stephanie Hooper**, and click the **Assign** button.

7   In the **Task Name** column, click the name of task 8, **Add dialog**.

8   In the **Resource Name** column in the **Assign Resources** dialog box, click **Sue Jackson** (located at the top of the **Resource Name** column), and then click the **Remove** button.

You have made two assignment changes in the sharer plan. Because the resource pool is opened as read-only, those changes have not been permanently saved in the resource pool. Next you will update the resource pool.

9   On the **Tools** menu, point to **Resource Sharing**, and then click **Update Resource Pool**.

Project updates the assignment information in the resource pool with the new details from the sharer plan. Anybody else who opens or refreshes the resource pool now will see the updated assignment information.

Note   Only assignment information is saved to the resource pool from the sharer plan. Any changes you make to resource details, such as maximum units, in the sharer plan are not saved in the resource pool when you update. When you want to change the resource details, open the resource pool as read-write. After it is open as read-write, you can change resource details in either the resource pool or the sharer plan, and the other project plans will be updated.

Next you will change an assignment in the sharer plan, close the project plan, and then update the resource pool.

10   In the **Task Name** column, click the name of task 3, **Sync sound.**

11   In the **Resource Name** column in the **Assign Resources** dialog box, click **Lane Sacksteder**, and then click the **Assign** button.

12   Click the **Close** button to close the **Assign Resources** dialog box.

13   On the **File** menu, click **Close.**

14   When prompted to save changes, click the **Yes** button.

Project determines that because the resource pool was open as read-only, the latest assignment changes from the sharer plans have not been updated in the resource pool. You are offered the choices shown in the following illustration:

15   Click **OK.**

Project updates the assignment information with the new details from the sharer plan. The resource pool remains open as read-only.

16   On the **File** menu, click **Close.**

Because the resource pool was opened as read-only, Project closes it without prompting you to save changes.

Troubleshooting   If a sharer plan is deleted, assignment information from that sharer is still stored in the resource pool. To clear this assignment information from the resource pool, you must break the link to the sharer plan. Open the resource pool as read-write. On the **Tools** menu, click **Resource Sharing**, and then click **Share Resources**. In the **Share Resources** dialog box, click the name of the now-deleted sharer, and click the **Break Link** button.

Working with Consolidated Projects

Most projects often involve several people working on tasks at different times, sometimes in different locations, and frequently for different supervisors. Although a resource pool can help you manage resource details across projects, it might not give you the level of control that you want over tasks and relationships between projects.

A good way to pull together far-flung project information is to use a *consolidated project*. This is a project plan that contains other project plans, called *inserted projects*. The inserted projects do not reside within the consolidated project plan, but they are linked to it in such a way that they can be viewed and edited from it. If an inserted project plan is edited outside of the consolidated project, the updated information appears in the consolidated project plan the next time it is opened.

Tip   Consolidated project plans are also known as master projects, and inserted project plans are also known as subprojects. This chapter uses the terms *consolidated* and *inserted*.

To learn more about consolidated project plans, type **About master and subprojects** into the **Search** box in the upper right corner of the Project window. The **Search** box initially contains the text *Type a question for help*.

Using consolidated project plans enables you to do the following:

■   See all tasks from your organization's project plans in a single view.

■   "Roll up" project information to higher levels of management. For example, one team's project plan might be an inserted project plan for the department's consolidated project plan, which in turn might be an inserted project plan for the organization's consolidated project plan.

■   Divide your project data into different project plans to match the nature of your project, for example, by phase, component, or location. Then you can pull the information back together in a consolidated project plan for a comprehensive look at the whole.

■   See all your projects' information in one location, so you can filter, sort, and group the data.

Consolidated project plans use Project's outlining features. An inserted project plan appears as a summary task in the consolidated project plan, except that its summary Gantt bar is gray and an inserted project icon appears in the Indicators column. When you save a consolidated project plan, you are also prompted to save any changes you have made to inserted project plans as well.

Tip   If you have a set of project plans that you normally work on, but you don't want to combine them into one consolidated project plan, consider saving them as part of a *workspace* instead. A workspace simply records the names and window sizes of the open project plans into one file that you can later open. On the **File** menu, click **Save Workspace**.

In this exercise, you create a new consolidated project plan and view the two inserted project plans.

1   On the Standard toolbar, click the **Open** button.

Open

   The **Open** dialog box appears.

2   Navigate to the Chapter 20 Consolidating folder, and double-click the **Parnell Aerospace Promo 20** file.

   Tip   You can also click the file name at the bottom of the **File** menu.

3   Project asks whether you want to open the resource pool. Click **Do not open other files** option, and then click **OK**.

4   On the Standard toolbar, click the **Open** button.

   The **Open** dialog box appears.

5   Navigate to the Chapter 20 Consolidating folder, and double-click the **Wingtip Toys Commercial 20** file.

6   Project asks whether you want to open the resource pool. Select the **Do not open other files** option, and then click **OK**.

   Next you will use a handy shortcut to insert both open project plans into a new plan, creating a consolidated project plan.

7   On the **Window** menu, click **New Window**.

   The **New Window** dialog box appears.

8   Under **Projects**, hold down the Ctrl key while clicking or drag to select the names of both open project plans, and then click **OK**.

   Project creates a new project plan that will become the consolidated project, and then inserts the two projects into the consolidated project as expanded summary tasks.

Show/Hide
Project Guide

9 Click the **Show/Hide Project Guide** button on the **Project Guide** toolbar.

The Project Guide closes.

10 On the **View** menu, click **Zoom**.

11 In the **Zoom** dialog box, click the **Entire Project** option, and then click **OK**.

Project adjusts the timescale in the Gantt chart so that the full duration of the two projects is visible. If necessary, double-click the right edge of any columns that display pound signs (###). Your screen should look similar to the following illustration:

Inserted projects appear as expanded summary tasks in the consolidated project plan. Note the Inserted Project icon in the Indicators column and the gray project summary tasks bars.

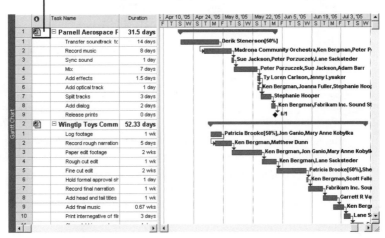

Tip   If you point to the Inserted Project icon in the Indicators column, Project displays the full path to the inserted project plan.

To conclude this exercise, you will save the consolidated project plan and display its project summary task.

12 On the **File** menu, click **Save As**.

13 In the **File name** box, type Consolidated Projects 20, and then click the **Save** button.

14 When prompted to save changes to the inserted projects, click the **Yes To All** button.

Next you will display the project summary task for the consolidated project.

15 On the **Tools** menu, click **Options**.

16 In the **Options** dialog box, click the **View** tab.

17 Under **Outline options**, select the **Show project summary task** box, and then click **OK**.

Project displays the Consolidated Projects 20 summary task. Your screen should look similar to the following illustration:

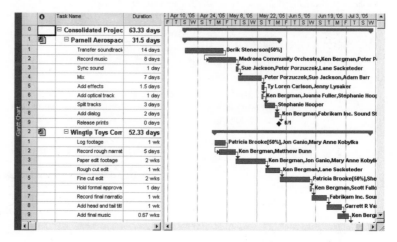

The values of this summary task, such as duration and work, represent the rolled-up values of both inserted projects. As Southridge Video takes on more projects, inserting them into the consolidated project plan in this way gives you a single location in which to view all activities of the organization.

Tip To add project plans to a consolidated project, on the **Insert** menu, click **Project**.

Creating Dependencies Between Projects

Most projects do not exist in a vacuum. Tasks or phases in one project might depend on tasks in other projects. You can show such dependencies by linking tasks between projects.

Reasons that you might need to create dependencies between projects include the following:

■ The completion of one task in a project might enable the start of a task in another project. For example, another project manager might need to complete an environmental impact statement before you can start to construct a building. Even if these two tasks are managed in separate project plans (perhaps because separate departments of a development company are completing them), one project has a logical dependency on the other.

■ A person or a piece of equipment might be assigned to a task in one project, and you need to delay the start of a task in another project until that resource completes the first task. The two tasks might have nothing in common other than needing that resource.

Task relationships between project plans look similar to links between tasks within a project plan, except that external predecessor and successor tasks have gray task names and Gantt bars. Such tasks are sometimes referred to as *ghost tasks*, because they are not linked to tasks within the project plan, only to tasks in other project plans.

In this exercise, you link tasks in two project plans, and you see the results in the two project plans, as well as in a consolidated project plan.

1   On the **Window** menu, click **Parnell Aerospace Promo 20**.

2   In the **Task Name** column, click the name of task 8, **Add dialog**.

Go To Selected
Task

3   On the Standard toolbar, click the **Go To Selected Task** button.

To the right of the task's Gantt bar, one of the resources assigned to this task is named Fabrikam Inc. Sound Studio. You want to use this studio for work on the Wingtip Toys project after this task is completed. Next you will link task 8 to a task in the Wingtip Toys Commercial 20 project plan.

4   On the **Window** menu, click **Wingtip Toys Commercial 20**.

5   On the **View** menu, click **Gantt Chart**.

6   Click the name of task 5, **Fine cut edit**.

7   On the Standard toolbar, click the **Go To Selected Task** button.

Project scrolls the Gantt Chart view to display task 5.

Task
Information

8   On the Standard toolbar, click the **Task Information** button.

The **Task Information** dialog box appears. In the next two steps you will enter the file name and task ID of the predecessor task in this format: File Name\Task ID.

9   Click the **Predecessors** tab.

10 In the **ID** column, click the next empty cell below task 4, and type Parnell Aerospace Promo 20\8.

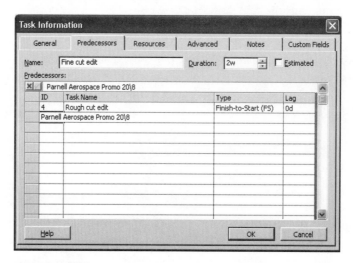

11 Press the [Enter] key, and then click **OK** to close the **Task Information** dialog box.

Project inserts the ghost task named *Add dialog* in the project. The ghost task represents task 8 from the Parnell project.

The ghost task appears in the project to which it is linked with a gray task name.

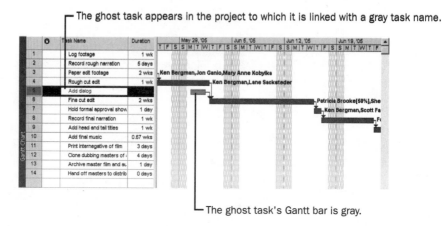

The ghost task's Gantt bar is gray.

Tip If you point to the ghost task's Gantt bar, Project displays a ScreenTip that contains details about the ghost task, including the full path to the external project plan where the external predecessor task (the ghost task) resides.

Next you'll look at the ghost task in the Parnell project.

12 On the **Window** menu, click **Parnell Aerospace Promo 20**.

Here you can see that ghost task 9, *Fine cut edit,* is a successor for task 8, *Add dialog.* Because task 9 is a successor task with no other links to this project, it has no effect on other tasks here.

The link between these two project plans will remain until you break it. Deleting a task in the source plan or the ghost task in the destination plan deletes the corresponding task or ghost task in the other plan.

To conclude this exercise, you will display the link between these two projects in the consolidated project plan.

13 On the **Window** menu, click **Consolidated Projects 20**.

You can see the link line between the task *Add dialog* in the first inserted project and the task *Fine cut edit* in the second inserted project.

Your screen should look similar to the following illustration:

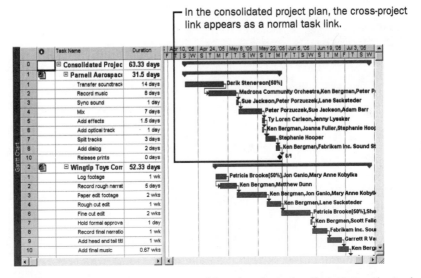

In the consolidated project plan, the cross-project link appears as a normal task link.

Because you are looking at a consolidated project plan that shows the tasks from both project plans, the cross-project link does not appear as a ghost task.

Here are a few more tips and suggestions for working with consolidated projects and cross-project links:

- If you do not want to see cross-project links, on the **Tools** menu, click **Options**. On the **View** tab, clear the **Show external successors** or **Show external predecessors** check box.

Link Tasks

- When viewing a consolidated project, you can quickly create cross-project links by clicking the **Link Tasks** button on the Standard toolbar. Dragging the mouse between two task bars will do the same thing.

- Each time you open a project plan with cross-project links, Project will prompt you to update the cross-project links. You can suppress this prompt if you would rather not be reminded, or you can tell Project to automatically accept updated data from the linked project plan. On the **Tools** menu, click **Options**, and then click the **View** tab. Under **Cross project linking options for <File Name>**, select the options you want.

CLOSE: all open files.

Key Points

- If you have resource information duplicated in more than one project plan, a resource pool is an excellent way to collect resource information across project plans and spot problems such as resource overallocation.

- Besides indicating individual resources' nonworking time in a resource pool, you can edit the project calendar in a resource pool (for example marking holidays as nonworking time) and that information will be propagated to all sharer files of the resource pool file.

- Resource assignment details from all sharer files are available for viewing (but not editing) in the resource pool file.

- Consolidating project plans into a single plan is useful when you want to see all of the aggregate details in one place (the consolidated project plan), yet continue to work with the individual project plans (or allow multiple Project users to work with them).

- When a task in one project plan has a logical dependency on a task in another project plan, you can link the two with a cross-project link. This produces what is sometimes called a ghost task (the predecessor or successor task) in both project plans.

IV
Introducing Project Server

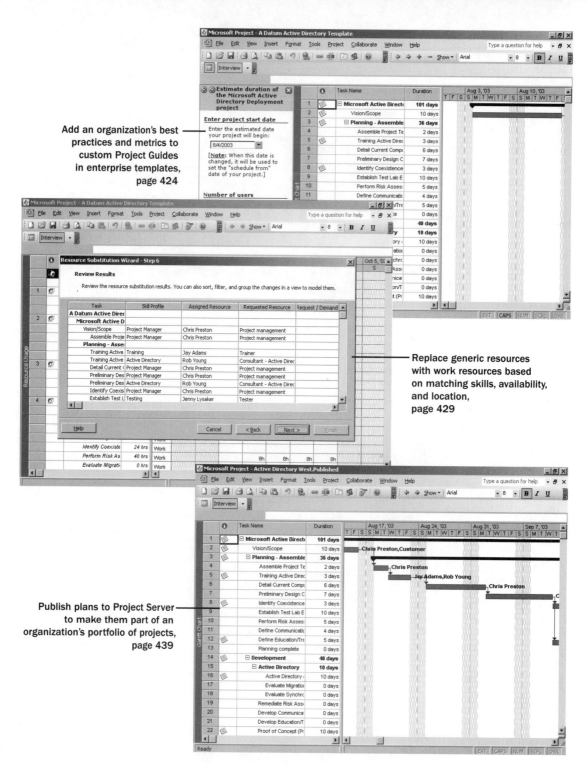

Add an organization's best practices and metrics to custom Project Guides in enterprise templates, page 424

Replace generic resources with work resources based on matching skills, availability, and location, page 429

Publish plans to Project Server to make them part of an organization's portfolio of projects, page 439

Chapter 21 at a Glance

21 Planning Work with Project Server

In this chapter you will learn to:

✔ Understand the components of a Project Server–based enterprise project management solution.

✔ Create a new project plan based on an enterprise template.

✔ Assign work resources from an enterprise resource pool based on criteria such as location and availability.

✔ Publish a plan to Project Server after developing it in Project Professional.

This chapter introduces some of the key differences between desktop project management (as you've practiced it in this book, probably using Project Standard) and Project Server–based *enterprise project management*. Project Server is the cornerstone of the *Microsoft Office System Enterprise Project Management Solution* (we'll refer to this as *Project Server–based EPM*). Enterprise project management is one of the more complex but potentially rewarding practices a large organization can adopt.

Although you might be the sole user of Project in your organization, the real "user" of enterprise project management is the entire organization, and thus the software toolset is correspondingly more complex than it is with Project running on a single computer. For this reason, fully addressing the details of enterprise project management is far beyond the scope of this book. However, we want to illustrate the key features and processes of Project Server–based EPM, so that you can start to determine whether it can serve a useful role in your organization. For most organizations we think the answer will be "Yes," but getting from initial interest in Project Server–based EPM to full implementation is a series of complex steps. We hope that this and the following chapters can help you formulate some ideas of how Project Server–based EPM can improve your organization's performance.

Chances are you currently don't have easy access to Project Server. In fact it takes quite a bit of software planning and deployment to get to the point where you can see the Project Server interface. For this reason, we don't require you to purchase and install Project Server to complete the exercises in this chapter. Instead, we'll play tour guide and walk you through the planning (this chapter), tracking (Chapter 22), and information management (Chapter 23) aspects of Project Server–based EPM.

Understanding the Key Pieces
of Enterprise Project Management

If you've completed the previous chapters in this book, you have a good introduction to project management on the scale of a single project manager with projects that have dozens of resources working on hundreds of tasks. You may be practicing project management at this scale now. Indeed, with a resource pool and multi-project features such as master projects, a single project manager should be able to stay on top of several different projects in various stages of completion with Project Standard running on a single computer.

Now imagine dozens of project managers planning and tracking hundreds of projects, each with hundreds or even thousands of resources and tasks—all within a single organization. Project management at this scale requires a high degree of planning, coordination, and standardization. This is the realm of enterprise project management: a large organization planning, coordinating, and executing a large number of projects simultaneously.

Think about any past or current experiences you've had working on projects in a large organization, and try answering these questions:

■ Were the projects defined and scoped in a consistent way that would enable apples-to-apples comparisons?

■ Were resource assignments made with full knowledge of each resource's skills, location, and availability?

■ Did the executive leadership of the organization have a clear picture of the status of each project?

If your answer to these questions is "No," the organization was probably not practicing enterprise project management. There is no question that many large organizations can gain great benefits by adopting enterprise project management. However, this is no easy task, or they would have implemented EPM already. Succeeding with enterprise project management requires a strong willingness from the leadership of the organization (executive sponsorship), a well-trained group of administrators, project and resource managers, and a software infrastructure capable of enabling it.

The Project Server–based enterprise project management toolset consists of the following:

■ Project Professional 2003

■ Project Web Access, the browser-based interface to Project Server

- Project Server 2003, running on Windows Server 2000 or later

- SQL Server 2000, the database for enterprise project and resource data

In addition, to enable document, issue, and risk tracking (described in Chapter 23, "Managing Risks, Issues, and Documents with Project Server"), Project Server can integrate with Windows SharePoint Services.

Deploying a complete Project Server–based EPM system requires considerable research, planning, and coordination within an organization that is well beyond the scope of this book. However, we want to give you a chance to see what Project Server–based enterprise project management looks like and determine whether it could play a beneficial role in your organization. To illustrate the capabilities of Project Server, we'll use a sample database that's included with Project Server. If your organization decides to move to a Project Server–based enterprise project management solution, we strongly recommend that you also use this sample database to get a closer look at enterprise project management. In fact, here is a list of key resources to help you with your evaluation, planning, and deployment of a Project Server–based enterprise project management solution:

- Review all of the relevant material on the main Project marketing page, *http://www.microsoft.com/office/project*.

- Review the Project Server Resource Kit published on TechNet: *http://www.microsoft.com/technet*.

- Complete a pre-deployment analysis contained in the Enterprise Implementation Framework (EIF). Search for it on *http://www.microsoft.com/technet*.

- Once your organization commits to a pilot program with Project Server–based EPM, install the sample database for Project Server and complete the two "Day in the Life of" evaluation guides included with Project Server. To view them from the Project Server installation CD, navigate to the *prjsvr\support\sample\ 1033* folder. The files are named *sampepm.htm* (project management focused) and *samprm.htm* (resource management focused).

If you are in an organization that is relatively new to the project management discipline or lacks an experienced internal Information Technology (IT) group, consider working through the Project Server deployment process with a recognized Project Partner.

Building a New Plan from an Enterprise Template

One of the principal goals of practicing enterprise project management is to have standard ways of describing work in projects across the organization. Previously in this book you've been introduced to templates for Project on the desktop. Templates are an excellent way to help ensure consistent project structures and schedule logic, task names, and even initial resource assignments. Such consistency is essential for multi-project or portfolio management within an organization.

In a Project Server–based EPM setting, an organization can implement *enterprise templates* that reside in Project Server and are available to Project Professional users. Enterprise templates can help enforce organizational standards and give project managers a quicker start when developing new project plans. In this section, you'll see two of the enterprise templates that are part of the A. Datum Corporation sample database included with Project Server. These enterprise templates will introduce you to *generic resources* and a customized Project Guide.

As noted above, we don't require you to have access to Project Server. Instead, we will guide you through some common Project Server–based EPM scenarios. We'll do this by playing the roles of various Project Server–based EPM users in the A. Datum sample database.

1　　Eva Corets, a project manager at A. Datum Corporation, starts Project Professional.

2　　On the **File** menu Eva clicks **New,** and then selects options in the New Project task pane to view the enterprise templates for Project Professional.

In a Project Server–based EPM system, enterprise templates are stored in Project Server and are available to Project Professional users in the organization.

Like all enterprise templates, these are stored in Project Server and are available to Project Professional users at A. Datum Corporation. The people who set up Project Server–based EPM at A. Datum Corporation created the enterprise templates for the most common types of projects the organization does and populated each enterprise template with task lists, schedule logic, and other information that reflects the best practices of the organization.

3 Eva creates a new project plan based on the A. Datum New Product Template.

An enterprise template can include not only task lists and dependencies, but generic resources assigned to tasks.

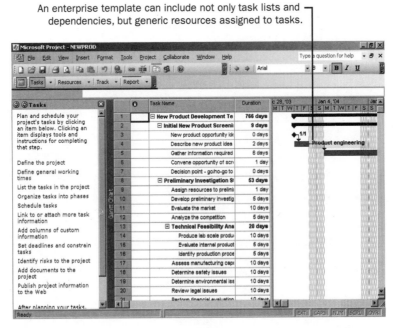

This project plan has a task list and links between tasks, and generic resources assigned to tasks.

4 Eva switches to the Resource Sheet view, and sees that this project plan already includes several generic resources.

Generic resources serve as placeholders for specific types of work resources; as part of planning an enterprise project you replace generic resources with real work resources.

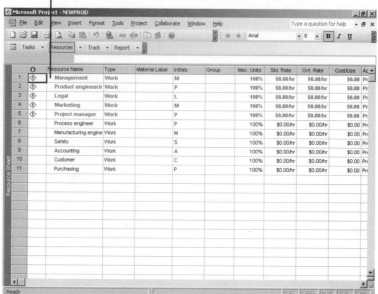

Like regular work resources in a resource pool, generic resources reside in the *enterprise resource pool* that all Project Server–based EPM users share. Generic resources, as the name suggests, are placeholder resources usually identified by a specific role or job title, such as *Manufacturing engineer* or *Safety*. Just like a regular enterprise resource, a generic resource can include cost and skills details. One way to think of a generic resource is as a resource starting point; a certain type of task should be performed by a certain type of resource. The generic resource describes that type of resource but doesn't represent a specific person or group of people. As a project manager develops a project plan, he or she can initially work with generic resources to make sure the right kinds of roles are assigned to the right tasks and then replace the generic resources with real resources before the tracking stage of the project begins. This replacement can be manual or automated, and is shown later in this chapter.

Elsewhere at A. Datum Corporation another project manager, Steve Masters, is also developing a new project plan.

5   Steve starts Project Professional and opens a different enterprise template, the
A. Datum Active Directory Template.

A customized Project Guide, associated with a specific enterprise
template, can be a powerful tool to help project managers within an
organization use a consistent approach to planning a new project.

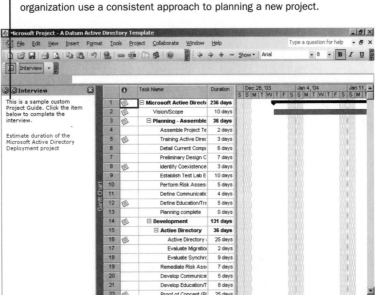

Like the enterprise project template that Eva is working with, this template also
includes generic resources assigned to tasks. It also includes a customized Project
Guide, which interviews Steve for a few key pieces of information that then affect
the project plan.

6   Steve completes the customized Project Guide for this template and enters some essential date and project scope information.

This customized Project Guide modifies the durations of some tasks based on the scope of the project's deliverable. With Project Server it is possible to codify your organization's schedule metrics into an enterprise template.

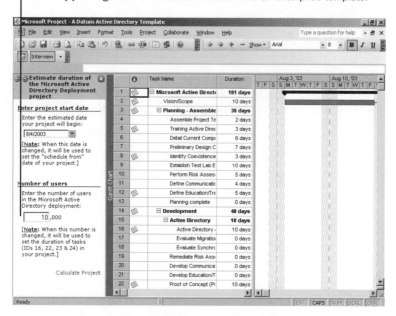

With the information that Steve has provided in the customized Project Guide, Project Professional recalculates the durations of several tasks, as well as sets the correct project start date.

The customization of the Project Guide in the A. Datum Active Directory enterprise template is modest in scope. However, it demonstrates two important things: First, this customized Project Guide shows you that you can, with some development effort, put whatever kind of information you care to into the Project Guide. In mature project management organizations, for example, it is common to find a rigorous and standardized project management methodology that defines how the organization does project management. Such a methodology could be described within a custom Project Guide that is integrated with enterprise templates. Second, this customized Project Guide supplies data, such as the project start date, to the active project plan. More interestingly, it acts on user-entered data, such as a scope estimate (the expected number of Active Directory users, in this case), to modify other values, such as the durations of several tasks. A robust customized Project Guide can serve as the first point of contact and guidance for Project Server–based EPM users in an organization, providing them assistance just when they need it most—as they are building new project plans.

Tip   To learn more about developing customized Project Guides, connect to MSDN (*www.msdn.microsoft.com*) and enter the search query **Microsoft Project Guide Architecture and Extensibility.**

Staffing an Enterprise Project with Resources

As with a single project plan on the desktop (in Project Standard, for example), one key result of the planning stage in Project Server–based EPM is identifying the correct resources to perform work in the project and assigning them to the correct tasks. The combination of the enterprise resource pool (stored in Project Server) and the features in Project Professional makes the task of resource identification and assignment a sophisticated and powerful step in planning an enterprise project.

The Project Professional feature that we'll investigate in this section is the Resource Substitution Wizard. A related feature that we won't look at here, Build Team from Enterprise, enables you to filter and query enterprise resources to locate those with the skills or other attributes (such as location or availability) that you want. Both of these features rely on the enterprise resource pool and certain information recorded within it.

1   Steve Masters, a project manager at A. Datum Corporation, is developing a new project plan in Project Professional based on the A. Datum Active Directory enterprise template.

The customized Project Guide remains available after initial use so that you can come back to it as needed in the planning stage.

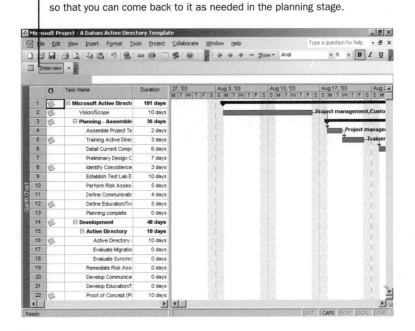

So far Steve has adjusted the project start date and scope via the customized Project Guide (described in the previous section). Next he's ready to look at the resource assignments.

2　Steve switches to the Resource Usage view and sees that this enterprise template includes generic resources assigned to tasks and that only a single task, a milestone, does not have a generic resource assigned.

The Resource Usage view shows the tasks to which generic resources (indicated by a gray resource icon) are assigned in this project plan. The plan was based on an enterprise template.

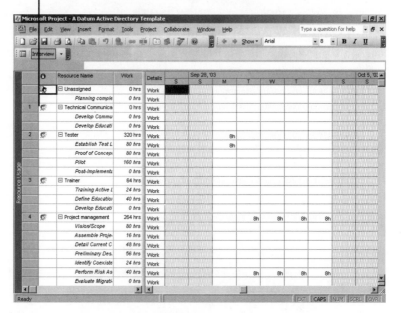

Steve switches back to the Gantt Chart view and is ready to replace the generic resources assigned to tasks in this project with real work resources (that is, specific people and teams) from the enterprise resource pool. He'd like to do this by most closely matching the skills required for the tasks in the project plan (as indicated by the specific generic resources assigned to each task) with work resources who have the matching skills.

3 On the **Tools** menu, Steve clicks **Substitute Resources** to start the Resource Substitution Wizard.

The Resource Substitution Wizard is useful for replacing generic resources with real work resources based on the work resources' location, availability, or other criteria. The work resources receive the task assignments that the generic resources initially had.

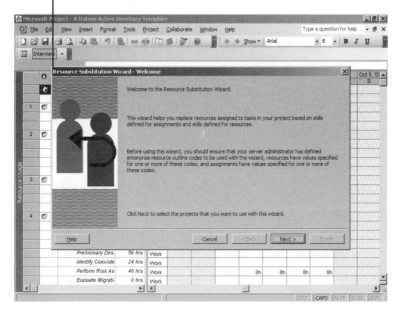

The Welcome page of the wizard reminds Steve that this wizard is dependent on enterprise resource outline codes in Project Server. Resource outline codes identify geographic location of resources as well as skills each resource possesses, such as particular technical or language abilities. A skills-based outline within an organization is also called a *resource breakdown structure (RBS)*.

4 Steve continues on to the next page of the wizard.

The Resource Substitution Wizard can act on several open project plans at once or, as shown here, on a single project plan.

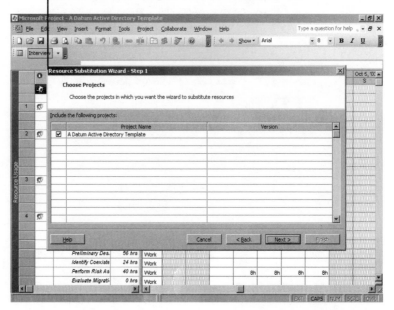

The Resource Substitution Wizard can act on several project plans at once, but Steve is focused only on the single project plan he has open in Project Professional.

5   Steve continues on to the next page of the wizard. Here Steve chooses which resources Project Professional can evaluate when staffing this project plan. Steve wants resources based within the western United States, so he chooses this option in the resource breakdown structure.

Here the project manager identifies the location (West) from which he wants the Resource Substitution Wizard to identify work resources that could replace generic resources in this project plan. Such location information is part of the resource breakdown structure (RBS) of the enterprise resource pool in Project Server.

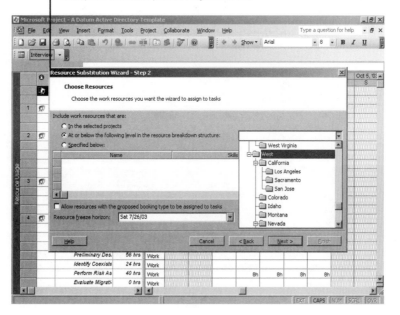

6   Steve continues on to the next page of the wizard. Project Professional has deter-mined that several other A. Datum Corporation projects stored in Project Server contain links to this Active Directory project, or share resources with it.

The project manager can substitute resources in any project plans
that share resource assignments or links to the active project plan.

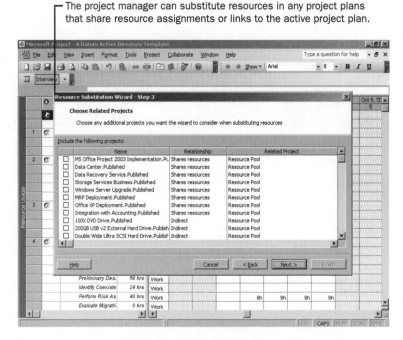

Because Steve knows that at this point the Active Directory project contains only generic resources, he is not concerned with this step and continues on with the resource substitution for this project.

7   Steve continues on to the next page of the wizard. Steve verifies that the resource substitution will use resources from the enterprise resource pool.

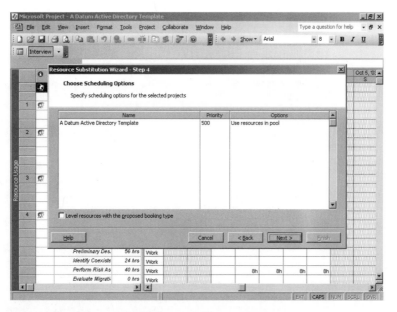

8   Steve continues on to the next page of the wizard.

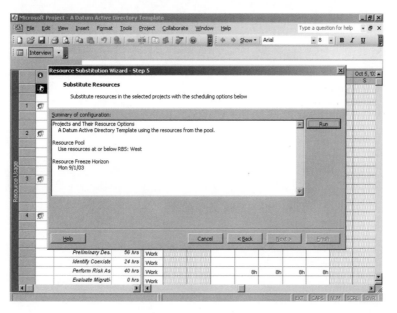

Steve sees a summary of the options he has selected and is now ready to start the resource substitution process.

9   Steve runs the resource substitution process.

The Resource Substitution Wizard runs and then presents a summary of the proposed substitutions. Steve reviews this list.

After the Resource Substitution Wizard runs, the project manager sees the substitutions of real work resources for generic in this summary form.

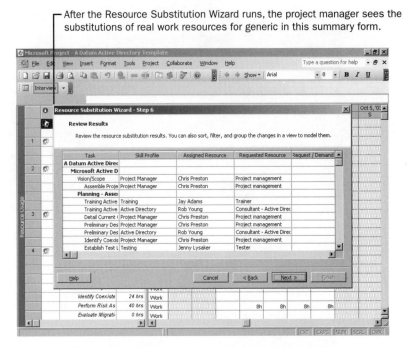

At this point Steve can either accept the substitutions in the project plan or save the list for later analysis. Steve decides to accept the proposed substitutions. He completes the wizard.

The project manager can choose to make the resource substitutions or save the substitution data to a file for later consideration.

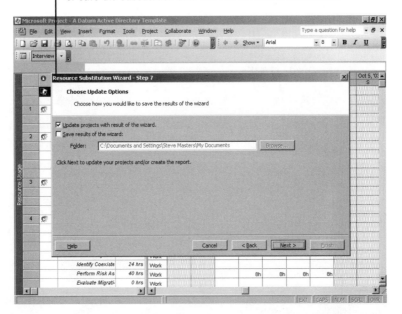

To wrap up his work for now, Steve takes a look at the Gantt Chart view to see the new work resources assigned to tasks in the project plan.

After accepting the results of the Resource Substitution Wizard, the real work resources are given the tasks that the generic resources were originally assigned to. There are no other changes to the project plan.

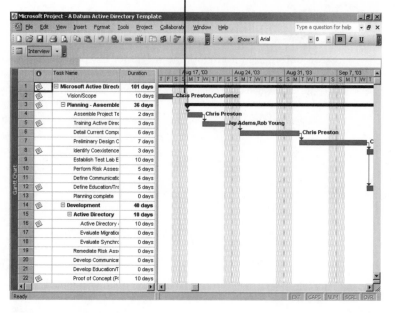

Steve's next steps would be to review the work resources that now have assignments in this project plan and, if he wished, to fine-tune the assignments before publishing the plan to Project Server.

Publishing a Plan to Project Server

To make a project plan viewable by other *stakeholders* (such as resources with assignments in the project plan), the project manager must publish the project plan to Project Server. Once a project plan is published to Project Server, its name is appended with *.Published*, which is a specific *version* of the project plan. Other possible version values include Archive and Offline, or increments of the same version value (such as *.Published*, *.Published2*, and so on). Project Server administrators can also create custom version values that are unique to their organization.

After initially publishing a project plan to Project Server, the project manager should republish updated information to keep fresh the data that stakeholders and others see. In the following example, a project manager will initially publish a project plan to Project Server and then later publish updated information.

1   Steve Masters, a project manager at A. Datum Corporation, is ready to publish his new project plan based on the A. Datum Active Directory enterprise template. In Project Professional, Steve points to **Publish** on the **Collaborate** menu and then clicks **All Information**.

Because Steve has not previously saved this project plan, he is prompted to save it now.

2   Steve enters the information he wants for the plan he is publishing.

When used consistently within an organization, custom enterprise fields help stakeholders make good cross-project comparisons and clearly see project status in Project Server.

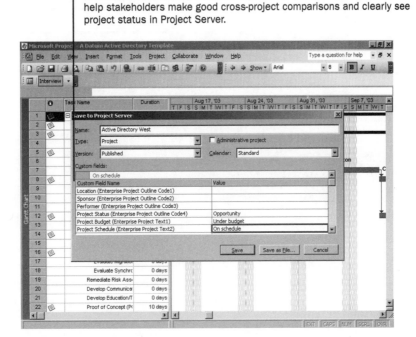

In the **Custom fields** section of the **Save to Project Server** dialog box, Steve sees several custom enterprise fields that he can edit for this project plan if he wishes. These enterprise fields help identify key values—especially when compared to other project plans—in Project Professional.

After Steve clicks **Save**, Project publishes the plan to Project Server and updates the plan's name in the title bar of the Project window.

Once a project plan is published to Project Server, *.Published* is appended to its name. Note that this is not a single file like an MPP but a set of data within the Project Server database.

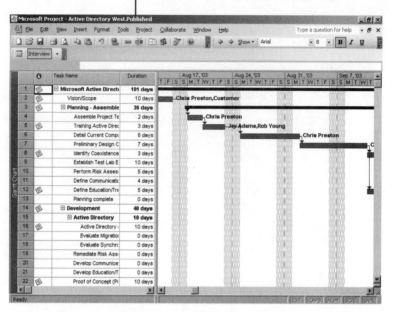

3   Later, after making changes to assignments in the Active Directory West project plan, Steve is ready to publish the updated information. Steve points to **Publish** on the **Collaborate** menu and then clicks **New and Changed Assignments**.

After confirming that he wants to resave the project plan, Steve sees a summary of the assignment changes he has made.

When publishing updated information to Project Server, the project manager sees a summary of the update and has the option to notify affected resources of the changes via e-mail.

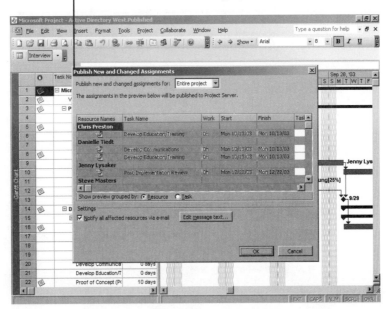

Project Professional saves the updated information to Project Server, where it is available for viewing by other people at A. Datum Corporation, depending on their roles.

Key Points

- Project Server–based enterprise project management enables an organization to practice project management in a consistent, efficient way.

- Enterprise templates are available to Project Professional users in a Project Server–based EPM system and help ensure consistent schedules within an organization.

- Customized enterprise templates can include custom Project Guide content to help the user fine-tune a project plan, for example by changing the durations of key tasks based on the scope of the project's deliverable.

- The Resource Substitution Wizard and Build Team from Enterprise are both features enabled by Project Server that help identify the optimal work resources for task assignments.

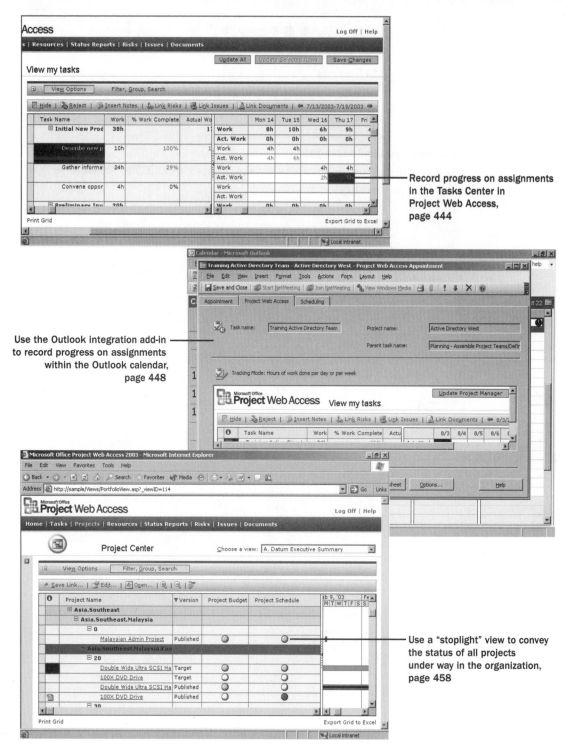

Record progress on assignments in the Tasks Center in Project Web Access, page 444

Use the Outlook integration add-in to record progress on assignments within the Outlook calendar, page 448

Use a "stoplight" view to convey the status of all projects under way in the organization, page 458

Chapter 22 at a Glance

22 Tracking Work with Project Server

In this chapter you will learn to:

✔ See how resources report their progress on assignments and nonworking time through the timesheet in Project Web Access.

✔ See how resources report their progress from the Outlook calendar to Project Server via the Outlook integration add-in.

✔ See how project managers approve task changes (such as actual work) from resources in Project Web Access and update project plans in Project Professional.

✔ See how executives and other stakeholders can see project status at a glance and drill into the details that most interest them in Project Web Access.

This chapter focuses on the role of a Project Server–based *enterprise project management* (EPM) system in tracking *actual* work and other schedule-related details in projects that are under way. The specific tools involved can vary with the role of the user—Project Web Access serves the needs of resources, project managers, and executive *stakeholders*. Resources can also use their Outlook calendars as timesheets for submission to Project Server, and project managers also use Project Professional to manage the schedule changes processed through Project Server.

Note This chapter does not use practice files and is not written for hands-on practice. We don't assume you have access to Project Professional and Project Server, or to the sample database in Project Server that we illustrate here. Instead, this and the other chapters in Part 4 describe and illustrate important features of a Project Server–based EPM system.

For more information, see "Understanding the Key Pieces of Enterprise Project Management," on page 420.

Reporting Actual Work Through Project Web Access

After the project manager has published a project plan to Project Server, resources can review their assignments in Project Web Access, the browser-based interface for Project Server. Resources can also report their personal nonworking time through Project Web Access. They can enter this information directly into Project Web Access or import it from Outlook into Project Web Access. For example, a resource can import as nonworking time any Outlook calendar appointments or events that are longer than four hours and are marked *Busy* or *Out of Office*. The project manager reviews these submissions and then can post them to the individual resource calendar in the project plan. This method is a great way to simplify the task of keeping resource calendars accurate and avoid scheduling work for a resource when he or she will not be available.

In this example, a resource records actual work and upcoming nonworking time in Project Web Access and then submits that information to a project manager.

1   Brad Sutton, a resource at A. Datum Corporation, logs on to Project Web Access to view his assignments that have been published to Project Server.

After logging on, Brad sees a personalized Home page that lists any new tasks or other items that affect him.

Every Project Server–based EPM user who logs on to Project Web Access sees a customized Home page. The tabs available also vary per user, depending on the roles to which they are assigned.

The links or tabs at the top of the screen lead to the major areas of Project Web Access, called *centers*. The **Tasks** link displays the Tasks Center, for example.

2   Brad clicks **Tasks** at the top of the screen to view his Tasks Center.

In the Tasks Center, resources see all their current assignments and can record progress on those assignments.

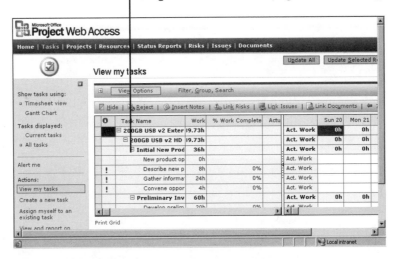

Here Brad can see his assignments for multiple projects. Brad can view this information in a timesheet format (the default) or as a personal Gantt chart.

In the Gantt Chart view, the resource's assignments appear as Gantt bars under summary tasks and projects.

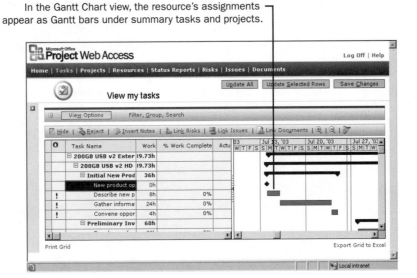

3   Brad switches back to the Timesheet view in the Tasks Center and changes the view options to show his scheduled work for the week. He then reports his actual work.

Resources can display the scheduled work on their assignments (that is, the amount of work for which they were scheduled) and enter actual work below that.

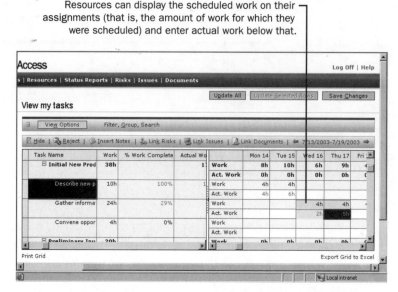

4   Brad clicks **Update All** to submit the actuals he has recorded to his project manager, Steve Masters.

Next, Brad needs to let his project manager know that he will be unavailable to work July 24 and 25. Brad does not use Outlook for recording his free/busy time, so he'll report the nonworking time directly in Project Web Access.

5   Brad clicks **Notify your manager of time you will not be available for project work** in the pane on the left.

Resources can report a variety of types of nonworking time. When nonworking times are approved by the project manager, they affect the resource's working time in their resource calendar.

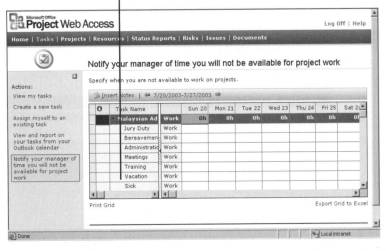

Brad sees that he can specify not only the time and duration but also the nature of his absences.

6 Brad records his upcoming out-of-office time.

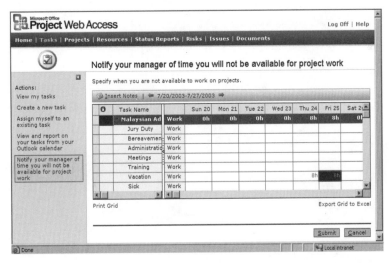

After Brad clicks **Submit,** Project Web Access confirms the submission, and Brad is able to continue with his work in the Tasks Center.

Reporting Actual Work Through Outlook

Project Server includes a COM add-in for Outlook that enables Outlook users to see their task assignments and report their status. This information is submitted to Project Server for project manager approval and is eventually incorporated into the project plan as actual work. The Outlook integration add-in allows team members who would rather work in Outlook than in the Tasks Center in Project Web Access to see their assignments and keep the project manager up-to-date on their status.

In this section we'll illustrate how a team member works with his Project Server–based EPM task assignments in Outlook.

1 Rob Young, a team member at A. Datum Corporation, has task assignments in several active and upcoming project plans. Rob has previously installed the Outlook integration add-in from Project Server. The add-in adds a toolbar and a new tab, **Project Web Access**, to the **Options** dialog box (**Tools** menu) that Rob sees:

The Outlook integration add-in (installed via Project Server) enables resources to use the Outlook calendar interface to manage their assignments in Project Server. These options allow resources to fine-tune how they interact with Project Server.

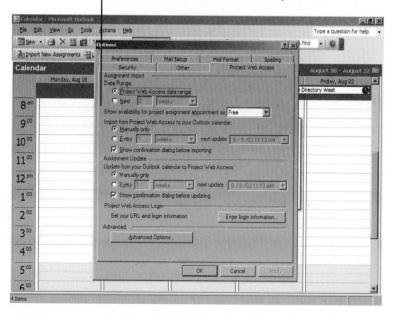

2 Rob clicks the **Import New Assignments** button on the **Project Web Access** toolbar in Outlook. After he enters his Project Server login information, he sees that a new task assignment is available for him to import into Outlook.

When importing assignment information from Project Server into Outlook, the resource sees the essential schedule details of the assignment.

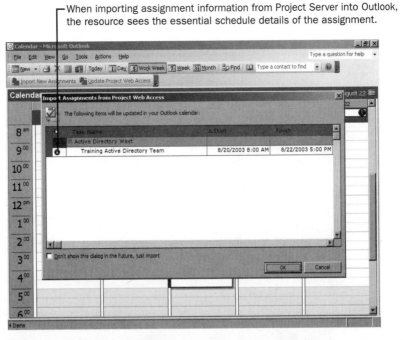

3   Rob checks his appointments for the week of August 18 and sees the multi-day appointment that is a task assignment in the Active Directory West project.

Imported assignments appear as appointments in the Outlook calendar. If the duration of the assignment is more than a single day, it appears as a multi-day appointment in Outlook.

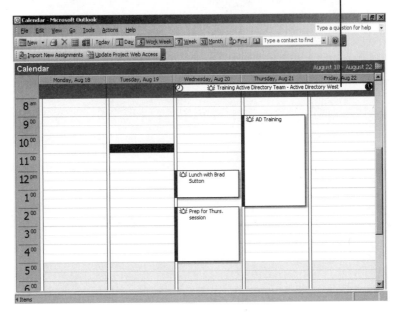

4 Rob double-clicks the multi-day appointment. Between the **Appointment** and **Scheduling** tabs in the **Project Web Access Appointment** dialog box, the Outlook integration add-in adds the **Project Web Access** tab. Rob clicks that tab.

Opening an appointment and then clicking the Project Web Access tab displays the schedule information about the assignment from Project Server.

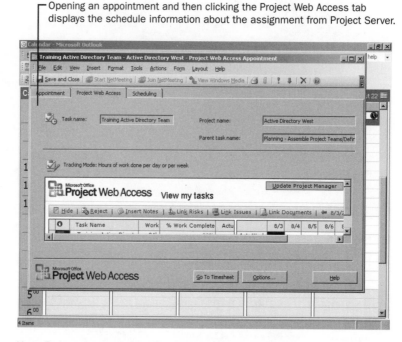

Here Rob sees the key information for this assignment—the task and project it is part of, and his timesheet view.

If Rob wants to, he can display this and his other tasks in Project Web Access by clicking the **Go To Timesheet** button. However, the timesheet grid for the task that's visible here is fine for his reporting needs.

5 Rob records his recent actual work on this task and verifies that the remaining work is zero.

The resource can record actual work or other details on this assignment here and then submit the information to the project manager—without ever leaving Outlook.

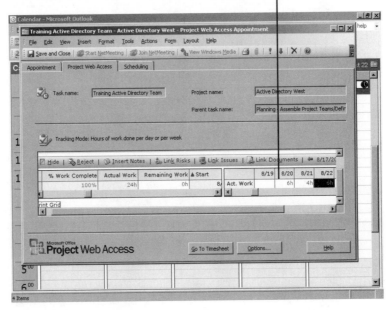

At this point his actuals are recorded locally but haven't been submitted to the project manager. Rob takes care of this next.

6   Rob clicks the **Update Project Manager** button in the **Project Web Access Appointment** dialog box.

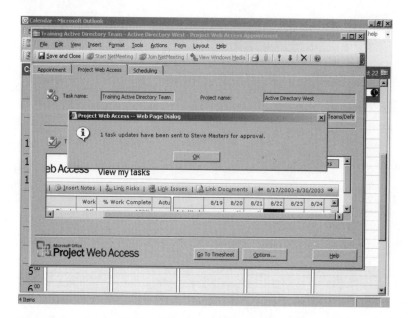

The add-in submits Rob's actuals to Steve Masters, the project manager of the Active Directory West project. This update will remain in Project Server until the project manager approves it, and then it will be recorded in the Active Directory West project plan.

As far as the project manager is concerned, the actual work submitted through Outlook is essentially the same as actuals submitted through Project Web Access. For handling assignment details, the Outlook integration add-in makes Outlook a reasonable substitute for Project Web Access for resources who prefer to work in Outlook.

Handling Actuals from Resources

When the project manger logs on to Project Web Access, he or she sees immediately whether resources have submitted new actual work, nonworking time, or other information. The project manager can then review the submissions and have them posted to the project plan. After they are in the project plan, Project Professional responds to actuals by recalculating task durations and rescheduling remaining work, as needed.

In this section we'll illustrate how a project manager reviews and processes information submitted by resources.

1   Steve Masters, a project manager at A. Datum Corporation, logs on to Project Web Access. Steve immediately sees that he has pending task changes from resources.

Project managers, like all Project Web Access users, see a custom Home page when they log on. In this case, the project manager sees that he has new task changes from resources to evaluate.

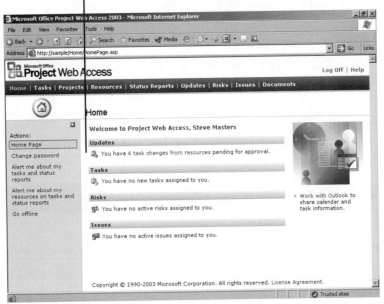

Steve could also have navigated to the Updates Center in Project Web Access to see this information.

2 Steve clicks the **6 task changes from resources** link, and Project Web Access switches to the Updates Center, where Steve can see the details of the task changes from resources.

In the Updates Center, project managers can see the details of task changes submitted by resources, and approve, reject, or hold on to all or some of them.

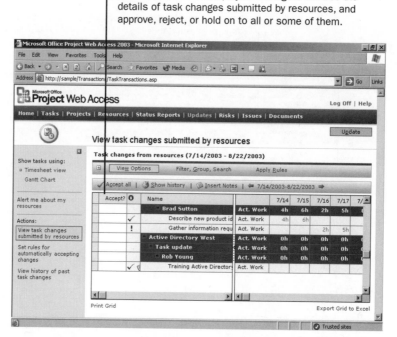

3 Steve switches to the Gantt Chart view and then clicks the **View Options** link to see how he can change the view of the task updates.

Expanding the View Options area of a view in Project Web Access shows the display options available for the active view. These options vary, depending on the type of view.

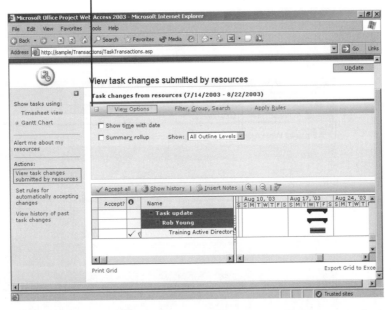

4 Steve switches to the Timesheet view and then adjusts the View Options to show scheduled work as well as actual work submitted by the resources. He also hides the task pane in Project Web Access to see more of the Timesheet view.

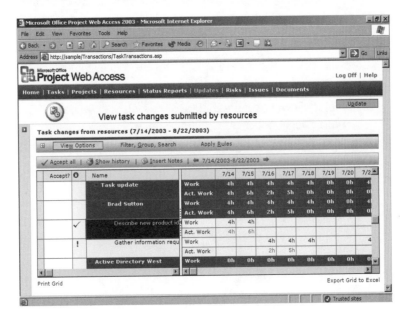

5 Today Steve is mainly focused on Brad Sutton's most recent work on the 200GB USB v2 External Hard Drive project. For the two tasks in this project for which Brad has submitted actuals, Steve clicks in the **Accept?** column and, in the drop-down list that appears, clicks **Accept**.

When a project manager approves only some task changes, the other task changes remain in the project manager's Update Center for future action.

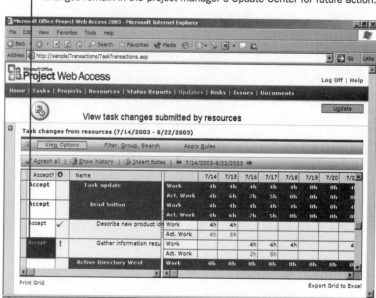

The other task changes that resources have submitted to Steve will remain in the Updates Center until Steve acts on them.

6 To conclude the update process for these assignments, Steve clicks the **Update** button.

Project Server opens the 200GB USB v2 External Hard Drive project in Project Professional, records the actual work against Brad Sutton's assignments, and prompts Steve to save the project plan.

Once the project manager approves the task changes
from resources, Project Server updates the schedule
in Project Professional and displays the results.

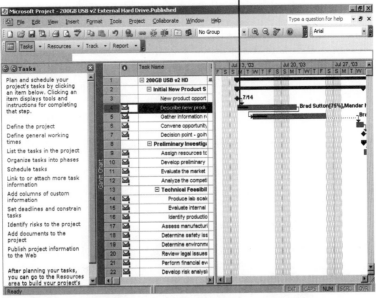

The project plan remains open in Project Server, where Steve can evaluate the
actual work submitted by Brad Sutton and other resources and make schedule
adjustments as needed.

With Project Web Access and the Outlook integration add-in, all the actual work and
resource working time settings recorded in the project plan can come directly from
the resources; the project manager does not have to reenter this information into the
project plan. However, the project manager always maintains control over what information is and is not incorporated into the project plan.

Keeping Stakeholders Informed

One of the primary purposes of a Project Server–based EPM system is to keep the
status of active projects accurate, timely, and visible. Executive stakeholders and
sponsors are often especially interested in the high-level status of a collection of
related projects, often called a *portfolio* or *program,* and want to drill into the details

of a specific project only when they see some indication of a problem. The Project Center in Project Web Access is where executives and other stakeholders can most easily see multi-project status at a glance. The Project Center can be substantially customized with display options and custom views, as we'll see here.

Jo Brown is an executive at A. Datum Corporation and oversees several of the projects under way there (she manages the project managers). Jo relies on the project managers within her organization to keep their project status accurate and uses the Project Center as the primary way to view project status. When she sees something there that concerns, her, she digs deeper into the project details and then consults with the project manager.

1   Jo Brown logs on to Project Web Access and displays the Project Center.

In the Project Center, each project appears as an item in the Gantt Chart view. Every project name is clickable, and displays the details of each project.

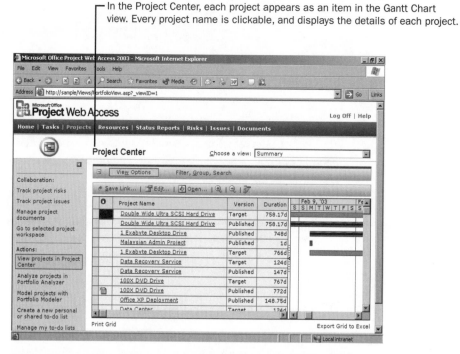

The Summary view, which is currently applied in the Project Center, shows each project as an item on a Gantt chart. As with other views in Project Web Access, Jo can alter this view to focus on the data she's most interested in or switch to another view. The Project Server administrators at A. Datum Corporation have created custom views specifically for executives such as Jo. Next Jo switches to a custom view.

2 Jo selects **A. Datum Executive Summary** in the **Choose a view** box and then closes the task pane in Project Web Access to see more of the view.

In this customized stoplight view, red, yellow, and green icons indicate key schedule status values (in this case, budget and schedule variance) for each project.

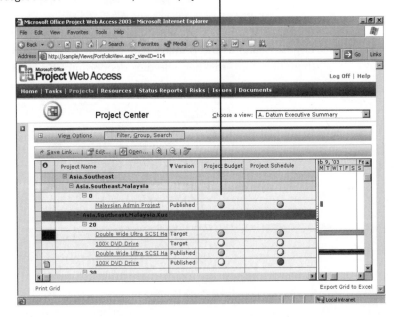

This type of custom view is sometimes called a *stoplight view* because it represents key project status measures (in this case, budget and schedule) with green (good), yellow (moderate problem), or red (major problem) indicators. This view also groups project by location.

Jo likes this view because she can scan for the "red light" projects and focus her limited time on those projects to see what is causing the budget or schedule variance.

3 Jo scrolls through the projects listed and sees a few with a red light for project schedule status. She hovers the mouse pointer over the red light in the **Project Schedule** column of the published version of the 100X DVD Drive project.

In this custom stoplight view, the Project Budget and Project Schedule indicators are determined by predefined thresholds. In this case, a project's completion date that has more than five days variance is identified with a red indicator. Hovering the mouse pointer over the indicator reveals the threshold.

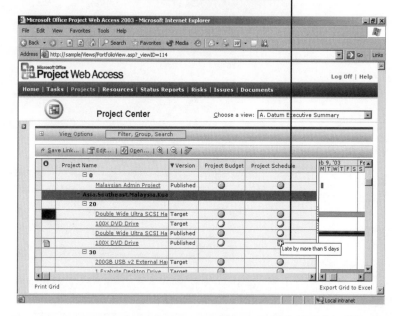

A ScreenTip appears that informs Jo that the project's schedule status is red because it's scheduled completion date is more than five days after the baseline completion date. Five days is the "red light" threshold specified by this view for schedule variance.

4   Jo scrolls the project list to the right to see that this project has moderate exposure
(as indicated by the yellow flag in the **Project Exposure** column) and that the project
manager is Steve Masters.

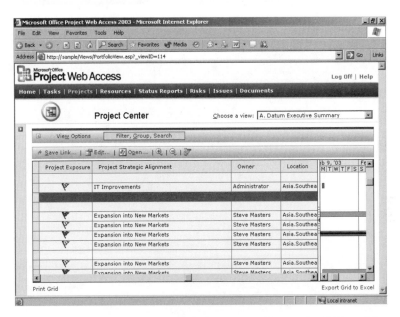

Before Jo discusses this project's status with Steve, she'd like a bit more detail
about the schedule variance in the project.

5   Jo scrolls the project list back to the left and then clicks the name of the project.

The project appears in the Project Center in the Gantt Chart view.

6 Jo switches to the Tasks Tracking view and locates the first schedule variance in the project.

The Gantt Chart view in the Project Center looks very similar to the same view in Project Professional and is ideal for drilling into project details.

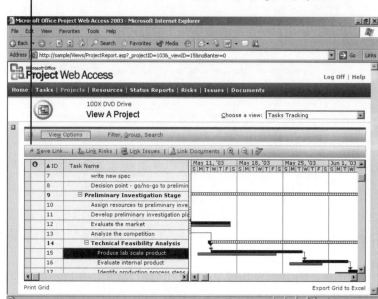

Jo can see that the first task in the Technical Feasibility Analysis phase of the project started later than planned. She can locate later variance in the project plan as well. This will help her focus her discussion with the project manager, Steve Masters.

Key Points

- Both the Tasks Center in Project Web Access and calendar appointments in Outlook (with the support of the Outlook integration add-in) serve as time-sheets for resources to report progress on their assignments.

- The Updates Center in Project Web Access allows project managers to evaluate, approve, or reject task change submissions from resources. Approved task changes cause Project Server to update the affected project plans in Project Professional.

- The Project Center in Project Web Access enables executives and other stake-holders to see project status across the organization and drill into the project plans that most interest them.

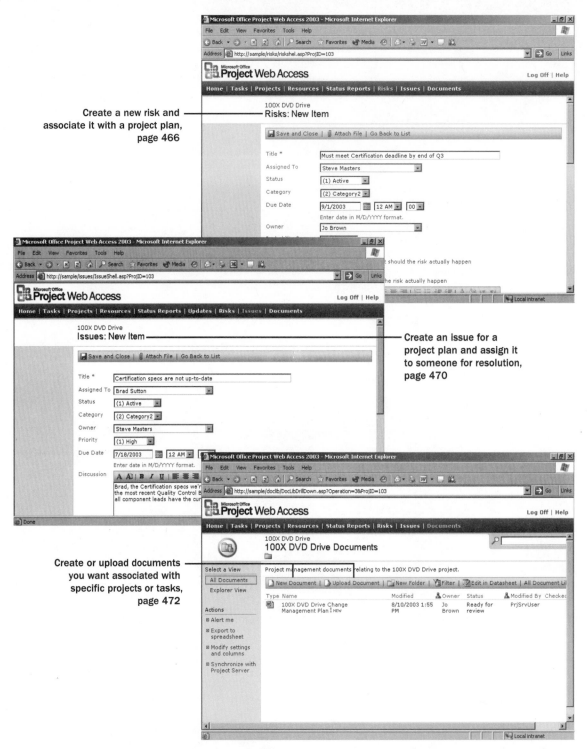

Create a new risk and associate it with a project plan, page 466

Create an issue for a project plan and assign it to someone for resolution, page 470

Create or upload documents you want associated with specific projects or tasks, page 472

Chapter 23 at a Glance

23 Managing Risks, Issues, and Documents with Project Server

In this chapter you will learn to:

✔ Create a risk in Project Web Access and associate it with a project.

✔ Create an issue, associate it with a project, and assign it to someone for resolution.

✔ Create a document library for a project and upload a document.

Project Server can integrate with Windows SharePoint Services (abbreviated as WSS, and previously called SharePoint Team Services). This integration adds the risk, issue, and document management capabilities of WSS to a Project Server–based *enterprise project management* (EPM) system.

When WSS is integrated with Project Server, some features of WSS are applied in ways that make them more applicable to enterprise project management. Document lists in WSS, for example, can now be associated with specific projects in the Project Server database, or with tasks within those projects. Note that WSS is not included with Project Server. Windows SharePoint Services is included with and requires the Windows Server 2003 operating system.

Each project published to Project Server gets a WSS subweb provisioned for it. Project Web Access users then interact with the WSS Risks, Issues, and Documents pages directly in Project Web Access. Risks, issues, and documents can all play essential roles in supporting Project Server–based EPM, and we'll walk through each of these on the following pages.

Note   This chapter does not use practice files and is not written for hands-on practice. We don't assume you have access to Project Professional and Project Server, or to the sample database in Project Server that we illustrate here. Instead, this and the other chapters in Part 4 describe and illustrate important features of a Project Server–based enterprise project management (EPM) system.

For more information, see "Understanding the Key Pieces of Enterprise Project Management," on page 420.

Managing Risks

The WSS integration with Project Server affords an excellent tool for identifying, tracking, and mitigating threats to project success, that is, for risk management. As the term is used in Project Server, a *risk* is a record of a potential threat (or less likely, an opportunity) that could affect the completion of a task or project. The Risks functionality in Project Server allows an organization to identify, rank, and track the risks they are most interested in. You can also associate risks with issues, documents, or other risks.

Risks and issues (another feature enabled in Project Server by WSS, and described in the next section) have some similarities. However, one distinguishing aspect of a risk is the trigger. A trigger is the criteria or threshold that needs to be met before a risk's contingency plan goes into effect. In a large organization, different people may be involved in defining or quantifying risks, developing contingency plans, and specifying a risk's trigger. Should a risk materialize into an actionable item, it may become an issue for ongoing tracking and mitigation. You can enable e-mail notification and alerts to keep track of risk status and see the status on all risks associated with a project, or all risks within an organization.

In this section, we'll see how to create a new risk (that is, formally identify something as a risk) for a project.

1   Jo Brown, an executive at A. Datum Corporation, logs in to Project Server and navigates to the Risks Center.

Jo sees the projects that have been published to Project Server.

Risks, which are potential problems or opportunities, can be associated with projects published to Project Server; with tasks within those projects; or with other risks, issues, or documents.

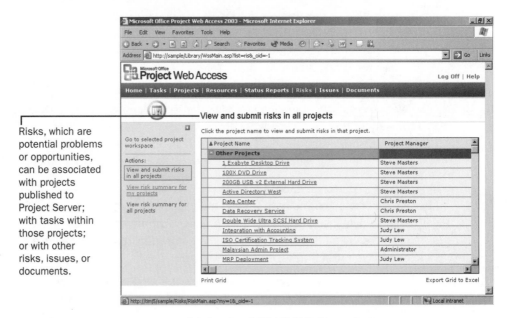

Jo wants to create a new risk for the 100X DVD Drive project.

2   Jo clicks the **100X DVD Drive** project name and displays the Risks page for that project.

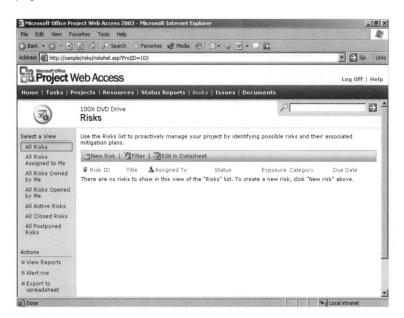

Currently this project has no risks associated with it.

3   Jo clicks **New Risk** and displays the Risks: New Item page.

┌─ The values contained within a risk help identify the nature of the risk
   (threat or opportunity), trigger points, mitigation plans, and owner.

4 Jo enters the risk information, and assigns the risk to the project manager of the 100X DVD Drive project, Steve Masters.

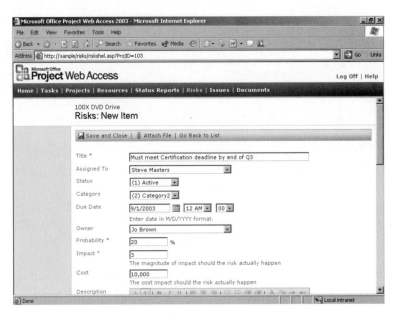

5 Jo clicks **Save and Close** to record the risk and returns to the Risks page for this project. The new risk appears there.

After a risk is created, its status and owner are visible on the Risks page for the project with which the risk is associated.

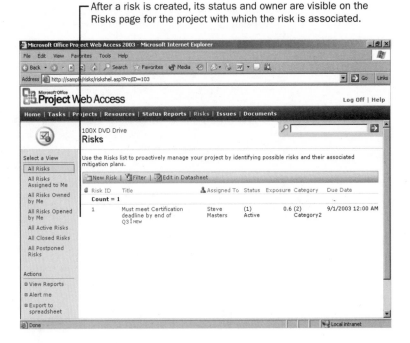

Managing Issues

Issues, as the term is used in Project Server, are action items with a structured discussion about a specific topic. At all times an issue has an owner (such as a project manager or a team member) and a status (such as active or resolved). Use of issues is an excellent way to keep track of action items about projects, when the action items shouldn't appear in the projects themselves. You can also think of issues as risks that evolved into actionable items and require tracking and mitigation.

As with risks and documents (described in the next section), you can associate issues with specific projects or tasks. You can also enable e-mail notification and alerts to keep track of issue status and see the status on all issues associated with a project.

In this section, we'll see how to create a new issue and assign it to someone for resolution.

1 Steve Masters, a project manager at A. Datum Corporation, logs in to Project Server and navigates to the Issues Center.

Here Steve sees the list of the projects he manages (under **My Projects**) and other projects at A. Datum that he can view.

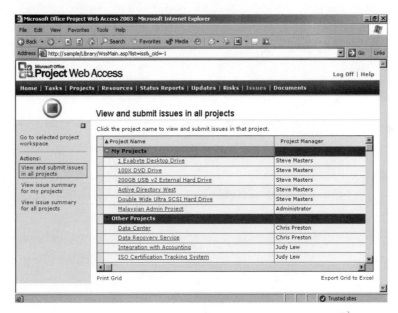

2 Steve wants to create a new issue for a task in the 100X DVD Drive project, so he clicks that project's name.

The Issues page for the 100X DVD Drive project appears; currently it has no issues.

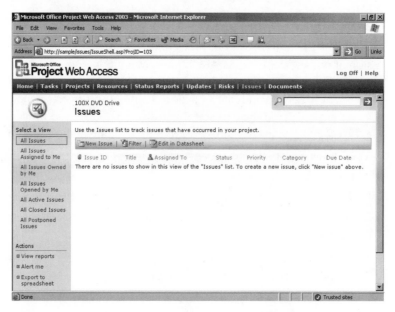

3   Steve clicks **New Issue** and, in the page that appears, enters the information he wants for the issue. Steve assigns the issue to Brad Sutton, a resource who has assignments in the 100X DVD Drive project.

4   Steve enters the issue information he wants Brad to act upon.

Unlike a risk, an issue is an actual, actionable item. The issue properties specify the nature of the issue, owner, and importance.

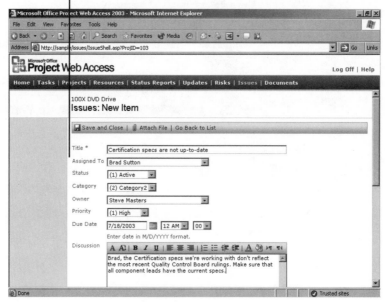

5   When he's finished, Steve clicks **Save and Close**.

The new issue appears on the project's Issues page, ready for Brad Sutton to resolve.

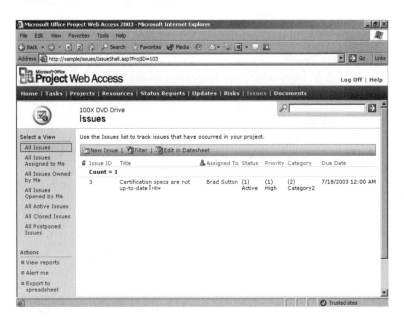

Managing Documents

Associating documents with projects or tasks is an extremely useful capability afforded by the Project Server–WSS integration. Common types of documents you might want to link to projects or tasks include specifications, budgets, and various project management documents such as risk management plans.

There are two types of document libraries: project and public. For project document libraries, project managers set up the properties of the document libraries associated with their projects. Project managers can specify options such as the default templates to use for Office documents and access permissions to the documents. With public document libraries, all Project Server users have access unless the server administrator specifies otherwise. Both types of libraries support e-mail notification when a document has been changed. For documents in a project document library you'll see visual indicators and links to those documents in the Project Center and Tasks Center.

In this section, we'll see how to create a document library for a project and upload a document to the library.

1   Jo Brown, an executive at A. Datum Corporation, logs in to Project Server and navigates to the Documents Center.

2   Jo clicks the name of the **100X DVD Drive** project, the project for which she wants to upload a document.

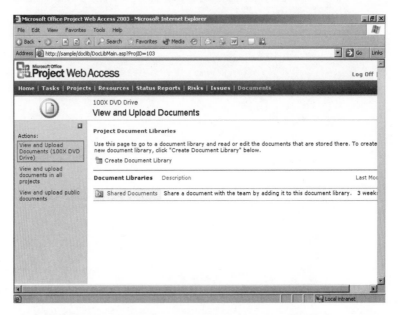

Jo sees that this project has not yet had a document library created for it, so she'll do that next.

3   Jo clicks the **Create Document Library** link.

Project Server prompts Jo to enter information about this project's document library and how she wants it to appear to Project Web Access users.

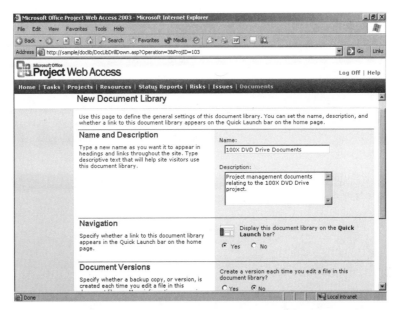

4   After recording the document library information she wants, Jo clicks **Create**.

Project server creates the new document library.

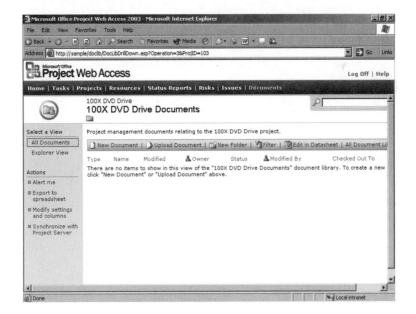

5   Jo already has the document she wants to add to this project's document library, so she clicks **Upload Document**.

6   Jo browses to the document she wants and clicks **Save and Close**.

The uploaded document appears in the project's document library.

Key Points

- Project Server can integrate with Windows SharePoint Services (WSS) for document, issue, and risk management with an enterprise project management focus.

- Risks and issues are similar, but risks are potential problems or opportunities whereas issues are actionable items.

- Documents, issues, and risks can be associated with projects; tasks within in projects; or with other documents, issues, or risks.

V
Appendixes

A   A Short Course in Project Management

Throughout this book, we've included advice on how best to use Microsoft Office Project 2003 while following sound project management practices. This appendix focuses on the basics of project management, regardless of any software tools you may use to help you manage projects. Although project management is a broad subject, this appendix uses the "project triangle" model. In this model, you consider projects in terms of time, cost, and scope.

Understanding What Defines a Project

Succeeding as a project manager requires that you complete your projects on time, finish within budget, and make sure your customers are happy with what you deliver. That sounds simple enough, but how many projects have you heard of (or worked on) that were completed late, or cost too much, or didn't meet the needs of their customers?

A Guide to the Project Management Body of Knowledge (published by the Project Management Institute, 2000)—referred to as the PMBOK, pronounced "pimbok"—defines a *project* as "a temporary endeavor undertaken to create a unique product or service." Let's walk through this definition to clarify what a project is and is not.

Tip   For more information about the Project Management Institute and the PMBOK, see Appendix B, "What's Next?"

First, a project is *temporary*. A project's duration might be just a week, or it might go on for years, but every project has an end date. You might not know that end date when the project starts, but it's out there somewhere in the future. Projects are not the same as *ongoing operations*, although the two have a lot in common. Ongoing operations, as the name suggests, go on indefinitely; you don't establish an end date. Examples include most activities of accounting and human resources departments. People who run ongoing operations might also manage projects; for example, a manager of a human resources department for a large organization might plan a college recruiting fair. But projects are distinguished from ongoing operations by an expected end date, such as the date of the recruiting fair.

Next, a project is an *endeavor*. *Resources*, such as people and equipment, need to do work. The endeavor is undertaken by a team or an organization, so projects have a sense of being intentional, planned events. Successful projects don't happen spontaneously; some amount of preparation and planning happens first.

475

Finally, every project *creates a unique product or service*. This is the *deliverable* for the project, the reason that the project was undertaken. A refinery that produces gasoline does not produce a unique product. The whole idea, in this case, is to produce a standardized commodity; you usually don't want to buy gas from one station that is significantly different from gas at another station. On the other hand, commercial airplanes are unique products. Although all Boeing 777 airplanes might look about the same to most of us, each is, in fact, highly customized for the needs of its purchaser.

By now, you may be getting the idea that a lot of the work that goes on in the world is project work. If you schedule, track, or manage any of this work, then congratulations are in order: you are already doing some project management work!

Project management has been a recognized profession since about the 1950s, but project management work in some form has been going on as long as people have been doing complex work. When the Great Pyramids in Egypt were built, somebody somewhere was tracking resources, schedule, and the specifications for the final deliverable.

Tip   Project management is now a well-recognized job in most industries. To learn more about organizations that train project managers and advance project management as a profession, see Appendix B, "What's Next?"

The Project Triangle: Seeing Projects in Terms of Time, Cost, and Scope

You can visualize project work in many ways, but our favorite is what's sometimes called the *project triangle*:

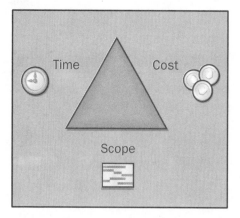

This theme has many variations, but the basic idea is that every project has some element of a time constraint, has some type of budget, and requires some amount of work to complete. (In other words, it has a defined scope.) The term *constraint* has a specific meaning in Project, but here we're using the more general meaning of a limiting factor. Let's consider these constraints one at a time.

Time

Have you ever worked on a project that had a deadline? (Maybe we should ask whether you've ever worked on a project that did not have a deadline.) Limited time is the one constraint of any project with which we are all probably most familiar. If you're working on a project right now, ask your team members what the project deadline is. They might not know the project budget or the scope of work in great detail, but chances are they all know the project deadline.

Here are some examples of time constraints:

- You're building a house and you must finish the roof before the rainy season arrives.

- You are assembling a large display booth for a trade show that starts in two months.

- You are developing a new inventory tracking system that must be tested and running by the start of the next fiscal year.

Most of us have been trained to understand time since we were children, and we carry wristwatches, paper and electronic organizers, and other tools to help us manage time. For many projects that create a product or result in an event, time is the most important constraint to manage.

Cost

You might think of cost simply as dollars, but project cost has a broader meaning: costs include all the resources required to carry out the project. Costs include the people and equipment who do the work, the materials they use, and all the other events and issues that require money or someone's attention in a project.

Here are some examples of cost constraints:

- You have signed a fixed-price contract to deliver an inventory-tracking software system to a client. If your costs exceed the agreed-upon price, your customer might be sympathetic but probably won't be willing to renegotiate the contract.

- The president of your organization has directed you to carry out a customer-research project using only the staff and equipment in your department.

- You have received a $5,000 grant to create a public art installation. You have no other funds.

For virtually all projects, cost is ultimately a limiting constraint; few projects could go over budget without eventually requiring corrective action.

Scope

You should consider two aspects of *scope*: product scope and project scope. Every successful project produces a unique product: a tangible item or a service. You might develop some products for one customer you know by name. You might develop other products for millions of potential customers waiting to buy them (you hope). Customers usually have some expectations about the features and functions of products they consider purchasing. *Product scope* describes the intended quality, features, and functions of the product—often in minute detail. Documents that outline this information are sometimes called product specifications. A service or an event usually has some expected features as well. We all have expectations about what we'll do or see at a party, a concert, or a sporting event.

Project scope, on the other hand, describes the work required to deliver a product or a service with the intended product scope. Whereas product scope focuses on the customer or the user of the product, project scope is mainly the concern of the people who will carry out the project. Project scope is usually measured in tasks and phases.

Here are some examples of scope constraints:

- Your organization won a contract to develop an automotive product that has exact requirements—for example, physical dimensions measured to 0.01 mm. This is a product scope constraint that will influence project scope plans.

- You are constructing a building on a lot that has a height restriction of 50 feet.

- You can use only internal services to develop part of your product, and those services follow a product development methodology that is different from what you had planned.

Product scope and project scope are closely related. The project manager who manages project scope well must also understand product scope or must know how to communicate with those who do.

Time, Cost, and Scope: Managing Project Constraints

Project management gets most interesting when you have to balance the time, cost, and scope constraints of your projects—"balance" as on a high wire. You could also think of juggling these constraints, or juggling them while on a high wire…well, you get the idea. Let's return to the project triangle model. The project triangle illustrates the process of balancing constraints because the three sides of the triangle are connected, and changing one side of a triangle affects at least one other side. Here are some examples of constraint balance:

■ If the duration (time) of your project schedule decreases, you might need to increase budget (cost) because you must hire more resources to do the same work in less time. If you can't increase the budget, you might need to reduce the scope because the resources you have can't do all of the planned work in less time.

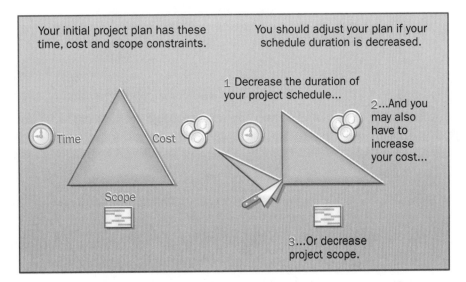

If you must decrease a project's duration, make sure that overall project quality is not unintentionally lowered. For example, testing and quality control often occur last in a software development project; if the project duration is decreased late in the project, those tasks might be the ones cut back. You must weigh the benefits of decreasing the project duration against the potential downside of a deliverable with poorer quality.

■ If the budget (cost) of your project decreases, you might need more time because you can't pay for as many resources or for resources of the same efficiency. If you can't increase the time, you might need to reduce project scope because fewer resources can't do all of the planned work in the time you have.

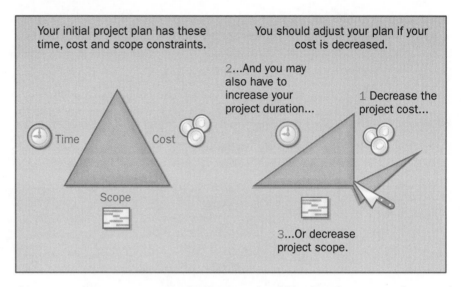

If you must decrease a project's budget, you could look at the *grades* of material resources for which you had budgeted. For example, did you plan to shoot a film in 35 mm when cheaper 16 mm film would do? A lower-grade material is not necessarily a lower-quality material. As long as the grade of material is appropriate for its intended use, it might still be of high quality. Another example: fast food and gourmet are two grades of restaurant food, but you may find high-quality and low-quality examples of each.

You should also look at the costs of the human and equipment resources you have planned to use. Can you hire less experienced people for less money to carry out simpler tasks? Reducing project costs can lead to a poorer-quality deliverable, however. As a project manager, you must consider (or more likely, communicate to the decision makers) the benefits versus the risks of reducing costs.

If your project scope increases, you might need more time or more resources (cost) to do the additional work. If the project scope increases after the project has started, it's called *scope creep*. Changing project scope midway through a project is not necessarily a bad thing; for example, your intended customer might have changed and you need to deliver a different product to the new customer. Changing project scope is a bad thing only if the project manager doesn't recognize and plan for the new requirements—that is, when other constraints (cost, time) are not correspondingly examined and, if necessary, adjusted.

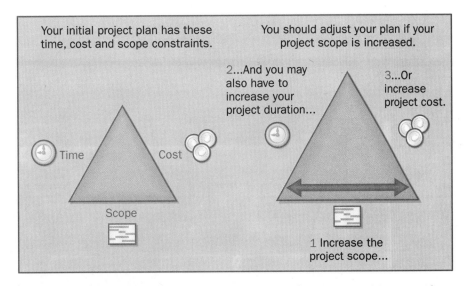

Time, cost, and scope are the three essential elements of any project. To succeed as a project manager, you'll have to know quite a bit about how all three of these constraints apply to your projects. You need a tool to help manage them.

Managing Your Projects with Project

The best project management tool in the world can never replace your good judgment. However, the right tool can and should help you accomplish the following while looking and feeling like other productivity programs you might use frequently:

- Track all the information you gather about the work, duration, and resource requirements for your project.

- Visualize your project plan in standard, well-defined formats.

- Schedule tasks and resources consistently and effectively.

- Exchange project information with all *stakeholders* over an intranet or the Internet.

- Communicate with resources and other stakeholders, while leaving ultimate control in the hands of the project manager.

In the chapters of this book, you were introduced to the rich functionality of Project in a realistic context: managing a project from conception to completion.

Not everything in this book might have applied to your needs, and you probably have needs that this book didn't address. But, after completing this tutorial, you're off to a great start with Project.

B   What's Next?

If you've completed most or all the chapters in this book, you're well on your way to mastering Microsoft Office Project 2003. However, one book can only get you so far. To help further your Project and project management knowledge, here are a few sources available to you.

Joining a Project Learning Community

If there's one thing we can say about Project users, it's that they love to talk about the program and their work with it and to share ideas with others. Whether you work in a large organization or independently, you're likely to find a community of Project users nearby.

If you're in a large organization, especially one with a strong project management focus, you might find an internal Project user group or support group there. Such groups often meet informally to provide peer training and support, to critique project plans, and to share best practices. If there isn't such a group in your organization, you might well start one.

In the public realm, there are many Project user groups around the world. These groups typically meet on a regular basis to share tips and tricks about Project. For example, in the Puget Sound area in the northwest United States, where the authors live and work, there's an active Microsoft Project User Group (MPUG) chapter that meets most months for informal idea sharing and for formal presentations by industry experts. Joining a user group is a great way to broaden your exposure to Project usage; it also can be a great source for informal product support, training, and career networking.

Here are a few places where you can investigate Project user groups and related resources:

- The official Project area of the Office Online Web site at microsoft.com includes a variety of tools from Microsoft and other Project users to help you manage your projects. Find it on the Web at *www.office.microsoft.com*

- The Microsoft Project Users Group (MPUG) offers both free and subscription-based information about a variety of Project and project management resources, as well as a directory of Project user groups around the world. Find it on the Web at *www.mpug.org*

- Msproject.com is an independent clearinghouse of information about Project. The Web site contains links to a variety of resources that would interest any Project user. Find it on the Web at *www.msproject.com*

- The official Project newsgroup offers help and discussions with other users of Project, including Microsoft Most Valuable Professionals (MVPs). You can use any newsreader software to access this newsgroup. To view or subscribe to this newsgroup, point your newsreader to *news://msnews.microsoft.com/ microsoft.public.project*

- For help with Visual Basic for Applications (VBA) in Microsoft Project, point your newsreader to *news://msnews.microsoft.com/microsoft.public.project.vba*

Joining a Project Management Learning Community

Probably more than most other desktop programs, Project requires you to be involved in a specific formal activity: project management. Project management can be an exciting mix of technical, organizational, and social challenges. The Project Management Institute (PMI) is the leading organization of professional project management. PMI focuses on setting project management standards, developing and offering educational programs, and certifying Project Management Professionals (PMPs) and Certified Associates in Project Management (CAPMs).

PMI's *A Guide to the Project Management Body of Knowledge* (PMBOK Guide 2000 Edition) describes generally accepted project management practices, knowledge areas, and terminology. In addition, PMI publishes the journals *Project Management Journal* and *PM Network*. You can learn more about PMI on the Web at *www.pmi.org*

Two Web sites or "portals" that might interest you are Project Connections and GanttHead. You can find these subscription-based sites at the following Web addresses:

- *www.projectconnections.com*
- *www.gantthead.com*

Both sites offer a wide variety of training, discussion forums, and industry-specific metrics and best practices for project management.

Final Words

There are, of course, many worthwhile commercial and nonprofit organizations dedicated to Project and project management besides those we've described here. Project enjoys a leading position in the diverse, sometimes contentious, but always interesting world of project management. Wherever you are in your own Project and project management knowledge and career development, you can find a great variety of supporting organizations and peers today. Good luck!

Glossary

accrual The method by which a project incurs the cost of a task or a resource. The three types of accrual are start, prorated, and end.

actual The details about task completion recorded in a Project plan. Prior to recording actuals, the project plan contains scheduled or planned information. Comparing planned project information to actuals helps the project manager better control project execution.

ACWP An earned value indicator; the acronym stands for Actual Cost of Work Performed. In earned value analysis, this is the actual costs of tasks that have been completed (or the portion completed of each) by the status date.

allocation The portion of the capacity of a resource devoted to work on a specific task.

assignment The matching of a work resource (a person or a piece of equipment) to a task. You can also assign a material resource to a task, but those resources have no effect on work or duration.

AutoFilter A quick way to view in a table only the task or resource information that meets the criteria you choose. To turn on AutoFilter, on the **Project** menu, point to **Filtered For <filter name>,** and then click **AutoFilter.** To filter a table with AutoFilter, click the arrow next to a column heading, and choose the criteria you want.

BAC An earned value indicator; the acronym stands for Budget At Completion. This is the same as baseline cost.

base calendar A calendar that can serve as the project calendar or a task calendar. A base calendar defines the default working times for resources. Project includes three base calendars, named Standard, 24 Hours, and Night Shift. You can customize these, or you can use them as a basis for your own base calendar.

baseline The original project plan, saved for later comparison. The baseline includes the planned start and finish dates of tasks and assignments, as well as their planned costs. Project plans can have up to 11 baselines.

BCWP An earned value indicator; the acronym stands for Budgeted Cost of Work Performed. In earned value analysis, this is the budgeted cost of tasks that have been completed (or the portion completed of each) by the status date. BCWP also is called earned value, because it represents the value earned in the project by the status date.

BCWS   An earned value indicator; the acronym stands for Budgeted Cost of Work Scheduled. In earned value analysis, this is the portion of the project's budget that is scheduled to be spent by the status date.

bottom-up planning   A method of developing a project plan that starts with the lowest-level tasks and organizes them into broad phases.

burdened labor rate   A resource cost rate that reflects not only the resource's direct payroll cost, but also some portion of the organization's costs not directly related to the resource's assignments on a project. Note that Project doesn't support a burdened labor rate directly; if you want to use one, simply enter it as a resource's standard or overtime cost rate.

calendar   The settings that define the working days and time for a project, resources, and tasks.

consolidated project   A Project plan that contains one or more inserted project plans. The inserted projects are linked to the consolidated project so that any changes to the inserted projects are reflected in the consolidated plan, and vice versa. A consolidated project plan is also known as a master project plan.

constraint   A restriction, such as Must Start On (MSO) or Finish No Later Than (FNLT), that you can place on the start or finish date of a task.

contour   The manner in which a resource's work on a task is scheduled over time. Project includes several predefined work contours that you can apply to an assignment. For example, a back-loaded contour schedules a small amount of work at the beginning of an assignment and then schedules increasing amounts of work as time progresses. You can also manually contour an assignment by editing work values in a usage view, such as the Resource Usage. Applying a predefined contour or manually contouring an assignment causes Project to display a work contour icon in the Indicators column.

Copy Picture   The feature that enables you to copy images and create snapshots of a view.

cost rate table   The resource pay rates that are stored on the **Costs** tab of the **Resource Information** dialog box. You can have up to five separate cost rate tables per resource.

cost   The resources required to carry out a project, including the people who do the work, the equipment used, and the materials consumed as the work is completed. Cost is one side of the project triangle model.

CPI   An earned value indicator; the acronym stands for Cost Performance Index. In earned value analysis, this is the ratio of budgeted to actual cost (CPI = BCWP / ACWP).

critical path   A series of tasks that, if delayed, will push out the end date of a project.

CV An earned value indicator; the acronym stands for Cost Variance. In earned value analysis, this is the difference between budgeted and actual cost (CV = BCWP – ACWP).

CV% The ratio of cost variance to BCWS, expressed as a percentage (CV% = [(BCWP – ACWP) / BCWP] × 100). This is an earned value indicator.

deadline A date value you can enter for a task that indicates the latest date by which you want the task to be completed. If the scheduled completion date of a task is later than its deadline, you are notified. The benefit of entering deadline dates is that they do not constrain tasks.

deliverable The final product, service, or event a project is intended to create.

dependency A link between a predecessor task and a successor task. A dependency controls the start or finish of one task relative to the start or finish of the other task. The most common dependency is finish-to-start, in which the finish date of the predecessor task determines the start date of the successor task.

destination program The program into which you place the data when exchanging data between Project and another program.

duration The span of working time you expect it will take to complete a task.

EAC An earned value indicator; the acronym stands for Estimate At Completion. In earned value analysis, this is the forecasted cost to complete a task based on performance up to the status date (EAC = ACWP + [BAC – BCWP] / CPI).

earned value analysis A sophisticated form of project performance analysis that focuses on schedule and budget performance as compared to baseline plans. Earned value uses your original baseline estimates and progress to date to show whether you're ahead, behind, or on schedule as compared with the actual costs incurred.

effort-driven scheduling A scheduling method in which the work of a task remains constant regardless of the number of resources assigned to it. As resources are added to a task, the duration decreases, but the work remains the same and is distributed among the assigned resources. Effort-driven scheduling is the default scheduling method in Project, but it can be turned off for any task.

elapsed duration The amount of time it will take to finish a task, based on a 24-hour day and a 7-day week.

enterprise project management Project management practiced in a formal, consistent way throughout an organization.

enterprise resource pool When using a Project Server–based enterprise project management system, a central repository of generic and work resources that can be shared by all projects published to Project Server.

enterprise template   When using a Project Server–based enterprise project management system, templates that are stored in Project Server and available to Project Professional users. Enterprise templates help ensure consistent use of best practices and metrics within an organization.

Entry table   The grid on the left side of the default Gantt Chart view.

export map   The specifications for exporting fields from Project to other file formats, such as HTML. Project includes several export maps, which you can use as they are or modify.

field   The lowest-level information about a task, resource, or assignment.

filtering   A way to see or highlight in a view only the task or resource information that meets the criteria you choose.

fixed consumption rate   A fixed quantity of a material resource to be consumed in the completion of an assignment.

fixed cost   A set amount of money budgeted for a task. This amount is independent of resource costs and task duration.

fixed duration   A task type in which the duration value is fixed. If you change the amount of work you expect a task to require, Project recalculates units for each resource. If you change duration or units, Project recalculates work.

fixed units   A task type in which the units value is fixed. If you change the duration of a task, Project recalculates the amount of work scheduled for the task. If you change units or work, Project recalculates duration.

fixed work   A task type in which the work value is fixed. If you change the duration of the task, Project recalculates units for each resource. If you change units or work, Project recalculates duration.

flexible constraint   A constraint type that gives Project the flexibility to change the start and finish dates (but not the duration) of a task. As Soon As Possible (ASAP) and As Late As Possible (ALAP) are both flexible constraints.

free slack   The amount of time that a task can be delayed without delaying the start date of another task.

fully allocated   The condition of a resource when the total work of his or her task assignments is exactly equal to his or her work capacity.

Gantt Chart view   A predefined view in Project consisting of a table (the Entry table by default) on the left and a graphical bar chart on the right that shows the project plan over time.

generic resource   When using a Project Server–based enterprise project management system, a special type of resource that can describe the expected skills of a specific type of work resource. Project managers can plan with generic resources and then replace them with work resources based on matching skills (and other factors).

ghost task   A task that represents a link from one Project plan to another. Ghost tasks appear as gray bars.

Global template   A Project template named Global.mpt that contains the default views, tables, filters, and other items that Project uses.

group   A way to reorder task or resource information in a table and display summary values for each group. You can specify several levels of groups. (The term *group* is also used to refer to the Resource Group field, which is unrelated.)

Group field   A field in which you can specify a group name (such as a department) with which you want to associate a resource. If you organize resources into groups, you can sort, filter, or group resources by group.

HTML template   A set of HTML tags and codes applied to Project data as it's exported through a map. Project includes several HTML templates, which you can use as they are or modify.

hyperlink   A link to another file, a specific location in a file, a page on the World Wide Web, or a page on an intranet.

import/export map   A set of specifications for importing specific data to or from Project fields. Project includes several built-in maps, which you can use as they are or modify. Import and export maps are sometimes referred to as data maps.

inflexible constraint   A constraint type that forces a task to begin or end on a certain date. Must Start On (MSO) and Must Finish On (MFO) are both inflexible constraints.

inserted project   A Project plan that is inserted into another Project plan, called a consolidated plan. An inserted project is also known as a subproject.

interim plan   A task's start and finish values, saved for later comparison. Each Project plan can have, at most, 10 interim plans.

lag time   A delay between tasks that have a task relationship. For example, lag time causes the successor task in a finish-to-start relationship to begin some time after its predecessor task concludes.

lead time   An overlap between tasks that have a task relationship. For example, lead time causes the successor task in a finish-to-start relationship to begin before its predecessor task concludes. In the Project interface, you enter lead time as negative lag time.

line manager   A manager of a group of resources; also called a functional manager. A line manager might also have project management skills and responsibilities, depending on the organization's structure.

link   A logical relationship between tasks that controls sequence and dependency. In the Gantt Chart and Network Diagram views, links appear as lines between tasks.

macro   A recorded or programmed set of instructions that carry out a specific action when initiated. Macros in Project use Visual Basic for Applications.

material resources   The consumables that are used up as a project progresses. As with work resources, you assign material resources to tasks. Unlike work resources, material resources have no effect on the total amount of work scheduled on a task.

maximum units   The maximum capacity (as entered in the **Max. Units** field) of a resource to accomplish tasks. If you allocate the resource beyond capacity, Project alerts you that the resource is overallocated.

Microsoft Office System Enterprise Project Management Solution   The set of tools and practices built upon Project Server and (optionally) Windows SharePoint Services.

milestone   A significant event that is reached within the project or imposed upon the project. In Project, milestones are normally represented as tasks with zero duration.

negative slack   The amount of time that tasks overlap due to a conflict between task relationships and constraints.

night shift   A base calendar included with Project designed to accommodate an 11:00 P.M.–8:00 A.M. "graveyard" work shift.

noncritical tasks   The tasks that have slack. Noncritical tasks can finish within their slack time without affecting the project completion date.

note   The information (including linked or embedded files) that you want to associate with a task, resource, or assignment.

OLE   A protocol that enables you to transfer information, such as a chart or text (called an object), to documents in different programs.

ongoing operation   An activity that has no planned end date and is repetitive in nature. Examples include accounting, managing human resources, and some manufacturing.

Organizer   A dialog box with which you can copy views, tables, filters, and other items between the Global.mpt template and other Project plans, or between two different Project plans.

outline   A hierarchy of summary tasks and subtasks within Project, usually corresponding to major phases of work.

outline number   Numbers that indicate the position of a task in the project's hierarchy. For example, a task with an outline number of 4.2 indicates that it's the second subtask under the fourth top-level task.

overallocated   The condition of resources when they are assigned to do more work than is their normal work capacity.

phase   A sequence of tasks that represent a major portion of the project's work. In Project, phases are represented by summary tasks.

planning   The first major phase of project management work. Planning includes all the work in developing a project schedule up to the point where the tracking of actual work begins.

predecessor   A task whose start or end date determines the start or finish of another task or tasks, called successor tasks.

product scope   The quality, features, and functions (often called specifications) of the deliverable of the project.

program office   A department within an organization that oversees a collection of projects (such as producing wings and producing engines), each of which contributes to a complete deliverable (such as an airplane) and the organization's strategic objectives.

progress bar   A graphical representation on a bar in the Gantt Chart view that shows how much of a task has been completed.

project   A temporary endeavor undertaken to create a unique product or service.

project calendar   The base calendar that is used by the entire project. The project calendar defines normal working and nonworking days and times.

project scope   The work required to produce a deliverable with agreed-upon quality, features, and functions.

project summary task   A summary task that contains top-level information such as duration, work, and costs for the entire project. The project summary task has a task ID of 0 and is displayed through the **View** tab of the **Options** dialog box, which is available by clicking the **Options** command on the **Tools** menu.

project triangle   A popular model of project management in which time, cost, and scope are represented as the three sides of a triangle. A change to one side will affect at least one of the other two sides. There are many variations on this model.

recurring task   A task that repeats at established intervals. You can create a recurring task that repeats for a fixed number of times or that ends by a specific date.

relationship   The type of dependency between two tasks, visually indicated by a link line. The types of relationships include finish-to-start, start-to-start, finish-to-finish, and start-to-finish. Also known as a link, a logical relationship, a task dependency, or a precedence relationship.

report   A format designed for printing. Project includes several predefined reports, each focusing on specific aspects of your project data. You can also define your own reports.

resource calendar   The working and nonworking days and times of an individual work resource.

resource leveling   A method of resolving resource overallocation by delaying the start date of an assignment or an entire task or splitting up the work on a task. Project can level resources automatically or you can do it manually.

resource manager   A person who oversees resource usage in project activities specifically to manage the time and costs of resources. A resource manager might also have project management skills and responsibilities, depending on the organization's structure.

resource pool   A Project plan that other projects use for their resource information. Resource pools contain information about resources' task assignments from all project plans (called sharer plans) linked to the resource pool.

resources   People, equipment, and material (and the associated costs of each) needed to complete the work on a project.

risk   An event that decreases the likelihood of completing the project on time, within budget, and to specification (or, less likely, an opportunity to improve project performance).

scheduling formula   A representation of how Project calculates work, based on the duration and resource units of an assignment. The scheduling formula is Duration × Units = Work.

scope   The products or services to be provided by a project, and the work required to deliver it. For project planning, it's useful to distinguish between product scope and project scope. Scope is one side of the project triangle model.

ScreenTip   A short description of an item on the screen, such as a toolbar, button, or bar. To see a ScreenTip, point to an item until the ScreenTip appears.

semi-flexible constraint   A constraint type that gives Project the flexibility to change the start and finish dates of a task within one date boundary. Start No Earlier Than (SNET), Start No Later Than (SNLT), Finish No Earlier Than (FNET), and Finish No Later Than (FNLT) are all semi-flexible constraints.

sequence   The chronological order in which tasks occur. A sequence is ordered from left to right in most views that include a timescale, for example, the Gantt Chart view.

sharer plan   A project plan that is linked to a resource pool. Sharer plans use resources from a resource pool.

shortcut menu   A menu you display by pointing to an item on the screen and then right-clicking. Shortcut menus contain only the commands that apply to the item to which you are pointing.

slack   The amount of time that a task can be delayed without delaying a successor task (free slack) or the project end date (total slack). Slack is also known as float.

sorting   A way of ordering task or resource information in a view by the criteria you choose.

source program   When exchanging data between Project and another program, the program in which the data resided originally.

SPI   An earned value indicator; the acronym stands for Schedule Performance Index. In earned value analysis, this is the ratio of performed to scheduled work (SPI = BCWP / BCWS).

split   An interruption in a task, represented in the Gantt bar as a dotted line between segments of a task. You can split a task multiple times.

sponsor   An individual or organization that both provides financial support and champions the project team within the larger organization.

stakeholders   The people or organizations that might be affected by project activities (those who "have a stake" in its success). These also include the resources working on the project as well as others (such as customers) external to the project work.

Standard base calendar   A base calendar included with Project designed to accommodate an 8:00 A.M.–5:00 P.M. Monday through Friday work shift.

status date   The date you specify (not necessarily the current date) that determines how Project calculates earned value indicators.

successor   A task whose start or finish is driven by another task or tasks, called predecessor tasks.

summary task   A task that is made up of and summarizes the subtasks below it. In Project, phases of project work are represented by summary tasks.

SV   An earned value indicator; the acronym stands for Schedule Variance. In earned value analysis, this is the difference between current progress and the baseline plan (SV = BCWP − BCWS).

SV%   The ratio of schedule variance to BCWS, expressed as a percentage (SV% = [SV / BCWS] × 100). This is an earned value indicator.

table   A spreadsheet-like presentation of project data, organized in vertical columns and horizontal rows. Each column represents one of the many fields in Project, and each row represents a single task or resource. In a usage view, additional rows represent assignments.

task   A project activity that has a starting and finishing point. A task is the basic building block of a project.

task calendar   The base calendar that is used by a single task. A task calendar defines working and nonworking times for a task, regardless of settings in the project calendar.

task ID   A unique number that Project assigns to each task in a project. In the Entry table, the task ID appears in the far left column.

task priority   A numeric ranking between 0 and 1000 of a task's importance and appropriateness for leveling. Tasks with the lowest priority are delayed or split first. The default value is 500.

task type   A setting applied to a task that determines how Project schedules the task, based on which of the three scheduling formula values is fixed. The three task types are fixed units, fixed duration, and fixed work.

TCPI   An earned value indicator; the acronym stands for To Complete Performance Index. In earned value analysis, this is the ratio of remaining work to remaining budget, as of the status date (TCPI = [BAC − BCWP] / [BAC − ACWP]).

template   A Project file format that enables you to reuse existing project plans as the basis for new project plans. Project includes several templates that relate to a variety of industries, and you can create your own templates.

time   The scheduled durations of individual tasks and the overall project. Time is one side of the project triangle model.

timephased field   The task, resource, or assignment values that are distributed over time. The values of timephased fields appear in the timescale grid on the right side of views such as the Task Usage or Resource Usage view.

timescale   The timescale appears in views such as the Gantt Chart and Resource Usage views as a band across the top of the grid and denotes units of time. You can customize the timescale in the **Timescale** dialog box, which you can open from the **Format** menu.

top-down planning   A method of developing a project plan by identifying the highest-level phases or summary tasks before breaking them into lower-level components or subtasks.

total slack   The amount of time that a task can be delayed without delaying the project's end date.

tracking   The second major phase of project management work. Tracking includes all the collecting, entering, and analyzing of actual project performance values such as work on tasks and actual durations.

underallocated   The condition of resources when they are assigned to do less work than is their normal work capacity. For example, a full-time resource who has only 25 hours of work assigned in a 40-hour work week is underallocated.

units   A standard way of measuring the capacity of a resource to work when you assign the resource to a task in Project. Units are one variable in the scheduling formula: Duration × Units = Work.

VAC   An earned value indicator; the acronym stands for Variance At Completion. In earned value analysis, this is the forecasted cost variance to complete a task based on performance up to the status date (VAC = BAC − EAC).

variable consumption rate   A quantity of a material resource to be consumed that will change if the duration of the task to which it is assigned changes.

variance   A deviation from the schedule or budget established by the baseline plan.

view   A visual representation of the tasks or resources in your project. The three categories of views are charts, sheets, and forms. Views enable you to enter, organize, and examine information in a variety of formats.

WBS (work breakdown structure)   The identification of every task in a project that reflects that task's location in the hierarchy of the project.

work resources   The people and equipment that do the work of the project.

work   The total scheduled effort for a task, resource, resource assignment, or entire project. Work is measured in person-hours and might not match the duration of the task. Work is one variable in the scheduling formula: Duration × Units = Work.

workspace   A set of project plans and settings that you can save and reopen by opening a single workspace file. Workspace files have the .mpw extension.

Index

Symbols

A

B

About the Authors

Carl S. Chatfield

Carl is the site manager for Project and FrontPage on Office Online (*www.office.microsoft.com*). Prior to his assignment to Office Online, Carl had worked on Office applications since 1991. Carl is also a technical communication instructor at the University of Washington. He is a graduate of the Masters program in Technical Communication at the University of Washington and has been certified as a Project Management Professional (PMP) by the Project Management Institute. He lives in Kirkland, Washington.

Timothy D. Johnson

Tim is a technical editor in the Project User Assistance team at Microsoft. Prior to joining the Project User Assistance team in 2000, he was a Project support professional for six years (going all the way back to Project 3.0—if you called Microsoft Product Support Services with a Project question, there's a good chance you talked to Tim). Tim lives in Issaquah, Washington.

Acknowledgments

We would like to thank our families for their patience while we developed this book. *From Carl:* thank you Rebecca, Alden, Lathan, and Mona. *From Tim:* thank you Ratsamy (Mimi), Brian, and Brenda.

The authors also wish to acknowledge the members of the Project Business Unit at Microsoft—Adrian Jenkins in particular—who provided valuable and timely answers to our technical questions.

seriously
Satisfying

Penny Stephens

WeightWatchers®

SIMON &
SCHUSTER
ILLUSTRATED

London · New York · Sydney · Toronto · New Delhi

A CBS COMPANY

Powys

37218 00312754 0

First published in Great Britain by Simon & Schuster UK Ltd, 2011

This edition first published in 2014 by Simon & Schuster UK Ltd

A CBS Company

SIMON & SCHUSTER
ILLUSTRATED BOOKS
Simon & Schuster UK
222 Gray's Inn Road
London WC1X 8HB
www.simonandschuster.co.uk

Simon & Schuster Australia, Sydney
Simon & Schuster India, New Delhi

Photography: Steve Baxter
Prop styling: Rachel Jukes
Food preparation: Carol Tennant
Design and typesetting: Jane Humphrey

Colour reproduction by Dot Gradations Ltd, UK
Printed and bound in China

A CIP catalogue for this book is available from the British Library
ISBN 978-1-47113-261-2

Pictured on the front cover: Slow Roast Lamb, page 80

Pictured on the back cover from left to right and top to bottom:
One Pan Ham 'n' Egg on Toast, page 8; Pasta with Tomato Pesto, page 100;
Beef and Ale Pot Pie, page 120; Marbled Chocolate Cheesecake, page 160

Pictured on the spine: Strawberry Trifle Loaf, page 172

If you would like to find out more about Weight Watchers
and the *ProPoints* Plan, please visit:
www.weightwatchers.co.uk

(V) This symbol denotes a vegetarian recipe and assumes
that, where relevant, free range eggs, vegetarian cheese,
vegetarian virtually fat free fromage frais, vegetarian low
fat crème fraîche and vegetarian low fat yogurts are used.
Virtually fat free fromage frais, low fat crème fraîche and
low fat yogurts may contain traces of gelatine so they are
not always vegetarian. Please check the labels.

(❄) This symbol denotes a dish that can be frozen.

Recipe notes

Egg size Medium, unless otherwise stated.

All fruits and vegetables Medium size unless otherwise
stated.

Raw eggs Only the freshest eggs should be used. Pregnant
women, the elderly and children should avoid recipes with
eggs which are not fully cooked or raw.

Recipe timings These are approximate and meant to be
guidelines. Please note that the preparation time includes
all the steps up to and following the main cooking time(s).

Low fat spread Where a recipe states to use a low fat
spread, a light spread with a fat content of no less than 38%
should be used.

Stock Stock cubes should be used in the recipes, unless
otherwise stated. Prepare them according to the packet
instructions, unless directed otherwise.

Microwaves Microwave timings are for an 850 watt
microwave oven.

ProPoints values Should you require the *ProPoints*
values for any of the recipes within this book, you can call
Customer Services on 0845 345 1500 and we will provide
you with the relevant information on a recipe-by-recipe
basis. Please allow 28 days for us to provide you with this
information.

Penny Stephens is an experienced and well-travelled
food writer who enjoys creating healthy and delicious
recipes that appeal to everyone. She regularly contributes
to *Weight Watchers Magazine* as well as *Your Week* magazine.
She has written several cookbooks for Weight Watchers.